Pakistan
a travel survival kit

Jose Roleo Sar

D1344459

Pakistan - a travel survival kit
  3rd edition

Published by
  Lonely Planet Publications
  Head Office: PO Box 88, South Yarra 3141, Australia
  Also: PO Box 2001A, Berkeley, CA 94702, USA

Printed by
  Colorcraft, Hong Kong

Photographs by
  Jose Roleo Santiago, cover
  Peter Campbell (PC)
  Phyllis Elving (Pacific Travel News) (PE)
  Pakistan Tourism Development Corporation (PTDC)

Illustrations by
  Peter Campbell

First published
  October 1981

This edition
  September 1987

Although the author and publisher have tried to make the information as accurate as possible, they accept no responsibility for any loss, injury or inconvenience sustained by any traveller using this book.

National Library of Australia
Cataloguing-in-publication entry

Santiago, Jose Roleo.
  Pakistan, a travel survival kit.

  3rd edition
  Includes index.
  ISBN 0 86442 013 7.

  1. Pakistan – Description and travel –
  Guide-books. I. Title.

915.49'1045

Introduction

Pakistan is one of the more misunderstood countries in Asia. During the heyday of the Asia overland trip it was the country overlanders rushed through – a transit zone from the exotic colours of Afghanistan to the mysticism of India. Now with the continuing upheavals and uncertainties in Afghanistan and Iran, it is almost as if Pakistan has been left out on a limb.

Although part of the subcontinent, Pakistan is quite different. It is an Islamic country with its own history and cultural heritage and fascinating in its own right. Pakistan was the site for some of the world's earliest human settlements, the centre of the great prehistoric Indus Valley Civilisation, the crucible of ancient empires, religions and cultures. Alexander the Great ended his long march eastward here and built Greek towns and cities which later gave impetus to the fusion of the Graeco-Roman and Indian art styles that emerged in the superb Gandhara culture.

Pakistan is also archaeologically significant – a museum and gallery of historic rock carvings and inscriptions – particularly along the Karakoram Highway, which follows the ancient Silk Trade Route from what is now known as the Grand Trunk Rd, all the way to Mintaka Pass.

The magnificent city of Lahore is a Moghul masterpiece, as important as any of the Moghul cities of India, while to the west is Peshawar, the capital of the swashbuckling Pathans and gateway to the Khyber Pass, the romantic western approach to the subcontinent. In the south is Hyderabad and the metropolis of Karachi, but Pakistan saves its best for the north – craggy and forbidding but nonetheless stunning in its beauty.

Places like the Swat Valley, Chitral Valley, Gilgit, Hunza and Baltistan are among the most beautiful and unspoilt regions in the world. Set against the background of the spectacular Trans-Himalayas, they offer unique cultures, fascinating rock carvings, the highest peaks and the largest and longest glaciers in the world, as well as trekking through this untouristed and untrammelled wilderness area.

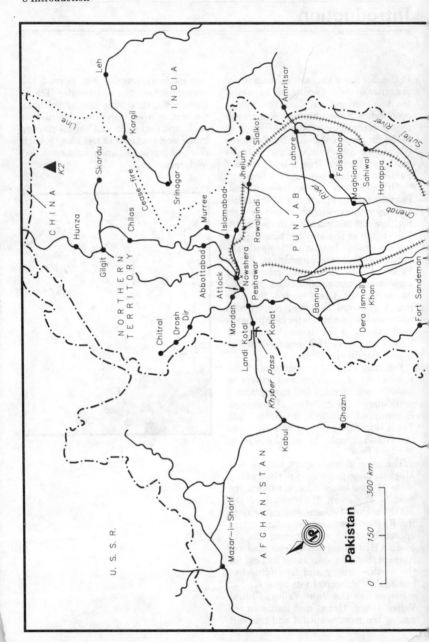

Pakistan

0   150   300 km

Jose Roleo Santiago

Jose Roleo Santiago has been 'on the road' for almost three decades, travelling extensively in South-east Asia, the subcontinent, the Middle East, Europe, Africa, the Americas and recently China. He has supported himself along the way as a jack-of-all-trades including travel writing. As well as this book he has also written another Lonely Planet guide, *Bangladesh – a travel survival kit*.

Editor	Peter Turner
Maps & Cover Design	Todd Pierce
Design & Illustrations	Valerie Tellini

Acknowledgements
This book would not have been possible without the kindness and assistance extended by the PTDC (Pakistan Tourism Development Corporation) tourist officers, by local and foreign travellers and the many hospitable Pakistanis I met on my travels in the country. In one way or another they provided information on places that I failed to visit.

For the 3rd edition thanks must go to all those who took the time to write and provided valuable information:

Barbro Andersson (UK), Anders Blonqvist (Swe), Gordon Bonin (USA), Christina Bos (Neth), Michael Brown (Aus), John Cocks (NZ), Brian Cooke (USA), S & L Cooper (UK), James Crestin (Sw), Gerard Custer (USA), Max de Wan (Aus), Ian Ditchfield (Aus), Dianne Eaton (USA), Martin Ellison (Aus), Patrick Frew (NZ), Meinhard Gurn (FDR), Ali Hassan (Pak), Peter Hedges (UK), Richard S Jones (UK), Mary Kowalchuk (Can), Margaret Lesjak (Aus), John Lowe (UK), Bernhard Magnouloux (Fr), Julian McIntosh (UK), Richard Meixsel (USA), Frank Metzler (Den), Nasir Abbas Mirza (Pak), O H Mollyneux (Aus), George Moore (USA), Richard Naish (UK), Margaret Peil (UK), Al & Charlotte Peters (USA), Andrew Powell (UK), Nick Quantock, Paul Rogers (Aus), Peter Ross (UK), Syed Sajid Ali (Can), Tahanga (Aus), David Thomas (UK), Dick Thompson (Aus), Paula Turkey (NI), Dave Wagland (Aus), Russell Woodhouse (Aus)

(Aus – Australia, Can – Canada, Den – Denmark, FDR – West Germany, Fr – France, Neth – Netherlands, NI – Northern Ireland, NZ – New Zealand, Pak – Pakistan, Sw – Switzerland, Swe – Sweden)

At Lonely Planet thanks must also go to Alison Porter for typesetting.

And the Next Edition
Things change – prices go up, good places go bad, bad places go bankrupt, and nothing stays the same. So if you find that something in this book is now dearer, worse or non-existent, don't blame the author or Lonely Planet, but do write and tell us about it. The best letters score a copy of the next edition – or another LP guide if you prefer.

Contents

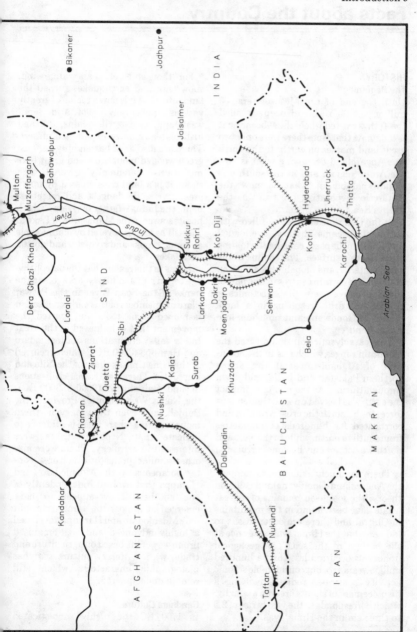

Facts about the Country

HISTORY
The Beginning

Until the end of the Mesozoic era, 65 million years ago, a broad, deep sea called the Tethys existed where the subcontinent is today. At that time there were only two great land masses on earth: to the north was Angaraland occupying what is now the Arctic region, and in the south was Gondwanaland in what is now the Antarctic. Separating the two was the Tethys Sea.

In the Cenozoic era the sea filled with sediment, became shallow, overloaded and finally collapsed, causing the folding of the earth's surface. The cooling of the earth's interior, and probably the explosion of magma at certain centres in this part of the globe, gave rise to plate tectonics or continental drift, resulting in a large section of Gondwanaland smashing into Angaraland.

This cataclysmic collision created the mountain ranges which rise in the northwest of Afghanistan and run across northern Pakistan and India, and down through Burma. At the points of impact the earth was heaved up with tremendous force. In the north the crust wrinkled and corrugated for hundreds of kilometres from south to north, while in the west and north-west it not only became corrugated but also cracked.

There is much evidence to support the Angaraland-Gondwanaland collision theory: the fossilised remains of a great whale have been found in the mountains in Chitral and there are other fossils to indicate that the Himalayas were once at the bottom of the sea. The geological upheavals occurred less than a hundred million years ago, but considerable seismic activity continues today, involving a displacement of about three cm annually, which corresponds to the yearly rise of 2.5 to three cm in the Himalayas.

For thousands of years rain, wind, snow, sun and earthquakes turned the land into what it is now a region of greatly varying topography – of arid semi-wasteland, vast fertile plains, dry and lush plateaux, huge expanses of desert. There are also arid, barren hilly regions; green wooded mountains and great bare mountains, perennially covered with snow. It is a land criss-crossed by many great rivers, the longest and mightiest being the Indus – father of rivers – which has its source in the Manasarowar Lake in Tibet. The land is covered by innumerable streams, brooks and rivulets, and dotted with lakes.

It was in this region that the paleolithic age began half a million years ago. On the banks of the Soan River in the Potwar Plateau, members of this early civilisation fashioned stone tools and started the movement that culminated in the great Indus Valley civilisations of Moenjodaro and Harappa (3000 BC), which occurred at the same time as those of the Nile and Euphrates. There were earlier civilisations in Sind, Baluchistan (6000 to 3000 BC), the North West Frontier Province, the Punjab, and even the craggy northern mountain area where there is evidence to indicate that Neolithic tribes were interested in astrology. There were also other similar prehistoric cultures contemporaneous with Moenjodaro and Harappa that evolved independently of one another. They appear to have emerged at almost the same time, but only Moenjodaro and Harappa developed a highly advanced and well-organised urban way of life based on agriculture and trade, with a literary culture that has pictographic characters, which still remain undeciphered.

Gandhara Culture

In 1700 BC the highly sophisticated

culture of the Indus Valley civilisation suddenly disappeared. This period coincided with the arrival of the neolithic Aryans from Siberia and the Urals. The fine wheel-turned 'painted black on red' pottery disappeared and was replaced with a crude, primitive pottery. The art style drastically reverted back to the ithyphallic art form (representations of the erect penis) and there was a break in the cultural development of the area, which regressed back to the neolithic art style. The Aryans settled there and adopted much of the culture they discovered. They refined Hinduism from worship of the Brahman bull and developed a script known as *pakrthi*, which remains undeciphered and is considered to be the precursor of Sanskrit.

In the 6th century BC, at about the same time that Buddhism emerged, the land now known as Pakistan became the 20th satrapy of the Persian Achaemenian Empire of Cyrus the Great, and later of Darius. In the 4th century BC this region was conquered by Alexander the Great of Macedonia. Greek rule was brief. In the latter part of the same century Chandragupta founded the Mauryan Empire and during the reign of his grandson, Ashoka, Buddhism took root and flourished in the Peshawar Valley. On the death of Ashoka in the 2nd century BC, the Bactrian-Greeks arrived, followed by the Scythians from Central Asia, who were in turn succeeded by the Parthians from Persia.

In the 1st century AD Kanishka led the Kushans from Afghanistan into the region and established an empire which extended from the Aral Sea up to the Gangetic Plains of India, and spread from Sind and Baluchistan to the Pamirs and Tibet. It became one of the major commercial *entrepots* on the Silk Trade Route which linked Rome and Chang'an (now Xian) in China with the sub-continent. During this period the Graeco-Roman and Indo art style fused and gave rise to the emergence of the Gandhara culture. Buddhism, along with the Gandhara art genre, swept through the Karakorams into Central Asia and influenced the Buddhist art form in China and Tibet. However, Gandhara was not merely a commercial hub, it was also a centre for pilgrims, religion and education. It was the Buddhist holy land.

Chinese pilgrims were greatly impressed by Gandhara, but in the 3rd century AD it was annexed by the Persian Sassanians and under them, the Buddhist Gupta Empire emerged in the 4th century AD. The latter continued cultural and commercial links with Byzantium, Persia and China. In the 5th century AD, at about the same time that Rome entered into a 'dark age', the White Huns or Hepthalites pillaged the region, putting

Moenjodaro Priest

the population to the sword and the cities to the torch– a disaster from which the Gandhara culture never recovered. Xuan Zhang, a Chinese pilgrim who visited the region in the early 7th century AD, was greatly impressed by the cities, but by then Gandhara was already in decline.

The Advent of Islam

In the 7th century AD the Arabs invaded Persia. In the early 8th century AD, led by Mohammed Ibn Qasim, they invaded Sind, introduced Islam, and gradually expelled the Hindus. In the middle of the 10th century, Mahmud of Ghazni conquered the northern region of the subcontinent which had gradually reverted to Hinduism. The northern mountainous frontierland was occupied by the Chinese in the middle of the 8th century AD until they were booted out by the Tibetans in the 9th century AD, but by the 10th century it finally fell under the sway of Islam.

At the end of the 12th century Shahabuddin Ghauri occupied Delhi and the land up to the Gangetic Plains, but in 1206 General Qutb-ud-din Aibak established the Sultanate of Delhi. A few years later, however, Tartar-Mongol hordes burst onto the plains of Russia, Persia and the subcontinent, and in 1249 Lahore and Delhi were sacked and depopulated. Late in the 14th century the Mongol hold over Russia began to wane and the Mongol empire, which had once stretched from the Sea of China to the Baltic, began to decline, finally fragmenting on the death of Kublai Khan, the last great emperor of China. Fighting amongst the Khanates in central Asia continued to blow up until the empire finally faded away.

The Moghul Empire

The Tartar-Mongol hordes were to reappear in the subcontinent as Moghuls under Amir Timur or Tamerlane. At this stage they had 'progressed' from being pagans and animists to adopting the tenets of Islam, but it wasn't until 1526 under the leadership of Babar that the last of the Afghan kings were defeated and the Moghul dynasty founded. This was expanded further by his grandson, Akbar (1556 to 1605).

In this period architecture took on the distinctive Moghul style, which featured exquisite designs that verged on the fantastic. Moghul art, culture and literary activity flourished and there was a proliferation of magnificent buildings, mosques, forts, palaces and gardens. Forts with battlemented ramparts were massive and resplendent palaces, beautifully designed and richly embellished with all the comforts sought after by oriental potentates. Most of the mosques were constructed along massive proportions, but at the same time managed to appear dreamlike and delicate with slender minarets tapering up to a cupola.

This artistic, cultural and literary activity, along with the construction of buildings and roads, continued under Akbar's son, Jehangir (1605-1627) and his grandson, Aurangzeb (1658-1707), who almost brought the entire subcontinent under his rule. However, the dynasty came to a sticky end on his death as his sons fought and murdered each other in their battle for the throne. The decline of Muslim power which followed gave impetus to the rise of the Sikhs in the Punjab and the British in Bengal in the latter half of the 18th century. The Moghul Empire survived for some time afterwards but its power base was destroyed.

The Sikhs

The Sikhs rise to power began with incursions into the frontier provinces where Moghul power had weakened. They established their influence in Kashmir, further north to Ladakh, northwest as far as Gilgit and to the west as far as the Peshawar Valley in the 1840s. Meanwhile the British were moving slowly but inexorably from Bengal southward, then north-west.

The British first came to the region for trade during the reign of Akbar at the beginning of the 17th century. Akbar's son, Jehangir, received Sir Thomas Roe as the ambassador of James I of England and shortly afterwards the British East India Company was established in Bengal. When the Moghuls began to lose power in the middle of the 18th century the British became involved in the internecine battles that flared up in the subcontinent in order to protect their commercial interests. In 1757 Robert Clive defeated Nawab Siraj-ud-daula at Plassey.

This victory was the signal for the British East India Company to carry out a piecemeal conquest of the entire subcontinent, overtaking the Sikhs in 1849 and imposing their power in Kashmir, Baltistan, Gilgit and the region beyond the Punjab later known as the North West Frontier Province. The Sind was taken in 1843 before the final collapse of Moghul power. Mismanagement by 'John & Company' made the British Imperial Government take over direct administration of their vast empire after the Great Mutiny of 1857. Expansion continued. However, they failed in several mighty attempts to annex Afghanistan, the last province of the Moghuls in the west. Hunza, under the leadership of Colonel Durand, was the last bit of territory in the subcontinent to be conquered by the British. It fell in 1891.

British India

Euro-Asian trade and commerce, conducted overland along the numerous camel caravan trails of the ancient Silk Trade Route, ceased with the emergence of the Ottoman Empire in the middle of the 15th century. Any likelihood of it being re-established was put to rest in the latter part of the same century with the discovery of a sea route to India and the East Indies by the Portuguese navigator, Vasco Da Gama. From then on Euro-Asian trade and commerce was conducted by sea. In effect, Da Gama's discovery resulted in the conquest of the subcontinent by the British merchants, the only invading power to come by sea via the Cape of Good Hope. Historically they were the only invading power to go westward against the major eastward current into Afghanistan.

With the arrival of the British, Moghul art, culture, literature and architecture were replaced along with the old monarchic Moghul system of government. British art, culture and language were introduced and a colonial government administration, from the district officer to the viceroy, was established. The period saw a resurgence in the construction of public buildings, housing, courts of justice, police stations, military cantonments, churches and cathedrals – generally located in the districts of towns and cities known as The Mall. There was a fusion of Moghul and Victorian architecture in public buildings, but the churches and cathedrals retained their Norman or traditional Gothic design while a more modern architectural approach was developed for the houses.

The British began the construction of an immense network of highways, roads and rail tracks that spanned the entire length and breadth of the subcontinent from the coastal regions of Dacca, Calcutta, Madras, Cochin, Bombay and Karachi to the mountainous regions of Darjeeling, Kashmir, Baluchistan and the North West Frontier Province. Clear-cut definitions of boundaries were also introduced for kingdoms, states and empires that surrounded the subcontinent from the west to the north and east. Explorers, travellers and adventurers proliferated, most of them going deep into the mountainous regions of the Himalayas, the Karakorams, the Hindu Kush, and beyond into Afghanistan, China and Tibet.

The subcontinent was mapped down to the last centimetre and the so-called Durand Line came into being to define its length and breadth. This generally followed the natural geographical barriers, such as the dry rugged deserts in the south-west which demarcate the borders with Iran and Afghanistan. To the north and the north-east the stupendous mountains of the Hindu Kush, the Karakorams and the Himalayas formed the borders with China and Burma.

Evolution of a State

From the outset the Muslims were naturally hostile to the British, who applied the policy of 'divide and rule' to secure their hold on the subcontinent. The Muslims felt deprived of the privileges they had enjoyed under the Moghuls, denied the educational and economic opportunities available under the new regime, and resented their degradation as a minority group. They knew, however, that the British were a people to be reckoned with.

Sir Syed Ahmed Khan (1817 to 1898) aspired to restore Muslim prestige in the subcontinent and thus began the Aligarh Movement, from which evolved the Muslim League. The Indian National Congress, which was set up mainly for the struggle for independence, amalgamated with the Muslim League. However, the Muslims considered that it was primarily a Hindu political organisation. Since they were specifically concerned with the protection of their religion, culture and way of life, and in securing their social, economic and political rights under British rule, the Muslim League finally broke away.

In 1930 the concept of a separate Muslim state was put forward by Alama Iqbal, the great Muslim poet. Three years later in London, the word Pakistan was coined for the first time by Chowdry Ramat Ali. Apparently *pak* means pure, while *istan* stands for land. It means therefore the 'land of the pure'. Another theory is that it is composed of acronyms of the first letters or syllables of the names of the provinces which make up the whole country. It doesn't really matter which is

the correct theory for it was adopted by Mohammed Ali Jinnah, also known as *Quaid-i-Azam*, who took up the political goal of the poet Iqbal.

The political aspirations of the Muslim League before, during and after WW II, posed a seemingly insoluble problem for the British government. British missions failed to find any answer to the problem and the plan to make Muslim majority provinces in the west and east of India into autonomous Muslim states under a unified central government was rejected both by the Muslim League and by Congress. Mohammed Ali Jinnah steadfastly objected to any other solution except that of the formation of a completely separate Muslim state, to which both Congress and the British eventually capitulated.

Having decided that the only 'solution' was to partition the country into separate Hindu and Muslim states, the British appointed Sir Cyril Radcliffe to draw the dividing line. Nehru, Jinnah and Mountbatten all insisted that the line be drawn by 15 August – the date of independence which had already been decided upon before Radcliffe arrived in India. That gave Radcliffe little more than seven weeks to work out the division of the country. Furthermore, convinced that relations between the two new states would be friendly, Field Marshal Auchinleck (Commander-in-Chief of the Indian Army), authorised Radcliffe to ignore considerations of natural defence.

The decision was made to carve the subcontinent into a central, predominantly Hindu region, which would retain the name of India, and this would be flanked on either side by the doubleheaded state of 'Pakistan'. The result was a disaster. The main problem centred on the Punjab, the region encompassing the great Muslim city of Lahore and the holy city of the Sikhs, Amritsar. Partition of the country resulted in the migration of millions of people; the Muslims headed west to Pakistan and the Sikhs and

Hindus headed east to India. This mass migration was accompanied by riots and massacres instigated by both sides, which led to a bloodbath of unforeseen violence and ferocity.

Nor were the wholesale exchange of population and riots the only problems, for Pakistan ended up short of many of the commercial skills the Hindus supplied. Worse, the borders were a subject of dispute. During the build up to independence, Kashmir remained undecided as to which way to go, but finally the Rajah of Kashmir, Hari Singh, signed the instrument of accession to India. Subsequently an armed struggle took place with Pakistan retaining a slice of Kashmir on the western side, with the rest falling under Indian control. To this day both sides claim the predominately Muslim region of Kashmir. Each time India and Pakistan find themselves at each other's throat, which over the last 30 odd years has been often, the Kashmir question is inevitably a central issue.

In the long term Pakistan's most serious problem was simply the fact that there were two Pakistans. When, on 15 August 1947, Pakistan emerged on the map, it was as a double-sided nation, with one side in the extreme west of the subcontinent, the other in the extreme east. Stretched between them was almost 2000 km of hostile India.

West Pakistan comprised Sind, West Punjab, the North West Frontier Province, Baluchistan and the former British political agencies in the northern region, while East Bengal and a great part of the Sylhet district formed East Pakistan. The western half was always the dominant partner despite the fact that it was the Bengalis in East Pakistan who supplied the majority of the country's export earnings. Basically the only real connection between the two halves was that they were both followers of Islam.

From the outset everything about the country had an air of impermanence; things were set up with a view towards

reorganisation later. Even the new country's name was tentative. In 1953 the country was renamed the Islamic Republic of Pakistan, only to be switched back to Pakistan in 1958. Initially Karachi, the port city of Sind, became the temporary capital. Then a new capital, Islamabad, was to be sited on the Potwar Plateau, but before it was finished the capital was moved, in 1959, to nearby Rawalpindi.

After 11 years of inefficient and corrupt 'democratic' government, General Ayub Khan set up the first military government in 1958. He introduced reforms in the agrarian and industrial sectors of the nation's economy, but in 1969 he was succeeded by General Yahya Khan who proved to be rather ineffective. All this time, discontent had been growing in the eastern half. The standard of living there was lower; their representation in the government, civil service and military was far smaller and their share of overseas aid and development projects was also disproportionately small.

In 1970 two events shook the country apart. A disastrous cyclone wreaked havoc on the eastern half, and the assistance the Bengalis received from West Pakistan was shamefully indifferent. Then in December 1970, elections took place to return the country to civilian rule. A general election was held in each wing on a one-person, one-vote franchise. The Awami League, led by Mujibur Rahman, won in East Pakistan with an overwhelming majority of 167 of the 169 seats, while the Pakistan People's Party headed by Zulfikar Ali Bhutto emerged the dominant political party in West Pakistan, taking 88 of the 144 seats. A constitutional dispute then arose over which political party should form a government, resulting in Mujibur Rahman being arrested and slapped into jail. This sparked off an insurrection in East Pakistan which led to the army taking over. The army's cruelty prompted a bitter guerrilla opposition and finally India, flooded with Bengali refugees, stepped in and declared war against Pakistan. The Pakistan army was defeated in the east, culminating in the creation of Bangladesh.

Back in the west Bhutto came to power and governed Pakistan from that time until 1977 when he was ousted in a bloodless coup d'etat over his re-election. Bitterness arose over whether or not Bhutto had rigged the votes, and whether or not there should be a re-run of the election, until it appeared that the country was on the brink of civil war. The army took over and Bhutto was arrested and imprisoned. Eventually the Supreme Court found him guilty of direct involvement in the murder of a political opponent and, despite the protests and appeals from leaders all over the world, he was hanged on 4 April 1979.

Since then General Zia-ul-Haq has governed the country under martial law. There has also been a steady swing towards a more fundamentalist Islamic rule in line with much of Islamic Asia. Today Pakistan is relatively quiet and stable, pursuing a policy of non-alignment and normalisation of relations with India. It is also trying to improve relations with neighbouring countries like China and Iran and, even more importantly, with the oil-rich states in the Middle East and the Gulf region.

Pakistan has gradually acquired a prominent position, not only in the Islamic world, but also in world affairs at large.

POPULATION & PEOPLE
Pakistan has a population approaching 94 million with a large percentage being concentrated in urban areas such as Karachi, which has slightly less than seven million, and Lahore with three million. It is composed of heterogeneous racial stocks which include Dravidians, Aryans, Arabs and Mongols.

The population is far from evenly distributed due mainly to Pakistan's diverse topography. The Indus Plains of the Punjab and Sind are heavily populated in contrast to the deserts and barren hilly regions of Baluchistan, the North West Frontier and the arid desolate northern mountain zone.

The racial groups are amazingly diverse in complexion, physique and culture. The more numerous Punjabis and Sindhis who settled along the Indus River are similar to the people of India; the Baluchis and Pathans of the deserts and hilly regions in the western frontier are closer to the Turkish racial stock of Afghanistan and Iran; while, with the exception of the Baltis who are related to the Tibetans, the people of the Northern Territory are a hybrid population of the Caucasian and Mongoloid racial stocks.

Each group or tribe retains its cultural and traditional customs, language, social system, attire, headwear and songs. Generally they are traditionally hospitable. 'Their simplicity ... is part of their charm,' wrote Camille Mirepois, author of *See Pakistan Again*, 'which has not yet, like elsewhere, been eroded by tourism.' Islam is the cohesive force which binds them all together.

ECONOMY
The land of the Indus is basically agrarian, self-sufficient in grains – mainly wheat – and is presently developing a number of light engineering and electrical industrial complexes. Pakistan produces 20% of its oil requirement and has coal mines and a tremendous quantity of gas. Its vast mineral resources remain unexplored and unexploited. It exports textiles to the west, and foodstuff and technological know-how to the Middle East, but the bulk of its foreign exchange earnings comes from its overseas workers in the oil states. This is presently tapering off as oil production in the Middle East and the Gulf region has diminished with the corresponding lowering of oil prices. This is offset by the six billion dollars that is being poured into the country by the United States of America, and an

improvement in the tourist industry. On the whole the general trend of the economy is on the upswing.

GEOGRAPHY

Pakistan stretches from the Arabian Sea in the south to the Tibetan Plateau in the north, over a total area of 796,000 square km. It consists of four provinces: the Sind, the Punjab, Baluchistan, and the North West Frontier Province; plus the northern territory of Gilgit-Hunza, Baltistan and Azad Kashmir & Jammu.

In the west it is bounded by 800 km of desert along the Iranian border and by the 2200-km Durand Line drawn in 1897 to separate British India from Afghanistan. It runs from the Chagai Range up the rugged Hindu Kush, up the Pamirs where a 15-km wide strip of Afghan land is all that separates Pakistan from the USSR. In the north the great Karakorams form the border with China, while in the north-east a ceasefire line demarcates the Pakistan and Indian sections of Kashmir & Jammu. From Jammu to the Punjab, the border with India is clearly delineated by the Radcliffe Line drawn in 1947. It runs south for 1500 km through the Punjab and the Rajaputana Desert to the Arabian Sea. In the south of Pakistan is the 800-km long Arabian Sea coastline.

The country is divided into six geographical regions: the Lower Indus Plain, the Upper Indus Plain, the Salt Range, the Baluchistan Plateau, the Western Border Mountains, and the Northern Mountain Zone. The Indus forms the backbone of the whole country. From Tibet it crosses Ladakh close to the Chinese border and traverses the Karakorams into the plains. Other rivers like the Jhelum, the Chenab, the Ravi and the Sutlej rush down to join the Indus as it sweeps across the long plains to the Arabian Sea.

The coastline is semi-tropical, rich in marine life and has mangroves in the Indus delta. Moving north, the land where the Indus flows is green and fertile, but dry and sandy on its lateral peripheries to the east and west. The plains end abruptly with the Salt Range of the Potwar Plateau where the land appears scarred and eroded. From here the land rises steeply to wooded massifs, which finally meet the convoluted glacial regions of the Hindu Kush, the Karakorams and the Himalayas. Except for the Indus Plains, which constitute about a third of the country, Pakistan is all hilly deserts, plateaux and great mountains.

FLORA & FAUNA

Along the coast there is a variety of marine life which includes shellfish, dolphins and sharks, while the Indus delta has crocodiles, reptiles and hog deer. Wheat, barley, oats, sugar-cane and cotton as well as a wide variety of tropical fruits such as mangoes, guavas, papayas and bananas are grown on the plains. Wildlife in the southern plains includes boar, deer, goats, porcupine, rodents and reptiles; while water buffalo, cattle, camels, donkeys, sheep, horses and goats are the most widely used domestic animals.

The barren sandy wasteland away from the Indus has sparse and stunted vegetation except for the oases with their date palm trees. Camels, jackals, hyenas, feral cats, panthers and leopards are to be found here.

In the more temperate areas apples, pears, plums, peaches, walnuts, mulberries, grapes and berries are grown. The trees up in the northern mountain zone include fir, pine, spruce, willow, eucalyptus, juniper and the Himalayan *chenar*.

Some of the rarest wildlife in the world exists in this area, including the Marco Polo sheep; the markhor, a wild mountain goat, which grows to about 1.5 metres; the ibex, another kind of mountain goat; the urial, a wild sheep; the snow leopard, which is believed to be almost extinct; and black and brown Himalayan bears. Reptiles, and various species of rodents and birdlife also abound here. The latter includes the Indian roller, the crested hopoe, the kingfisher, the common kite and a number of migratory birds from Siberia. The northern mountain zone is noted for its hawks, falcons and eagles. Flowers in the glacial region of the Himalayas include the wild rose, sunflower and edelweiss among others. Numerous herbs such as alfalfa and thyme grow in profusion in this craggy country.

RELIGION

The state of Pakistan was founded on Islam, and is consequently overwhelmingly Islamic. Hindus compose only about a million of the total population, a far smaller percentage than the number of Muslims in India.

However, historically it has been the site for a great number of religions. Hinduism evolved here from the original Aryan invaders, and the Buddhist empire of Ashoka extended into much of present day Pakistan.

Other religious minority groups include a number of Christians, Parsees and the Kalash Kafirs of the Chitral region. In Karachi there is a small but influential group of Zoroastrians who form an important, but unofficial, line of communication to their fellow fire-worshippers in Bombay in India. Even the Muslims are divided into three major sects: the Sunnis, orthodox Muslims; the Shi'ites or Shias, followers of Imam Ali who was killed in the Karbala; and the Ismailis or Maulais, followers of the Agha Khan. With the exception of countries like Iran where the Shi'ites are in the majority, the Sunnis predominate throughout the Islamic world.

The influence of the Islamic fundamentalist movement in neighbouring countries moved the government in Pakistan to codify Islamic tenets into the body of laws of the country. The severe penal code upheld in Saudia Arabia of cutting the hands off thieves and of flogging lovers convicted of adultery has been adopted by Pakistan. Disparaging the prophet Mohammed is now punishable by death.

Marco Polo Sheep

Islam

The founder of Islam was the Arab prophet, Mohammed, who was born in Mecca in 571, and began his teachings in 612 AD. His descent is traditionally traced back to Abraham who had two wives, Hagar and Sarah. Hagar gave birth to Ismail, and Sarah had a son named Isaac. As the first wife, Sarah demanded that Hagar and Ismail be banished from the tribe. According to the Koran, the holy book of Islam, Ismail then went to Mecca, and apparently his descendants can be traced through to Mohammed.

The initial reaction to Mohammed's message was one of hostility. The uncompromising monotheism – Allah is the one true God, all-powerful, all-pervading – threatened the polytheism and idolatry of the Arabs. Mohammed's teachings conflicted with what he believed was a corrupt and decadent social order, and in a society which was afflicted with class divisions, he was preaching a universal brotherhood in which all people are equal in the eyes of God. Mohammed did not claim to have supernatural powers. He taught that he was the chosen teacher of God's message – the only true prophet charged with the divine mission of conveying the word of God.

By 622 Mohammed was beginning to gain adherents and enemies. In the same year he and his followers were forced to flee from Mecca to Medina. This flight or *hegira* is the starting point for the Muslim lunar calendar. There he managed to build a political base and an army, which eventually defeated Mecca and brought all Arabia under his control. Mohammed died in 632 AD, two years after taking Mecca, but within a century the Arab Muslims had forged a huge empire which stretched all the way from Persia to Spain. Though the power of the Arabs was eventually superseded by the Turks, Islam continues to be a powerful force.

At an early stage Islam suffered a fundamental split which remains to this day. The third caliph, successor to Mohammed, was murdered and followed by Ali, the prophet's son-in-law, in 656. Ali was assassinated in 661 by the Governor of Syria, who set himself up as caliph in preference to the descendents of Ali. Today 90% of all Muslims are Sunnis, followers of the succession from the caliph, whilst the remainder are Shi'ites who follow the descendants of Ali. Iran is the only country where the Shi'ites form a majority. The Shi'ites further split into two groups after a dispute regarding belief and scriptural interpretation and from this evolved the Ismailis who are followers of the Agha Khan.

The teachings of Mohammed are contained in the Muslim holy book, the Koran, which was compiled after his death. It is divided into 114 chapters and is considered to be the very word of Allah. Much of the Koran is devoted to codes of behaviour and much emphasis is placed on God's mercy to mankind. The other main source for Muslim social conduct and behaviour is the Sunna, as reported in the Hadith, based on the deeds and utterances of Mohammed and chronicled by his contemporaries.

Mohammed's teachings are heavily influenced by Judaism and Christianity, and there are many similarities. These include a belief in hell, heaven and one true God, a creation theory almost identical to the Garden of Eden, and myths like Noah's Ark and Aaron's Rod.

The name Islam is derived from the word *salam* which means 'peace', but it has a secondary connotation, 'surrender'. The true meaning is something like 'the peace which comes by surrendering to God' and the corresponding adjective is *Muslim*. The fundamental tenet of Islam is the expression *'La ilaha illa Ilah'* – there is no God but Allah. Islam is a faith that demands unconditional surrender to the wisdom of Allah and means far more than a mere set of beliefs or rules. It involves total commitment to a way of life, philosophy and law. Theoretically it is a democratic faith in which devotion is the responsibility of the individual, unrestricted by hierarchy and petty social prerequisites, and concerned with encouraging initiative and independence in the believer. Nor, in theory, is worship bound to a particular locale – the faithful can worship in a rice field, house, mosque or on a mountain. But in practice it is a moralistic religion and its followers are duty-bound to fulfil many restrictive rituals and laws, such as the washing of hands and face, worshipping five times a day at a mosque, constant recitation of the Koran, almsgiving, fasting annually during the month of Ramadan and saving to make the pilgrimage *Hadj* to Mecca. It is also a fatalistic faith in which every-thing is rationalised as the will of Allah.

Sufism - Islamic Mysticism

Sufism emerged in ancient Persia. It was spread across the Middle East and to the west and east of the Indo-Pakistan subcontinent in the 12th and 13th centuries, by Shah Abdul Latif Bhitai, Sachal Sarwart, Lal Shahbaz Qalandar and Hazrat Bahauddin Zakaria of Multan, who were all followers of the Sufi saint, Shahabuddin Suhrawardy.

Shah Latif Bhitai is considered the greatest Sufi mystic and poet/philosopher of Sind followed by Sachal and Qalandar. These Sufis were pirs, dervishes or fakirs, who preached brotherhood, love and peace. They relied mainly on their own moral and spiritual resources and were impressive for their tolerance of other creeds, recognising them all as avenues to Allah.

Like the sadhus of India they were ascetic wanderers. They wandered through the deserts, renounced vanity, protested against worldliness and sought knowledge through their nomadic existence. When they did settle, like Lal Shahbaz Qalandar in Sehwan Sharif or Shah Abdul Latif Bhitai who lived in a sand dune in Hala

near Hyderabad, they tended to choose to live in caves. In Gholra Sharif near Rawalpindi there are man-made caves, now in ruins, where the *pirs* retired for months and even years to meditate on life, the universe and Allah.

They wrote verses about the love of God which they set to music and sang and danced to, first slowly then faster and faster until in a frenzy they fell into a trance. Legend has it that when Sachal went into an ecstatic trance through the rhythmic sounds of various musical instruments, including his own voice, his long hair stood on end. Qalandar is remembered by his followers for his loud music and wild dancing.

Sufism influenced the literature, art, culture and music of the land as well as giving rise to another religion – Sikhism. Guru Nanak, founder of Sikhism, and Kabir, a Muslim saint, propagated the belief in oneness. Nanak was a Hindu but was claimed as a leader by the Muslims who called him Nanak Shah, while the Hindus regarded Kabir as their greatest teacher. This united both the Hindus and the Muslims and gave impetus to the emergence of Sikhism.

The shrines of Qalandar in Sehwan Sharif, of Latif Bhitai in Hala, of Datta Ganj Baksh in Lahore and of Imam Bari (Shiah Sufi) in Islamabad – retain a profound air of mysticism despite pot-smoking malangs, dervishes or fakirs, who dance in a frenzied manner to the beating of drums. They are usually hung with pennants or colourful flags during *urs* or anniversaries of saints when hundreds of thousands of their followers gather there. At these times, despite the massed crowds, they manage to impart a strict, sacred, religious festival mood.

Each Sufi mystic shrine has a particular characteristic to differentiate it; peacocks abound around the mausoleum of Shah Hu Bahu in the Kallarkahar area in the Salt Range; ravens in Gujarat at the shrine of Pir Kaman Wallah; and singers and musicians gather at Sehwan Sharif shrine of Qalandar; snake charmers go to Umarkot for the shrine of Pir Namana Shah, and at the shrine of Hazrat Sakhi Qadir in Pakpattan fakirs bind themselves in chains.

In Baltistan, the Sufis of the Valley of Khapulu, the Nurbuksh, have distinctive temples that are to be seen nowhere else in the world. They are also more liberal in their philosophy and behaviour towards others.

Life in Pakistan

Pakistan is a tapestry of bright and dazzling oriental colours set against the sounds of plodding camels, the clip-clop of horse-drawn tongas and victorias, the sputtering and skittering of auto-rickshaws and, above all, the wail of the muezzin. That cry from the minarets is an ever-present reminder of the power of religion in this intensely Islamic country. The call to prayer, long and passionate, emanates from loudspeakers jutting out of the minarets of mosques in towns and villages throughout the country. Out in the fields a tractor will stop and a Sindhi or Punjabi farmer will spread his prayer mat on the ground facing Mecca.

Except in the very remote villages, purdah (seclusion of women) is slowly being put aside. In those hidden areas of Baluchistan, amongst the Pathans of the North West Frontier Province and in the high northern mountains, any local woman caught unveiled hastily slips on her purdah, or if without a veil, turns her back and hides her face. In the wilder tribal areas of the mountains, life is hard and insecure. The men walk around armed, not merely to hunt, but to protect themselves from their tribal enemies. Women seldom venture far from their houses, which are walled in and built with towers like forts.

These fortified villages are usually autonomous. They have a *jirga* – a village council of elders – who adjudicate disputes and make decisions concerning village life. There is usually a *malik* who

generally speaks Urdu and English, and acts as a kind of political agent or liaison officer between the tribes and the government. Higher up in the mountains the small groups of villages, which have merged into mirdoms, are more peaceful and, unlike the people of Baluchistan and the North West Frontier Province, are no longer tribal. Despite their snowbound isolation, the new roads have rapidly brought even the Kalash Kafirs into contact with the outside world.

Life for the pastoral nomads is different again. In spring and summer they load up their camels and move to the upland pastures. The men herd the cattle, sheep and goats. The women, unveiled and unselfconscious, trudge along carrying their babies in one arm while balancing large wicker baskets on their heads. In the winter they return to the desert where young children, still only toddlers, are taught to look after the family animals. Even in these remote regions the muezzin call to prayer can be heard.

Pakistan is a land of mosques, but it is also one of graveyards and shrines known as *derghas*, bristling with flags where country people come to pay homage, make requests or offer prayers to those legendary saints who flew like eagles or turned the course of rivers. These legendary times are still part of every day life in Pakistan. In and around Hund the children use writing tablets and reed pens like those of the Gandhara period. The turbans, footwear and musical instruments have scarcely changed over the centuries and in the valleys of the Kalash Kafirs the way of life remains much as it was over 2000 years ago. In the Larkana region bullock carts are the same as those used in Harappa and Moenjodaro, 5000 years ago.

People appear to be almost contemptuous of time, refusing to be driven to a hectic way of life despite encroaching progress. This dichotomy between old and new is becoming increasingly obvious, impinging on all aspects of life. Islamic fundamentalism is dragging the country back into mediaeval times while modern trends are pulling in the opposite direction.

Despite the strictures of Islam many travellers report that Pakistan can be an amazingly friendly country, and that the people are courteous and outgoing. However, women may find it oppressive. It is important to remember that women in Muslim society remain segregated, hidden in the background and totally subject to patriarchal rule.

Pakistan has undergone many changes since this book was first written. Progress has been fast in some areas, slow in others. With the economy improving and prosperity in the air, Pakistan is gradually assuming the trappings of a modern, developing country. It is losing some of its 'romanticism' as a result, but becoming more efficient, less exasperating and a little more comfortable.

ARCHAEOLOGY

Pakistan is one of the most interesting and fascinating archaeological areas in the world. Here one can trace human development from the paleolithic, neolithic, prehistoric, proto-historic and historic ages.

Paleolithic tribes developed the Soan Pebble Culture in the Potwar Plateau 500,000 years ago. Neolithic tribes, already occupied with the study of the stars, developed their megalithic culture up in the Northern Territory; and in Amri in Sind and Mehr Ghar in Baluchistan, neolithic tribes (6000 to 3000 BC) were the first to domesticate the buffalo. They also had trade relations with Persia and Central Asia.

Around 3000 BC, the pre-Aryans developed settlements, and the Indus Valley civilisation emerged. The pre-Aryans produced sophisticated artefacts which are now on show in the major museums of the country. Their steatite seals, which display advanced artistry in the craft, are of great interest. Etched in a highly sophisticated art style, they are engraved with animals like the humped Brahman bull they venerated, or tigers, elephants, antelopes, fish-eating crocodiles and rhinoceros. A seal found in Harappa has a cross on one side and a splayed eagle with a snake above each wing on the other. The motif is similar to those found in Mesopotamia, Susa, and Tall-Brak in Syria. They are often engraved with characters believed to be the precursor of hieroglyphs, which were later developed in this region.

Moenjodaro, which means 'Mound of the Dead', has surprisingly revealed no regular cemetery, but in Harappa they have found two. The graves point north-south and were large enough to contain between 15 and 20 clay pots. Shell bangles, necklaces and amulets of steatite, paste beads, copper finger-rings, earrings of thin copper wire, lamps of clay and bones of fowls were found at the foot of the graves.

Other cities of the great prehistoric Indus Valley civilisation include: Kot Diji, now the site of a great fort near Rohri in Sind, Rehman Deri in the southern region of the North West Frontier Province, and Taxila. In the valley of Peshawar and in the area of the Potwar Plateau, Alexander the Great built towns and cities, supposedly to guard the eastern frontier of the Hellenic empire.

Of the Mauryan empire of Chandragupta, who superseded Alexander the Great, the only inscriptions that remain are those of Ashoka, the greatest of the Mauryan emperors. The Kushan empire, developers of the Gandhara culture, left ruins of their cities like Taxila, Charsadda and Pushkalavati, the ancient capital of Peshawar. Their artistic sculptures, Buddhist monasteries, stupas, rock carvings and inscriptions are strewn all over the valley of Peshawar, Swat, Dir, Taxila and right up to the northern upper highland, particularly along the Karakoram Highway which follows the ancient Silk Trade Route, from what is

now known as the Grand Trunk Road, up to Gilgit and beyond the Mintaka Pass.

The upper highland of the Northern Territory is a craggy gallery and museum of rock carvings and inscriptions which date back to neolithic times. The petroglyphs point to the significant role of this area in the history of Eurasia, particularly during the period of the Silk Trade Route civilisation. These rock records show the arrival of the Aryans, and later the Achaemenians, the Greeks, the Scythians, the Parthians, the Sassanians, the Hepthalites and the Chinese and Tibetans, who engraved their passage through what the ancient Chinese described as the 'suspended crossing'. This 'suspended crossing' was a major section of the ancient Silk Trade Route until about the 9th century AD. They recorded the details of daily life from animals, activities, imperial visits – to symbols, coats-of-arms and scripts.

HOLIDAYS & FESTIVALS

Holidays in Pakistan are generally either Muslim religious festivals or concerned with independence and the memory of Mohammed Ali Jinnah, father of modern Pakistan. The Muslim holidays are based on the lunar calendar which is at least 10 days shorter than ours each year, so each year they occur 10 days earlier.

Public Holidays

23 March	Pakistan Day – celebrates the 1940 decision to press for a Muslim nation independent of India
1 May	May Day – Labour Day
1 July	Bank holiday: other offices and businesses remain open
14 August	Independence Day – commemorates Pakistan's founding in 1947
6 September	Defence of Pakistan Day – commemorates the India-Pakistan war of 1965 over Kashmir
11 September	Anniversary of Quaid-i-Azam (Jinnah's) death
25 December	Birthday of Quaid-i-Azam (Mohammed Ali Jinnah)
31 December	Bank holiday: other offices and businesses remain open

Muslim Religious Holidays

For 1988 they fall approximately on:

18 April	Start of the month of Ramadan
17 May	Eid-ul-Fitr – two-day feast to celebrate the end of Ramadan
25 July	Eid-ul-Azha – sacrifice of Ismail, this is the time for the pilgrimage to Mecca
25 August	Azhura (Muharram) – death of Imam Hussain, during this period Shi'ites scourge themselves and work themselves up into an emotional frenzy over the event
23 October	Eid-Milad-un-Nabi – birthday of the prophet, Mohammed

LANGUAGE

English is widely spoken throughout Pakistan but Urdu is the major local language. In the Punjab the people speak Punjabi, while close to the Afghanistan border, around Peshawar, they speak Pushto. Other major languages are Sindhi and Baluchi. Shina, Khowari, Burushuski and Balti are the Northern Territory languages.

A relatively recent language is Urdu, which was used in the Moghul encampments by a motley collection of troops mainly from Central Asia, Persia and India. It became the lingua franca of the camps and evolved into a language spoken mainly in the north-west of the subcontinent.

A knowledge of this language will improve your chances of having a good time in Pakistan. It is also spoken in parts of India and consequently is extremely useful.

Below is a list of commonly used words and phrases.

hello/goodbye	*salaam*
thank you	*shukria*
sir	*jenab*
yes	*haan/ji haan*
no	*nahin*
well/OK	*thik*
good/yes	*achchah*
why	*kyon*
I'm well	*thik hun*
bad	*kharab*
where	*kidhar*
how much?	*kitna?*
expensive	*mahenga*
much	*bahut*
little	*tora*
enough	*bas*
stop	*rukiya*
difficult	*mushkil*
and/more	*aur*
or	*ya*
that/he/she/it	*voh*
I/we	*main/hum*
you	*aap*
I go	*men jata hun (m)*
	men jati hun (f)
I am going	*ja raha hun (m)*
	ja rahi hun (f)
went	*gaya (m) gayi (f)*
know	*malum*
understand	*janta*
room	*kamra*
bedding	*bistar*
bus	*bas*
country	*mulk*
watchman	*chowkidar*
year	*sal*
month	*mahaina*
tomorrow/yesterday	*kal*
morning	*subha*
time	*waqt*
hour	*ghanta*

half (as in time)	*sarheh*
1½	*derh*
half	*adha*
water	*pani*
tea	*chai*
food	*khana*
hot(food)	*garam*
cold (food)	*tanda*
meat	*gosht*
roasted skewered meat	*kebab*
chicken	*murgi*
roasted chicken	*tikka*
rice	*chawal/pulau*
potato	*alu*
vegetable	*sabzi*
lentils	*dahl*
onions	*piyaz*
egg	*anda*
bread	*roti*
unleavened flat round bread	*chapati*
Persian bread	*nan*
garlic	*lashun*
salt	*namak*
sugar	*chinni*
hot weather	*garmi*
cold weather	*sardi*
rain	*barash*

Greetings

Peace be unto you!	*Asallah-allaikhum!*
Unto you also peace!	*Wallaikhum salaam!*
How are you?	*Kya aap kaise hai?*
What is your name?	*Aapka nam kya hai?*
God willing!	*Inshallah*

Some phrases: I would like food – *mujhe khana chahiye* or *mujhe chai chahiye* – I would like tea. *Mujhe kamra chahiye* – I would like a room. To ask a question the verb *hai* (to have) is almost always used, for example 'Where is the GPO' is translated as *GPO kidhar hai?*

If you want sugar and milk in your tea another useful phrase to remember is *chai duod-chinni.*

Numbers

1	*ek*	20	*bis*
2	*do*	30	*tis*
3	*tin*	40	*chalis*
4	*char*	50	*pachas*
5	*panch*	60	*sath*
6	*chhe*	70	*sat tar*
7	*saat*	80	*assi*
8	*ath*	90	*nabbe*
9	*nau*	100	*ek sau*
10	*das*	1000	*hazar*
11	*gyarah*	100,000	*ek lakh*
12	*barah*	10 million	*ek crore*
13	*terah*	10 billion	*ek arab*
14	*chauda*		
15	*pandra*		
16	*sullah*		
17	*satra*		
18	*atharra*		
19	*unnis*		

Note The difficulty with Urdu numbers is that they have different terms running in a consecutive manner. For example 25 is not *bis-panch* but *pachis*; 24 is not *bis-char* but *chau-bis*. Take care not to confuse *pachis* (25) with *pachas* (50).

Facts for the Visitor

VISAS

A passport that is valid for Pakistan is required by all visitors. Visa requirements have toughened up and almost all visitors now require a visa for Pakistan. The good old days of unlimited stay for British and Commonwealth citizens is over. Visas are free for Australians, Canadians and New Zealanders but hapless Brits will have to pay a hefty fee of around £25.

Visas are issued for up to three months, but if you ask for two that's all you'll get. For most nationalities there is no visa fee, this includes the USA. Pakistan also issues multi-entry visas which allow six trips within a period of one year. Check with the nearest Pakistan embassy or consulate.

Those in transit do not require a visa provided that they continue their journey within 72 hours and hold confirmed onward tickets.

All visitors staying for more than one month are required to register with the Foreigners Registration Office at police headquarters in the nearest city. It is not necessary to do this until the one month period is up.

Visa Extensions Visa extensions are denied or granted according to the treaty agreement of the government of Pakistan with the government of the traveller. However, foreign registration officers in the hinterland are often not aware of these treaty agreements.

Tribal or special areas have different rules and regulations. Commissioners and/or superintendents of police have no authority to extend visas. They can only issue a permit allowing an extension for a limited period of time. This varies in different regions, but usually does not extend beyond a week.

Travellers seeking a visa extension in the Punjab – particularly if in Rawalpindi or Islamabad – should see Abdul Salaam

of the Interior Ministry, Block R, Room 512, 5th floor, the Secretariat, Islamabad.

Registration When a visa extension is granted, this amounts to registration in some areas such as Karachi, but not in Rawalpindi or Islamabad where registration at another office is the next step.

Karakoram Highway Permits are no longer required for the Karakoram Highway from Rawalpindi to Gilgit and as far as Baturo Bridge beyond Hunza.

MONEY

Approximate exchange rates (1987) are:

US$1	Rs 17.21
£1	Rs 27.64
A$1	Rs 12.05
C$1	Rs 13.18

The rupee (Rs) is divided into 100 paise but you may still occasionally hear prices referred to in annas – the rupee used to be divided into 16 annas, and in markets the term is still used occasionally. Twenty-five paise is equal to four annas. When you're changing money, always check that you have been given the correct amount and flip through the paper bills received. If you have been handed any really dirty, tatty-looking notes that have obviously been in circulation for years, try to exchange them for newer ones there and then if possible. As in India you may have some difficulty in them being accepted elsewhere if you don't.

You can bring in any amount of foreign currency or travellers' cheques but only Rs 100 in Pakistan currency. Inflation has hit Pakistan rather badly and prices are spiralling. Sterling pounds and US dollars have good exchange rates, but not quite good enough to offset the effect of inflation. Deutschemarks are also good. As usual, American Express travellers' cheques, which are available in any of these currencies, have the advantage of being replaceable at their offices in Karachi, Lahore, Islamabad and Rawalpindi. Offices at the latter two cities are apparently unreliable, fraught with hassles and offer service very reluctantly. Don't rely on having your money or mail sent to you here either. You will probably have to wait for ages for them, even if they have already arrived. If you need money from home urgently, it's better to have it sent across by bank draft as registered airmail to a specific address, preferably your embassy, consulate or a friend's place in Karachi or Lahore, than to have it transferred from bank to bank via telex or cable. There are too many delays via the latter method.

If you have US dollars, Indian rupees or any other negotiable foreign currency on you when you arrive in Pakistan, hide it well. Officials – police, customs officers, etc. – will have no hesitation in using threats and intimidation to relieve you of it.

On departure you can reconvert up to Rs 500 into foreign currency but be sure you have your encashment receipts. You can only take Rs 20 out of the country in Pakistan currency. Applications to the State Bank of Pakistan, or through its authorised outlets, must be made for larger sums.

CUSTOMS

The usual duty-free regulations apply to Pakistan with the exception that you should not bring liquor with you. There are generally no restrictions on what you may export, so long as you show foreign exchange receipts to the value of the items you're taking out. You are not allowed to take antiques out of the country. If you are worried about something you've purchased check with the museums at Lahore or Karachi to see whether you can export it.

Liquor SRO(1)/79 of the customs rules

and regulations of Pakistan unequivocally bans the import of liquor. It should be noted, however, that mountaineering, trekking and scientific expeditions often bring in consumables (foodstuffs) which include a supply of liquor.

Different rules apply to different categories of travellers. People who stay more than 24 hours but not more than six months are defined as travellers not tourists.

HEALTH

You need an International Health Certificate showing you have been immunised against cholera. If you are not immunised against cholera and find yourself at the border, you can obtain a certificate at Wagah for Rs 5 – Wagah is only 27 km from Lahore. Pakistan is in the malarial area and it is necessary to take a weekly or daily dose of prescribed anti-malarial tablets.

Avoid drinking any water that you are not sure has been boiled or purified wherever possible. This is a lot easier to say than to do, but take every precaution that you can. Water is more likely to be purer and less harmful in the monsoon season than at any other period during the year. As in India, care in where and what you eat will help protect your gut and bowels from the often savage effects of a radical change in diet.

Malaria Malaria is spread by the bite of the mosquito which transmits the parasite that causes the disease. This disease has an unpleasant habit of recurring from time to time, even if you get over it quite easily the first time. Occasionally, it can be fatal.

As yet, you can't be innoculated against malaria – although the medicos have been hinting that they're close to a breakthrough – but you can take simple precautions. These amount to taking either a daily or weekly tablet – depending on which brand your doctor recommends – which kill any parasites that manage to get into the bloodstream. You usually have to start taking the tablets about two weeks before entering the malarial zone and continue taking them for several weeks after you've left it. Another precaution is to try and avoid being bitten in the first place by using mosquito repellent, coils and nets.

Hepatitis Hepatitis is a disease of the liver which generally occurs in countries with poor sanitation. It's spread from person to person by contaminated food, water, or cooking and eating utensils. Possible sources of this disease are: salads which have been washed in contaminated water, food that has been handled by an infected person, or sharing a chillum (smoking pipe) with an infected person.

Symptoms appear from between 15 to 50 days after infection – generally around 25 days – and consist of fever, loss of appetite, nausea, depression, complete lack of energy and pains around the bottom of your rib cage (the location of the liver). Your skin turns progressively yellow and the whites of your eyes turn yellow to orange. The best way to detect it is to check your eyes and urine. The latter will also turn a deep orange, no matter how much liquid you drink. However, if you haven't drunk much liquid and/or you're sweating a lot, don't jump to hasty conclusions. Drink plenty of boiled or purified water and then, if your urine is still bright orange go to the nearest hospital for a check.

However, the severity of the disease varies. It may last less than two weeks and give you only a few bad days, or it may last for several months and give you a few bad weeks. And you could feel depleted of energy for several months.

The usual protection against hepatitis is a gamma-globulin injection, this has been improved over the last few years and now can give protection for up to six months. The best way to guard against hepatitis is to be careful about what you eat and drink.

Diarrhoea Diarrhoea is often due simply to a change of diet. A lot depends on what your digestive system is used to and whether or not you've got an iron gut. If you do get diarrhoea, the first thing to do is nothing – it rarely lasts more than a few days. Fasting will often cure diarrhoea, but make sure you drink enough liquids to avoid dehydration. If you have to travel, Lomotil will stop the symptoms but it will not cure you. You need a prescription to obtain this drug, so ask your doctor for a supply before you leave.

If diarrhoea persists for several days and is accompanied by severe abdominal pain, fever, or blood in your stools, then it may be dysentery. Whilst diarrhoea is unfortunately all-too-common, it is rare to contract dysentery. There are two types – amoebic and bacillary. Both require a course of drugs and medical advice should be sought.

Dehydration It's easy to become dehydrated if you don't drink enough, which is one reason why it's a good idea to carry a water bottle with you. You will know you are dehydrated if you find you are urinating infrequently or if it is a deep yellow or orange colour. A secondary symptom is headaches. Remember, you sweat just as much in hot, dry climates like Pakistan's as you do in hot, humid climates. The only difference is that in dry climates the sweat evaporates, whereas in humid climates the sweat is unable to evaporate because the air itself is already moist, and you end up in a lather of sweat.

If you're sweating profusely, you're going to lose a lot of salt, which leads to fatigue and muscle cramps. Make it up by putting extra salt in your food – a teaspoon a day is enough – but don't increase your salt intake unless you also increase your water intake.

Medical Facilities There are a number of excellent hospitals in urban areas which can correctly and quickly diagnose ailments, prescribe medical treatment and even provide free medicine. Doctors specialise in local diseases and they know their business. Medical assistants in Pakistan also appear to know what they are doing, even if they simply dump pills into your lap.

CLIMATE

Pakistan has some real climatic extremes – from the broiling heat of the southern deserts to the freezing cold of the northern mountains. The summer season begins in mid-April, but it starts to get uncomfortably hot in May. June, July and August are the hottest months of the year. On the plains temperatures are generally 30°C or more, but can soar to a very uncomfortable 45°C.

The monsoon arrives in mid-July and continues till mid-September but it is not as severe as it is in India. It brings 40 to 50 centimetres of rain on the plains, and between 150 to 200 centimetres to the lower regions of the northern highland. The monsoon never reaches the upper highland, although it gets cloudy enough to disrupt flights.

The best time to visit Pakistan is from mid-September until March – after the monsoon. The days are cool, clear and pleasant during this period, but it can get cold on the plains at night. In the depths of winter in the far north the temperature can dip well below freezing and bring bitterly cold nights.

BUSINESS HOURS

On Fridays, shops and offices are closed. The weekend begins on Thursday afternoon when public and private offices close at 12 noon, and other offices at 2 pm. Usual business hours are 9 am to 4 pm in winter, 7.30 am to 2.30 pm in summer. Banks are open from 9 am to 1 pm, Monday to Thursday and 9 to 11 am, Saturday and Sunday. Big stores are open from 8 am to 9 pm. Hours are more variable, but usually longer, in smaller shops and stalls. Post Offices keep normal business hours except during Ramadan when some are open only until 2 pm. GPO's are usually open for business on Fridays from 9 am to 1 pm.

BANKS

All banks, except the foreign ones, have been nationalised. Nearly all the major foreign banks are represented in the major cities, so there should be no problems cashing travellers' cheques. In urban areas foreign currency and travellers' cheques can be cashed in almost any bank, but particularly the Pakistan National Bank and the Habib Bank. In some special areas like Quetta, Peshawar and the Northern Territory only the Pakistan National Bank deals with foreign currencies and travellers' cheques. In the Northern Territory, particularly Gilgit and Baltistan, the Pakistan National Bank does not accept foreign currency apart from US dollars and pounds sterling. It must also be noted that banks in different regions offer different rates of exchange for foreign currency and travellers' cheques.

Never have money sent to a bank by telegraph or telex transfer, as already mentioned. This warning cannot be stressed often enough. A bankdraft must be addressed to a specific local bank to make encashing it easier. Grindlay's Bank in Islamabad (but not in Rawalpindi), which deals with diplomats' accounts, has the best reputation. If you need to have lost travellers' cheques replaced, plan to do so in Karachi and Lahore, but not Islamabad or Rawalpindi – for reasons already stated. American Express offices, particularly in Islamabad and Rawalpindi, have become notorious for inefficiency and inconvenience to visitors who have limited time in the country.

EMBASSIES

There are consular offices in Karachi, Quetta and Peshawar, but most of the embassies are in Islamabad.

MUSEUMS/GALLERIES/LIBRARIES

There are libraries, museums and art galleries in almost every major city in Pakistan, including small galleries and museums specialising in folk art or handicraft.

FILM

There are now photographic studios capable of excellent colour film processing in nearly every major city. Buying film to suit your camera is another matter, but there are specialist shops where you can get most kinds of film in Karachi, Lahore and Islamabad.

ENTERTAINMENT

The only entertainment readily available consists of television and cinemas which usually feature local, Indian and occasionally western films.

There are no massage parlours, night clubs, cabarets, bars or red light districts here. There is, of course, sport which includes cricket and hockey. Up in the Northern Territory they play polo and games like *bushkazi*, which was introduced by the Afghan refugees in the region. This is a wild, raging activity involving lots of thrills and spills, possibly what you would expect the wild, raging horsemen of the steppes to indulge in on their day off. It requires a large playing field – at least a couple of km long – some *chapandoz*, the swaggering horsemen who look like Genghis Khan (indeed, the latter would make an ideal captain were he still around) and a *boz*, the headless body of a goat. The chapandoz are divided into two teams and a marker peg is hammered into the ground at one end of the field. The boz is dropped at the other end, and then all hell breaks loose. The idea is to pick up the boz, carry it up and around the marker, then drop it back at its starting point. But it's not so easy to achieve when you've got a fierce team of superb Afghani riders trying to stop you by using any method they can!

TRAVEL & TREKKING AGENCIES

In almost every major city there are travel and tour agencies, but there are only a few mountaineering and trekking agencies, and most of these are in Islamabad and Rawalpindi.

BEACHES

There are a number of beaches where you can go water skiing and surfing, but this is usually only possible on those beaches controlled by hotels. Western women should not wear bikinis on any other beaches.

OTHER

There's duck shooting, wild boar hunting, fishing and bird-watching on the southern plains, and trout fishing up in the Northern Territory. Hunting has been banned since 1980.

PUBLICATIONS

Dawn and *Morning News* are the major English newspapers in Karachi and the *Pakistan Times* and *The Muslim* are available in Lahore, Rawalpindi and Islamabad. All other major magazines such as *Time* and *Newsweek* can be bought at major bookstores.

ELECTRICITY

220 volts, alternating current.

TIME

Pakistan is five hours ahead of GMT. When it is noon in Pakistan it is 7 am in London, 12.30 pm in India, 5 pm on the Australian east coast, and 2 am on the US east coast.

POST/TELEPHONE/TELEGRAPH

Mail services are fairly reliable although important letters should be registered or insured. It's best to use aerogrammes where possible. The postal service in the main cities is fairly reliable, but don't count on it elsewhere. Poste Restante is also reasonably reliable.

Telegraph and telephone offices are

everywhere, but telegrams should only be sent from the main cities. International phone calls can be made from major hotels, but as with India do not be surprised if you have to shout down the receiver.

INFORMATION

The Pakistan Tourism Development Corporation has its head office at the Hotel Metropole, Club Road, Karachi (tel 51 6031 or 51 0234). A number of brochures on most of the interesting regions are available here. There are also offices in Lahore, Rawalpindi, Peshawar, Quetta and most other places of interest to travellers, including the Northern Territory.

In Karachi there are also PTDC information centres at the airport and in the Hotel Pearl Continental.

ACCOMMODATION

Pakistan now has hotels of international standard in every major city, with such familiar names as *Holiday Inn*, *Hilton*, *Sheraton*, and the *Pearl Continental*. It has accommodation for every class and type of traveller from the international five-star hotels down to *mussafir khanas* – local inns – where charpoys (rope beds) are still available.

In most cases these local inns and the cheaper hotels do not accept foreigners except those in remote towns and villages where there is no alternative. In many cases you will find places of exceptional value, but it is also advisable to check the rooms and toilet facilities before booking in. In towns where specific recommendations are not listed you will generally find hotels clustered around railway or bus stations. Most hotels recommended are chosen for their location, cleanliness and safety, but they are not necessarily the best.

There are also a number of youth hostels but these are often not open and/ or located at an inconvenient distance from the cities. Karachi and Lahore have YMCA and YWCA hostels, non-members can pay a temporary membership fee to stay there. The Salvation Army hostels in these cities accept only foreign tourists and require no membership fee. Major railway stations usually have retiring rooms with beds available for railway passengers, but you will need a sleeping bag. Retiring rooms are available to air-con and 1st class passengers, but waiting rooms with chairs, sofas, toilet and shower rooms are available for other passengers.

Camping It is possible to camp in the gardens of *Dak Bungalows*, guest houses, rest houses and Youth Hostels in Pakistan. There are no official camp-sites apart from the *Tourist Camp* in Islamabad, which also has a few dorm rooms. Camping on roadsides or in tribal areas in Baluchistan and the North West Frontier Province is forbidden.

Showers Major railway stations usually have free shower rooms, which are handy in summer if you're on the road. In urban areas or villages there are also the *hammams*, attached to barber shops, where you can have a refreshing wash in little cubicles for a small fee. In winter they provide hot water. They are easily identifiable by the towels hanging out front to dry.

FOOD & DRINK

Pakistan is a country where a variety of different kinds of foods is available. In most cities you have a choice of Middle Eastern, Indian and Afghani food. In Peshawar what you eat is similar to the Pathan food of Afghanistan – *kebab* and *nan* – while in Lahore it is Moghul – tandoori chicken. By and large food here is similar to that in India, although the curries are generally not quite so hot.

Specialities include kebabs of various types. For example *sheikh kebab* is minced and grilled meat on a skewer, and *shami kebabs* are minced meatballs.

Top: Boats in Karachi harbour (PE)
Bottom: Gidani Beach near Karachi (PE)

Top: Typical Pakistani truck (PE)
Left: Shah Jahan Mosque, Thatta (PE)
Right: Chaukundi Tombs (PE)

Tikka is a tasty spiced and barbecued dish consisting of chunks of beef, mutton or chicken. One of the great Pakistani taste sensations is a whole roasted leg of lamb called *sajji*.

Note that there are meatless days, usually on Tuesdays or Wednesdays, when restaurants only serve poultry or fish. In general, however, Pakistan is not a good place for vegetarians.

The unleavened Indian-style bread known as *chappatis*, or the Iranian bread *nan* are usually an integral part of the meal, as is the lentil dish *dhal*. Seafood is particularly good in Karachi. Other popular dishes include *pulau*, rice cooked with spices mixed with chicken or lamb, and *samosas*, flaky pastry triangles filled with meat or vegetables. *Paratha* is unleavened bread but thicker than a chappati and fried until crisp, usually eaten at breakfast with fried eggs and tea. *Puri* is another type of bread but it is soaked in ghee and deep fried so that the mixture rises until the bread is puffed up and crisp. It is eaten with curry.

When you're in Lahore visit the Old Walled city and try *kalla pacha*, a thick soup made out of sheep or goat forelegs, or sample *karlai gosht*, tender mutton, stewed or crispy fried. In Karachi have some *nohari*, spicy meat in gravy; and in Peshawar ask for *chapli-kebab*, another spicy meat dish shaped like the *chappal* or sandal, hence the name. In Hyderabad and Quetta ask for *sajji*.

There is a wide range of desserts, which include the popular ice-cream-like sweet called *kulfi*. Small sweet pastries are also popular as desserts, and there's a wide variety of fresh fruits varying from the tropical mangoes, pomegranates, papayas and melons of the plains to the apricots, peaches, apples, mulberries and pears of the cooler hill regions. There is also a variety of nuts available, including walnuts and almonds.

As in India the iced curd (yoghurt) drink, *lassi*, is very popular and refreshing. Another tasty drink is *nimbu pani*, which is made from fresh limes – ask whether the water's been boiled or purified before drinking it, if you're worried. You can also get various soft drinks but not Coca Cola or Pepsi. Generally tea is served with milk and sugar already in it – often with far too much of each. You can also get the black tea of the plains *sulaimani* and coffee is available. The salted tea of the northern area as well as Tibetan-style tea, churned with butter, is available mainly in the upper highlands. Green tea, called *shabaz chai*, is also popular and is usually flavoured with cardamom or jasmin.

Restaurants In the better hotels and restaurants, western food is available, but generally local food is all that's available, except for western-style breakfasts. As with India, the railway station restaurants are good places to go for a rather bland local attempt to reproduce English food. In major towns you will also find a few Chinese restaurants. Except for the restaurants at railway stations, opening hours are generally only from 7.30 to 9.30 am for breakfast, 12 noon to 2 pm for lunch, and 7.30 to 10 pm for dinner. Outside these hours it's considered snack time, and a sandwich and tea or soft drink is about all you can find. There are a few restaurants which only serve Muslims.

Ramadan The month of Ramadan is the holiest time of the year for Muslims. During Ramadan all Muslims fast for the entire day. Breakfast is at 2.30 am and only when the sun has vanished from the horizon can the fast be broken. A shrill siren followed by a chorus of muezzin calls from all the mosques in the vicinity, signals that the fast is over for the day. Smoking is also forbidden. Except for railway restaurants and teastalls or eating places around bus stations in urban areas, all restaurants and eating places are closed for business from dawn to dusk. However, food stores are often open for business.

Restaurants in large tourist hotels are licensed to open for business during Ramadan, mid-level hotels only serve breakfast in your room. Travellers on trains can eat and smoke, but not on buses. For foreigners it is an extremely difficult time. With empty stomachs locals can become rather irritable, tempers flare and there are more accidents on the road. Villagers are particularly strict about fasting, even while travelling or at work when, traditionally, they are exempt from the strictures of Ramadan.

If you are in the country during this time, take a water bottle and food with you when you go out, but be discreet about eating or smoking when there are locals around.

Ramadan has its advantages. You feel cleansed after a while, particularly if you stop smoking, and it is an opportunity to lose weight. But take care not to overdo it!

Liquor Permits To have an alcoholic drink you need a liquor permit which first requires a Tourist Certificate from the tourist information centre. They will direct you to the Excise and Tax Office where a Rs 12 fee entitles you to six bottles of hard liquor or 60 bottles of beer in a month! You can apply for a three-month liquor permit if you wish. The Excise and Tax Office will tell you where you can buy alcohol. The *American Club* or *Flashman's* in Islamabad or Rawalpindi are places where you can purchase liquor.

THINGS TO BUY
Pakistan has a number of interesting local handicrafts which include the fine Persian-style carpets rated by connoisseurs as being almost as good as real Persian rugs.

It also has some of the finest embroidery and leather work you will come across anywhere. The leather bags, jackets and shoes are excellent buys. Pakistan also produces exquisite brass and copperware, jewellery and other articles made of onyx,

silver and gold. Pottery is another highly developed craft, as is carpentry. So if you like ornately carved wooden screens, trays and furniture this is a good place to get them. Less ornate wooden products that Pakistan is noted for, are cricket bats and squash racquets, which are rated as the best by connoisseurs of sporting equipment.

In major cities government-controlled handicraft shops have fixed prices. Lahore and Peshawar both have extensive bazaars where you can often find unusual articles and precious and semi-precious gems, but Karachi probably has the widest range of shops and articles. Bargaining here is essential to get good value for money.

Duty-Free Shopping Duty-free shops have sprung up in Karachi and Lahore. In Karachi they have one at the International Airport and another on Airport Rd, but in Lahore they have only one in the city. Available in these shops are the usual items – perfume, tobacco, cigarettes, liquor, cameras, televisions, films, wristwatches. In addition they display local handicrafts such as carpets, leatherwork and jewellery.

WHAT TO BRING
As little as possible is the golden rule of good travelling. It's usually better to leave it behind and have to get a replacement when you're there, rather than bring too much and have to lug unwanted items around.

However, if you intend to go trekking, take good mountaineering or trekking gear. See the section on Northern Territory for equipment and requirements.

Other useful items to bring with you are a plug for sinks and basins, a padlock for hotel doors which are often fastened with a latch, and plenty of film for your camera.

Clothing Except for the coldest mid-winter nights, you will need nothing more than light clothes on the plains. A sweater or light jacket may be necessary for cold nights. But it's a different story up in the mountains where it gets icy cold, particularly at high altitudes. You will need as much warm gear as possible. In the height of summer on the plains or in the thin air of the mountains, you will also need good sun hats and glasses for protection against sunstroke.

The usual rules of Asian decorum apply to dress standards. In particular, women should dress very discreetly, but men should also be careful about what they wear – shorts are frowned upon. In summer it's preferable to wear light cotton shirts rather than singlets or T-shirts.

WOMEN TRAVELLERS

The Muslim social code requires strict conformity to the accepted standards of decorum. Discipline is harsh with little flexibility. In order not to offend the Muslim 'sense of decency' and to spare yourself unpleasant hassles, western women travelling in Pakistan should try to fit in. You will not often see women in Pakistan – they don't seem to exist on the streets. At most you might briefly see a shadowy figure in the distance, covered from head to foot with the long robe of 'purdah'. Some brave pioneers are making their way into banks and offices, but in general they lead their own life behind the walls of their homes.

Wearing the *salwar kamis* or traditional costume (loose baggy pants and long flowing shirt) can go a long way to gaining some acceptance and preventing an unwanted Muslim response to 'free' western women. Any tailor will be happy to make up a costume for you, they are comfortable and cheap. A *chaddor* (scarf) completes the costume and is used to cover the head in public.

The following is an extract from a letter sent to us by an Australian woman which may be useful advice for other women

travelling on their own or together. She writes:

Nothing could be preparation for the actual experience of walking down the street, the culture shock was so great I spent a lot of my time in Karachi in self-imposed purdah.

The things I think should be noted by the lone female traveller are:

(a) Buy some *Shalwar Kamis* (local clothes) which are excellent to travel in and people appreciate that you're wearing them. They also make you 'invisible' to the local males to some extent.

(b) Make yourself get out and walk – start with the main street. This is easy to do if you stay near the city centre and it's good exercise (if you're like me and the Aussie girl I travelled with and like the food, you will need to unless you want to put on weight). By walking you get to see all the bazaars and everyday life close up, and it's cheaper.

(c) Get some idea of Pakistani pronunciation so that when you need to ask directions they will understand you.

(d) If you want attention in banks, post offices, etc become like a Pakistani male – aggressive.

(e) Brush up on sport – always one way of getting into a conversation (people seem to be pleased if you know who is in their national teams). Also a good way of diverting the conversation from sex – all the men I talked to in Pakistan always got round to sex and would ask the most personal questions, and they had no hesitation in telling me how sexually frustrated Pakistani men are. Though I don't think they expected me to do anything about it. Politics is another good subject to change the subject if all the sex talk gets too much.

DRUGS

Smoking dope is illegal everywhere in Pakistan. Jail sentences for offenders are getting rather hard – you run the risk of receiving an unlimited jail sentence or paying a hefty bribe to get out of it.

Warning to Dope Smokers Be very wary of anyone who approaches you offering drugs. Many local dealers have connections with the police and will set you up for a 20% cut in the price of the drugs confiscated. Do not be persuaded to do any drug-running in the hope of making a quick buck, a number of unsuspecting travellers are in jail because they were induced to be 'mules', the colloquial expression used in Pakistan for drug smugglers. You may find yourself busted for very little and end up in jail with a lot of hassles and no money.

A Japanese traveller recently had to pay US$500 to a Lahore policeman after his 'friendly' hotel owner had dropped him in it. In fact, in some of the seedier hotels in Lahore, it may be worth checking the room for drugs before you check in as there have been cases of drugs being 'planted' by the owners of the hotels on unsuspecting travellers.

Getting There

AIR

Karachi is the main international access point for air travellers, although there are also some flights through Lahore – mainly to and from India – and Islamabad. *Pakistan International Airline* has a wide range of services to other Asian countries, the Gulf states and Europe. There are flights to Bombay from Karachi and to Delhi from Lahore. On departure there is an embarkation airport tax of Rs 100 on international flights, and Rs 5 to Rs 50 on domestic flights.

Concessions

For foreigners there are no concessions on domestic flights except for accredited students and journalists. For foreigners whose stay in the country is more than six months – 20% discount applies on normal air fares to anywhere in the world. For foreign tourists, from Karachi to London – 48% discount on roundtrip air fares, good for 90 days. From Karachi to Amsterdam, Athens, Copenhagen, Paris, Zurich or Rome – 40% discount on roundtrip tickets, good for 90 days. From Karachi to New York – 40% discount on roundtrip fares, good for 120 days. Karachi to Bangkok, Hong Kong, Manila, Kuala Lumpur, Singapore, Seoul, Beijing or Tokyo – 40% discount on roundtrip fares, good for 120 days.

There are also special concessions during high and low seasons.

Arrival

PIA has buses between the airport and town in Karachi and Islamabad, but don't count on this. There are usually public buses and minibuses, auto-rickshaws and taxis at the airport. Buses and minibuses are Rs 2 to Rs 3; auto-rickshaws Rs 15 to 25; taxis Rs 40 to Rs 50. The latter usually have meters, but although sealed, they will most likely have been tampered with. Fix fares before you leave the airport otherwise the trip to town will take a very long time!

LAND

India

Most overlanders today will be arriving from India – there are numerous fascinating comparisons and contrasts between Pakistan and India, making it interesting to see the two countries one after the other. Since Partition, the border with India has been closed everywhere except in the Punjab – by road at Wagah and by rail at Attari (Lahore-Amritsar). Now these two access points are open only during the 3rd, 13th and 23rd of every month for vehicles, eg buses and tourist vans; for trains – Tuesdays, Thursdays and Saturdays every week. Those coming from India must have the Punjab Travel Pass issued by the Ministry of the Interior at Khan Market in New Delhi. With the Punjab problem remaining unresolved, the rail route between Rajasthan and Sind – between Barmer and Hyderabad through Khokhropar border – may soon be opened to international traffic.

There is a toll tax on all overland routes of Rs 2, it is seldom collected.

Afghanistan

There are two road entry points between Pakistan and Afghanistan, but since the Russian invasion these border routes have been sealed due to Afghan mujihadeen activity. The most popular land route previously was at Torkham on the famous Khyber Pass between Peshawar and Kabul. See Peshawar for details of this route just in case things change at this border. There is also a less frequented crossing at Chaman in the south between Quetta and Kandahar. See Quetta for details.

Iran

The land route between Pakistan and Iran is now open. It is a long trip across deserts between Taftan and Quetta. See Quetta for full details of this route and rail route.

China

The land route between Xinjiang and Northern Pakistan which goes through the 5000-metre-high Khunjerab Pass, was opened on 1 May 1986. It was first opened to Pakistani and Chinese nationals in the summer of 1983. The route is spectacular. It follows the ancient Silk Trade Route from the Grand Trunk Rd, through Gilgit-Hunza Valley and Gojal or Upper Hunza, into Taskurgan and Kashgar in Xinjiang, Chinese Turkistan.

Other

Overland road and railway lines are at Gandasinghwallah near Lahore and

Khokhropar in Sind on the Indo-Pakistan border, but they are still closed.

SEA

India & Gulf States

There used to be boats plying between Bombay and the Gulf states via Karachi, but this ceased operation a couple of years back. Report has it that operation will be resumed, but no one knows when. At present there is only the *Hadji* or pilgrim boat that plies between Karachi and the Gulf states.

Africa

There are freighters plying between Karachi and Mombasa and Dar es Salaam via Aden and Mogadishu. They are not allowed to take passengers but apparently quite a few have made it by talking with the captains of the freighters.

Getting Around

AIR

Pakistan International Airline has an extensive domestic network with several flights daily between the major centres: Peshawar, Multan, Islamabad, Lahore and Karachi. There are also flights to Quetta, Hyderabad, Sukkur, Moenjodaro, Chitral, Gilgit, Skardu, Saidu Sharif, Gwaddar and Pasni. The services from Peshawar to Chitral and from Rawalpindi (Islamabad) to Gilgit and Skardu will probably be of particular interest to travellers. The flight to Skardu in particular is fantastic since the mountains are often higher than an F-27's maximum altitude, so you weave in and out of 7000-metre peaks.

The fares on these routes are artificially low since the government wants to emphasise the links with these remote regions which are often cut off by snow-blocked passes for most of the year. Unpredictable weather conditions for most of the year could make flights very uncertain, so if you're flying north you must be prepared for delays.

There's a limited tourist quota on these northern routes – only two daily. Since there are delays, flights to these areas tend to be crowded, it is necessary to book your tickets days before your actual date of departure.

Concessions

Local and foreign students *attending local colleges or universities* are granted 30% discount on domestic flights. Apply to the PRO (Public Relations Officer) with your student identity card. Maximum age limit is 26. Discounts are also available to journalists accredited to Pakistan and to groups of four to more than 20. PRO offices can be found at PIA offices in Karachi, Lahore, Rawalpindi, Peshawar, Multan and Quetta.

PIA has a fleet of 707s, 747s, DC10s, Airbuses and Fokker 27s.

RAIL

The main railway routes in Pakistan are from Karachi to Lahore, Rawalpindi and Peshawar, and from Karachi to Sukkur, Quetta and the Zahedan. There are several classes: air-conditioned 1st class sleepers and seats; 1st class sleepers and seats; and 2nd class sleepers and seats. There are two kinds of trains, express and ordinary mail trains. On the main rail routes there are usually several trains daily.

Trains are always overcrowded and between big cities it can be difficult to get seats. You must always reserve seats several days in advance for air-conditioned and 1st class seats. All sleepers also require advance reservation. If all else fails you can get a station porter to 'reserve' a seat for you for a nominal fee.

Concessions

Any foreign tourist irrespective of age – student or not – is eligible for a 25% discount for six months from normal rail fares. To get this discount you need a Tourist Certificate, obtainable from the local tourist info centre, which must be presented to the Regional Railway super-intendent. Foreign students are eligible for a 50% discount in all classes except the air-conditioned 1st class. As in India life is much easier if you can get a sleeper for long night trips.

BUSES

Buses are a good alternative to rail transport, particularly for short trips or where the trains are very crowded. Although there are buses operating at all hours between almost every reasonably sized town the most frequent services are along the Grand Trunk Road in northern Pakistan, from Lahore to Rawalpindi and Peshawar. Usually the bus stations are near railway stations and although you cannot reserve seats on the ordinary buses there are often minibuses where seats can be reserved. The minibuses are faster, more comfortable and only a little more expensive. They often operate out of a different station from the ordinary buses. The GTS – Government Transport System – buses run on schedule though for they do not have to wait to fill up and therefore are much more reliable and faster.

Concessions

NATCO (Northern Area Transport Company) and other bus lines operating between Rawalpindi and Gilgit and in the northern area offer 50% discount to both local and foreign students and it's not necessary to be attending local colleges or universities.

CARGO JEEPS

In the upper northern region of Pakistan the usual form of transport between towns and villages are the cargo jeeps which carry cargo and passengers along the narrow and steep mountain roads. Many of these roads are simply too severe or too narrow for any other form of transport. Note that cargo jeeps do not usually run to set schedules and they are not cheap. If PIA has a flight it will probably be cheaper than a jeep.

CAR RENTAL

There are now many car and jeep rental agencies in Pakistan from the plains up to the higher northern area. Consult the tourist offices for information on car and driver rental. PTDC has buses, minibuses, vans, jeeps and cars for hire.

CAR IMPORT

Check with your national motoring organisation about import regulations for bringing your own car to Pakistan. For some time it was, and may still be, possible to import a car for 15 days, extendable for a further 15 days, without the necessity of holding a *carnet de passage*. Longer stays do require a carnet or a bank guarantee that you will re-export the vehicle when you depart. The Automobile Association of Pakistan, 8 Multan Rd, Samanabad, Lahore, or the Karachi Automobile Association, Oriental Building, McLeod Rd, Karachi, can provide more information on driving in Pakistan.

ROADS

The major roads in Pakistan are generally sealed and in good condition but minor roads are much worse. This applies particularly to the northern region where the roads can be hair-raising and subject to damage by snow, landslide or earthquake. Driving in towns and cities can be a time-consuming and nerve-shattering experience due to the chaotic pedestrian, animal, bicycle and auto-rickshaw traffic. Try to avoid the rush hours in big cities, you could end up a cot case otherwise. When you're driving through tribal areas be very careful, if you have an accident you are likely to be a long way from medical treatment, on top of which you may also find yourself embroiled in a tribal conflict. Unless it's imperative, it's wise not to drive at night since very few bullock carts, bicycles or trucks have tail lights.

LOCAL TRANSPORT

For urban transport you've got a choice of taxis, auto-rickshaws, pedi-rickshaws and tongas, plus buses, minibuses and miniwagons. Fares for the latter are usually fixed. Buses cost from Rs 1 to Rs 2.50 depending on the city and on the distance. Minibuses are usually a little more expensive but are faster and more comfortable. Buses are always packed.

Taxis and auto-rickshaws (a motor scooter tri-wheeler) may have fare meters but they are unlikely to be functioning. Count on about Rs 2.50 per km for a taxi, half that for an auto-rickshaw. Bargain hard and always fix the fare before you start off. Pedi-rickshaws and tongas (two-wheeled horse carriages) are also subject to pre-departure fare negotiation. Since street signs are often invisible, non-existent or indecipherable, it is necessary to take a pedi-rickshaw or auto-rickshaw to get where you're going. It will prove less inconvenient, less hassle, less time and energy consuming and less costly in the end.

Sind

It was called the 'Unhappy Valley' or the 'Land of Uncertainties' by ancient travellers such as the Persians, Greeks and Arabs who marched through the scorching deserts of Persia and Baluchistan for long, wearying days and weeks towards the Valley of the Indus – seemingly a promised land – only to find it depressingly arid and barren. 'The skies are enormous. So much sheer space, so much parched land exposed under the pitiless sun, such endlessly monstrous horizons lie heavy on the spirit,' writes Jean Fairley. It is also a land of parrots that dart around; of the sheesham and pipal trees; of the brightly-plumaged kingfishers that flash along the canals and river banks; and of white herons perched on the backs of water buffaloes.

The province of Sind, the Lower Indus Plain, is almost 140,000 square km in area and most of it is dry alluvial deposits. Separated from the Upper Indus Plain by the rocky gorge above Sukkur-Rohri, it slopes southward down to the Arabian Sea, and from the edge of the Kirthar Range of the Baluchistan Plateau, which makes up the provincial boundary line in the west, it spreads eastward to the Thar Desert. In the middle of this plain flows the Indus River – its life and soul – down to the delta region and out into the Arabian Sea.

The climate is generally dry and hot with temperatures in summer rising to between 27° and 40°C. The coastal region does not suffer from extremes of temperature, mainly due to the sea, but does tend to be oppressively humid during the summer monsoon which sweeps up from the Arabian Sea and drops a little rain on the parched plain. In autumn and winter, when the winter monsoon wind from Central Asia blows across and over the great mountains of the north-west, the temperature can dip to as low as 7°C, but generally it stays around 20°C – a mild and pleasant climate.

Under these geographical and climatic circumstances it was only on the banks of the life-supporting Indus and its many tributaries that villages and towns sprang up. Here civilisation emerged – Moenjodaro on the west bank of the Indus and the earlier Kot Diji on the riverside just south of the Sukkur-Rohri region. The Indus Valley Civilisation reached its peak in Moenjodaro. The region from Thatta, south of the Indus, had also once been the centre of a very advanced civilisation. Its great cities were served by the port of Banbhore, believed to have been the landing site of Mohammed Bin Qasim, the Muslim conqueror of Sind, but, like Moenjodaro, they disappeared without a trace, leaving only their beautiful burial grounds.

These cities must have been contemporaneous with the historical periods discovered in Banbhore: the Scytho-Parthian (2nd century BC), the Hindu-Buddhist (1st century AD), and the early Islamic cultures (8th century AD). The prosperity they enjoyed could only be ascribed to the port town of Banbhore which, at that time, must have been linked up with the great trading area which began on the coast of East Africa and extended through Aden on the Arabian Peninsula to Persia. Banbhore was also connected by overland camel caravan routes from Basra through Persia into the Makran and also from Baluchistan and the Punjab. These were minor veins that formed part of the ancient Silk Trade Route of Eurasia.

What happened to these cities? 'In this place there was a great city whose inhabitants were so depraved they turned into stones,' the 12th-century Arab traveller from Morocco, Ibn Battuta, was told. And he himself saw an 'innumerable number of stones in the shape of man and animals, mostly broken, disfigured.' Now they are all gone; cities and all have disappeared without a trace, perhaps buried in the sand.

In the early 18th century the Indus changed course and must have closed up the port of Banbhore which was eventually replaced by Karachi. The pace of development in the southern region faltered and it never recovered its ancient glory.

At this time Thatta, on the west bank of the Indus to the south, and Hyderabad on the east bank and to the north, appear to have developed in importance. The coastal region was dotted with tiny fishing villages and Karachi was only beginning to emerge as a port town. Thatta was once the capital of the Moghuls in Sind but it declined when the Muslim rulers moved the capital to Khudabad and in turn Khudabad faded away when the Indus changed its course. Hyderabad eventually became the capital of Sind.

Karachi and the surrounding areas did not prosper as much as the ancient and medieval cities that previously flourished in the Banbhore-Thatta region. The coastal region was dotted with tiny fishing villages and Karachi was only beginning to emerge as a port town.

The whole Lower Indus Plain fell into a deep lethargy that disappeared only when the British added it to their Indian empire. Once again the banks of the Indus became alive with activity. Great highways were built, rail tracks were laid and irrigation canals and barrages were built. Unfortunately these put an end to traffic on the river itself. The plain, at once so dry and so green in patches, is interspersed with sprawling industrial cities and plant complexes, mediaeval cities, ageless villages and hamlets.

In the hot season the whole landscape shimmers and the grey, brown and even reddish colours all turn creamy-white. Dust and sand carried up by the wind create a haze which blots out the sun or turns it opaque. It is the season along the coast when fishing ceases and marriages take place, when on a full moon the villagers in their fine bright clothes, along with the fakirs, snake charmers and musicians trudge up to the mountain shrines for an all-night feast. They sometimes put on wrestling matches during this period, but more often it is a time for music, dancing and enjoying the moon.

In autumn, when fishing is resumed, the whole coastline, particularly in the late afternoon, is suffused with colours. The sky and the sea are generally tinted with crimson.

KARACHI
The city was originally a little fishing village where Kalachi, a dancing girl of great beauty, lived. Kalachi's fame was spread far and wide by boatmen, caravan traders, poets and minstrels. Tales of her loveliness and charm bedazzled strangers from far-flung lands and since then the fishing village has been called Karachi.

Alexander the Great was believed to have set sail from here on his way back to Syria. It replaced Banbhore as a port and, though small, was a thriving harbour where pilgrims embarked on their voyages to Mecca.

Ten years before the Great Mutiny took place in India, the British first showed their interest in Sind, and when General Dyer advocated its conquest, Lord Napier sent the *Wellesley* to Karachi. On the approach of the ship the Talpur rulers ordered cannons on the fortress of Manora Island to fire welcome salvoes. Whether it was intentionally misinterpreted or not, the friendly salvoes from the cannons brought about the capture of the town without bloodshed on 17 February 1843.

Richard Burton, later to become famous for his explorations of the Nile and for his literary achievements, shifted the capital of Sind from Hyderabad to Karachi. Construction works took on a hectic pace. Streets were laid and paved, highways and railways constructed, port facilities improved, and a number of buildings of varying architectural designs were built –including Gothic, Victorian and contemporary. Among them are Frere Hall, the Chief Courts, the Municipal Corporation Building, Cotton Exchange, the President's House, the Assembly Chambers, Port Trust Building, the Mereweather Tower, St Andrew's Church and St Patrick's Cathedral.

From then on Karachi overshadowed Hyderabad as the commercial, educational and administrative centre of Sind. It expanded into a great sprawling, bustling metropolis, and since Partition, when its population was 400,000, the population has rocketed to around seven million, many of them refugees.

For the first decade after independence in 1947 Karachi was the capital of Pakistan until the new city of Islamabad was ready for use in 1965. A dry, hot and dusty city, squeezed between the desert and the Arabian Sea, Karachi has little of obvious interest to the tourist, but it is still more than simply an arrival point and travel crossroads.

Information

There are Tourist Information Centres at Karachi International Airport (tel 48 2441); *Hotel Pearl Continental* (tel 5l 6397) in the city; and at *Hotel Metropole* on Club Rd (tel 51 0234).

The Immigration and Central Police Station of Sind, the GPO, the Telephone and Telegraph Office, and American Express are all on Chundigarh Rd which used to be known as McLeod Rd.

The best time to visit Karachi is from September until April. May and June are the hottest months of the year.

Consulates

India – India House 3 Fatimah Rd (tel 51 4310)

Sri Lanka – 44E Razi Rd, Block No 6, PECHS

Iran – 81 Shahrah-e-Iran, Clifton Beach (tel 53 0596)

USA – 8 Abdullah Haroon Rd (tel 51 5081)

UK – York Place, Runnymede Lane, Clifton Beach (tel 53 2041)

Film Processing

Colour films and slides – *Polaroid Co* opposite Metropole Hotel (tel 51 2494).

The City

Karachi's overall features are a composite of the Talpurian, the British and the modern elements, quite different from its contemporary sister-cities in India and the Punjab, as it does not have the ubiquitous Moghul features. Over the years it has acquired the usual trappings of a modern metropolis – towering hotels, banks, travel agencies, airline offices, tourist shops, cinemas, shopping centres, double-lane boulevards and an international airport. With their quaint architecture and sedate atmosphere, the buildings of the British era are distinctive and well preserved, contrasting with the bold, new concrete-and-glass structures. With the Talpurian bazaars they lend the city a historical air.

Tomb of Quaid-i-Azam

The most important city monument is the mausoleum of Quaid-i-Azam, Mohammed Ali Jinnah, the founder of Pakistan, who died in 1948. Its architecture combines both traditional and modern Islamic designs. It's about 31 metres high and is topped with a simple marble dome. Its ceiling is lined with blue-glazed tiles which were donated by Japan. The glass and gold chandelier came from China and a silver handrail from Iran. It is situated just north-east of Bohri Bazaar at the end of Jinnah Rd.

National Museum

In the centre of Burns Garden it is open daily, except Friday, from 10 am to 4 pm. Exhibits include relics excavated from the 5000-year-old city of Moenjodaro,

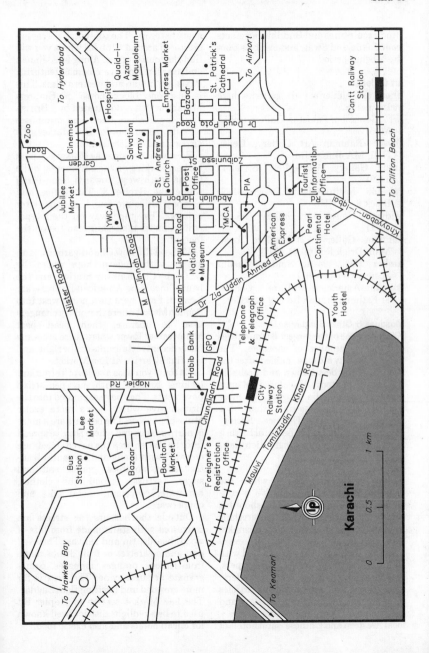

Hindu sculptures and Buddhist artefacts from Taxila and Swat, and exhibits from the Moghul period.

Art Galleries

There are numerous art galleries here including:

Art Council of Pakistan Gallery (tel 51 5108)

Faysee Rahman Art Gallery, Denso Hall, MA Jinnah Rd

Indus Gallery, 11-B/6, PECHS (tel 43 3229)

Pakistan Institute of Art & Designs, 61-N, Block 6, PECHS

Midway House Art Gallery (tel 48 1571)

Rehman Gallery, 12 Banglore Town, Main Drigh Rd (tel 41 4073)

Atelier BM, 194-A, Sindhi Muslim Society (tel 43 3867)

Pakistan-American Cultural Centre, 11 Fatimah Jinnah Rd (tel 51 3836).

Mosques & Other Buildings

Karachi is one of the largest Islamic cities and has a number of mosques. The **Defence Society Mosque**, named after the suburb, is the best known and probably the most visited. The large **Memon Mosque**, near Jodia Bazaar, is more traditionally mosque-like than the modern, low-slung Defence Society Mosque. **Frere Hall** in the peaceful Bagh-i-Jinnah gardens is imposingly Victorian.

Bazaars

Saddar is the city centre where the **Empress Market** is located. It's a conglomeration of bazaars, modern shopping centres and tourist shops selling everything from carpets and leather bags to snake-skin purses and fur coats. In every direction the footpaths are crowded with stalls selling fruit drinks, newspapers, second-hand clothing, fancy jewellery, spicy cakes and miscellaneous articles from combs and mirrors to scissors and ear cleaners. There are eating places – local, western and Chinese – and hotels of every category. The top-notch places are clustered around Club Rd where you will find the tourist office. Along M A Jinnah and Garden Rds are cinemas featuring Pakistan, Indian and western films. This is just one block north of Empress Market, which is dominated by a British clock tower where buses and minibuses pick up passengers for Lee Market, the airport, and Hyderabad.

Westward towards **Lee Market** you pass barbers working on the pavements, while to the south-west, towards Shah-i-Iraq where the Excise & Tax Office and passport office are found, are the letter writers. They tap away on their type-writers under makeshift lean-tos on the footpath.

McLeod Rd, now Chundigarh Rd, is an avenue with modern shops where the GPO, the City Railway Station, and the banks, including American Express, are located. From here turn north-west into **Boulton Market** where the money changers used to operate, then head past **Mereweather Tower** where there are some fairly decent restaurants on the right, and you finally arrive at Lee Market.

En route you pass a series of Talpurian-looking bazaars with no pedestrian pavements. They have expanded into the British area which has a more exotic atmosphere now. The bazaars are a maze of narrow lanes and where they've spread into the British area the paved streets are crowded with stalls and tarpaulin lean-tos selling potatoes, grains, salt and sugar, textiles, second-hand clothes, hardware, porcelain, metal pots and copperware.

Outside the bazaars the streets are congested with stalls made from bits of wood, boards, tin and canvas. They sell *pan* and cigarettes or fruit drinks made from lemons, oranges, mangoes, pomegranate or sugar cane. The area is far more crowded and bustling than Saddar. The Lee Market section of Napier Rd used to be a redlight district, well known for cheap hotels and also exotic food.

Streets

Karachi has well-paved streets, broad and well-lit avenues, even two-lane boulevards where traffic flows heavily from dawn till dusk, becoming even more frenetic during the rush hours. Only late in the evening does the pace slacken. There is a motley collection of plain-painted public government buses mixed with ornately and colourfully painted private buses; white and yellow minibuses and black and yellow taxis, lavishly decorated auto-rickshaws and garishly painted lorries and cargo trucks. The ingenious auto-rickshaws sputter, skitter and trundle their three-wheeled way in and out of a maze of buses and trucks, camel wagons and donkey carts, even carts drawn by men. On Wednesday afternoons the donkey cart drivers hold impromptu races along Mauripur Rd, west of the city towards Hawkes Bay.

In the swirl of traffic camels plod along pulling overloaded wagons, but managing to maintain their measured gait with heads high above the congestion of more lowly vehicles. It all seems chaotic but traffic flows quite smoothly except for occasional mishaps when an overloaded donkey cart or horse cart suddenly tilts back leaving the unfortunate animal dangling in the air. Apart from Saddar there do not appear to be bus stations anywhere in Karachi, people simply clamber on board while buses are still moving. Buses are impossibly crowded, but always seem to have room for one more passenger.

Beaches

With its coastal location, Karachi has some superb beaches. There is good swimming all year except in the June-August monsoon season when the currents can be tricky and jellyfish abound. To prevent offending the Muslim sense of decorum and to avoid hassles, bikinis should be worn only on private, hotel-controlled beaches.

Clifton Beach is as much amusement park as beach – and an excellent place for children. It has a fair ground which opens at 4 pm and an amusement park with merry-go-rounds, ferris wheels, flying saucers, lindy-loops, toy trains and self-drive cars for two and four. Another recent attraction is a dolphin pool. Towards Marine Drive camels and horses can be hired by the hour. Dotted along the shore, there are teashops and foodstalls which serve fried fish. There are also kiosks where you can buy soft drinks, stalls for *pan* and cigarettes, and tourists shops. Close by is the **Pigeon Temple** where there is a fresh water spring and aquarium at the Muslim shrine. As it is an amusement park it is crowded all week. Take Bus 20 from Shahrah-i-Iraq Rd.

Manora Island is another beach resort with a lighthouse that appears not to be in use any more. It is 15 minutes by minibus to Keamari, the Karachi port, where you can get a boat to the island. At Keamari you can also hire outrigger sailing boats – bunder boats – complete with crew for Rs 25 per hour. A popular activity is to hire a boat for five or six hours at Rs 100 per head. You can take the boats around the harbour, go scuba diving or dive for lobsters or fish. Boat trips can stretch deep into the night, particularly in autumn when turtles lay their eggs on the beaches, or if you decide to pig out on the seafood – crabs, fish, lobsters and shark.

Sandspit, Hawkes Bay & Paradise Point are connected beaches, merging into one long beach. There are saddled camels and horses for hire, teashops, soft-drink stalls, and even huts that you can rent by the day. But note that the currents become very treacherous here during the monsoon season, so take care at that time.

Sandspit is almost nondescript, but the scenery improves as the beach, lined with weather-beaten huts, arches around to Hawkes Bay and the beautiful Paradise Point. The land rises from the shore to semi-arable wasteland that is patched with green and spreads back to mountains topped with shrines. These beaches fill up on Thursdays and Fridays. Bikinis are really verboten then. The local females go into the water completely dressed!

Five years ago Hawkes Bay was becoming a junkies' and freaks' haunt, and was apparently also a smuggling area patrolled by police and coast guards in the wee hours of the morning. Avoid going to Paradise Point and beyond either on a dark or moonlit night, particularly if you are a woman or with a woman.

French Beach is the beach to go to at Hawkes Bay. People on foot are not allowed entry so you need to be in a car and look presentable. It's mostly foreigners here – a good place for women to relax away from the ogling locals.

The beaches are 40 km from Karachi, 1½ hours by bus from Lee Market, 45 minutes by car. Buses depart Karachi at 6 am, 2 and 5 pm. Returning buses leave at 9 am, 4 and 6 pm.

Gadani Beach is a developing resort about 50 km from Karachi. Take a look at the shipwrecking yard and workers' shanties while you're here. The hulking remains of once great ships are beached and gradually cut into scrap iron piled high in rusting heaps on the beach. Each house in the fishing village has a camel tied up outside and smuggling is said to supplement the income from fishing. It's a three-hour bus trip from Lee Market – an early bus leaves at 8 am and another at 1 pm. Even on the early bus you only get a few hours at Gadani if you're day-tripping.

Parsee Tower of Death

Traditionally, only Parsees were allowed here, but others can now visit this rather macabre place, provided they are accompanied by a Parsee. On Mehmudabad Rd, near Corporation and Parsee Gates in the Korangi area, it consists of two rather squat towers set in a large compound. You can't miss it, the vultures and buzzards circulating overhead are a dead give-away. Hmmm!

Other

A great way to spend a few hours is to wander around the fish harbour on the West Wharf. Hundreds of ornately-painted and decorated boats, and all kinds of other water craft dock there daily with fresh vegetables and fish.

Another interesting place to take a look at is the colourful **dhobi ghat** where laundry is done en masse. If you like zoos, the **Karachi Zoo** is worth going to, if only to see an elephant collecting rupees. It's a favourite trick of one of the elephants here.

Once the monsoon is over, crabbing, diving for lobsters, fishing, scuba diving, or simply boating at night are all great fun.

The Karachi Cultural Club puts on programmes regularly, except during religious festival when they are usually postponed. There are several venues including Adamjee Hall (tel 70 135); Fleet Club at the Star Hotel and Moti Mahal Auditorium at the Taj Mahal Hotel.

Places to Stay – bottom end

Accommodation in this bracket will cost between Rs 20 and Rs 50. The main area for cheap hotels is in the Saddar area around the Empress Market. Centrally located and cheapest is the *Estate Hotel* (tel 51 1411) on the corner of Rajagazanfar Rd, south of Empress Market. It's reasonably clean and popular with travellers. Ground floor rooms with bath are Rs 20/35 for singles/doubles. Upper floor rooms go for Rs 30/45.

Royal Hotel on Chundigarh Rd (tel 21 1089) has rooms with fans, some with attached bath for single Rs 25, double Rs 35. *Sunshine Hotel*, Cantt Railway Station (tel 51 2316), has the same facilities and rates.

Ambassador Hotel on Blenken St, off Dr Daud Pota Rd, is on the 1st floor. Rooms with bath and fan are Rs 35/45. It has a dining room serving local food only. The *Shalimar Hotel* (tel 52 9491) is on the same street and offers the same standard for slightly higher rates.

Hostels *Amin House* on Maulvi Tamizuddin Rd is a Youth Hostel, which accepts foreigners whether they are members or not. A dorm costs Rs 15, a single with attached shower and toilet is Rs 25. Recently renovated, it is not too far from the Cantonment Railway Station. Auto-rickshaw fare is Rs 5.

YMCA Hostel (tel 51 6927) on Stratchen Rd, is opposite the PIA office. It's a modern building with attached and common bathrooms. Only Christians admitted, non-members can use the facilities for a temporary membership fee of Rs 30. There's also a Rs 100 deposit, returnable on departure; Rs 25/50 for singles/doubles. The *YWCA Hostel* (tel 7 1662) a block away from Abdullah Haroon Rd on MA Jinnah Rd, is open only to female travellers. The *Salvation Army Hostel* on Frere Rd (tel 7 4262) has dorm only, Rs 30 per bed. It's just behind Empress Market.

If just in transit there are railway retiring rooms at the Cantt Railway Station and the City Railway Station, singles/doubles for Rs 20/36.

Places to Stay - middle

The *Khyber Hotel* (tel 71 0359) on Preedy St in the Saddar area, has attached baths and fans for singles Rs 50 to Rs 65, doubles Rs 90 to Rs 120. *Holiday Hotel* on Frere St, Saddar (tel 51 2081) is more modern with slightly better facilities. Singles are Rs 75, doubles Rs 150 and up. Other hotels of a similar standard include the *National City Hotel* and the *Royal City Hotel* near the Orient Cinema, Saddar.

The *Gulf Hotel* (tel 51 5834) and the *Palace Hotel* (tel 51 1011) on Dr Ziauddin Ahmad Rd, along with *Al Farooq Hotel* (tel 22 8112) off Zaibunnisa St, are of a slightly higher standard with rates from Rs 85 single, Rs 175 double.

The *Beach Luxury Hotel*, Maulvi Tamizuddin Rd (tel 55 1031), along with the *Imperial Hotel* on the same road (tel 55 1051), has rates from Rs 240 to Rs 480. Other hotels in this range include the *Colombus Hotel*, Clifton Rd (tel 51 1311); *Hotel Midway House*, Airport Rd (tel 48 0371) and *Hostelliere de France* Star Gate, Airport Rd (tel 48 1101).

Places to Stay - top end

Accommodation rates range from Rs 600 to Rs 1200 and upward, plus taxes. They are all of international standard from three-star to five-star hotels.

The *Metropole Hotel*, Club Rd (tel 51 2051), is the oldest in town and has rates from Rs 600 to Rs 1200. The *Mehran Hotel* is a modern building and has similar rates, as does the *Taj Mahal*, Shahrah-E-Faisal Rd (tel 52 0211).

The poshest hotels in town are: the *Karachi Holiday Inn* (tel 52 0111) on Abdullah Haroon Rd; *Pearl Continental* (tel 51 5021) on Club Rd, which used to be the *Intercontinental*; and the *Sheraton Hotel* (tel 52 1021) opposite the Pearl Continental. They range from Rs 1200 to Rs 2400 and up.

Places to Eat

Cheap eating places are in Lee Market, near the bus station and on Napier Rd. You will only find Pakistani food here and prices range from Rs 8 to Rs 16. The best cheapies in town are located near Mereweather Tower where Chinese soup and noodles, and fruit drinks are available. Exotic local food here for only Rs 8 to Rs 12, some are located around Empress Market where a meal could cost Rs 16 upward, and Clifton Beach where a fish dish with roti will be Rs 8.

Most of the medium class restaurants in town are run by Parsees where meals could cost Rs 20 and upwards. Fast food places have also sprung up which are good for snacks, hamburgers, chicken sandwiches, soft drinks and ice creams. Most are on Abdullah Haroon Rd.

For local exotic specialities *Hill Park* in PECHS area between Bond and Frere Rd has good, spicy food, but it is difficult to get to unless you have your own transport. *Farooq's Restaurant* is another place for hot, spicy, exotic food on Abdullah Haroon Rd.

For Chinese food there are many Chinese restaurants in town – *South China Restaurant* Shahrah-e-Iraq Rd, is open only in the evening; *ABC Chinese Restaurant* and *Hongkong Chinese Restaurant* the latter is the best but has 7% surtax. *Four Season Chinese Restaurant* (tel 511 971) located on the ground floor of the Metropole Hotel, is another good place for Chinese meals, prices start at Rs 40.

For international cuisine in flashy places, the *Horseshoe* on Airport Rd and the *Khekashan 11* at the airport are in this category. On Airport Rd the *Kee Chain* is good for all sorts of barbecues, *Omar Khayyam* has air-con luxury and excellent seafood, *Le Cafe* has tasty snacks, burgers and good music. *Shangrila* at Avari Tower is another place for snacks. *Samarquand* at the West Wharf is an excellent place for seafood; the *Casbah* at Beach Luxury Hotel is another place for seafood, also for shashliks, tikkas and Lebanese dishes; and for a real gourmet tour, the ground floor of the Sheraton has *Albustan* which has delicious seafood; or there's *Fanoos Lounge* for European snacks, ice-cream and fruit juices. The latter also has music. *Le Marquis*, on the mezzanine, has superb French food, and on the same floor is the *Maskada Lounge*, which specialises in pastries, capuccinos, espresso and Turkish coffees. The main *Sheraton Restaurant* offers what it calls a 'European Express', which consists of a variety of dishes from Brussels, Paris, Prague, Berlin, Bucharest, Athens and Istanbul.

The *Pirate Isles* at the Taj Mahal offers barbecued food in a different atmosphere. Another interesting place is the *Revolving Restaurant* at the Tower International at Shaheen Complex just above the American Express; and if you're into American food and atmosphere go to *Nadia's Coffee Shop* at the Holiday Inn.

For less spicy and hot exotic local dishes *Agha's Tavern* at the North Western or the *Village* adjacent to the Metropole, and for snacks try *Cafe Grand* and *Ampi's* in the same area. For vegetarians there's *Alfa* on Innervarity Rd which specialises in South Indian vegetarian food.

Liquor Getting a drink in fundamentalist Pakistan can be a difficult proposition. Generally foreigners are allowed to drink, but only in their hotel room. Most of the bars in the more expensive hotels are now closed. To get a drink apply for a Tourist Certificate at the tourist office on Club Rd. The staff here may pass you on to the Excise & Tax Office on Shahrah-i-Iraq Rd in the government complex compound, and they will redirect you to where you can buy alcohol.

Getting There

Air PIA has three flights to India from Karachi every week.

Karachi-Delhi	Rs 1475 plus airport tax Rs 100
Karachi Bombay	Rs 1190 plus airport tax Rs 100

Domestic flights have an airport tax of Rs 5. From Karachi to:

Quetta	three flights weekly	Rs 595
Lahore	four flights daily	Rs 950
	night coach	Rs 795
Rawalpindi	four flights daily	Rs 1155
	night coach	Rs 945
Peshawar	one flight daily	Rs 1155

Other There are now flights to other cities such as Multan, Bahawalpur and Moenjodaro from Karachi. Check with the PIA Office for these flights.

Warning The international airports in Karachi and Lahore now have trained German Shepherd dogs to sniff out nefarious drug smuggling.

Rail On the Karachi-Lahore-Rawalpindi-Peshawar route there are now six to eight trains daily; to Lahore takes 19 hours; Rawalpindi 26 hours; and to Peshawar 32 hours. There are also express trains which make the trip in 16 hours.

For concessions apply for a Tourist Certificate at the Metropole PTDC info centre. You have to present at the office of the Commercial Department, City Railway Station on Chundigarh Rd (tel 326 349, 513 965). Reservations can only be made for air-con and 1st class and these classes are often booked out two weeks in advance, particularly on the Karachi-Lahore route. There is still no priority tourist quota on trains in Pakistan.

From Karachi to:

		sleeper	seat
Khokhropar	air-con	Rs 283	Rs 165
	1st class	Rs 115	Rs 62
	2nd class	Rs 31	Rs 27
Quetta	air-con	Rs 575	Rs 330
	1st class	Rs 230	Rs 135
	2nd class	Rs 70	Rs 55
Lahore	air-con	Rs 775	Rs 445
	1st class	Rs 315	Rs 142
	2nd class	Rs 98	Rs 74

Buses Buses for Thatta and Hyderabad depart at ½ hour intervals from 6 am to 6 pm. The Thatta service leaves from Lee Market and the trip takes two hours. Hyderabad buses depart from Boulton Market and Empress Market, with some leaving from the cinema area on M A Jinnah Rd; trip takes 2½ hours.

Blue Lines has an office at the Palace Hotel Annexe opposite the Sheraton. This company has air-con minibuses making regular trips to Hyderabad which cost Rs 40; to Larkana and Sukkur it is a seven-hour trip costing Rs 110. The

Mirpurkhas Bus Company (tel 51 1011) has regular services to Hyderabad and Mirpurkhas.

There are also direct bus services to Peshawar via Saddiqabad, Dera Ghazi Khan and Mianwali. *Nasir Naytullah Buses* operate on this route. Also there is a direct bus service to Lahore via Saddiqabad, *New Khan Road Runner* air-con minibuses operate on this route.

Overland routes to the Makran coastal area remain closed to foreigners, but the Karachi-Khuzdar road via Bela in Baluchistan is now paved and open. It's still apparently unsafe and, for security, tourists with their own transport are advised to travel in convoy. If you are on your own, it would be better to take another route. See section on Baluchistan.

To India Despite persistent rumours that the Khokropar border will open soon, it is still closed. A lot of money has been spent on the restoration of the railway line between Barmer in Rajasthan and Hyderabad in Sind, so ask around – it may be open soon.

The Wagah road route is open for private vehicles on the 2nd, 12th and 22nd of every month, travelling in a police escorted convoy. Expect to pay.

Sea The ships plying between Bombay and the Gulf states via Karachi, which stopped operating a couple of years back, have not as yet resumed operation. There is presently only the *Hadj* or Pilgrims' boat which departs for the Gulf States.

Getting Around

Airport Transport From the international airport into the city centre it costs Rs 2.50 by minibus, Rs 1.75 by bus, Rs 20.25 by auto-rickshaw and Rs 35 to Rs 40 by taxi.

Local Transport From the Cantonment Railway Station to the city centre it's Rs 1 by bus, Rs 1.50 by minibus, Rs 10 by auto-rickshaw and Rs 20 to Rs 30 by taxi.

Around the city taxis cost Rs 5 upwards and auto-rickshaws Rs 5. Tongas are Rs 25 per hour for a ride around town. Both taxi and auto-rickshaw meters are notoriously unreliable so always agree on the fare before starting out. Cars with drivers can be hired from around US$30 a day with additional charges for fuel. City tours can be booked through the tourist office or private tour operators, usually for a minimum group of four.

Things to Buy

Karachi is a city of bazaars and shopping centres for all types and classes of local handicrafts; from the famous Baluchi embroidery, appliqued or patchwork quilts, to leather goods, brassware, beadwork, folk jewellery, onyx bric-a-brac, carved wooden chests, furniture and carpets.

Government handicraft centres and the more expensive emporia are located on Abdullah Haroon Rd, Zaibunnisa St and Club Rd. They, of course, offer the best quality and the highest prices. Bazaars are cheaper and if you are lucky you might even come across Kashmiri shawls of the same quality as those sold in the expensive shopping centres. The main bazaars are the traditional *Jodia Bazaar* behind Boulton Market, the new *Liaquat Market* to the north and the central *Bohri Bazaar* in the Saddar area. Across from the Hotel Pearl Continental the government-run *Sind Handicraft Centre* has fixed prices for locally produced items. In Saddar the shops sell embroidered Kashmiri shawls, carved onyx pieces and other Pakistani crafts. You will find most of the carpet shops along Zaibunnisa St near Bohri Bazaar. You can see carpets woven in the villages being trimmed and finished in Karachi. Visits can also be arranged to a small silk weaving factory and to a brasswork shop.

AROUND KARACHI

There are a number of interesting places to visit further out of Karachi accessible either by public bus service or on day tours, usually handled by the PTDC. North of Karachi it becomes dry and barren, and then gradually gets greener and more arable beyond Keenjhar Lake and Kotri Junction.

Chaukundi

The tombs at Chaukundi are archaeologically interesting, although it is not clear exactly how old the graves are. They are believed to date from the 13th to the 16th century. They are constructed out of slabs of rocks, stacked into elongated pyramids of cubical stone (Chaukundi means cubical) and carved with exquisite designs, the origins of which remains a mystery. Chaukundi is 27 km from Karachi. Buses depart regularly from Lee Market.

Manghopir

There is a sulphur thermal spring here which is apparently good for skin diseases, and other afflictions – including frigidity! Manghopir has a shrine to the Muslim Saint Mangho, which according to local legend, is guarded by crocodiles. It is about 40 km from Karachi and buses depart from Lee Market. There are no hotels here, only sheds for local travellers and pilgrims.

Banbhore

This ancient sea port is believed to have been the landing site of the Muslim conqueror, Mohammed Bin Qasim, in the early 8th century. It is interesting for the ruins of three different historical periods which have been uncovered here: Scythian-Parthian, Hindu-Buddhist and Islamic. Banbhore is about 64 km from Karachi and five km off the National Highway to Thatta. Buses go from Lee Market.

Haleji Lake

Situated 85 km from Karachi, 15 km before Thatta, Haleji Lake is considered to be the largest waterfowl sanctuary in Asia, and is the main reservoir for Karachi. It's 1½ km off the Thatta road from the village of Gujjo. Thousands of birds of over 70 species migrate here in winter from Siberia and stay through January and February. The birds include flamingoes, pelicans, pheasant-tailed jacanas, herons, ducks, partridges and egrets. There is a rest house here where you can stay for Rs 30 a day. The PTDC has huts from Rs 75 to Rs 200 plus 15% surtax.

THATTA

At one time Thatta was important as Sind's capital city and as a centre for Islamic arts. From the 14th century four Muslim dynasties ruled Sind from Thatta, but in 1739 the capital was moved elsewhere and Thatta declined.

It was believed that this was the place where Alexander the Great rested his legions after their long march. His admiral of the fleet, Nearchus, sailed from here back to the Persian Gulf. Today most of the remaining monuments only date back to the 16th and 17th centuries.

Makli Hill - City of Mausoleums

A couple of km before Thatta, this vast necropolis covers 15 square km and is said to contain over one million graves.

They are mainly made of sandstone, exquisitely carved with geometric and floral designs. Most of them date back to the Summas, the dynasty which ruled the Sind from the mid-14th to the early 16th centuries. Others are from the Moghul period. The carvings are so regular they seem to have been stamped into the stones. Some of the mausoleums are being restored. Recent tombs from the Arghun and Moghul periods have beautifully glazed or enamelled tiles and bricks, which they still continue to manufacture, particularly the Thatta blue tile.

Amongst the more important tombs is that of Mirza Jani Beg. Built in 1599 for the last of the Turkhan rulers, it is made

of glazed bricks. North of this is the imposing mausoleum of Nawab Isa Khan, the Moghul governor of Sind. Its design is similar to those found in Fatehpur Sikri in India. A low building similarly designed, a little to the east, houses the tombs of the women of his zenana – the part of a house where high caste Muslim women were cloistered. There is a fine view from here, across the lake to the town of Thatta. The mausoleum of Diwan Shurfa Khan built in 1638 is slightly to the north-west, and is a square solid structure with squat round towers at each corner. A couple of km north, the tomb of Nizam-ud-din is a square stone building constructed out of the materials of a Hindu temple.

The Town The town is dominated by the great mosque built by the Moghul Emperor Shah Jahan, which has been carefully restored to its original condition. The mosque's 33 arched domes give it superb acoustics and the tilework, a whole range of shades of blue, is equally fine. Situated on the outskirts of the new town it is surrounded by narrow lanes and multi-storey houses made of plaster and wood which are topped by *badgirs*, the wind-catchers designed to funnel cool breezes down into the interiors of buildings. They are also quite common in Hyderabad. The bazaars of Thatta are known for hand-printed fabrics, glass bangles, and the Sindhi embroidery work inlaid with tiny mirrors, one of the more well-known handicrafts of Pakistan.

Thatta is a fascinating town which appears to have scarcely moved out of the 18th century and is only slowly catching up with the modern world.

Places to Stay

Apart from the *muzzaffarkhanas* which range from Rs 15 to Rs 25, the *Agha Mohammed Hotel* is on the main street, has fans and common bath and is apparently the best in town.

Getting There

Thatta is 100 km north of Karachi, about half way to Hyderabad. The nearest railway station is at Jungshasi, about 21 km away. The PTDC arranges tours to Chaukundi-Banbhore-Makli Hill-Thatta but a minimum of four or five tourists are required. Public transport is not readily available for the first three. In summer it can get very hot with temperatures rarely dropping below 40°C.

The National Highway continues up to Hyderabad. Buses to Karachi or Hyderabad leave every hour.

AROUND THATTA

Keenjhar Lake

It is less than two hours from Thatta by bus, which goes all the way to Hyderabad. It is a beautiful lake resort with wooded areas. This is a good place to spend time boating, fishing and picnicking – a place to rest up before moving north to Hyderabad and Moenjodaro. There are motels, cabins and huts run by the PTDC, (tel 341), with rates from Rs 75 to Rs 500 per day plus 15% surtax.

Jherruk

On the banks of the Indus River, 56 km from Thatta, is another lake. Near the Jhimpir Railway Station the shrine of Amirpir is worth a side trip.

HYDERABAD

Hyderabad, 180 km north of Karachi, is the second largest city in Sind and one of the largest in Pakistan. Its population is about 1 million. Hyderabad is five km from the eastern bank of the Indus and is connected with Karachi by rail and a super-highway which goes over the Kotri Barrage.

It is one of the oldest cities on the subcontinent, dating back to the time of the Hindu ruler, Nerron. When the Indus changed its course away from Khudabad, at that time the capital of the region, the new capital was shifted to Hyderabad. In 1768 the Kalhora ruler constructed a fort half a square km in area and it still stands today. In 1843 the British arrived and defeated the Talpurs, completing their conquest of Sind.

Under the British, the Mall, a new section containing their government administrative offices, was added to the old city. It was centred around the old fort and Shahi Bazaar, one of the longest in the city at 2½ km. The bazaar is a labyrinth of narrow alleys where they produce Sindhi embroidery, block prints, gold and silver jewellery. You can also buy pointy-toed shoes, perfumes and most important, the glass bangles, for which this bazaar is famous.

In the old city, buildings are topped by *badgirs* that look like chimneys on roof tops. They catch the cool breezes which blow steadily in a south-west direction for 40 days from late April each year. Hyderabad is hot for most of the year, although in autumn and winter the temperature dips down to around 24°C. In the old sections of the town, cows still roam the streets giving it a distinctly mediaeval atmosphere.

On the northern side of the hill on which Hyderabad is sited there are tombs from the Talpur and Kalhora periods. The tomb of Ghulam Shah Kalhora is one of the finest, although its dome collapsed and has now been replaced by a flat roof.

Also worth a visit is the Institute of Sindhology's museum at the University of Sind. It has displays on all aspects of Sindhi history, music and culture depicting the lifestyles of the desert tribes. Infrequent GTS buses go to the campus, otherwise take a miniwagon to Jumshero, across the river from Hyderabad, and walk the 1½ km to the university.

Places to Stay

There are cheap and medium-priced hotels around Shahi Bazaar but they don't accept foreigners. However, hotels in the Ghari Khatta area, near the railway station, take travellers. *United Hotel* on Abdul Qayyum Rd has singles/doubles at Rs 20/35. The *Yasrab* and the *Firdaus Hotel* on Pasundar Rd are similarly priced. There are a number of more expensive hotels around the city. In Ghari Khatta the *Spinzar* (tel 26 049) has singles and doubles at Rs 120 upwards. Rooms are the same price at the *New Indus Hotel* (tel 25 276) and at *Sanjees* (tel 27 275-9) both in Thandi Sarak area. The *Faran* (tel 23 993) has similar rates in the Saddar area.

Places to Eat

Apart from the local restaurants, there are are two Chinese Restaurants in the Ghari Khatta area, *Sancha Chinese Restaurant* and the *Canton Chinese Restaurant* on Station Rd. The *Tung Fung Chinese Restaurant* which is said to be the best in town is located at the Spinzar Hotel.

The *Midway Restaurant* at the City Gate Hotel is also recommended.

Routes Out

Hyderabad is a road junction with highways west towards Manchar Lake and Sehwan Sharif; east towards Mirpurkhas and the Tharparkar Desert to the south-east; and north towards Kot Diji and Sukkur, Rohri and the Punjab.

MIRPURKHAS

Located 65 km east of Hyderabad, this town is worth a day trip if only to see the 15-metre-high Buddhist stupa with terracotta figures. Overland rail and road routes continue into the Rajaputana Desert in India. Hotels are on Station Rd and cost Rs 15/25 for singles/doubles.

The bus from Hyderabad costs Rs 7. From Mirpurkhas, *Brownlines* coaches go to Umarkot (Rs 10).

The *Khokhropar Special* departs from Mirpurkhas, for the border town of Khokhropar, at 2 am. It connects with a train on the Indian side of the Khokhropar checkpost which gets to

Monbao at 9 am. Monbao is the main station for Jodhpur in Rajasthan.

THARPARKAR DESERT

East of the Indus in Sind is another fascinating and extremely interesting facet of Pakistan. The Tharparkar Desert, which is over 28,100 square km in area, has its own culture, folklore, unique landscape and fauna and flora.

It is a curious combination of the ancient and modern, largely because it is a strategic defence region on the Indian border.

Major towns here are Umarkot in the north-west, Naukot to the west and Diplo to the south-west. There are numerous villages called *goths*, which still retain their feudal, socio-economic structure. The general atmosphere is mediaeval, but it has the modern trappings of trucks, jeeps, generators and electricity. The faithful, but often complaining, camel is still widely used, but trucks carry most of the cargo and mass transport. They ply between Naukot, Mithi and Islamkot regularly, and once a month they travel towards Sandhuri, north to the Rangers' border post, to fetch supplies.

Beyond Mirpurkhas or Thatta, traffic generally peters out as you progress deeper into the desert region. At **Naukot** the 586-km metalled road from Hyderabad tapers off. About three km from the outskirts of the town are the ruins of a fort, now inhabited by owls, pigeons, rats and other desert animals. The shrine of Pir Razi Shah Likyari, though venerated by both Hindus and Muslims, is in ruins.

From here the desert spreads out endlessly in all directions. **Mithi**, 67 km from Naukot, is a prosperous place linked to the outside world by telephone. What's more, many local people own transistors. There are a number of hotels with beds from Rs 5 a night here. If you're interested in craft this is where *rillis*, colourful patchwork bedspreads, are made.

In this part of the world Hindus and

Muslims live in harmony, though they retain their respective rituals and customs. The Hindus predominate with 56% of the population, while Muslims make up 44%. It is typical of the subcontinent, a kind of mini-India with Hindus, Muslims and Rajputs.

Islamkot, 40 km away, has well-laid out roads lined with trees, seven restaurants, but, strangely enough, not a single hotel. The Rajputs, who were originally driven out by the Moghuls, settled here and consequently there is a strong similarity to Rajasthan. It is prosperous and clean and retains its traditional songs, dances and festivals.

Though **Khario Ghulam Shah** is a very barren region, the tribes make do with what they've got and manage to enjoy life through dance and music. The **Kasbo** village, deep in the desert, is a fertile oasis inhabited by pastoral tribes, the Rabaris, who are snake worshippers. In this goth there are three Hindu temples, now in disrepair.

En route to **Virawah**, 68 km from Islamkot, are the **Abhe Ka Thar** goth of the Bheel tribe; **Lornian** of the Samma tribe; **Bhelwah** of the Moro tribe – this area is noted for succulent fruit; and **Dano Dandal**, another fertile spot where 400 families live. Then there's **Gori** goth, which has a thousand inhabitants, a primary school and an ancient Jain temple known as **Gori Mandar**. The latter is in disrepair but is still intact and its domes, tiny rooms and stone carvings are worth seeing.

From Gori it is 23 km to **Virawah** which also has a Jain temple with stone carvings. No Jains live here now, but nearby **Pari Nagar** also has a Jain temple. This goth is believed to have been a port for the Rann of Kutch region centuries ago.

Nagar Parkar is 23 km south of Virawah – part rocky, part sandy, part green. One of the primary products here is castor oil. It's not far from the Karonjhar Hills at the foot of which are streams that are considered sacred by the Hindus. The huts in this goth are built of local stone. Three km further on is a lake called **Bodeshar Talab** which features Hindu temples – now largely in ruins – as well as a white marble mosque built in 1436. This stands in a graveyard and dominates the whole goth.

North-east of Virawah is **Sami Ji Veri**, another Rangers' border post. Cacti in this area grow as high as two metres. From here it is only five km to Rann of Kutch where the surface of the land is crystalline white due to salinity. En route to Chachro is the peacock region, once so numerous when revered by the Hindus, now an endangered species, most of them having been devoured by the Muslims.

Umarkot, 70 km to the north-west, in the direction of Mirpur Khas, is a largish town with an urban lifestyle. There used to be yogis or fakirs here like those in the hilly area of Rawal in the Punjab, but they have disappeared. It is certainly the most touristed town in the Tharparkar Desert, so commercial that even the snake-charmers have become materialistic. You really know you are in the modern urban world of the subcontinent when you see the beggars. There is a crumbling old fort in the town – good views of the desert can be had from the tower and the small museum has a collection of Urdu and Persian books. A small memorial to the west of town marks the birthplace of the Moghul Emperor Akbar.

Beyond Umarkot to the north, the desert commences to expand endlessly again. There are isolated villages in this region, but they are not as fascinating or interesting as the goths in the south. At Khokhropar, the border town, is the overland route to India. There is also a railway line which begins from Bramer and goes through Mirpurkhas into Hyderabad. This sea of sand spreads up to the Cholistan Desert and beyond the border with India, it forms a continuous region of the Rajaputana Desert.

SEHWAN SHARIF

On the west bank of the Indus, Sehwan Sharif is 140 km north-west of Kotri. To get there from Hyderabad you must first take a minibus or miniwagon to Kotri Junction and then a train from there. The trip takes 2½ hours and the railway line passes through fairly arid, dusty and bleak countryside. The National Highway continues on this side of the Indus and there are buses.

Sehwan Sharif is an oasis in this dry wasteland and is noted for the shrine of Lal Qalandar Shah Baz which was built in 1274. The Muslim saint from Mervant, after wandering for decades, decided to settle in a cave here. He claimed to be the last of the true Syed or direct descendants of Mohammed. He lived here for 40 years helping villagers in times of flood and famine. It is claimed he was seen riding a lion, using a snake for a stick, and at other times flying like an eagle. Although his real name was Sheikh Usman Ali, he came to be known as Lal Qalandar Shah Baz which means 'Divine Spirit of the Eagle'.

The shrine is the main attraction of the town and pilgrims pour into it every day of the year but most particularly during *Urs*, the anniversary of his death, when they turn up in their thousands. Here you will see fakirs and malangs or spiritual mendicants garbed in long flowing robes, almost rags, and adorned with steel bracelets and beads. They dance like dervishes to the beating of drums, working themselves up into a trance-like state of total abandonment.

Things to See

North of Sehwan Sharif is Dadu. From here it is one-hour bus ride to Manchar Lake, worth a visit if you are headed in that direction. The people here are believed to have been descendants of the original pre-Aryan inhabitants of Moenjodaro. They have boats with a curiously broad panel in the bow. At one time they lived on these boats but nowadays they lead a more settled life.

From Dadu it is also an hour trip by jeep to Ranikot where the worlds' largest mud fort is located. The walls are 24 km in circumference and its origins and purpose are still a mystery. It is about 90 km north-west of Hyderabad. From Sann, there is a track heading west which goes for 21 km without any human settlements. There is no public transport to this place, you will need to hire a jeep. The fort was built in the 9th century AD, probably to guard the ancient Silk Trade Route north to Central Asia. Camping inside the fort is possible.

Another archaeological site is Amri, near Sann on the west bank of the Indus. It is neolithic (6000 to 3000 BC) and predates the Indus Valley Civilisation. It is believed that this civilisation had trade links with Persia and Central Asia before the Indus Valley Civilisation ever emerged.

Places to Stay

Sehwan Sharif has government rest houses, guest houses, muzzaffarkhanas, and tents for the poor pilgrims, for whom board and lodging is free. The government structures made of concrete are like ovens in the hot season.

MOENJODARO

History

Five thousand years ago, when the Mesopotamian civilisation flourished on the banks of the Euphrates, Moenjodaro began to develop as one of the great cities of the Indus Valley Civilisation. The 'Mound of the Dead' as the name means, thrived from 3000 to 1700 BC then abruptly declined, due, according to historians, to a violent invasion by the Aryans in 1700 BC.

It was certainly a thriving civilisation of a high order. Long after its demise Buddhist monks during the Kushan period erected a stupa over 70 metres high. It's now in ruins but it still rises above the surrounding area.

Moenjodaro has been restored and in the process lost its brooding air of mystery. The whole city is made of baked red bricks set in what is now semi wasteland. The architecture is unusual and alien, and evokes a great past.

The City

The city was planned on modern urban lines in square or rectangular blocks, with avenues up to 10 metres wide – some paved – which crossed at right angles, while residential areas had narrower streets. The elaborately designed buildings indicate a remarkably advanced knowledge of urban planning, architecture, engineering and sanitation. There are public buildings with pillared halls, baths, a state granary, colleges for priests, palaces, houses and shops. The highly developed drainage system compares with that of the Minoans of Crete.

It is divided into two parts: a lower area to the west and an upper area to the east, which was probably fortified. The excavated ruins cover about 100 hectares, but outer parts of the city are still buried.

People

The people from Moenjodaro are believed to have originated in Central Asia. Evidence suggest that they were of average size, brown in complexion, with long heads and faces and black hair. One of the busts found indicates that the men used razors. This particular Moenjodaron is depicted wearing fine muslin, which is embroidered with floral designs.

Women wore girdled skirts, beads, necklaces, gold bracelets or amulets, nose studs – still very common today in the subcontinent – anklets and earrings. They had a fan-shaped hair style and their children played with terracotta toys, such as carts and bullocks, which had sections that could be moved, like the head and tail. They also had dice and a kind of chess game, and lived in houses with paved floors.

Steatite seal from Moenjodaro. Many seals showing animal and human figures have been found, but the pictographic writing remains undeciphered.

Economy

The economy of Moenjodaro was based on agriculture with the main crops being wheat, barley, sesum, field peas and cotton. Objects discovered include statues, toys, jewellery embellished with precious and semi-precious stones, seals made of a steatite material, games and scales. These suggest it was a society which had thriving and diverse industries and trade links with other cultures, not merely neighbouring cities, but places like Mesopotamia, Persia, Central Asia, China, Tibet and Burma.

Culture

They had a very skilled and sophisticated art style, and developed a technique of fine wheel-turned pottery known archaeologically as 'black and red ware', as well as standard weights and measures for business transactions, and seals with animal figures and inscriptions etched on them. Their pictographic system of writing appears to have been based on astrological and zodiacal signs and the forms and shapes on fauna and flora. What is quite amazing is that they are almost identical with those discovered on Easter Island.

They also created kitchen utensils which were predominantly made from bronze and copper, while others were wrought from silver and lead. Weapons such as swords, knives and daggers were of bronze and their arts included sculpture in terracotta, ceramics and bronzeware. The government was likely to have been both secular and religious, based on a theocracy headed by a king-priest not unlike the present king-god of the Tibetans, the Dalai Lama.

Things to See
Buddhist Stupa
In the north-west of the city this stupa dates from the time of Vasudeva (182 to 230 AD), a Kushan emperor. It was whilst excavating this stupa in 1922 that British archaeologists stumbled upon the far older city beneath it. The stupa is on a high mound which was the fortress of the ancient city. It commands a panoramic view of the whole city.

Great Bath
West of the stupa the Great Bath was probably built for religious purposes. Twelve metres long, two metres deep and seven metres wide it was surrounded on three sides by halls, rooms and chambers. It was elaborately water-proofed and immediately west of it was the Great Granary.

Houses & Other Buildings
The better houses had courtyards reached through a side-alley gate, and a number of rooms including a kitchen, bathrooms, servants' quarters and a well. The most interesting aspect of the architecture was the chute dropping down into bins outside, which indicate that garbage was collected and dumped somewhere. There were also public buildings, residential dwellings and a number of shops. A

structure between the stupa and the Great Bath is believed to have been the palace of the priest-king.

Museum
The museum here, although small, contains a variety of artefacts from the archaeological site: engraved seals, terracotta children's toys, kitchen utensils, weapons, sculpture, jewellery and other ornaments. Other artefacts from Moenjodaro are distributed in major museums of Pakistan like Karachi and Lahore.

Getting There
Moenjodaro is 430 km north of Karachi and 168 km north of Sehwan Sharif. From Kotri the scenery is dry, arid and dusty. Approaching Larkana the scenery to the right of the railway tracks begins to get a little greener. The tiny station at Moenjodaro marks the dividing line between the dry, dusty region and the more fertile agricultural region.

The station is quite deserted, lonely and a long way by foot from the centre of town. If there is no tonga waiting at the station, backpackers should leave their gear there and walk to Dokri Village three km away, to collect a tonga to go to the archaeological site. It is about 11 km away and costs Rs 20. If you're travelling south from Lahore by train you will have to change trains at Sukkur. Get off at Larkhana and from there it's a 28-km taxi ride to the site. Buses also run from Larkhana to Dokri and cost Rs 5. You will still have to hire a tonga to get to the site. There are occasional minibuses that ply to some villages beyond Moenjodaro but they are irregular.

If you arrive early in the morning you can continue on the same afternoon; a day is plenty of time to see the site and museum. There is an airport near the museum and an information centre close to the site.

Places to Stay

There is an archaeological *Dak Bungalow* here, charging Rs 80 per person. Arrangements to stay there must be made in Karachi, though it's sometimes possible to get in without an advance reservation. Alternatively there is a *motel* run by the PTDC. In Larkana the *Sambara Inn* on Raza Shak Kabin Rd (tel 2291-3) has singles and doubles for Rs 200 to Rs 400. *Hotel Meran* Station Rd, has double rooms for Rs 75. The *Tourist Inn* Station Rd (tel 22 482), has singles/doubles for Rs 15/25.

KOT DIJI

Kot Diji is the site of another metropolis of the Indus Valley Civilisation. It is considered to be older than Moenjodaro. Prehistoric artefacts have also been unearthed here and can be seen in museums. Kot Diji is the site of a huge battlemented fort. This impressive building is visible from the highway.

It's between Ranipur and Khaipur on the highway from Hyderabad, on the east bank of the Indus close to Rohri. Worth a side trip.

SUKKUR & ROHRI

North of Larkhana the landscape becomes luxuriant, and in Sukkur the railway line and the highway split up, with a road and railtracks leading northwest to Quetta via Sibi and Jacobabad, while another highway and railway line go via Rahimyar Khan and Saddiqabad straight to Multan.

Sukkur is a sprawling town, with beautiful mosques, gardens, shrines and *madrazhis* (Muslim religious schools). A desert oasis town, similar to Jaisalmer in Rajasthan, it also boasts many havelis, however, unlike those of Jaisalmer, the Sukkur variety are decorated with geometric, floral designs and painted in a variety of bright, contrasting colours.

Sukkur is also the site of a huge *barrage* which is named after it. Built between 1923 and 1932, it stretches for 1400 metres, crosses the Indus in 46 spans and feeds seven main canals, totalling 650 km in length. One canal alone is wider and longer than the Suez or Panama canals. The Sukkur barrage irrigates 2½ million hectares of previously non-arable land and is the largest irrigation project in the world. This has greatly contributed to Sukkurs' position as a prosperous industrial and agricultural centre.

Just across the Indus is **Rohri**, also fairly prosperous and an important rail and road junction. The two towns, five km apart and 488 km north of Karachi, are linked by the Landsdowne and Ayub bridges, which are extremely beautiful. There is a medieval mosque with porcelain-tiled walls, and eight km away are what are believed to be the remains of the ancient city of *Arar* or *Alar* where Alexander the Great is said to have camped. In the middle of the Indus there is an island where the shrine of Khwajha Khizar is located. It is reputed to be more than a thousand years old and is venerated by Hindus and Muslims alike. Slightly south of this island is a larger island called Bhakkur, whose fort has a long and chequered history. The Landsdowne Bridge connects Bukkur to Rohri. The 27-metre high tower of Ma'sum Shah Bakhri, Nawab of Sukkur, provides a fine view over the town and the barrage. There is also a rock in the river where the picturesque temple of Sri Sadbella provides a fine view of the Landsdowne Bridge.

Places to Stay

Although it can be uncomfortably hot in summer, the towns have a quiet atmosphere and they are good places to stop off at on the journey north or south; places where you can shake off travel fatigue, reappraise your itinerary and do your laundry.

Sukkur *Al Firdous Hotel* (tel 3404), Barrage Rd and *Fazal Hotel*, Clock Tower area, are the cheapies with rates from Rs

15 for singles, and doubles Rs 18 to Rs 25. Hotels *Al-Hamra, Shalimar* and *Nusrat* on Barrage Rd and *Royal Hotel* (tel 4371), Clock Tower area, have rates from Rs 25 to Rs 50. Nusrat has a reasonably good restaurant. *Mehran Hotel* (tel 3792), on Station Rd, with air-con and dining hall, has singles from Rs 40, doubles from Rs 75. *Inter Pak Inn* (tel 3051), located on the outskirts near the barrage is the most expensive at Rs 200 to Rs 400.

Kushan statue representing a yakshi or female deity and dating from *circa* 100 AD.

Rohri The hotels are near the railway station and mostly charge the same rates.

Getting Around
Tonga, if shared with other passengers from the bus station to the city centre, is Rs 1 to Rs 2; alone Rs 5 to Rs 10. Auto-rickshaw within the city perimeter is Rs 3 to Rs 5. There are no rickshaws here.

Punjab

North of Sind is the Punjab or *Panj Nad* – Land of Five Rivers – the Jhelum, Chenab, Ravi, Beas and the Sutlej, which all flow south to join the Indus at Mithankot. This region is known geographically as the Upper Indus Plain. In area it is about 196,000 square km and is bounded in the west by the Sulaiman Ranges in Baluchistan and by the Indus in the North West Frontier Province. In the north it is bounded by the Hazara district and Azad Kashmir & Jammu, while in the east the Ravi and the Sutlej and the Rajaputana Desert in India form the boundary. To the south the rocky gorge in Sind demarcates the province.

The land rises to around 200 metres and gradually climbs up to 300 metres at the Potwar Plateau. It has a continental climate, but suffers from extreme heat in the summer when the temperature soars to 46°C, untempered by any breeze except the dry wind called *loo* which, like the *ghibli* in the Sahara, blows in the day time and stirs up dust and sand to darken the sky. This is occasionally broken by electrical sandstorms and thunderstorms accompanied by heavy rainfall, which usually causes a slight drop in the temperature. The region between Sibi in Baluchistan and Jacobabad in Sind is considered to be the hottest in Pakistan. It was in the latter area that the highest temperature – 51°C (126°F) – was recorded. In winter the temperature drops to a much more pleasant 24 to 30°C.

The Punjab is not only the granary of the country, but also an important industrial region. So amid grainfields of wheat, barley, rice and maize or fields of cotton, sugarcane and bananas there are industrial villages with modern plants and factories, all new and starkly alien to their surroundings. It is the only region which has diversified industries and many major industrial centres such as Faisalabad, Sargodha, Lahore, Sialkot, Rawalpindi, and Jhelum and Campbellpore, both oil-producing towns.

The land traversed by several rivers is lush green and fertile; a hospitable region where, half a million years ago, the Paleolithic Age flourished along the banks of the Soan River as it flowed down the Potwar Plateau across the Salt Range. Here the sister-cities of Moenjodaro – Harappa and Taxila – emerged to be wiped out later by the arrival of the pastoral Aryans, who adopted the culture they discovered here.

This was the region that Cyrus the Great (6th century BC) of the Achaemenian Empire conquered, and his successor, Darius, turned into a satrapy of the Persian Empire, only to be superseded by the Hellenic Empire of Alexander the Great in the 4th century BC. Alexander found the rulers of Taxila friendly and was able to make treaty agreements with them. This was consolidated by the marriage of a Greek princess with Chandragupta, who later set up the great Mauryan Empire.

Along the banks of the Jhelum River, Alexander of Macedon fought and won his last great battle, but it was here that Bucephalus, his faithful charger died. It was also here where Alexander, weary of endless military campaigns, finally decided to turn back homeward. His coming and going strongly influenced the emergence of the Buddhist Gandhara Culture of the Kushan Empire which had its capital in Taxila, once visited by Saint (Doubting) Thomas on his way to the coast of Malabar. It was this great 'Holy Land' of Buddhism that was to influence – through the ancient Silk Trade Route – the historical development of Central Asia, particularly of Chinese Turkestan and of Tibet.

The northern part of the Indus Plain developed faster than the southern region, not only because of its great rivers but because the main camel caravan route of the ancient Silk Trade – now making up the Euro-Asian Highway – ran from the Khyber Pass through the Valley of Peshawar to Lahore. This important overland trade route gave impetus to the development of villages into towns, towns into cities and cities into kingdoms. It is a very rich region, which nonetheless suffered greatly from the depredations of the Mongols, other invaders and conflicts. Its rich, natural resources have always allowed it a quick recovery.

It was only when the Moghuls invaded and had established their empire and secured the frontiers that this Upper Indus Plain began its 'golden age'. Huge forts, splendid palaces, mosques and other public buildings proliferated along the whole length and breadth of the land. Great and beautiful cities like Lahore, Rawalpindi, Bahawalpur and Multan emerged. When Moghul power began to decline in the late 18th and early 19th century the Sikhs came, only to be superseded by the British in 1849. The British similarly established their empire, secured the frontiers and continued the construction work begun by the Moghuls.

NORTH OF SUKKUR
North of Sukkur and Rohri in Sind the land, cut by the Indus and the highway, turns greener. A little beyond Ubauro a side road leads west to the Guddu barrage – about 60 km away – which bridges the Indus. This road continues on to Sui in Baluchistan to the west and then splits off to Dera Ghazi Khan in the north.

A short distance north – toward Rahimyar Khan – a road leads to Sadiqabad, while to the west the **Bhong Mosque** is 26 km off the highway. Described as a 'jewel of a mosque', it has mosaics of tiny mirrors on the walls. This is now the land of the Srikis, renowned for their valour as warriors.

Rahimyar Khan is about seven km off the main highway, an industrial town now, but once the site of towns of the Indus Valley Civilisation.

It is all flat open spaces until **Uch Sharif**, today a nondescript oasis, but during the 13th century it was a centre for religious, cultural and literary pursuits and attracted scholars, poets and pirs from Central Asia. A few interesting sights remain –the tomb of Jaial Surkh Bukhari, and the blue and white tiled tomb of Balial Halim. The buildings reflect the same peculiar, traditional architecture and artwork as that on the walls of the houses of Sukkur. The 13th century, octagonal Mazhar of Bibi Jawinda is of Central Asian design, tiled in blue and white faience and is about four km from the southern bus station.

If continuing up to Ahmadpur East you have to go to the northern bus station for Bahawalpur. Fare is Rs 2.50, takes half an hour. Ahmadpur East is another oasis, but much larger and more developed. It is now a military cantonment. This is a town with many palaces and tombs of previous rulers of Bahawalpur, but only the main palace is open to tourists. The town is known for its pointy-toed sandals with beadwork embroidered into the leather, and pottery which is considered the finest in the whole of Pakistan.

Out of Ahmadpur East is again flat desert, it is a half-hour trip to Bahawalpur by minibus and costs Rs 7.

BAHAWALPUR
From the bus station to the city centre costs Rs 5 by auto-rickshaw, and Rs 3 by rickshaw. Rickshaws here are quite different to those elsewhere in Pakistan. The town is growing quite fast and modern buildings are transforming this traditional desert oasis into a bustling centre for tourists wishing to explore the Cholistan Desert on camel or jeep safaris.

Bahawalpur was founded in 1748 and remained a kingdom until 1954. There are three palaces here, the main one *Nur*

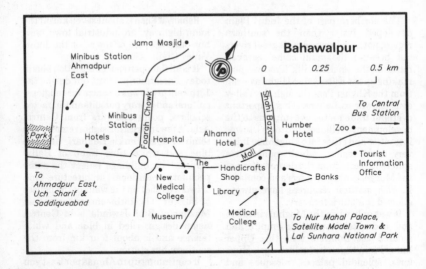

Mahal is occupied by the military. Bahawalpur is also known for its distinctively embroidered slippers and shoes and the filigree pottery which is made here. It has a marble mosque in the Foarah Chowk and a few British buildings like the Science College. About 15 km further east is the Lal Suhanra Park, which is actually a wildlife sanctuary – worth a visit. The Japanese have a fun park project here.

Information
The Tourist Information Centre is at the Stadium on the Mall. See Mohammed Yunus for assistance.

Festival
There is a tribal mela in the desert for seven weeks between January and February.

Places to Stay & Eat
Ehrun Hotel the most expensive in town, is adjacent to *Abaside Hotel*. The most pleasant is *Alhamra Hotel* singles/doubles Rs 35/60. It has a restaurant. *Humber Hotel* is cheaper but has no restaurant.

Getting There & Away
Air PIA has weekly flights to the major cities.

Rail Trains run to the south and north.

Bus There are buses and minibuses going in nearly every direction, including Bahawalnagar in the desert area. There are direct buses to Multan, Faisalabad and Lahore. Fares Rs 30 to Rs 45.

THE CHOLISTAN DESERT
East of Bahawalpur is the Cholistan Desert which covers an area of about 25,000 square km and extends into the Thar Desert of India. The region was once watered by the Hakra River, known as the Saravati in Vedic times. At one time there were 400 forts in the area and archaeological finds around the Darawar Fort, the only place with a perennial waterhole, indicate that it was contemporaneous with the Indus Valley Civilisation.

The average annual rainfall is only 12 cm, and the little cultivation there is, is made possible by underground wells, drawn up by camels. The water is stored

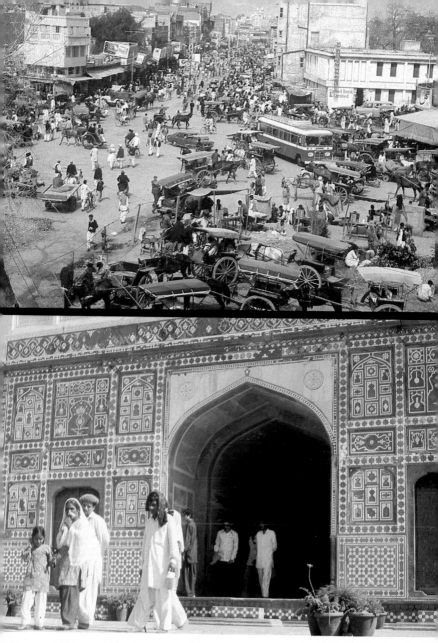

Top: Rajah Bazaar, old city, Rawalpindi (PTDC)
Bottom: Jehangir's Tomb, Lahore (PE)

Top: Tea stall in Peshawar (PTDC)
Left: Sindhi woman dancing (PTDC)
Right: Thatta embroidery (PE)

in troughs, built by the tribes, between sandhills and in waterholes called *tobas*.

The people are racially similar to those in Rajasthan – tall, with sharp features. They live in large, round, mud and grass huts, usually built on the top of sandhills. On the whole, they are pastoral and nomadic. The main tribes are the Chachar, Mehr, Lar, Paryar, Channar, Chandani and Bohar.

The forts here were built at 29 km intervals, which probably served as guard posts for the camel caravan routes. There were three rows of these forts. The first line of forts began from Phulra and ended in Lera, the second from Rukhanpur to Islamgarh, and the third from Bilcaner to Kapoo. They are all in ruins now, and you can see that they were built with double walls of gypsum blocks and mud. Some of them date back to 1000 BC, and were destroyed and rebuilt many times.

The Maujgarh Fort is in pretty bad shape, and so is the mosque in the area. There is also the tomb of a holy man which dates back to the Moghul period. The most impressive fort is the **Darawar Fort** which is the oldest, but has been rebuilt with bricks by the rulers of Bahawalpur. Apparently the bricks were transported by a human line from Uch Sharif where they were kilned, to Darawar, about 64 km way across the Desert. Near the fort is the marble **Jamia Mosque**. The tombs here of the rulers of Bahawalpur are adorned with blue glazed tiles and geometric patterns.

MULTAN

Multan, the 'City of Pirs and Shrines' is a prosperous city of bazaars, mosques, shrines and superbly designed tombs. It is also a city of dust, summer heat and beggars. It has a long history. Alexander the Great added it to his list of Indus conquests. In 641 AD Xuang Tzang found it 'agreeable and prosperous' – Mohammed Bin Qasim obviously agreed, he was the next to conqueror Multan in 712 AD. Mahmud of Ghazni invaded in 1005,

Timurlane in 1398. In the 16th century it was the Moghuls turn, followed by the Sikhs in 1752 and the British in 1849.

Multan is now a centre for agricultural produce and fruits and is fast becoming a modern town, however some old traditions remain, in particular Multan is known for its intricately glazed pottery, camel skin tiles and cotton fabrics. However Multans' main claim to fame is the many splendid shrines and tombs.

There are five of these mausoleums in the old fort, the most famous being that of Saint Rukni-i-Alam, also known as Rukn-ud-din. The tomb was originally built by the Emperor Tughlag Shah (1340-1350) for his own use, but his son decided it should be for the saint. The dome of the tomb, which is built on high ground, is visible many km away. One of the supporting towers was destroyed during the siege of 1848, but it was later carefully restored. This tomb is decorated with glazed tiles patterned in *bas relief*.

Other tombs include those of Baha-ud-din Zakharia (also known as Baha-il-Haq) which was very badly damaged in 1848 and the tomb of the Sufi, Shams-i-Tabriz, who was murdered in 1247. The old fort is called Ibn-i-Qasim Bagh and there is also a Hindu temple dedicated to Shiva's 'Narsingh' or lion-man incarnation, now in disrepair. The Chowk Bazaar in the centre of town is also a fascinating place to visit.

Places to Stay & Eat

The *Mahmood Hotel* on Sher Shah Rd, between the GTS bus stand and the cantonment station, is still the cheapest at Rs 15 for a single. The *Prince Hotel* on Nishtar Rd, *Al-Qamer Hotel* on Railway Rd, and *Hotel Plaza* near the GTS bus station have rates from Rs 25 to Rs 45. *Guilt Hotel* has singles/doubles for Rs 30/50.

Of the more expensive hotels, *Hotel Sindabad* (tel 72294) on Nishtar College Rd has a restaurant and rooms range from Rs 135 to Rs 275. *Hotel Silver Sand* (tel

33061) on Railway Rd and *Shezan Residence* (tel 30256) Kutchery Rd, have the same rates. The best place for eats is at *Rang-La Restaurant* on Kutchery Rd.

Getting Around
Rickshaws within the town are Rs 3, Rs 5 for auto-rickshaws.

Getting There & Away
Most buses leave from Hassan Parawana Rd. Opposite the Mavra Hotel are the minibuses for Lahore, Rs 42. Near the Rex Cinema is the station for: Bahawalpur, Rs 13; Rahimyar Khan, Rs 37; Mianwali, Rs 60. The buses for Sukkur and Karachi leave from the Guild Hotel. Shalimar Flying Coach on Sher Shah Rd has buses for Jhang and Sarghoda, Rs 60.

NORTH OF MULTAN
To the north of Multan is a region called Choti. The tribes in this area, the *Lagaris*, have an entirely different culture. In the district of Sanga are the *Hurs*, also culturally unique.

Climbing up onto the Potwar Plateau the land stands out to the south where the Salt Range begins and continues towards the Peshawar Valley. Just before reaching the valley, the range turns south to Bannu and Dera Ismail Khan. This is an unappealing stretch of land with its scarred red earth and sandstone rocks dissected by ridges, troughs, gulleys, crevasses, and salt and coal mines. But it's also an area with some attractive historical spots.

The route splits here and at Faisalabad one road leads to Sargodha while another runs on towards Lahore.

From Multan there is another road which goes through Khanewal via Harappa to Lahore.

FAISALABAD
It is Rs 5 by auto-rickshaw to the city centre from the bus station. The city appears compact but actually spreads out over a large area. It has a real 'oasis'

atmosphere with all the typical desert scents and sights, particularly common are the camels drawing carts loaded with grains and trading goods. It is fairly neat and clean, the city centre is designed like the British flag. The clock tower is in the middle and all around it are bazaars and mosques of varying architecture. It has also one of the largest agricultural colleges in Asia.

Not many tourists come here, although it is a pleasant jumping-off point for Lahore, Sargodha or Multan. There are many jewellery shops and money changers, but not many hotels or eating places, however those that exist are fairly good.

Places to Stay & Eat
Hotel Rays on Alama Iqbal Rd (tel 4006) is the best in town, it has a restaurant and rates are from Rs 125 to Rs 200. It will soon give way to *Serena Inn* presently under construction. *Super Hotel* (tel 22726) on Ghul Bhawana Bazaar has singles/doubles with attached bath for Rs 25/45. The *Shasha Hotel* on Kichari Bazaar and Chiniot Bazaar is of a similar standard and price. *Namat Kadah Hotel* on a corner of Clocktower Chowk is good for kebab-nan snacks. *Al Khayyam Hotel & Restaurant* on Aminpur Bazaar is an excellent place for meals, but the best in town is the restaurant in the Hotel Rays.

Getting There & Away
The city is linked by air and rail with major cities. Buses for Lahore are located at the Central Bus Station to the north of the town. Those for the western and southern areas like Sargodha, Jhang and Multan are located on Alama Iqbal Rd. The *Flying Coach* has its station near Hotel Rays and the *New Khan Road Runner* is on the same road.

The bus to Lahore takes 2½ hours and costs Rs 15. The Flying Coach air-con minibus is Rs 25 and takes two hours, but it has no definite schedule, unlike the GTS buses.

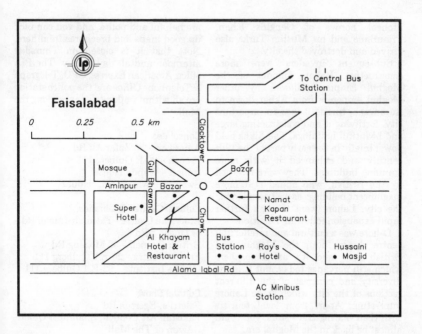

Faisalabad

0   0.25   0.5 km

To Central Bus Station

Clocktower

Mosque

Gul Bhawana

Aminpur

Bazar

Bazar

Super Hotel

Chowk

Namat Kapan Restaurant

Al Khayam Hotel & Restaurant

Bus Station

Ray's Hotel

Hussaini Masjid

Alama Iqbal Rd

AC Minibus Station

HARAPPA

This was the first of the Indus Valley Civilisation sites to be discovered, but in size and condition it is inferior to Moenjodaro. Located 186 km south-west of Lahore, Harappa is reached via the station at Sahiwal, formerly known as Montgomery. Situated beside an earlier course of the Ravi River, Harappa was discovered in 1920/21, but through the ages the site was quarried for bricks and most of the buildings so far excavated are in poor condition. Like Moenjodaro the excavations have revealed a series of cities, stacked one upon another. The site, with its citadel and great granary, seems similar in many ways to Moenjodaro and like its southern sister-city appears to have thrived around 3000 to 1700 BC with an economy based largely on agriculture and trade. The Harappan society seems to have been egalitarian, pursuing a rather simple way of life.

Things to See

There is a museum here which exhibits numerous artefacts discovered on the site: terracotta toys, chess boards, utensils and pieces of jewellery, indicating that they may have had trade relations with Burma! The museum is situated just off the main highway near the railway station.

LAHORE

Situated on the east bank of the Ravi River, Lahore is very old. Legend traces its origin to Loh, the son of Rama Chandra, the hero of the *Ramayana*, but history records that it began as a dependency of the 8th century AD Hindu ruler, Lalitiditya. In the early 11th century it came under Muslim rule and evolved as a centre of Islamic culture and learning as well as trade and commerce. In the 13th century it was depopulated and razed to the ground by the Tartar-

Mongol hordes of Genghis Khan, Timurlane and his Muslim Turks also arrived and destroyed the city.

Subsequent invaders were more constructive. Babar, founder of the Moghul Empire, followed by other Moghul emperors from Akbar down to Aurangzeb, turned it into an important city, fortifying it and constructing large and beautiful buildings. The Sikhs held power briefly in the early part of the 19th century and enhanced it with more stunning buildings. They were followed by the British, who added still more magnificent buildings as well as enlarging the city. Lahore went through further rapid expansion following Partition.

Lahore was a cultural and intellectual centre during both the Moghul and British eras, and it's an atmosphere which still pervades today, but it is the diversity and contrast of the different sections of the city which make Lahore interesting. Apart from local tourists with their blaring transistors, you could almost be back in the Moghul era.

Lahore is 213 metres above sea level and has a population of approximately 3 million. The temperature here drops down to 10°C in winter, but in summer can soar to 40°C or more. The best time to visit is straight after the monsoon period when the weather is cool and pleasant.

Warning

Whilst Lahore is a beautiful city with much to offer, there are unfortunate aspects of which the traveller should be aware. Cheapies near and around the railway station are not recommended – it is unwise to leave money and valuables in your hotel room here. The purchase of drugs of any kind should also be avoided, police informers abound in Lahore, especially in the aforementioned hotels.

Information

The Tourist Information Centres are at Lahore International Airport, and *Falettis* (tel 303660), Egerton Rd. The staff here are helpful and polite, and you can pick up good maps and brochures from here. Note that it is closed on Thursday afternoon and all day Friday. The PIA office, American Express, GPO, Telegraph & Telephone Office and the police station are all within walking distance along the Mall.

Consulates

American – 50 Zafar Ali Rd
French – 20-E Gulberg 111
Italian – Wapda House
Swedish – Walten Rd, Saddar

Cultural Centres & Libraries

American Centre – Fatimah Jinnah Rd – or Queen's Rd
British Council – 32 Mozang Rd
French Centre – 20-E/2 Gulberg 111
Goethe Institute – 92-E/1 Gulberg 111

Cultural Show

Faletti's, Egerton Rd
Pakistan Art Council, Shahrah-i-Quaid-i-Azam or The Mall
Salatin, on The Mall

Duty Free Shop (tel 222724) Montgomery Rd. The usual duty-free stuff is available.

Banks American Express, First National City Bank of New York and Grindlay's.

Foreigners' Registration Office

This is off the Lower Mall on Kutchery Rd near the District Court. Route is towards Badshahi Mosque. This is the place for extending visas, otherwise registration could be done at the police station near your hotel.

Things To See
Moghul City

Lahore is actually three cities in one. The old Moghul City is walled in by a 10-metre-high brick rampart overlooking its surrounding moat. The moat is now dry and the walls dismantled in certain places to make openings for streets and roads. Within the ramparts are shrines, mosques, bazaars and workshops where craftspeople still weave textiles and do traditional copper, silver and brass work using age-old methods. The city itself is ringed by Circular Rd.

Badshahi Mosque

The mosque at one corner of the walled city is imposing, both externally and internally. Built by Aurangzeb, it has huge gateways, tall towering minarets, three vast domes and a spacious courtyard. Take a look at it at dusk when the dark red bricks are fiery with the setting sun – a real 'Arabian nights' silhouette. Make sure you don't wear shorts or miniskirts – bare knees are not appreciated here.

Lahore Fort

Like many of its contemporaries, the great Fort of Lahore was also a palace. It was originally built by Akbar and later improved by Jehangir and Shah Jahan, both of whom gave free rein to their flair for architectural extravagance. The older gates are no longer used but inside the *Hathi Pol* – Elephant Gate – you can still see the *kashi* tile mosaics which date from the time of Shah Jahan. They were badly damaged during the Sikh wars but have now been restored. The mosaics show elephant and camel fights, polo games and scenes of court life.

The **Pearl Mosque** or *Moti Masjid* still stands in the fort and was restored in 1904. The *Diwan-i-Am* or Hall of Public Audience and the *jharoka* or balcony throne was the place where the emperor used to appear daily. Another interesting building is the **Shish Mahal** – palace of mirrors – which is decorated with glass mosaics and stands to the north of the square. Then there's the **Naulakha** which gets its name from its construction cost of nine lakhs (Rs 900,000). The north wall has fine kashi tilework. Also worth seeing here are the *choti khwabagh* or lesser bedchambers

and the *arzgah*, where noblemen would gather each morning to pay their respects to the emperor. Aurangzeb, the last of the great Moghuls, added the *Almiri Gate*. On his death the city began to decline.

On Mondays, Thursdays and Saturdays there is a *son et lumiere* show in English at the fort. Entrance to the fort is free for students.

If you're interested in collecting postcards there's a good selection of high quality cards available for Rs 1 each from the shop near the gate at the main entrance. The next best selection is at the Lahore Museum – same price.

Other Old City Buildings

Between the fort and the Badshahi Mosque is the **Gurudwara Arjun Singh**, a quaint, beautiful Sikh temple which is dwarfed by its large neighbours. The *samadhi*, facing the east wall of the fort, contains the ashes of Ranjit Singh, the Sikh ruler of Lahore who died in 1849. Seven concubines and four wives became *satis* at his cremation, burning themselves to death on his funeral pyre.

The **Sonehri Masjid** – Golden Mosque – has three gilt domes and dates from 1753. Its builder, Bokhari Khan, is said to have died in a rather unusual fashion, kicked to death by the female attendants of a widow he had displeased or scorned! The **Mosque of Wazir Khan**, also in the old city was built in 1634 by the Governor of the Punjab during the reign of Shah Jahan. It's well worth seeing as it's very beautiful and not only has some fine kashi tilework, but also offers an excellent view of the city. It's a little difficult to find but keep asking and you will eventually find it. Apparently auto-rickshaws are not allowed in as the alleys are really very narrow. It is not far from the Golden Mosque and through the bazaars.

Just beyond the Circular Rd in Iqbal Park is the **Minar-i-Pakistan** – a monument to the conception of Pakistan – designed like a flower bud just beginning to open with a long stamen jutting out to the sky.

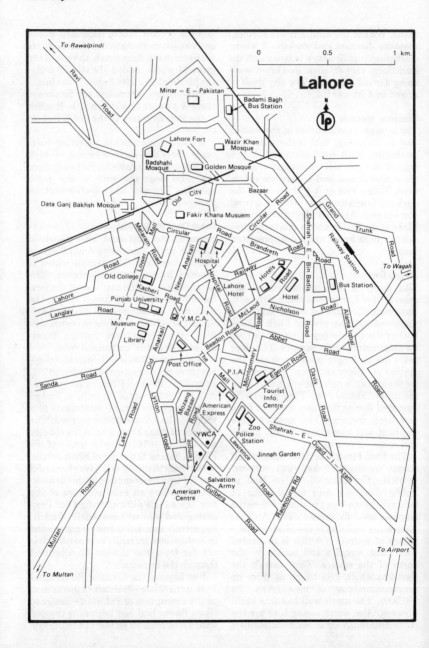

Lahore

0   0.5   1 km.

To Rawalpindi

Ravi Road

Minar – E – Pakistan

Badami Bagh Bus Station

Lahore Fort

Wazir Khan Mosque

Badshahi Mosque

Golden Mosque

Old City

Bazaar

Data Ganj Bakhsh Mosque

Fakir Khana Musuem

Circular Road

Circular Road

Shahrah – E – Bin Badis Road

Grand Trunk Road

Railway Station

To Wagah

Melaram Road

Mall

Brandreth

Lower Road

Hospital

New Anarkali Road

Hospital Road

Railway Road

Hotels Road

Bus Station

Old College

Lahore Road

Kacheri Road

Lahore Hotel

Punjab University

McLeod Road

Hotel

Nicholson Road

Langlay Road

Y.M.C.A.

Museum

Old Anarkali Road

Beadon Road

Montgomery Road

Abbet Road

Alama Iqbal Road

Library

The Mall

Post Office

P.I.A.

Egerton Road

Davis Road

Sanda Road

Lytton Road

Mozang Bazaar

American Express

Tourist Info. Centre

YWCA

Zoo Police Station

Lawrence Road

Shahrah – E – Quaid – I – Azam

Lake Road

Temple Road

Salvation Army

Jinnah Garden

American Centre

Gulberg

Racecourse Rd

To Airport

Multan Road

To Multan

There is a lift up to the top of the sightseeing tower.

Inside the Bhati Gate of the old city is the **Faqir Khana Museum** which contains a collection of paintings, carvings, manuscripts, old china, carpets and numerous other objets d'art. Outside the old city is the beautiful mosque of **Data Ganj Baksh** built on a high platform but presently being dwarfed by gigantic minarets which are under construction.

British City

The British built their city adjacent to the old Moghul city. It begins with the **New Anarkali Bazaar**, named after the famous courtesan of Akbar, off Circular Rd to the south. Anarkali – pomegranate blossom – was entombed alive by the emperor for smiling at Prince Salim, who later became Emperor Jehangir. Her tomb is near the bazaar, which is a paved street with narrow alleys off each side. It's lined with traditional shops now crowded with stalls selling everything from glass bangles to transistor radios, beaten gold to tape recorders and refrigerators – most of it at bargain prices!

The Mall

From here the Mall runs south-east towards the airport. It is the most modern section of the city where the government buildings, big hotels, churches, modern mosques, restaurants, cafes, banks, airline offices and travel agencies are. Lined with shady trees, it is quiet, sedate, well-paved, neat and clean and has a completely different atmosphere from the rest of the city. Most of the imposing government buildings like the **High Court**, the **Punjab University** and the **Museum** are of Moghul-Victorian design, while the churches and cathedrals are either Norman or Gothic. There are also modern structures here such as the **Shohada Mosque**, the **Islamic Summit Minar** and the **WAPDA** building.

From the Mall, streets and alleys branch off towards the British-built railway station. It is here that the section of the old Moghul city merges with the modern part of Lahore. The railway station, of Moghul-Victorian design, is surrounded with bazaars, cheap and medium-class hotels, cafes and eating places. The central bus station is just a block away and nearby are minibuses, buses, auto-rickshaws, taxis and tongas all waiting to pick up passengers. It's chaotic, crowded, congested, confusing and dusty.

Close to the police station and opposite the Lahore Hilton in a wooded section of the Mall is the **Jinnah-i-Bagh** zoo which contains peacocks, Bengal tigers, giraffes, ostriches, Bactrian camels, elephants, deer and other animals.

Lahore Museum & Kim's Gun

Opposite the Punjab University on the Mall, the **Lahore Museum** houses collections from various historical periods of Pakistan – from the paleolithic age to the Indus Valley civilisation, the Gandhara culture and the Moghul and British periods. It's a smallish museum, but is noted particularly for its Gandhara sculptures – the most famous of which is the *Fasting Siddartha* – and for its Moghul paintings. You are not allowed to take bags inside. From 1875 to 1893 Rudyard Kipling's father was the curator of this museum. On an island in the Mall in front of the museum is **Kim's gun**, the *zamzama*. This huge, menacing-looking gun, known as the 'lion's roar', was immortalised by Kipling as Kim's gun – last used in the Battle of Panipat in 1761. A Persian inscription indicates that it was cast in 1760.

Other Museums

Faqir Khana Museum in the Old Walled City, **Shaker Ali Museum** and **Chugtai Museum** are all worth visiting.

Tombs of Jehangir & Nur Jehan

Five km north-west of the city is the quiet secluded village of Shaddara. From here it is two km to the mausoleums of the Moghul Emperor Jehangir and Empress Nur Jehan – Light of the World. In their serene setting, they are separated only by a canal. Nur Jehan's tomb is in an open garden but Jehangir's is huge and enclosed by high walls. The building has four 30-metre-high minarets; the cenotaph is inlaid with *pietra dura* work like the Taj Mahal in Agra; and on the east and west side of the tomb the 99 names of Allah are finely carved. You can see across the Ravi River to Lahore from the minarets. Close to the tomb of Nur Jehan is the tomb of Asaf Khan, her brother, but unfortunately most of the kashi tilework has been stripped off this beautiful Persian-style tomb.

Entry fee to all three tombs is Rs 2 which you pay at either Jehangir's or Nur Jehan's tomb. It's about a 10-minute walk from the bus stop to Nur Jehan's tomb, and the shortest way from there to Jehangir's tomb is to jump the back wall, cross the tracks, find the break in the loose rock wall – it's easy – then follow it along the right side and you'll come to the entrance to the compound. You are not allowed to climb up via the minarets to the roof.

Shalimar Gardens

Laid out by Shah Jahan in 1642, the Shalimar Gardens are typical Moghul gardens. Designed along the lines of the imperial Persian gardens, they are an imposing 32 hectares in area. The gardens are 10 km east of the city and are built in three tiers with pools, fountains and pavilions. Entrance fee to the gardens is Rs 2. The best times to visit them are between 11 am and noon or 4 to 5 pm in summer, or from 11 am and noon and 3 to 4 pm during winter, when the fountains – some of them anyway – are turned on.

Take bus 3, 12 or 17 from the bus station near the railway station. On the way to the gardens you will pass the gate of the **Balabi Bagh** or rose garden which was designed and planted in 1655. Notice the

exquisite, coloured tiles decorating this gate. Close to the Shalimar Gardens is the tomb of their builder, Ali Mardan Khan.

Around Lahore

Sheikhpura, once known as Jehangirabad, is 42 km from Lahore. Here there is a building once used as a hunting lodge by the emperor, now occupied by the Pakistan police. Nearby is the **Hiran Minar**, a large stone sculpture built by Jehangir in memory of his pet antelope, *Manaraj*. Sixty-seven km out of Lahore, is the **Changa Manga Forest** which has a lake and a miniature railway that meanders through and around the forest.

Things to Buy

Most handicraft shops are expensive and located along the Mall. The APWA Cottage Industries and Pakistan Handicrafts shops have fixed prices. Anarkali Bazaar, Gulberg Market, Shah Alam Market and the Old City bazaars have lower prices, and you can bargain here.

Places to Stay – bottom end

Cheap hotels are near and around the railway station, but they are simply not recommended because of the many rip-offs and set-ups reported over the years – particularly in the hotels along McLeod and Badrenath Rds. There have been lots of hassles here ranging from stolen travellers' cheques to planting hashish in rooms in order to blackmail tourists. If you have to stay in a cheapie check that your room is secure and take care.

If you're in transit try the *Railway Retiring Rooms* where singles cost Rs 30 and doubles Rs 60. If you're on your way to India via Wagah at the border, there's a *PTDC Motel* right there with dorm accommodation. It's clean and pleasant and costs Rs 30 for a bed. It also provides a good breakfast.

One of the safest cheapos is the *Youth Hostel* at 110 B Firdous Market, Gulberg 111 (tel 8 3145). Dorm beds cost Rs 10. Many travellers recommend this place, but its biggest disadvantage is being too far out of town. Not only that but it's a long and complicated way out there. You have to take bus 25 or wagon 15 south from the terminus at the end of McLeod Rd near the railway station.

The *YMCA Hostel* on the Mall (tel 5 4433) is next to the GPO in a section of a large building and is easy to miss, so keep your eyes open for the entrance. It's a popular place with dorm beds for Rs 20, but is often packed with local Christians.

The *Salvation Army Hostel*, 35 Fatimah Jinnah Rd, (also known as Queen's Rd), has three-bed dorms, Rs 30 per bed, doubles Rs 60, beds in the outside hall for Rs 10. There is also a common room and a kitchen. They look after you well here. The *YWCA Hostel* on the same road near to the PIA office, has dorm beds for Rs 30, singles/doubles Rs 45/75, and is friendly and pleasant.

Campers can put up their tents or park their vehicles in the gardens of the YWCA or in the grounds of the Sally Army Hostel. Camping is also possible at the Youth Hostel.

Places to Stay - middle
Both the *Orient Hotel* and *Lahore Hotel*, which are adjacent to each other on McLeod Rd have rooms with fans and attached toilets and showers for Rs 80 to Rs 150. While both these hotels are very good, they are not recommended in summer as the rooms are like ovens then. The *Modern Hotel* on Station Rd, has singles/doubles for Rs 70/140. The *Menora Hotel* (tel 30 3557) McLeod Rd has air-con and non air-con rooms with rates from Rs 50 to Rs 175. There are other middle level hotels on McLeod Rd but most of them do not accept foreign tourists.

Places to Stay - top end
Lahore's international hotels are mainly along the Mall and Airport Rd. All have rates from Rs 600 to Rs 1500. The *Hilton International* (tel 6 2294) on the Mall, is

apparently the poshest in town. *Pearl Continental* (tel 6 7931), also on the Mall, is the renamed Intercontinental. *Faletti's* (tel 30 3660) is on Egerton Rd.

At a lower price level the *Hotel Ambassador* (tel 30 1861), Davis Rd, the *Indus Hotel* (tel 30 2856) and the *Country Club Hotel* (tel 31 1361) both on the Mall are all good class hotels.

Places to Eat
Cheapies are near and around the railway station and are good value. Others are at and around Mozang Bazaar, an area especially good for chicken tikka. The Gamal Mandi area is good for fried fish, the Old Walled City for more exotic dishes.

More upmarket places are generally located on the Mall. Opposite Lord's is *Kim Mun Chinese Restaurant* on the 1st floor. Adjacent is the *Regina Restaurant* which is in a cellar. The Hilton International has three recommended restaurants: *Fort Grills* is reputedly the best in town, while for snacks, *Kim's* is good, and for barbecue, the *Barbecue* (what else?). Other five-star hotels offer exotic and continental dishes. There is a *Wimpy* and a *Salt-n-Pepper Restaurant*, both on the Mall, both offering burgers, chicken sandwiches and french fries.

Getting Around
From the airport to the city centre costs Rs 40 by taxi; Rs 2.25 by minibus and auto-rickshaws cost Rs 20 to Rs 25. Within the city perimeter auto-rickshaws are Rs 5 to Rs 8, minibuses Rs 1.25, tongas Rs 2 to Rs 8. Taxis and auto-rickshaws use meters, but unless you know exactly where you are going it is wise to fix fares before setting off.

Bus Below is a list of buses which may be useful for getting around the city.

Number	Starting Point & Destination
17	Railway Station to Shalimar Gardens

6 & 23	Railway Station to Jehangir's Tomb
6	Railway Station to Lahore Museum
1 & 24	Lawrence Rd to Airport
12	Wagah to Airport

Getting Away
Lahore is a rail, road and air junction on the great Euro-Asian Highway which spans Peshawar and Amritsar to Delhi.

Air PIA has domestic flights to the following:-
Quetta, three flights daily – Rs 715
Karachi, four flights daily – Rs 950 (night flight Rs 795)
Rawalpindi, five flights weekly – Rs 240
Peshawar, every Saturday – Rs 370

Rail Get a Tourist Certificate from the Tourist Information Centre and apply for railway concessions at the office of the railway superintendent (tel 320343).

There are six to eight trains a day that make the 19 to 21 hour trip from Lahore to Karachi. Express trains like the *Shalimar Express* and *Super Express* services depart from Lahore at 6 am and arrive in Karachi 16 hours later at 10 pm. For details on fares to Karachi and Quetta, see those sections.

The fares to Hyderabad (1040 km) and Rawalpindi (290 km) are:

		sleeper	seat
Hyderabad	air-con	Rs 675	Rs 395
	1st class	Rs 275	Rs 162
	2nd class	Rs 124	Rs 85
Rawalpindi	air-con	Rs 225	Rs 130
	1st class	Rs 90	Rs 47
	2nd class	Rs 25	Rs 21

To Attari, distance 24 km – to the border of India – Rs 7.

To India The Wagah Route to India via the Punjab is open only three days in a month: on the 2nd, 12th and the 22nd. International buses like *Top Deck*, *Exodus*, the German and Turkish buses

are stationed at the International Hotel on Airport Rd and depart on these days at 8 am. From Lahore to Delhi is Rs 330 by bus. Those on a very strict budget can go to Wagah a day before the border is opened and hitch rides to Delhi from there.

There are special trains from Lahore to Delhi and these depart at 2 pm on Sunday, Tuesday and Thursday every week. You have to change trains at Attari and in Amritsar for the train to Delhi. Lahore-Attari train fare is Rs 7; Attari-Amritsar-Delhi is Indian Rs 42, 1st class Rs 180.

From Pakistan you require no Punjab travel permit, but from Delhi the permit is obtainable at Khan market from the CBI or Interior Ministry bureau.

There is a Tourist Advisor on platform no 4 at the railway station. The quota for tourist reservations is only open in first class.

Bus *GTS* – Government Transport System – buses are near the railway station, they depart on schedule. *Flying Coach, Skyway Coach* and the *New Khan Road Runner* are all near the railway station, others, the private buses, are stationed at Badami Bagh, a little way beyond the old walled city.

Some GTS bus fares are:

		air-con
Rawalpindi	Rs 31.50	Rs 65
Sarghoda	Rs 22	
Faisalabad	Rs 15	Rs 25
Bahawalpur	Rs 20	Rs 45
Multan	Rs 20	Rs 30

Money Lahore International Airport has a bank which changes your local currency. Although they don't always ask to see your air ticket or encashment receipts, it is best to have them with you. At Attari there are official money changers, in Wagah they have unofficial money changers. On the Pakistan side of the border you get a little more for your local currency than on the Indian side.

LAHORE-RAWALPINDI

The Grand Trunk Rd is presently being turned into a double-lane superhighway. Out of Lahore the landscape becomes more arid and dusty, then gives way to expansive grainfields followed by a sprawling industrial area. After the industrial region you pass through a number of towns and villages with attractive, small mosques usually painted white, yellow and green. Traffic on the Grand Trunk Rd is fairly heavy and you will see ornately-painted trucks and buses glinting with chrome from front to back.

At Gujranwallah the highway splits off to the south and to the north. To the south is Faisalabad, formerly known as Lyallpur, which was laid out at the turn of the 20th century in the pattern of the Union Jack. It is an important centre for higher education in the field of technology and is also a major market for agricultural produce. To the north is Sialkot, the site of another religious shrine but also the centre for the manufacture of sports equipment, surgical tools, rubber and plastic products, ceramics and light electrical devices.

A village which used to be a military cantonment during the British period is presided over by the forlorn spire of an English church. The bus passes through numerous villages and towns and stops at a teashop and restaurant where ice-cream and soft drinks are available. The stops make it more interesting than the train trip, apart from which it is less crowded and you see more of the landscape.

At Jhelum the land begins to ascend to the Potwar Plateau. It becomes undulating and rolling, then hilly. The lush green countryside is occasionally broken by rugged terrain and dry mountains. There is a sealed road to Islamabad but buses by-pass it and take the route straight to Rawalpindi.

Places to Stay

Jhelum is a nondescript town, but the road which crosses the Grand Trunk Rd here leads north to Muzzaffarabad in Azad Kashmir and Jammu or to the south towards Kallarkahar in the Salt Range. For places to stay try the *Hotel Mehwish* (tel 3048), near the GTS bus station, singles/doubles Rs 60/70; *Hotel Paradise* (tel 3533), near the bus station has a dining hall, singles/doubles Rs 30/50; *Sandar Hotel* (tel 3333) Raja Bazaar, singles/doubles Rs 15/25.

Kharian is a nearby town and there are some places to stay here:– *New Gulf Hotel* (tel 704) near the GTS bus station, singles/doubles Rs 20/40; *Shahzad Hotel* (tel 749) on GT Rd has singles/doubles Rs 25/40. In Gujrat the *Imran Hotel* has singles for Rs 20 and doubles at Rs 35. The *Melody Inn* (tel 3751) on Railway Rd has air-con rooms from Rs 100/150 for singles/doubles. *Hotel Grace* and *Hotel Nasheman* are nearby and have rates from Rs 25 to Rs 40.

Things to See

Twenty one km from Rawalpindi and over 200 km from Lahore is **Manikyala**, an ancient Buddhist site with a stupa over 60 metres high. The main structure is well preserved but there is nothing much left of the rest.

About 10 km before you reach Manikyala on the Grand Trunk Rd is **Rewat Fort**, a fortified village of the early Islamic period. It's east of the road and has six gates, a mosque and a mausoleum.

Rohtas Fort built by Sher Shah Suri, architect of the original Grand Trunk Rd, is to the right of the town of Dina, 98 km from Islamabad. On the left is Mangla Dam and the fort is seven km to the right. It's a rough track over sand and streams. The fort itself is five km in circumference with battlemented ramparts. Along the riverside the walls are doubled. It's an impressive, little-known structure, which once guarded the old trade route.

RAWALPINDI

On the Grand Trunk Rd between Peshawar and Lahore, Rawalpindi, with a population close to a million, is not of great interest in itself. It is, however, an important transit point, as it was a couple of millennia ago when it formed part of the main artery of the ancient Silk Trade Route.

It is one of the oldest settlements along the Khyber-Peshawar-Lahore route which, even before the ancient Silk Trade Route was developed, must have formed a section of the neolithic trade routes that criss-crossed the region of Central Asia, Persia, Asia Minor and this western part of the Indian subcontinent in 6000 BC.

Cyrus the Great, Darius, Alexander of Macedon, the rulers of the Bactrian-Greeks, the Scythians, the Parthians, the Kushans, the Sassanians, the Hephthalites and later Genghis Khan, all stopped off here with their armies. During the British campaign to take control of the Khyber Pass and establish their political influence over Afghanistan, Rawalpindi developed as a major military cantonment. Today it is the headquarters of the Pakistan Armed Forces. Traditionally an important commercial and trading centre, it remains so today.

Only 20 km away from Rawalpindi is Islamabad, the new capital of Pakistan. Since its conception in 1961 the two cities have been sprawling towards each other and will probably merge eventually.

Like Lahore, Rawalpindi is really several cities in one. Once again they can be divided into the British area around the Mall, the old city area and the modern Saddar area, which is squeezed between the two.

Information

There are Tourist Information Centres at the Pearl Continental Hotel (tel 66011) and Flashman's Hotel (tel 164811 telex 52620FH PK), both in the Mall. American Express, on Shahrah-i-Reza Pehlavi Rd, three blocks from the Mall, has a signboard on the roadside. The GPO is on Kashmir Rd in Saddar Bazaar just off the Mall, and the Telephone & Telegraph Office is in the Mall. There is a Foreigner's Registration Office on Rashid Minhas Rd, within walking distance or Rs 5 by auto-rickshaw. It is open from 8 am to 2 pm, but it does not extend visas.

Banks American Express, Grindlay's, The First National City Bank of New York and the State Bank of Pakistan are all represented. The latter apparently accepts hard foreign currencies except for the yen. For cashing bankdrafts try the Bank of America and Grindlay's in Islamabad.

British City

The Mall was built on the edge of the old town and not on such a grand scale as Lahore's. As usual it is in a wooded, shady section with a relaxed and tranquil atmosphere, in contrast to the hustle of the old city. The Mall forms part of the Grand Trunk Rd through Rawalpindi.

Saddar Area

If the old city is the distant past and the Mall the immediate past, then Saddar is the present. Here you will find most of the banks, hotels, shops, airlines, travel agencies and all the trappings of a modern metropolis.

Old City

It can no longer be classified realistically as old, but fine old buildings with traditional trellised balconies still predominate. Modern buildings that manage to retain a traditional air have sprung up in the more prosperous sections of the city, but it is the bazaars, with their exotic wares spilling out into the maze of narrow alleys, that make the old city so exciting and fascinating. The muzzaffarkhanas and traditional eating places with kitchens out front on the sidewalk and hunks of meat and chicken hanging from smoke-darkened ceilings have disappeared.

Craftsmen, nonetheless, still continue to work on the pavement since their stalls are too small and crowded. In the barbershops you can have a shave, a haircut, a bath or all three. Towels that are hung outside to dry, flap like flags in front of these *hammams*.

Stalls are stacked with green watermelons, sweetmelons, apples, grapes, oranges, plums, pomegranates and a variety of nuts. Walk around here in winter but take a tonga in summer. It's magic to clip-clop through the swirl of city traffic, missing everything by centimetres, slipping through gaps that are only there for a split second.

However the old city is changing, with sections of the bazaar being demolished and renovated.

Other

South of the city is the 900-hectare **National Park** which has a lake, an aquarium, an *al fresco* restaurant, a Japanese garden, several km of road and a bridle path for horse riding. The *Youth Hostel* is here, but it's just a bit too far out of the way to be convenient. Since 1963 Rawalpindi has expanded in all directions, particularly towards Islamabad where, at that time, there were only a few buildings in Aabpara. Today they stretch all along the route between the two cities.

Places to Stay - bottom end

The cheapies around the railway station are not recommended. More secure cheapies are located in Hatti Chowk, the best of these are the *Shah Taj* and *Al Hamra* hotels, at Massey Gate. They are fairly clean with singles/doubles at Rs 25/40. *Hotel Al Khalil* in the same area has singles/doubles for Rs 25/50. At Raja Bazaar the *Deluxe Hotel* near *7-Brothers Restaurant* has rooms for Rs 20/40. If in transit try the Railway Retiring Rooms, Rs 20 to Rs 35 or the waiting rooms where sofas are available, and they're free. The

Youth Hostel 25 Gulistan Colony is too far out and difficult to find. It's Rs 15 a night. Bus 10 from the GPO takes you there and you still have to walk across the park. Ask directions as you go.

Pir Wadhai near the Central Bus Station, has cheapies for Rs 15 single, Rs 8 for a rope bed. The *Corner Hotel* and the *Nadir Hotel* are recommended, singles/doubles Rs 25/40. This is the place to stay if en route by bus to the sub northern area and the upper northern area.

Places to Stay - middle

Marhaba Hotel Kashmir Rd (tel 66021) has singles/doubles for Rs 40/70. *Al-Azam Hotel*, *Good Luck Hotel* and *Cantt View Hotel* all on Hatti Chowk have rates from Rs 40 for singles, Rs 70 to Rs 185 for doubles and family rooms. Murree Rd near Liaquat Bagh is the place where middle level hotels are located. *Shama Hotel* (tel 70341) opposite Moti Mahal Cinema has air-con rooms but ordinary rooms are from Rs 50 to Rs 75. *Shangrila Hotel* (tel 74501) has singles/doubles Rs 50/75. *National City Hotel* (tel 71411) charges Rs 75/100. *Park Hotel* (tel 74161) singles at Rs 35 and doubles Rs 85 to Rs 150. *Al Hayat Hotel* has singles/doubles Rs 35/70.

Further up on Committee Chowk are the *Queen's Hotel* (tel 75240), singles/doubles Rs 40/75; *Pilot Hotel* (tel 73503) College Rd near Liaquat Bagh, Rs 30/50. *Carlton Hotel* on the same road has the same rates. *Park Hotel* farther up Murree Rd, where most mountain porters and guides stay, has rooms from Rs 80 up.

Places to Stay - top end

Pearl Continental (tel 62700, telex 5736 HICR PK) The Mall, is the poshest in town and has rates from Rs 1000 to Rs 3200. Non-guests can use their pool for Rs 60. *Flashman's* (tel 4 4811, telex 5620 FH PK) has rates from Rs 320 to Rs 1200. The Tourist Info Centre is located here. *Shalimar Hotel* in Saddar has the same rates. Other hotels with lower rates in this

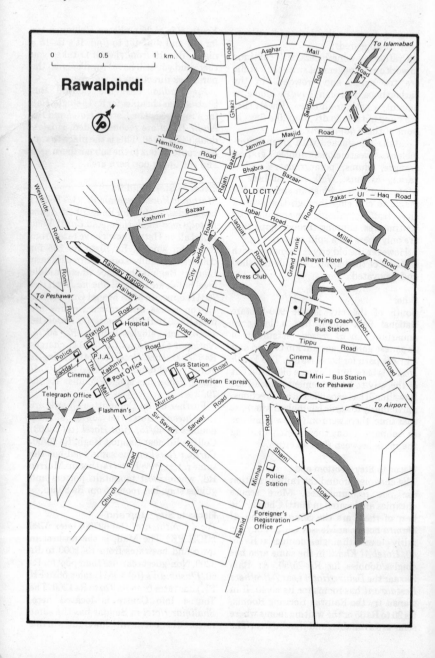

bracket are *Potohar Hotel* (tel 844303), Murree Rd; *Gatmell's Hotel* (tel 65123) Airport Rd and *Silver Grill* (tel 64729) the Mall.

Places To Eat

Inexpensive eating places are generally around the railway station, Rajah Bazaar, Pir Wadhai and Saddar Bazaar. Good, local food for Rs 8 to Rs 12.

For snacks the *Kamran Restaurant* on Bank Rd is a bit pricey but good value. *7-Brothers Restaurant* in Rajah Bazaar is a modern version of the Pathan traditional eating place. For Chinese meals there are Chinese restaurants on Murree Rd and Khyber Rd usually with generous helpings from Rs 30 up. Middle level hotels usually have restaurants that are good value. For a real gourmet tour, the top-notch hotels are the places to go. The *Brasserie* at the Pearl Continental is known for local dishes as well as continental food. They also have the *Little Hut Bakery* where confectionery, French cakes or pastries and bread are available. At *Shalimar* they offer European, Pakistani and Chinese dishes.

Liquor The Excise & Tax Office is just off Liaquat Bagh Rd on College Rd, next to the *City Hotel*. The monthly allocation is two units or two bottles of hard liquor or 32 bottles of beer. Liquor is usually available at the five-star hotels like Flashman's or the Pearl Continental.

Getting Around

Taxis cost Rs 10 within city limits, Rs 20 to Pir Wadhai; auto-rickshaws Rs 5 to Rs 8; tonga Rs 2 to Rs 5 mainly for Rajah Bazaar. Buses Rs 1.25; minibuses Rs 1.50 to Rs 2.50 mainly to Aabpara in Islamabad Miniwagons Rs 1 mainly to the airport and Pir Wadhai.

Route to Pir Wadhai The tongas for Rajah Bazaar are around the corner from the GTS bus station in the Saddar Bazaar area. It is Rs 2 and in Rajah Bazaar there

are miniwagons a block away, straight up from the corner where the tongas drop you. It's Rs 1 to Pir Wadhai.

Getting Away

Rawalpindi is 274 km west of Lahore, 166 km east of Peshawar, 1570 km north of Karachi and about 375 km south of Gilgit.

Air PIA on the Mall, just off Saddar Bazaar has flights to major cities in the country:

Lahore	five weekly	Rs 240
Peshawar	every Saturday	Rs 180
Quetta	three daily	Rs 670
Karachi	four daily	Rs 1155
	night coach	Rs 945
Saidu Sharif	weekly	Rs 180

Special Fares Area

Skardu	two to three daily	Rs 160
	plus Rs 5 airport tax	
Gilgit	two to three daily	Rs 160
	plus Rs 5 airport tax	

There is a tourist quota of two seats on flights to Skardu or Gilgit. This is a priority quota and you have to apply for a tourist certificate from the Tourist Info Office in Rawalpindi at Flashman's Hotel. Flights to these areas are very uncertain, and depend on weather conditions. Departure time is at 6 am, 9 am and 1 pm. There are usually only two flights but the third takes place when the first is cancelled. Flight delays or cancellations are not unusual or uncommon and can be caused by the monsoon or winter weather conditions, to name a few.

It is advisable to book flights to these areas as soon as you get into town, or if you are in a rush, the bus is the alternative.

Rail Services are rather crowded and slow. Going by bus or minibus to either Peshawar or Lahore is more comfortable and faster.

Bus The central bus station is in Pir Wadhai which is a fascinating place to go. Here are some of the most ornately and garishly painted and decorated buses in the world, all shiny chrome and gleaming bright colours. Most often, they have geometric designs and Islamic calligraphy painted on them and are covered in scenes of mosques against backdrops of desert and date palm trees. Bristling with antennae and ribbons, the buses look almost extra-terrestrial.

Natco – Northern Area Transport Company – are stationed here. They have four daily departures to Gilgit, 9 am, 1 pm, 7 pm and 11 pm. The fare is Rs 86 and the trip takes 18 to 21 hours. There is a student concession of 50% discount on normal fare. There are also deluxe minibuses which make the trip in 16 hours but they are rather irregular, mainly depending on availability of sufficient passengers; the fare is Rs 120. Minibus to Saidu Sharif is Rs 25/40.

Other bus stations are: Moti Mahal Cinema off Murree Rd mainly for minibuses to Peshawar; fare is Rs 20. GTS bus station, Saddar Bazaar for every direction. Fare to Lahore is Rs 31.50. The minibus bus stand for Lahore and the Salt Range is near the Committee Chowk on Murree Rd. Lahore fare is Rs 35. *Flying Coach* and *Skyways* have air-con deluxe coaches. The Flying Coach station is near the Shangrila Hotel on Murree Rd, coaches depart every hour from 4 or 5 am in summer, 6 am the rest of the year, they also have night services for Rs 65 to Lahore. *Skyway* has video, same fare as the Flying Coach.

RAWALPINDI TO ISLAMABAD

A well-paved double-lane superhighway links the two cities. Buses and minibuses usually wait till they're full before leaving. The last sound you'll hear when you leave Rawalpindi is the call of the muezzin echoing from the mosques. The sound will ring in your ears all the way to Islamabad. Mosques – their usual mini-minarets topped with cupolas in a variety of brilliant colours – are jostled next to each other along the whole stretch.

If en route to Islamabad from Pir Wadhai, it is not necessary to go to Rawalpindi. Take a wagon to Faizabad (Rs 1) and from there another Suzuki wagon to Aabpara (Rs 1).

ISLAMABAD

This modern capital of Pakistan, planned like Brasilia or Canberra, was only begun in 1961 and is still far from complete. Laid out over undulating land it used to be a barren plateau with a few scraggy trees and tufts of green at the foot of the Marghalla Hills. From one or two long, low buildings – the offices of the *Pakistan Times* at Aabpara in 1963 – it has grown into a whole, new city designed by planners and architects of world reputation.

It is divided into residential, business, recreational, industrial, government and religious sections with buildings painted in clean, clear lines that are solid and neat, yet blend harmoniously with the environment. The huge Islamabad Secretariat complex is made up of a series of long, multi-storey white buildings against a backdrop of green hills, while the State Bank of Pakistan rises in solitary splendour, almost like a tower. Other impressive buildings are the Holiday Inn and the British and American embassies.

The city has numerous high-rise apartments of about 12 to 14 storeys like those in Singapore. The streets and avenues are paved, clean and lined with flowering shade trees that flash with colour in spring. Rawalpindi is lush and green with many parks and gardens. All the embassies of countries which maintain diplomatic relations with Pakistan are located in this city, as is the University of Quaid-i-Azam. Like any other city in Pakistan there are numerous mosques and shrines, varying in architecture from modern to traditional. One of the most outstanding and one of the largest mosques in the world, the Shah Faisal Masjid, is in the process of being built here. Nestling at the foot of the Marghalla Hills on rising land, its gleaming white, tent-like design is extraordinarily arresting. But unlike most other cities in Pakistan there are no tongas or bullock carts in Rawalpindi.

Also noteworthy is the shrine of Bari Imam near the Marghalla foothills. Just across Aabpara, in the wooded area near the Rose & Jasmine Gardens, is Bari Imam's father's shrine. Here fakirs, malangs and pilgrims flock during the saint's urs when a *mela* is held. The smell of marijuana hangs heavily in the air and *tablas* (drums) beat out a frenzied dancing tune that becomes faster and faster. Islamabad would be a quiet place were it not for this local colour.

With its patches of vacant land and streets and roads ending in cul-de-sacs, the city still looks unfinished.

Information
The Tourist Information Centre is in the Islamabad Hotel, Municipal Rd, Ramma 6, and American Express is at Aabpara on the Grand Trunk Rd.

Note that the American Express offices in Rawalpindi and Islamabad have a bad reputation for inefficiency and poor service. The mail service is also unreliable and the wait for replacements for lost travellers' cheques seems endless. It appears that in many instances both mail and travellers' cheques are often there, but staff will not hand them over even if your visa is about to expire the following day, causing a great deal of delay, frustration and inconvenience to travellers with limited time.

The GPO is on Municipal Rd in the Civic Centre, while the Telephone & Telegraph Office is at Shalimar 5. The Foreigner's Registration Office is at Zafar Chowk near Peshawar Mor. This is only for registration and not for visa extensions. For visa extensions see Mr Abdul

Salaam of the Interior Ministry, Block R, Room 512, 5th Floor, The Secretariat, Islamabad.

The Ministry of Tourism is on College Rd, F-7/2. Mountaineering and trekking permits are obtained here. Take minibus 1A behind Aabpara Market to get there. Almost all the embassies are in the Diplomatic Enclave on Constitution Avenue.

Visas
India Usually you can get your visa the same day – apply at 9 am and pick it up at 4 pm. Open every day, except Saturday, from 9 to 11 am and 12 noon to 4 pm. Two passport photos are required, the visa fee is erratic and depends upon nationality (USA Rs 73, France Rs 99, Australia Rs 61, UK Rs 181). Most westerners require a letter of introduction from their embassy. This makes it easier and quicker getting a visa. Double and triple entry visas are also available. The Indian Embassy is on Constitution Avenue.

Iran It takes two weeks to get a reply to your application. Note that it is only in Islamabad that you can apply for a visa for Iran – you cannot get one in Quetta or Peshawar any more. Most nationalities require a letter of introduction from their embassy. The office is open every day except Thursday and Friday and is at Street No 17, F-6/2.

China Usually takes only a couple of days – two passport photos and Rs 100. Open every day except Sunday from 9 am to 1 pm and till 4 pm. The Embassy is at House No 6 , Street No 2, F-7/3 (tel 81 1053).

Things to See
Institute of Folk Heritage, G House No 6, Street 63, F-7/3. It has a library of folk music and a museum of musical instruments, folk costumes and jewellery.

Pakistan National Council of Arts on H-4,

Street 11, F-7/2, has an art gallery on Sher Shah Rd. The **Contemporary Art Gallery** is at 26 Civil Lines.

Daman-e-koh, on Marghalla Hills, is a terraced garden which offers a scenic view of the whole city. It is a pleasant spot for sightseeing and relaxing.

Rose & Jasmine Gardens offer a sweeping panorama of both Islamabad and Rawalpindi. They are just off the Grand Trunk Rd behind the Shakaparian Hill. Further to the east is **Rawal Lake**, a waterfowl sanctuary where you can go boating and fishing or swimming. Behind the Secretariat Block is the old village of **Nur Shahan** and south-east of this village is the **university**.

Places to Stay – bottom end

There are no inexpensive hotels in Islamabad, and travellers usually prefer to stay in Rawalpindi where accommodation is cheaper. However, there's a *Tourist Camp* opposite the Rose & Jasmine Gardens. Camping is Rs 8 per person, Rs 2 to Rs 15 for vehicles. There are dorms for Rs 15 per bed. It is popular with tourists who have their own vehicles.

Places to Stay – middle

A few middle level hotels have sprung up in and around Islamabad with rates from Rs 80 to Rs 120; some of them are located in the Shalimar Shopping centre area. The *Blue Star Hotel* in the T/T Colony has slightly lower rates. It is modern and has a pleasant atmosphere. To get there take the bus to Zero Point, then get a Suzuki wagon for Peshawar Mor. If you're near the Islamabad Hotel, British Council Library or the GPO, you can get Suzuki wagons to Peshawar Mor for Rs 1. There's a direct bus, No 17, to Pir Wadhai from the Blue Star Hotel.

The *Motel Inn Garden* on Shahrah-e-Kashmir Rd (tel 82 5273) has rates from Rs 160 to Rs 250. This is a little distance from the city.

Places to Stay – top end

The *Holiday Inn* on Agha Khan Rd (tel 82 6121) has 122 rooms with rates from Rs 1000 to Rs 2500. The *Islamabad Hotel* in the Civic Centre (tel 82 7311), has 135 rooms with rates from Rs 500 to Rs 800. Just above the American Express on Shahrah-i-Kashmir Rd, the *Ambassador Hotel* (tel 82 4011) charges from Rs 300 to Rs 600.

Places to Eat

The cheapies are just behind Aabpara where you can get a meal for Rs 5 to Rs 8 per person. In front is the *Danbar Restaurant* which has the TV going in the evening, and just around the corner is the *Kamran Restaurant* with local and western food for between Rs 20 and Rs 30. Both are popular with those staying at the Tourist Camp. There are also Chinese restaurants at Aabpara and the Shalimar Shopping Centre, which are open in the evening.

Liquor If you're thirsty get a Tourist Certificate, then go to the Excise & Tax Office for a permit to buy alcohol. You could also try the American Club.

Getting Around

There are buses, minibuses and miniwagons that ply to most areas of importance. In most cases you still have to walk long distances to your destination. Taxis within the city limits cost Rs 10 to Rs 15.

Getting Away

There are rail services to Haripur and Peshawar from Rawalpindi but they are hardly used by tourists as buses and minibuses are faster and more comfortable. Murree buses depart from the GTS bus station just opposite Aabpara in Islamabad – fare Rs 10.

Around Islamabad

Shrine of Imam Bari This is east of Islamabad at the foot of the Marghalla

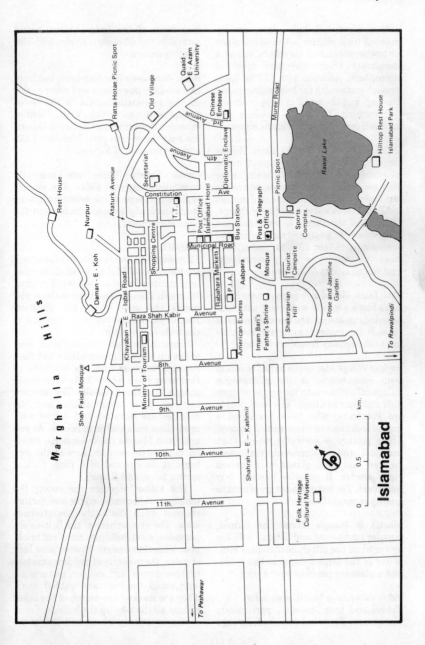

Islamabad

Quaid - E - Azam University
Ratta Hotae Picnic Spot
Old Village
Chinese Embassy
Hilltop Rest House
Islamabad Park
3rd Avenue
Diplomatic Enclave
Murree Road
Rawal Lake
4th Avenue
Secretariat
Ataturk Avenue
Rest House
Constitution Ave
Post & Telegraph Office
Picnic Spot
Nurpur
Post Office
Islamabad Hotel
T.T.
Bus Station
Sports Complex
Daman - E - Koh
Shopping Centre
Municipal Road
Aabpara
Mosque
Tourist Campsite
Rabahara Markets
P.I.A.
Iqbal Road
Shakarparian Hill
Rose and Jasmine Garden
To Rawalpindi
Raza Shah Kabir Avenue
American Express
Imam Bari's Father's Shrine
Khayaban - E -
Marghalla Hills
Shah Faisal Mosque
Ministry of Tourism
8th. Avenue
9th. Avenue
10th. Avenue
Shahrah - E - Kashmir
11th. Avenue
Folk Heritage Cultural Museum
To Peshawar
0   0.5   1 km.

Hills in a wooded, hilly place, usually crowded with pilgrims. A meeting place for townspeople and travellers, it has a completely traditional and mystical atmosphere. Adorned with Shi'ite flags, it reverberates with the beat of drums and dancing, and the smell of dope is almost overpowering. Numerous hawkers and stalls sell tea, food and religious objects.

Shrine of Pir Syed Mir Ali Shah This is about eight km east of Rawalpindi in the village of Gholra Sharif. In this shrine are man-made caves, now in ruins, where the saint spent much of his time in devotion to Allah. You can stay here free of charge. The site of the shrine is warm but it's often windy. It's situated on hilly ground overlooking distant villages, and offers a great opportunity to see a fascinating, traditional aspect of Pakistan.

Shah Faizal Masjid You cannot miss it – it looks like a gigantic white tent with four towering minarets at the foot of Marghalla Hills. It dominates the city and is visible from the highway from Rawalpindi.

Saidpur Village Also in the foothills, 32 km from Rawalpindi, is the picturesque village of Saidpur with its jumble of stone huts and narrow alleys. The local people are Potoharis, who have developed a unique technique in wheel-turned pottery. Their pottery is aesthetic rather than practical and is engraved, embossed, painted and then glazed with melted glass powder. If you like pottery, buy some here. The output is not great but the quality is magnificent.

Misriot & Mangla Dams The former, popular for boating and fishing, is 19 km away; while the latter, near Rohtas Fort, is one of the largest dams in the world, and a pleasant place to have a picnic.

Indus Valley Jeep Tour/Camel Safari
Travel and tour agencies, particularly *Karakoram Tours* in Islamabad, arrange

jeep tours of the Indus Valley, camel safaris in the Cholistan Desert and also hunting safaris.

Indus Valley Jeep Tour Jeep tours last from two weeks to one month and cover nearly all the interesting sights in the Indus Plains and the North West Frontier Province including the Cholistan Desert, the Salt Range and even Manchar Lake and the beaches of Karachi.

Camel Safaris These are generally combined with jeep tours. The camels replace the jeeps in the desert for a more traditional trip around the forts in the Cholistan Desert.

MURREE
Fifty-nine km north-east of Islamabad, the hill resort of Murree is one of the most important and most accessible in Pakistan. Murree is 2295 metres above sea level and marks the spot where the Kashmir Himalayan Range begins to descend to the wide Indus plain.

From Islamabad the surfaced road winds up through grassy plains and then through terraced and wooded hills to Company Bagh where it starts to climb steeply to Ghora Ghali. The scenery becomes more mountainous and the hillsides are terraced and dotted with mud-stone huts and farm houses. As you approach Murree the mountains, which for most of the way are bare at the top, begin to be covered with pine, fir and spruce trees, and flowers.

The higher you get the cooler the temperature becomes and the architecture changes to a distinctly mountainous style. The atmosphere of the British era pervades, most buildings are of red brick, post-Victorian design. To overcome lack of space, the majority of buildings are two to three-storeys high and very picturesque with small windows and gabled roofs. They are stacked one on top of the other almost all the way up the hillside.

Murree is only about two km at its

longest and half a km at its widest. During the British period living was literally split level, with the British ensconced higher up the hillside than the locals below. Today the distinction still holds true, the upper section of town being more expensive than the lower one. There are places in Murree which have commanding views of the entire country-side below. In the distance the mountains are such a light blue that they almost merge with the sky. There are some excellent hiking and trekking trails around Murree.

Information

The Tourist Information Centre is near the GPO on Jinnah Rd (tel 2420) and is only open during the season.

Places to Stay

Being a popular tourist resort, Murree tends to be expensive. During the off-season prices drop dramatically. Accommodation varies with altitude. Cheapies are of course located on the lower level, the more expensive on the top level.

The *Cecil Hotel* on Mount View Rd (tel 2247), is one of the top places and rooms vary from Rs 250 to Rs 750 and up. The *Blue Pines Motel* (tel 2233) has rates from Rs 150 to Rs 300 and up.

At a lower level, the *Central Hotel* (tel 2053) has singles/doubles for Rs 80/120. *Hotel Lalazar* (tel 2150) has rooms for Rs 65/120. The *Lockwood Hotel* (tel 2112) and the *Ritz Hotel*, near the GPO, both charge Rs 60/105 for singles/doubles.

Further down the scale are the *Kashmir Villa* near the GPO (tel 2408) and the *Gulberg Hotel* on Cart Rd (tel 2301). Both have singles/doubles for Rs 35/75. The *New Kashmir Hotel* and the *New Green Hotel* at Lower Jinnah Rd and Motor Agency Rd, have singles/doubles for Rs 20/35.

Seven km north to Burbhan is a *Youth Hostel*. However, it is often closed during the high season, but the chowkidar here has his own little hut which he offers for only Rs 40 to couples or groups. This is the place for quiet relaxation.

Getting There

Buses leave Rawalpindi at 8 am and Islamabad at 9 am. The trip takes about two hours.

Around Murree

Although part of the Punjab, Murree is an offshoot of the Himalayas that rise up to the North West Frontier Province hill stations of **Ayubia** and **Nathiagali**. There are other lovely hill resorts – smaller, greener and wooded – but with fewer facilities. These hills are known as *ghalies*, and in the spring there are numerous beautiful walks through the woods – all with fine views of the Himalayas.

Stations in the ghalies include **Ghora Dhaka**, **Khanspur**, **Changlagali** and **Khairagali**, the latter having guest houses and rest houses. Another excellent place to stay is at the *Galliat View Hotel* in Nathiagali. The service here is good and doubles cost Rs 40. If you want a splurge you could try the *Pines International*, also in Nathiagali, with rates from Rs 200 to Rs 400. Further north, near the Tourist Information Centre, is *Dine's Hotel*, (tel 505), which has rooms for Rs 200 and up.

ABBOTTABAD

North of Murree at an altitude of 1223 metres this popular hill station is a transit point for Muzzaffarabad in Azad Kashmir & Jammu to the east, the Kaghan Valley to the north, the Swat Valley to the west and Taxila and Rawalpindi to the south. It was named after Major Abbott, the British officer who 'pacified' the area between 1849 and 1853. It is here where Kakul, the West Point or Sandhurst of Pakistan, is located.

Places to Stay

The *Palm Hotel* on the Mall (tel 2241)

has 16 rooms with rates from Rs 105 to Rs 200 plus 15% tax. Both *Sharban Hotel,* (tel 2376/78 and *Spring Field* (tel 2334) have rooms for Rs 105 to Rs 175.

The *Youth Hostel* is five km north of town on the way to Balakot near Burn Hall Senior School. It costs Rs 1 by Suzuki wagon to get there. In the centre of town the *Pine View Hotel* has singles/ doubles for Rs 25/35. If you've got a sweet tooth, the *Modern Bakery*, opposite the post office, has a selection of cakes and pastries.

Getting There

The railway line from Taxila terminates about 15 km before Abbottabad at Havelian leaving you in the middle of nowhere. It's much more convenient to catch a bus as there are regular services between Murree, Taxila and Rawalpindi to Abbottabad.

TAXILA

This famous archaeological site thrived from around 3000 BC to the 16th century. Situated 35 km north-east of Rawalpindi, it is on the railway line, just off the Grand Trunk Rd. Buses are faster than the trains. At an altitude of 500 to 700 metres, Taxila is girdled by the foothills of the Himalayan Kashmir Range. It's flat, semi-arid, and in summer can get uncomfortably warm and dusty. The best time to visit the area is in spring and autumn.

Archaeologically impressive, its structures are made of dry baked mud bricks with cubicles for rooms. Taxila is not a place to spend just a few hours before rushing back to Rawalpindi or moving further north, because it is scattered over a wide area. Located north-east of Bhir Mound, the museum alone needs several hours to see.

The remains of Taxila were discovered in 1852 and so far the excavations have revealed three distinct cities. Bhir Mound is the earliest of the three and dates to around 180 BC. To the north-east

is Sirkup originally built by the Bactrian Greeks who were followed by the Scythians, who grafted onto it their own structures. The Scythians were in turn followed by the Parthians and later by the Kushans, who transformed it into a great centre of the Gandhara Culture. It eventually became the Buddhist 'Holy Land'.

The excavated site reveals a wide street, running south-north, lined with buildings – usually two or three storeys high – with walled-in open courtyards. The most recent, Sirsukh, was founded around 130 AD during the Kushan period and has only been partially excavated. It is surrounded by a five-km long wall.

Things to See

Structures reveal that successive waves of invaders settled here. The **Temple of Jandhial**, north of Sirkup, is 2500 years

Fasting Buddha, Taxila

old, and appears to be Zoroastrian – a fire worshipping place – but is built like a Greek temple. Buddhist monasteries and stupas are scattered at **Mohra Moradu**, **Kalwan** and, at the far end, **Jaulian**, which is considered to be the most interesting. The **Stupa of Kunala**, the prince whose eyes were gouged out at the order of his step-mother whom he had scorned, and the **Dharmarajika Stupa**, also known as Chir Tope, are both worth seeing.

A visit to the **museum** is a must. Just opposite the PTDC motel, it was opened in 1928 and has a priceless collection of Gandhara busts of the Buddha, the period which produced a style of art which evolved out of the fusion of Graeco-Roman and Indian art forms. Earlier, it must have been neolithic, then a site for the prehistoric Indus Valley Civilisation, then Aryan, followed a millennium later by the Achaemenians and the Greeks. The rulers in this area had enough wisdom not to be antagonistic to Alexander the Great when he arrived.

Other exhibits include bas reliefs depicting the Buddha's life; gold, bronze, silver and copper coins; kitchen utensils made of copper and bronze; pottery and earthenware jars and utensils; jewellery made of gold and precious and semi-precious stones; a primitive, two-piece condenser made of clay; manuscripts on bark; a marble slab with Aramaic inscriptions; carpenter's and surgical tools and instruments; weights for scales, and terracotta children's toys, similar to those discovered in Moenjodaro and Harappa.

Places to Stay

The *Youth Hostel* only accepts card-holding members at Rs 10 for a dorm bed, Rs 15 a single and Rs 25 a double. It's reasonably clean and provides breakfast. If you wish to have lunch or dinner you must let the manager know in advance. A little further on is the *PTDC Motel* where the Tourist Information Centre is. Rooms here cost Rs 120 and over, plus 15% tax.

Getting There

Taxila is three km off the Grand Trunk Rd to the north beyond the rail tracks. A paved road leads to it and a tonga for six should be about Rs 1.50 each. From this direction the Youth Hostel is on the left, surrounded by a high wall and gate.

Around Taxila

About 13 km west of Taxila is a **Sikh Temple** at Hasanabdal. It houses the sacred rock on which Guru Nanak, founder and religious leader of the Sikhs, is said to have left his handprints. The Sikhs call it Panja Sahib; the Muslims know it as Baba Wali. Near here is the tomb of **Lalla Rookh**, and two km away is the **Wah Garden** built by Akbar. The Tarbela Dam is just to the north-west of here and further west the Grand Trunk Rd continues to Attock, Campbellpore and Peshawar.

The Salt Range

A little known, seldom visited area, the Salt Range records 600 million years of the earth's geological evolution and is often described by geologists as the 'Museum of Geology'. It is desolate, barren and bleak, except for a few patches that are green and fertile with trees fruit orchards.

It was here that the pebble culture emerged during the Paleolithic Age. It is also the site of Hindu temples, Buddhist monasteries and, more recently, Muslim mosques. This was where the earth cracked and the ocean stagnated until it dried and solidified into salt.

The Salt Range starts at the edge of the Potwar Plateau near the town of Jhelum, heads off south-west, then snakes north-west, turning south just above the Kalabagh towards Bannu and Dera Ismail Khan. Here it reaches an elevation of 600 to 1500 metres. Although superficially not terribly attractive, it is geologically, archaeologically and historically important and has some pleasant spots to visit.

Not far out of Rewat, the road follows the river south to Pind Dadan Khan, 105 km away. About midway along and just off it is **Jallalpur Sharif**, plonked on the edge of the plateau at an elevation of 1100 metres. From here you get a commanding view of the range and the Jhelum River. This was climbed by al-Biruni, a Central Asian Muslim scholar, in the 11th century. Immediately to the south is **Misar Shah**, where a shrine in the style of the Taj Mahal can be seen. This is the area where Bucephalus, Alexander the Great's famous white horse, is believed to have been buried. Lower down and south-west is an ancient fort which overlooks and guards the range and the river.

From **Mandra**, a small town 45 km north-west along the Grand Trunk Rd, a road and railway line turn southward to **Chakwal**, the transit point here. It is five hours by bus from Rawalpindi to here and though the road is surfaced it is still bumpy. The railway line continues to **Bhaun**, but the road turns south-east towards **Choa Said Shah**, a lovely little town, six km away from **Kutas**, once the site of Buddhist and Hindu temples. Nothing much remains today. About half-way to Kutas is **Dhok Tahlian Dam**, which has a rest house and fishing boats for hire.

The road descends for nine km down a steep escarpment with suspension bridges over gorges into **Kewra** where the biggest salt mine in the world exists. The salt seams span the whole length of the range and in some places are crystal clear, while in others they are pinkish red. Certain areas, which have been mined, are like huge caves; others are filled with amazingly clear, pure water; still others have stalactites.

If you're going on a tour, check at the Pakistan Mineral Development Corporation here and get a visiting permit. It's advisable to take a torch with you.

The road continues on to **Pind Dadan Khan**, site of a Hindu shrine, then crosses the Jhelum River and continues on towards Sargodha. South-west of Chao Saidu Shah, immediately below Bhaun, is **Kallar Kahar**, a town originally built by Babar. There is a salt lake here, not unlike the Dead Sea, which is the site of the **Buddhist Mahot Temples**, circa 10th century AD. From here the road continues towards Sargodha via Katha and Khusab.

In Khusab it forks into two: one road leads west to Talagang and Fatehgang then on to Campbellpore, while the other leads off towards Mianwali. From the Salt Range you can go north to Jhelum, south to Sargodha, east to Lahore or west to Kohat and Peshawar Valley.

Places to Stay

Chakwal *Awami Hotel* on Civili Hospital Rd, has a restaurant and rooms with fans for singles/doubles Rs 20/35. *Hotel Neemat Kada* on Chappar Rd is of a similar standard and price.

Choa Saidan Shah The *Hadji Hotel* on P D Khan Rd, has rooms for Rs 20/35.

Kutas There is a *Youth Hostel* here and a rest house, but they are often closed and in disrepair.

Sargodha The *Al-Farooq Hotel* on Railway Rd (tel 2323) has rooms with fans and bath for singles/doubles Rs 25/40. They also have a T V room. *Hotel Marlbro* Kutchery Rd (tel 3444) has rooms for Rs 30/50.

North West Frontier Province

Of Pakistan's four provinces, the North West Frontier Province is the smallest with an area, excluding the federally administered tribal areas, of only 49,400 square km. The province is almost entirely made up of tribal areas with a few political agencies, that in reality are also tribal, the difference being that they were consolidated into one political entity during the British period and still retain this status. While tribal areas are autonomous, political agencies, although they have their own tribal laws, are administered by the federal government.

The central government has jurisdiction along the sealed Khyber Pass in the Khyber Agency, but to the north and south of the highway tribal law prevails, as it does south of the Peshawar Valley from Darra to Waziristan. To the north, Bajaur – with the exception of Dir – the Malakhand Division, the Swat Valley, the Hazara district and Chitral, remain tribal. Gradually, their status will be transformed and inevitably they will fall within the jurisdiction of the general law of the land.

Although the province is small, it has the most variegated topography, climate, history, social and political set-up in Pakistan. In the south at the border of Baluchistan the land is flat and barren with oases where villages and towns have sprung up. The Indus River forms the natural boundary with the Punjab to the east, while to the west the mountains here form the border with Afghanistan. Higher up the terrain continues to be as barren and forbidding as that of Baluchistan. This is where the Salt Range ends. It continues north and just below the Peshawar Valley it turns south-east skirting the Potwar Plateau.

Beyond the lush valley of Peshawar and the Kabul River the mountainous forest belt rises from 1000 to over 4000 metres, to where snowcapped mountains and deep valleys are dissected by cascading streams. Most of the southern part of the province is out of the monsoon belt and is therefore generally dry and hot. This is the native territory of the swashbuckling Pathans, a people given to fiercely defending themselves against any invaders, as well as fighting amongst themselves. None of the conquering nations, the Moghuls, the Afghans, the Sikhs or the British were ever able to unite them. They were able to hold onto the Peshawar Valley to safeguard the strategic Khyber Pass, but were forced to leave the Pathans to administer their own laws and fight their own battles.

The North West Frontier Province, the name given by the British to the region, was the centre of early civilisations such as the Grave Culture of Dir and Swat, quite different from the Indus Valley Civilisation. Conquered by Cyrus the Great it became a satrapy of Darius in the 6th century BC and later a part of the Hellenic Empire of Alexander the Great in the 4th century BC. The Mauryan and Kushan empires also rose in this region giving impetus to the development of the Buddhist Gandhara Culture. These civilisations were swept away by successive waves of barbarian invasions; the Bactrian-Greeks, the Scythians, Parthians, the Sassanians, the Hephthalites and the Tartar-Mongol hordes. The establishment of Pax Britannica brought some stability to the region.

Historical evidence based on anthropological studies of the Afghan people, the Pathans, who claim to be Children of Israel (*Bani Israel*), indicates that they belonged to the lost tribes of Judea who migrated eastward after Moses, their leader, had been denied the right to settle in the 'Promised Land'. Somewhere along the way, they became Muslims, followed the invading armies eastward to Hindustan, and finally settled in the valleys where they must have become assimilated with the Greeks already settled there. In the isolated valleys these people, and successive invaders, fragmented into different and independent tribal domains.

In the south the Waziristan region is divided into two agencies – the southern and northern political agencies. The southern agency is inhabited by the Mashuds and the Ahmadzais, with the former being dominant. Their principal town of Wanna is connected by sealed road with Tank and Dera Ismail Khan. The northern agency is populated by Utmanzais and Ahmadzais and the capital, Miram Shah, is linked to Bannu. In the upper region are the Kurram Agency and Peshawar Valley. To the west the Khyber Agency up to Landi Kotal and Torkham is inhabited by the Afridis and Azakzais, while in the Malakhand Division and the Hazara district are the Yussufzais and the Kohistanis.

Generally the Pathans speak a language called Pushto, but in the isolation of their remote valleys they developed different dialects and fought with one another, tribe against tribe, clan against clan. In the border regions the tribes became professional thieves and lived in a state of continual warfare which was finally halted, and then only partially, with the arrival of the British. Some powerful tribes actually carved out tiny kingdoms or mirdoms, which were to become political agencies during the British era.

The western frontier areas to the south had far easier mountain passes than in the north; some of these were actually used by invaders more often than the northern passes, such as the Khyber Pass. Alexander the Great led his Greek legions over Kot Kala Pass, which is just below Chitral into the region of Dir. In the Parachinar area is the Kurram Pass, while to the south the Tochi and Gomal passes were used by invaders, traders and nomads alike. To a degree these passes contributed to the instability of the region and its continuing poverty. Women are often unable to afford purdah and simply turn their backs when they come across strangers. Like Baluchistan the women you are likely to see here are invariably nomads. They are treated with the deepest respect and reverence and men automatically move out of their way. Try to observe this yourself if you meet up with one when you are out walking.

In the upper northern region of Chitral the same kind of development of tiny kingdoms or mirdoms took place, but the process went even deeper with the major mirdoms of Chitral attaining control or influence over other minor mirdoms. The Moghuls did not penetrate as far as this region, and the isolated people developed their own peculiar culture, temperament and architecture, with clearly Central Asian influence, being linked up by trade routes with Bokhara and Samarkhand and Chinese Turkestan.

This region has tougher mountain passes which are open only during the summer. From the north the Tartar-Mongols were the only ones able to scale the passes and penetrate the region while the Afghans were the sole invaders able to get in from the west. In many ways Chitral belongs to the upper northern mountainous zone rather than to the North West Frontier Province, it was largely its political evolution that made it part of the latter. After the Partition the government of Pakistan took over and continued the process the British had begun, although in many ways 'the restless ... difficult to lead and impossible to control' Pathans seem almost impermeable to alien culture.

Tribal Areas

All tribal areas are off-limits to westerners as protection cannot be guaranteed for political reasons, such as the Afghan refugee encampments and smuggling.

Landi Kotal on the Khyber Agency Highway is now closed to foreigners indefinitely due to US pressure to stop the outflow of narcotics. It remains a nexus of smuggling with feuding tribes vying to control the smuggling business. Foreigners are only allowed as far as Jamrud. The Khyber permit beyond Jamrud is available to accredited journalists, diplomats and UNO officials and is not normally extended to anyone else.

The Darra gun factories are also closed to foreigners – again due to US pressure – but you can still travel to Bannu, Dera Ismail Khan and down to Quetta by direct bus. You still need a permit for Loralai from Dera Ghazi Khan. The short cut to Quetta is via Dera Ghazi Khan across the Baluchistan Desert through Loralai into Ziarat. A Travel Permit from the Ministry of Interior in Islamabad is required, but when you are already there, you can invariably proceed towards Quetta with no hassles. The bandits or dacoits that used to plunder villages and rob bus passengers have altogether disappeared.

There are tribal police checkposts at Jamrud on the Khyber Highway and others before Darra on the Peshawar-Kohat Rd.

In some restricted areas, travellers can get to Landi Kotal, Darra or other tribal areas dressed in local garb with woollen cap or turban. But it is too risky here, despite the fact that travellers are often invited by the chiefs of tribes or by Afghan refugees, sometimes to cross the border into Afghanistan. But you would be ill-advised to attempt this now, it's far too dangerous. Russian troops have gradually taken control of the border, and in the spring of 1983 they pursued mujahadeens right across the Kurram Agency in Parachinar, took them back into Afghan territory and apparently executed them.

Afghan Refugee Camps

These used to be open to foreigners so long as they had business with the Afghan refugees. The camps were a show window to display refugees to the eyes of the world and to allow them to earn a little from their industry by selling rugs and other handicrafts. Nowadays it is impossible to obtain a permit unless you have a special purpose for wishing to visit the camps. In that case you must apply to the State and Frontier Region Division, Civil Secretariat, tel 20624, Islamabad. Generally permits are only issued to accredited journalists, diplomats, UNO or International Red Cross Officials and members of other charitable voluntary institutions. If a tourist group does get a permit, it is likely that a visit means an official guided tour around the camp, and it is most unlikely that an individual traveller would get such a permit.

Most of the large Afghan refugee camps are along Jamrud and Charsadda Rds. If you wander into the area you may get invited in by the Afghans themselves, particularly if they are interested in doing business – selling carpets and other items – and talking about their plight. However care should be taken that no problems arise out of an unofficial visit as the political repercussions are endless. Problems that have arisen in the past which have caused trouble are disagreements over prices of goods, political arguments and hassles with the authorities.

The subject of Afghan camps is a potentially explosive political situation which must be treated with care otherwise many people will be put in jeopardy.

PESHAWAR

Peshawar, population 750,000, is the capital city of the North West Frontier Province. It is a place in transition – some districts are ultra modern, others cling to the romantic past. Historically, this has been the gateway between Central Asia and the subcontinent. It has never quite developed into a great metropolis, although for centuries it was the centre of remarkable civilisations, such as the Gandhara Culture of the Kushan Empire headed by Kanishka (60 AD). This highly sophisticated civilisation had diplomatic, cultural and commercial links with Rome, Persia and China through the ancient Silk Trade Route.

Peshawar's strategic location meant that innumerable destructive hordes came, trampled upon it and left it in ruins, for the Khyber Pass, though narrow, was not easy to defend. Unlike Lahore, which was able to survive ruinous attacks, recover and prosper, Peshawar was not so resilient. Peshawar's frontline position – the name actually means 'Frontier Town' – contributed to its style of development. It was always a frontier guardpost or a commercial trading place, a place where camel caravans loaded and unloaded, a transit town on the way to Lahore, Delhi or Multan. It was really only with Babar, founder of the Moghul Empire and builder of Peshawar's Bala Hissar Fort, that the city developed a kind of security.

With the decline of the Moghuls the Sikhs came, saw and conquered the region, and then in turn were followed and supplanted by the British, who also had a tough time with the Pathans but somehow managed to subdue the whole region. Since then it has evolved into what it is now – City of the Pathans – though it remains a dispersal point, a strategic region and recently, a watching post over the troubles afflicting Central Asia.

Peshawar is affected by the monsoon and can be warm and uncomfortably humid for part of the year. In winter the atmosphere is completely different, although cold, the landscape is charming and attractive.

Information

There is a Tourist Information Centre at Peshawar Airport, and another at Dean's Hotel (tel 2428), on Shahrah-e-Reza Rd. The Foreigner's Registration Office is on Police Rd; the banks and the GPO are on Saddar Bazaar. The Telegraph & Telephone Office is in the Mall.

Consulates

Afghanistan – Tel 73418 is on Sahibzada A Qayyum Rd; officially open but no longer issues visas

Iran – Tel 7306 is on the same road, does not issue visas

British – Tel 72562 is on Khalid Rd

USA – Tel 73061 is on Hospital Rd

Libraries

British Council Library – The Mall off Arbab Rd

National Central Library – Saddar opposite the GPO

Peshawar Municipal Library – Grand Trunk Rd near the Bala Hissar Fort

Money Exchange

The State Bank of Pakistan in Peshawar does not deal in foreign currency. If you need money changed try the National Bank of Pakistan or United Bank Ltd among others.

At Quissa Khani Bazaar there are money changers who will change any currency including Arab and Iranian rials, but for hard currencies only large notes are accepted.

Things to See & Do

If you arrive in Peshawar between the end of April and around mid-May, you're in for a treat. This is festival time, the Khyber Jashne (mela), an almost month-long celebration.

Old City

Just like its counterparts in the Punjab or Sind, the old city of Peshawar is a maze of narrow lanes, buildings with overhanging trellised balconies, bazaars, local inns, eating places and mosques. It is the busiest and most bustling area of the city and is usually crowded with gun-toting Pathans, colourfully clad in turbans and long flowing quamis and baggy shalwars that resemble pyjamas. It is here that you sense Peshawar's exotic frontier atmosphere most strongly.

An extension of the old city continues behind **Saddar Bazaar** where the familiar old buildings, muzzaffar khanas, mosques and bazaars have cropped up. It is now modernised with the old traditional area receding. The alleys have been widened and the eating places are gone.

The city is surrounded by the ruins of a wall which used to have 20 gates. Within these walls are bazaars with twisting streets that have trading quarters for businesses as esoteric as sword-making. The Kabul Gate leads to one of Peshawar's most famous streets, the **Kissa Kahani** (Street of Story-Tellers) where all the tall tales are supposed to be swapped over hookahs and endless cups of green tea.

Nearby is the **Bater Bazen** named after the bird market that used to be here, but now a centre for copper and brassware. Also in this area is the **Mochilara Bazaar** (the shoemakers bazaar), the place to go for an exotic pair of embroidered Pathan chappals. Near the **Gunj Gate** is a 2nd century BC stupa, a wooden building with 13 tiers crowned by an iron steeple, called **Shahji-ki-Dehri**. Close to it are the ruins of a large Buddhist monastery built during the Kushan period by King Kanishka.

At the central square – **Chowk Yadgar** – is a clock tower and a little way up is the Mahabat Khan Mosque, a beautiful ornate structure, which is over two hundred years old. Farther up to the east is probably the really old part with structures made of mud bricks with wooden braces; there used to be a Buddhist stupa and a Hindu temple here, but later it was turned into a serai. In the opposite direction westward is the most modern area of Peshawar, for here are situated research and educational centres – the Teacher's Training College, the North Regional Laboratories of the Council of Scientific and Industrial Research and the University of Peshawar.

British City

The British left the old city intact, just as they had done elsewhere, and grafted on a new section which began as a military cantonment. Here the ubiquitous Mall emerged, typically lined with large, shady trees behind which are the government buildings, the churches, official residences, the banks, library, travel agencies and now Chinese restaurants. The **Saddar Bazaar** has become the city centre and a buffer zone between the old and the new where the shops, cinemas, local modern hotels, cafes and restaurants are located.

A block away is the Mall which is beginning to lose its Victorian style as new buildings emerge. Like other malls in Pakistan it has a sedate and quiet atmosphere and hints of the British era still live on in the old military buildings with their cannons. Except for the **Bala Hissar Fort** and the Moghul gardens such as the **Khalid Bin Walid Garden** and the **Shahi Bagh** there is very little of the Moghul period left here.

Museum & Art Gallery

On the Grand Trunk Rd in the Cantonment area the museum was originally the Victoria Memorial Building. It has a particularly fine collection of objects from the Graeco-Buddhist Gandhara period and a small bookstore mainly on the archaeology and history of the Gandhara era. There is also an art gallery, **Abasin Art Gallery**.

Bala Hissar Fort

Originally built by Babar in 1519 on the north-west edge of the city. In its present form it dates from the Sikh period (1791-1849) when they controlled the Peshawar Valley. Today it is being used, once again, as a military fort. While no tourists are allowed in, the Bala Hissar Fort is clearly visible from most parts of Peshawar and occasionally you will see tanks and heavy military trucks surrounding it.

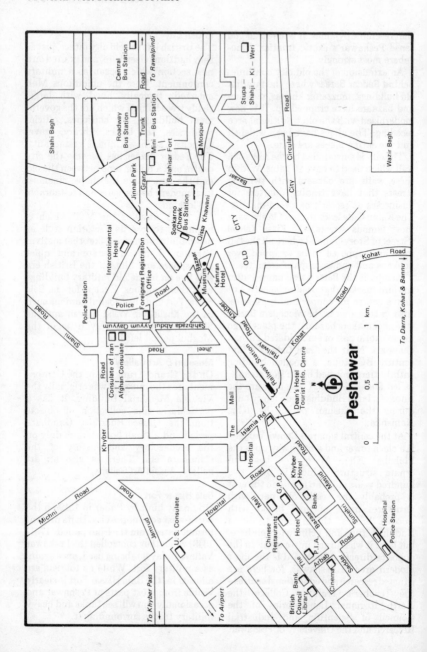

Around Peshawar

Jamrud Fort, 15 km from Peshawar, is a rambling collection of towers and walls, and a major landmark on the Khyber Pass. It's now military property and also off-limits to foreigners.

Charsadda, 29 km north-east of Peshawar, captured by Alexander the Great in 324 BC, has been identified as the pre-Kushan capital – Pushkalavati. **Shaikhan Deri** nearby is the site of a Greek town recently excavated.

The **Warsak Dam**, 29 km north of Peshawar, deep inside tribal territory on the banks of the Kabul River, is held up as a symbol of changing tribal attitudes. **Barra Bazaar** 7 km in the direction of Darra, is the place where smuggled goods are available including of course, drugs of the border variety, sold here by the kilo or tonne.

Places to Stay – bottom end

The cheapies are generally in the bazaar area. Well-known are the *Rainbow Hotel*, the *National* and *Kamran Hotel*, all in Khyber Bazaar. They are reasonably clean, have fans and dorm accommodation with four to six beds for Rs 15, and singles/doubles for Rs 20/30. Many travellers recommend the *Khyber Hotel Tourist Inn*, Saddar Bazaar, which has fans and share bathrooms with hot water and costs Rs 15 for a single and Rs 25 to Rs 30 for a double. Slightly more expensive is the *Moonlight Hotel & Restaurant* just across the street from the Khyber. There are other hotels around with rooftop beds that are fine in summer for Rs 8.

The *Youth Hostel* on the university campus on Jamrud Rd is too far out of town to be convenient. There is a camp site about 100 metres from Jan's Hotel which costs Rs 10 for a car and two people. If just in transit the railway retiring rooms cost Rs 15 to Rs 20 for a single, double Rs 30.

Places to Stay – middle

Guls Hotel, Saddar Bazaar, has singles/ doubles for Rs 25/50. *Hotel Shahzad* and *Sabir Hotel* just off Saddar on Chowk Foarah, have the same rates. *International Hotel* Saddar Rd (tel 72100), charges Rs 35/60. *Skyline Hotel* Sunehri Masjid Rd (tel 74031), has rooms for Rs 30/50. *Sindabad Hotel* Saddar Rd (tel 75020) has singles/doubles Rs 40/70. *Habib Hotel* and *Neelab Hotel* Khyber Bazaar, have rates from Rs 80 upward. *Jan's Hotel* Islamia Rd (tel 73006), just off Saddar Bazaar, has rates from Rs 120 up.

Places to Stay – top end

The *Khyber Pearl Continental* Khyber Rd (tel 76360), has 150 rooms from Rs 800 to Rs 1800. It has everything from a coffee shop to a swimming pool and tennis courts, but the bar is now out of business. The PTDC-run *Dean's Hotel* is at 3 Islamia Rd (tel 76481-4), and has 47 rooms with singles/doubles for Rs 400/600 plus taxes. *Galaxie Hotel* (tel 72738) Khyber Rd, has rates from Rs 300 upwards. *Green's Hotel* (tel 74304) on Saddar St, has less expensive rooms.

Places to Eat

The cheaper eating places are along and behind Saddar Bazaar and in the old city in the bazaar area. You can get good food here for Rs 12 to Rs 16. Cheaper still are the Khyber and Quissa bazaars where you can get kebabs, nan, fish and tea. Try the *Salatin Hotel* for a splurge on excellent Pakistani dishes. The top end hotels like Dean's provide excellent local, Chinese and western dishes. There are many middle level restaurants and two Chinese restaurants, the *Hongkong* and the *Nanking*, on the Mall, where a meal could cost Rs 30 up.

Liquor Even Peshawar is becoming a 'dry' city. If you do get 'thirsty' there's always the Tourist Info Centre at Dean's, staff in the hotel might also be of help. It used to be that you simply showed your passport, but things have changed.

Getting Around

Taxis within city limits are Rs 10 to Rs 15, while auto-rickshaws are generally around Rs 6. The meters on the latter usually aren't working, so get the fare sorted out before you take a ride. Tongas are Rs 5 to Rs 10 if you are alone, if with others, Rs 2 per person. Numerous buses, minibuses and miniwagons ply between Saddar Bazaar, bazaars in the Old City and bus stations on Grand Trunk Rd for Rs 0.50 for buses, Rs 1 on minibuses and miniwagons Rs 1.25.

Getting Away

Air The PIA office is at the corner of Arbab Rd and the Mall. They have flights to the following:

Saidu Sharif	Rs 105
Chitral	Rs 120
Islamabad	Rs 130
Lahore	Rs 370
Quetta	Rs 540

Airport tax of Rs 5 is additional to these fares.

Rail Trains are not used much, as buses, minibuses and coaches are available for any direction. They are faster, less crowded and more comfortable.

Bus There are a number of bus stations around Peshawar: *Soekarno Chowk* is for buses for Jamrud, Landi Kotal, Torkham, and it used to be up to Jallalabad and Kabul; *Broadway House* on the Grand Trunk Rd is for Darra, Kohat, Bannu and Dera Ismail Khan. *Bala Hissar Fort* minibus station is for Charsadda, Mardan, Swat and Dir. The *Central Bus Terminal* is for Attock, Hasanabdal, Taxila and Rawalpindi. There are also minibus stations on the Grand Trunk Rd, eg the Flying Coach deluxe minibuses and others plying between Peshawar and Rawalpindi-Lahore. Fares and journey times are:

Rawalpindi	Rs 20-25	three hours
Mingora	Rs 15-20	two hours
Dir	Rs 25-35	six hours
Kohat	Rs 12-15	two hours

THE KHYBER PASS

This famous historical pass is in the Sulaiman Hills in the Western Border Mountains. About 1000 metres high, the pass is 1½km at its widest and only 16 metres at its narrowest. It's reckoned to begin at Jamrud Fort and end at Torkham, 58 km away.

The Khyber Agency is the only Afghan outpost to be annexed by the British. Its recorded history is long and colourful and begins with the arrival of the Achaemenians, followed by the Greek legions of Alexander the Great, who were in turn succeeded by a series of invading hordes who thundered through on their way to the lush valley of Peshawar, tapering off with the British-Indian expeditionary forces who marched in so bravely and stumbled out so disastrously. Numerous memorials were carved on the rock faces to the British-Indian regiments who gradually wrested the pass from the Pathans and the Afghans.

The immigration and customs checkposts used to be at Torkham, the border town here, which has shops, hotels, cafes, restaurants, banks, bakeries and government offices. Most of the buildings are low-roofed and seem to huddle together as if for security. Landi Kotal, the next town along towards Peshawar, is very much the same. Beyond this everything is dry, barren and flat, but there is not the sense of desolation there is on the Salt Range. Landi Kotal is famous for its smuggling and items from all over the world are openly on sale here at astonishingly low prices.

This is now the Khyber Agency, a tribal political agency, where signboards begin to appear by the roadside warning motorists not to wander off the main highway. Only along this metalled highway do the laws of Pakistan apply –

Top: Kohistani man (PTDC)
Left: In the bazaar at Peshawar (PE)
Right: Gilgit (PE)

Top: In a Peshawar cafe (PC)
Bottom: Road up the Khyber Pass (PE)

tribal laws take over on either side of the road.

You will rarely see any women apart from the nomadic tribeswomen, who are usually dressed in red or maroon. The black and grey tents of the nomads hug the sand, while camels wander around grazing on the sparse vegetation. You will also see children, young shepherds and shepherdesses and their flocks of sheep and goats. Except for the nomads, all the men appear to be literally armed to the teeth.

As you approach Peshawar the land becomes greener and less wild, and the turbans, guns and bandoliers give way to urban denizens in western attire.

The Afghanistan border is still officially open but in practice it's virtually closed. Likewise the Afghan consulate is, in theory, open for business as usual, but in fact is closed. There used to be a daily bus from Peshawar to Kabul, but the service has completely stopped. A barrier consisting of a waist-high barbed wire fence with an opening is now part of the scenery at Landi Kotal. There are also numerous signs including a 'Welcome to Pakistan' sign, a warning to get to Peshawar by nightfall and a small board on the Afghani side with a few propaganda posters plastered on it in Urdu.

The Khyber Pass double-engined train to Landi Kotal still operates once a week on this route, but it is mainly for locals.

DARRA

Only 42 km south of Peshawar, the town of Darra is in a tribal area on the main highway to Kohat and Bannu. It is off limits to foreigners. The situation won't change until the Afghan question is resolved. Ask around before you attempt to go there.

If you do manage to get there, it's a nondescript little place like the wild west towns in the movies – one main bazaar lined with shops, local hotels and places to eat. At first glance it looks like any other small town, but when you take a

look at the shops you will be struck by display after display of a surprising commodity – guns and weapons of all types both locally manufactured and imported (smuggled). Darra is the arms capital of the North West Frontier Province and here even pens and walking sticks may conceal lethal weapons. It has been manufacturing guns or making perfect replicas of foreign firearms and supplying the warring tribes for over a century. Despite this, Darra doesn't seem to have prospered as much as one would expect, and is still a smallish town.

Apart from guns and heavier weapons, the local people seem to deal in every kind of contraband you can think of, including marijuana and heavier drugs and not

Pen gun

merely in kilograms but in tonnes. On this scale even illegal businesses acquire a kind of legitimacy and deals are made quite openly, without fear of any interference from the authorities. Strangers, however, are likely to find themselves hassled by the police should they try to dabble! Darra is not a sinister place, despite its nefarious businesses. Hot and dusty though it is, Darra has become something of a tourist attraction.

SOUTH TO DERA ISMAIL KHAN

On the way to Dera Ismail Khan from Peshawar, the road goes through Kohat, a largish, bustling township with fairly good hotels such as *Jan's Hotel*, *Pughman Hotel* and *Nadria Hotel* with rates for singles from Rs 15 to Rs 90 and doubles from Rs 25 to Rs 120. It is mainly a transit point to Parachinar to the west and Bannu in the south, 189 km away and 4½ hours by bus. There is a hotel in the Tea Bazaar in Bannu, the *Farid Hotel* (tel 4242), which also has a restaurant and charges Rs 12 to Rs 15 for rooms.

Eventually you arrive in Dera Ismail Khan, 340 km south of Peshawar, the bus travels a little faster and stops less often as the land opens up into a vast wasteland. Further south a travel permit is required through Waziristan and Fort Sandeman in Baluchistan, although three Americans from Texas pedalled through on their bikes a few years ago without any travel permit. They were, however, escorted out of the area by heavily armed police officers in a jeep. Despite their being of true Texan stature, it was apparently not an experience to be repeated.

In Dera Ismail Khan the *New Shahra Hotel* and *Al-Habib Hotel* both have the same rates, singles/doubles Rs 15/25. *Hotel Gulbahar* has rooms for Rs 20/30. Dera Ghazi Khan, farther south in the Punjab, has many more hotels, among them *Al-Fateh Hotel*, Faridi Bazaar has singles/doubles for Rs 10/20. *Victory Hotel* Azmat Rd has doubles only for Rs

40. *Pak Land Hotel* (tel 3022) Faridi Bazaar, has rates from Rs 75 up. Dera Ghazi Khan is an important transit area, as roads split off in nearly every direction, towards Multan farther to the south in the Punjab, towards Loralai in Baluchistan to the west, and to Peshawar to the north.

Parachinar in the Kurram Agency is another tribal area where a special permit is required. Apparently the restriction is not merely because it is a tribal area, but because of its proximity to Kabul, which is less than 100 km away.

Although the country is green just out of Peshawar, it gradually becomes dry again and is dominated by barren hills and mountains. The route passes through the scenic Darra Pass with mountains to one side and wide plains below. A little beyond Kohat you will see the craggy, jagged Salt Range in the distance. In summer the dry, white powdery salt looks almost like wind-blown snow. The desolate landscape is alien and forbidding, but has its own fascination, and once again becomes greener and flatter towards Bannu.

Bannu is smaller than Kohat, a peaceful place. Beyond the town the land remains flat and green most of the way to Dera Ismail Khan, 145 km further on and 3½ hours by bus. But slowly it becomes dry again and sandy with the horizon shimmering in the distance. Dera Ismail Khan is a fairly large, sprawling oasis, the last major town in the south of the North West Frontier Province. Immediately south is Baluchistan and to the southeast is the Punjab. About 20 km before Dera Ismail Khan is another Indus Valley Civilisation archaeological site known as Rehman Dheri. It is built to the same design and in the same materials as the cities of Moenjodaro and Harappa.

The next nearest town is Dera Ghazi Khan, 256 km away in the Punjab, and six hours by bus. Usually buses go to Multan, but you can get off at Taunsa and from there take another bus. Dera Ghazi Khan is another fairly largish town, more developed than Bannu or Dera Ismail Khan, but still quite provincial. From here you can either proceed to Multan back to Lahore or continue straight to Karachi, Jacobabad and then to Quetta, or alternatively bus it to Loralai – travel permits are just an impossibility – anyway when you are already there they may allow you to continue on to Ziarat – good luck!

Tribal areas are generally restricted to tourists. Waziristan in particular is semi-wild, a place where feuding continues and kidnapping for ransom is still practised. Houses here are generally fortified with towers and men are always suspicious and armed.

Southward to Dera Ismail Khan there is a small-gauge train to Bannu, but it's virtually unused and most of the stations along the way are closed. The road leads down from Peshawar to Kalabagh where you can either go into the Salt Range in the Punjab or down to Mianwali, a small town, similar to Dera Ismail Khan. From Mianwali travelling further south is generally by bus or train, both of which are irritatingly slow, particularly in the hot season when you would probably prefer to explore on your own along the banks of the Indus on this side of the Punjab.

Exploration of the banks of the Indus is also possible on the North West Frontier Province side, where you may encounter tribes that sill live on the islands in the Indus River. Apparently there is a ferry that plies between towns along the river as well as pontoon bridges that span it, which allow you to travel from one little-visited village to another.

Try to avoid travelling around here during the summer and monsoon period up to October as it is scorching on either side of the Indus then. It is semi-wasteland, mottled with desert scrub, flat at times, undulating at others, with a sparse covering of trees and interspersed oases. During the winter from December to February you'll find it a lot easier to move around and observe the culture of the different tribes. Further south you may even come across tribes with unique cultures.

NORTH TO CHITRAL

From Peshawar you can travel north, visiting a number of interesting archaeological sites, to the Swat Valley or Chitral via Dir. The north-east of the Peshawar Valley has a concentration of archaeological sites of the Gandhara period, like nowhere else in Pakistan. On the road to Mardan, en route to the valley of Swat is **Charsadda** (2nd century BC) and nearby is **Pushkalavati**, the Lotus City, capital of the Mauryan Empire. Originally this consisted of three cities: Bala Hissar founded in the 6th century BC; Shaikhan Dehri, the second city founded by the Bactrian-Greeks in the 2nd century BC; and Prang, the third city, which is still to be excavated. Charsadda has an ancient Buddhist stupa known as the **Eye Gift**, and near this are the remains of an ancient Greek town.

Takht-i-Dehri, 44 km away from Mardan, is a well-preserved Buddhist monastery with monks' cells, halls of stupas, assembly halls and meditation rooms below. From the hill is a marvellous view of the plains of Mardan to the south and to the north is the Malakhand Pass. Three km from here is **Shari Balelol**, a village which, when excavated, revealed a walled city and a Buddhist monastery with well-preserved Gandharan sculptures. Local people here make a living producing perfect replicas of the stonework. **Kotlang**, 24 km away, is known for pink topaz and is another archaeological Buddhist site.

On the road to Swabi is **Shahbaz Ghari**, the site of Ashoka's rock inscriptions, which reveal his remorse for the destruction and terrible slaughter in the Kalinga Kingdom of eastern India. One of the trails of the Silk Trade Route passed through this area. At Swabi, the road forks off to the left to Tarbella and to the right to Attock. Not far away is Hund.

The road continues on to Mardan, 65 km away. The ruins of a Buddhist monastery at **Chanaka Dehri** are interesting and worth a visit. Up a hill on the same Malakhand Rd is another Buddhist site. This is the region described by Churchill as a land of 'savage brilliancy' and it was here where he is said to have developed a taste for whisky.

The Malakhand Pass begins at Dargai and the drive is particularly scenic. There is a fort at the top of a hill on the left, and on the other side is **Bat Khela**, which has a Hindu fort perched just above it.

Unless you have your own transport it is quite difficult to reach any of the archaeological sites. There is no public transport to any of these areas. In Mardan the *Zamran* and *Puskaiz* hotels are Rs 10 to Rs 20.

The Malakhand Rd splits up at Chakdara with one fork leading to Chitral via Dir and the other leading towards the Valley of Swat. From the foothills of the Hindu Kush upwards the landscape is scarred and eroded and the road runs through wide, flat valleys which narrow further north through the Malakhand Pass, then widen again until Chakdara and the Swat Valley. From Chakdara the land opens up until Dir, a transit town to Chitral, over the 3125-metre-high Lowari Pass. There are some reasonably clean, medium class hotels around the bus station in Dir if you want somewhere to stay overnight. Up in the town are other, slightly more expensive hotels, but they are inconvenient if you intend to take the early bus for either Swat or Peshawar.

Further to the east is Hund, formerly known as Udabhanpur – City of Waterpots. This is where the Indus becomes really broad and until recently it used to be crossed by rafts held up by huge waterpots. It was here also that Genghis Khan finally caught up with Jallaludin, emperor of the Khwarzem Empire, who

had murdered the Mongol emissaries. One of the routes of the ancient Silk Trade went through this region and it was also once a Buddhist pilgrimage centre. While crossing the Indus on his way back to China, Xuan Zhang (643 AD) lost every one of the irreplaceable Buddhist manuscripts he had collected in India.

There is nothing left in Hund now, even its ancient air has faded away, but it remains a quiet, pleasant place to visit. There are no hotels here. If on the Grand Trunk Rd from Peshawar get off at Topi near Tarbella – there is a rest house here – and take another bus. You have to make enquiries, tell the bus conductor where you intend to get off. They will drop you in the area of Hund but you still have to walk up to the village. From here upwards is a trekking area, but hardly touristed, although hilly, wooded and historical. In Buner and in the surrounding areas are other archaeological sites, primitive rock shelters, carvings and inscriptions.

PESHAWAR TO RAWALPINDI

Out of Peshawar on the Grand Trunk Rd towards Noushera and Rawalpindi, beautiful residential buildings and modern industrial plants and factories have cropped up on both sides of the highway, but beyond unfolds wide, open grassy spaces, military cantonments and airfields, and approaching Noushera it becomes wooded. Noushera is another military cantonment, and another transit zone with routes to the north and south. If you wish to stop over here the *Noor Mahal Hotel* and *Shobra Hotel*, both on the GT Rd, have rooms from Rs 20 to Rs 40.

Beyond Noushera the Indus is now spanned by a new modern bridge which offers you an excellent view of the **Attock Fort** with its great battlements and ramparts. It guards the route to Rawalpindi and Lahore. Built by Akbar in 1583 it covers the crest of a hill and slopes down to the banks of the Indus. A few km farther up where buses stop for tea, is an old Moghul structure right in the middle of the highway, perhaps once an outpost where tax was collected.

The highway continues towards Hasanabdal passing the **Wah Garden**. The sandstone hills on the southside of the highway are honeycombed with holes which are actually doorways dug by cave-dwelling gypsies. They live here much in the manner of the gypsies of Andalusia in southern Spain.

Further east, beyond Hasanabdal and Taxila, on a spur of a ridge, there is a tower built in memory of John Nicholson, a slightly strange British officer who died in the assault of Delhi following the Indian Mutiny. On the northside, just on the highway side directly opposite the memorial tower, are three structures that look like Greek temples, perhaps ruins of Greek towns built here.

Baluchistan

West of the Indus Plains is Baluchistan, the largest province in Pakistan with an area of about 343,000 square km. But though it's bigger than the British Isles, it only has a population of about one million, due mainly to its daunting arid geography.

In the south of the province, Makran is almost entirely desert with low, dry hills rising from 300 metres to 2500 metres in the north. In the west there is a large salt lake, Hammum-i-Maskhel, and more expansive desert plains. This is where the Chagai and Toba Kakar Mountain Ranges form the borders of Iran, Afghanistan and Pakistan. Around Quetta and Ziarat are fertile plateaux but to the east, tracts of desert and semi-wasteland are dissected by the Sulaiman Ranges which stretch south-north through the Khulu Agency up to the Waziristan area of the North West Frontier Province. There are four reasonably big rivers here which include the Zhob, Porali, Hingal and Dasht – all flowing south. Around Quetta the high peaks are Tukatu, a little less than 400 metres high, Chiltan, a little over 3000 metres and Khalifat, about 3500 metres. To the east, just west of Dera Ismail Khan is Takht-i-Sulaiman, over 3750 metres high.

Baluchistan is outside the monsoon zone and has, with the exception of the hilly and arid mountainous regions, a pleasant climate. In winter the temperature falls to as low as –30°C while in summer it ranges from 18° to 30°C. The province has been influenced by the civilisations in the Indus, Dir and Swat Valleys. One of the oldest neolithic sites (6000 BC) is to be found at Mehr Ghar, just south of Bolan Pass. This culture faded away in 3000 BC about the same time that the Indus Valley Civilisation emerged.

The Indus Valley influence emerged in the Kutli Culture of Sind in the south of Baluchistan while the Dir and Swat Culture (grave culture – 1500 to 600 BC) emerged in the Red Ware or Zhat Culture and the Buff Culture of northern Baluchistan. Along with Sind, the Punjab and part of the North West Frontier Province, Baluchistan fell under the sway of the Achaemenian Empire in the 6th century BC. Archaeological findings indicate that in the 1st century AD the Kushan Empire also had some influence and that Buddhism thrived and flourished in Baluchistan until the re-emergence of Hinduism in the 5th century AD. The latter endured until Islam burst into the region in the 7th century AD.

Some historical evidence suggests that the Baluchis may have belonged to the Ten Lost Tribes of Israel and formed part of the army of the Achaemenian emperor, Kaikhusro – Cyrus the Great (558 to 530 BC). A thousand years on they re-appeared in history as part of the standing army of the Sassanian king, Nausheran (531 to 578 AD), marching towards Hindustan in the 5th century AD. In the 7th century AD, they appeared as supporters of Imam Ali, and after the Karbala they were again on the march towards Persia, only to turn up in the 10th century AD with Mahmud of Ghazni. After that they attached themselves to every conquering Muslim horde of the subcontinent and finally settled in this region when Babar appeared on the scene.

Fiercely independent Baluchistan never really became part of the Moghul Empire, but effectively remained an autonomous frontier tributary. In India they fought the Hindus and gained some influence in the Punjab and Sind. In order to survive they expediently changed their loyalty and allegiance when necessary: at one time with the Moghuls, then the Persians and the Afghans, but their constant was the fight for Islam. When the Moghul power declined they took on the Sikhs, the Marathis and finally the British, who arrived in 1841.

When they were not fighting wars to prop up Muslim empires, they pursued brigandage in the same manner as the Khanjuts of Hunza, waylaying camel caravans or plundering villages in the deserts. They were later described as 'races of barbarous people who inhabit the mountains ... whose employments are fighting and shedding blood'. Due to these 'wild tribes on the banks of the Indus' who were 'war-like' and 'good archers', the Baluchistan desert region became a 'no-man's land, belonging to no province where robbers from every district found shelter and where permanent villages, except in three instances, were conspicuously absent.'

Makran, once a thriving region with its capital in Panjgur and a commercial entrepot in Tiz with 'great warehouses, palm groves and a beautiful mosque, with people of all nations', simply dried up.

When the British came in 1841, the Baluchis gave them the toughest fight they ever had on the subcontinent. They were reckless fighters, often throwing away their matchlocks to attack with the sword, only to fall to bullets and bayonets. Since their defeat they seem to have lived in a non-existent world, isolated in their inhospitable land, they reminisce about their romantic exploits of the past, and cling desperately to a tribal way of life.

In the war of independence in 1947, they supported the political goal of Quaid-i-Azam for a separate Muslim state, never quite being able to surrender their autonomy and independence, and consequently giving the Pakistan government a hard time for quite a while.

Camel Caravan in the Baluchistan Desert

Despite continuing problems, Baluchistan is an integral part of the country, fairly prosperous and potentially immensely rich in mineral resources, which so far remain in the ground. Today, while Baluchistan is largely tribal from the Khulu Agency up to Fort Sandeman in the north and Kalat to Las Bela and the Makran coast in the south, it is gradually being weaned away from tribalism and drawn into the orbit of modern civilisation.

When the British finally defeated the Baluchis, they found that there were no cities or towns in the province, just villages and tribes. To this day the majority of the people are nomads who migrate to the hills in spring and summer with their cattle, goats, sheep, camels, donkeys and horses, where they set up tents – *khizdis* and huts – *jhuggis* – made of twigs and branches of trees, grass, reeds or straw. In the winter they retreat to mud huts on the plains. All the towns in Baluchistan – Quetta, Ziarat, Sibi, Fort Sandeman, Loralai and others – were built by the British. Except for these strategic areas, the British left the region alone.

They blasted tunnels through the mountains for rail tracks to Quetta and from here to Taftan in the west, Chaman in the north-west and Fort Sandeman in the north. In the main, they only set up military cantonments and tentative administrative centres. Even now Baluchistan appears to be a place where progress is almost an aberration. Apart from Quetta most places are still really villages or towns, most of them around oases and separated by hundreds of km of sand. Basically, the villages are hidden deep in the valleys of the mountains, while the plains are left to the nomads.

Baluchistan is where the alternative route of the Euro-Asian Highway passes from Zahedan in Iran to Taftan in Baluchistan and on to Quetta. Another alternative road turns south from Kandahar in Afghanistan into Chaman

in Baluchistan – this was the route for freight bound for Afghanistan arriving through Karachi harbour. Apart from its importance as a transit area, there are mineral resources which are just beginning to be tapped. The Sui district has one of the largest gas deposits in the world.

Baluchistan is a province of contrasts. It has some of the bleakest landscape in the country with grim, jagged mountains, barren and arid land where the sparse greenery shrivels and wilts, but hidden away are some stunningly beautiful places.

QUETTA

The capital city of Baluchistan has none of the Moghul features of other major cities of the subcontinent, no ancient bazaars, grand forts or beautiful palaces. Nor does it have the spectacular structures of the British era. Its history begins with the arrival of Islam in the 10th century with the Chakkars laying the foundation of the city, but it declined largely because of internecine fighting, and in 1730 came under the ruler of Kalat. In 1935, a disastrous earthquake virtually wiped out the city and all the present buildings date from that time.

Today is has a population of over 100,000 and although it is of no particular interest in itself, it is an important road junction with routes leading into Afghanistan and Iran. Situated at 1700 metres, the city is a pleasant escape from the heat of the plains in summer, but it gets extremely cold in the winter. Its name is derived from the Pushto word *kwatta*, which means fort.

Originally the fort was all there was to Quetta which guarded the overland approaches to the western frontier for at that time the capital was at Kalat in the south. The British-built city was laid out in blocks with the Mall, which they could never do without, set in a quiet, attractive area. Around this administrative centre the rest of the city clustered.

Today it is spacious and, unlike most

cities, does not suffer from traffic congestion. Apart from the bazaars, which are bustling and colourful, the city is quiet and the houses spaced well apart with walled compounds and lawns. There are many shady trees which emphasise the quiet and sedate atmosphere. Today Quetta is prosperous and flourishing, partly because of its continuing military importance, but mainly because it is a transit point and commercial centre for Iran and Afghanistan.

Information

The Tourist Information Centres are at Quetta Airport (tel 72053) and *Hotel Imdadi* on Jinnah Rd. There is an Afghani Consulate (tel 74160), in the Mall and an Iranian Consulate (tel 75054) on Hali Rd. The office of the Deputy Commissioner is on the corner of Shahrah-e-Iqbal and Club Rds. The main banks are on Jinnah Rd in the town centre and the GPO is in the Mall.

Liquor Liquor permits are available from the Excise & Tax Office on Alandar Rd where all the licensed liquor shops are. Like everywhere else you have to obtain a Tourist Certificate first. Passports aren't enough these days.

Things to Buy

Baluchistan produces some of the finest carpets in Pakistan as well as the most beautiful embroidery works, usually in strong, vibrant colours with geometrical patterns inlaid with tiny mirrors.

Around Quetta

Chiltan Hill on Brewery Rd is a good vantage place for a view of the surrounding country. Ten km out of town the greenish-blue waters of **Lake Hanna** encircled by brick-red hills is a pleasant place to visit, there is no public transport direct to the lake. A further 11 km brings you to **Urak Tangi**, which is enchanting with its mass of flowers and delicious fruit. **Pishin**, 50 km away, is another region noted for its

fruit: apples, peaches, plums, apricots and grapes. Then there's **Bund Khusdil Khan**, 18 km away, which is a sanctuary for migratory birds in winter. There is public transport to these three places, although often crowded and loaded with merchandise going up, and fruits and vegetables going down. There is a Planetarium underway.

Places to Stay - bottom end

The *Allah-Wallah Hotel*, MA Jinnah Rd has singles/doubles with attached bath for Rs 20/40. Nearby is the *Muslim Hotel & Restaurant*, which has singles/doubles for Rs 25/40. *Tourist Hotel* off Jinnah Rd in an alley, has similar rates, so does *Hotel City Baluchistan* on Prince Rd.

Close to the New Adda bus station, terminal for Taftan, is the *Osmani Hotel*, good for an overnight stay, dorm bed costs Rs 15. On Shirki Rd also near the Taftan bus terminal, the *Mohammed Tanzabee Hotel* has much lower rates, dorm bed Rs 10. There is a restaurant here which is open till 11 pm, cheap and good value, and nearby is a fascinating bazaar seldom visited by tourists. These are all places to stay if en route to Taftan for Iran.

In summer, accommodation here could be a problem, hotels on Jinnah Rd usually have charpois – rope beds – for Rs 8 out in the open courtyard, with your pack stored away. An alternative is the railway station retiring rooms; singles/doubles are Rs 25/30. *Lourdes* has a camping and parking site, Rs 15 per vehicle.

Places to Stay - middle

Faran Hotel (tel 73514), Shahrah-e-Liaquat Rd, singles/doubles Rs 55/75. *Imdadi Hotel* (tel 70166), Jinnah Rd – Tourist Info Centre is located here – has rooms for Rs 45/75. *Asia Hotel* has lower rates, and is clean with share bathrooms. Also *Shabistan Hotel* on Shahrah-e-Adalat St which has attached bathrooms. *Hotel Zufaqhir* on the same road has a pleasant courtyard and a good restaurant for almost the same rates.

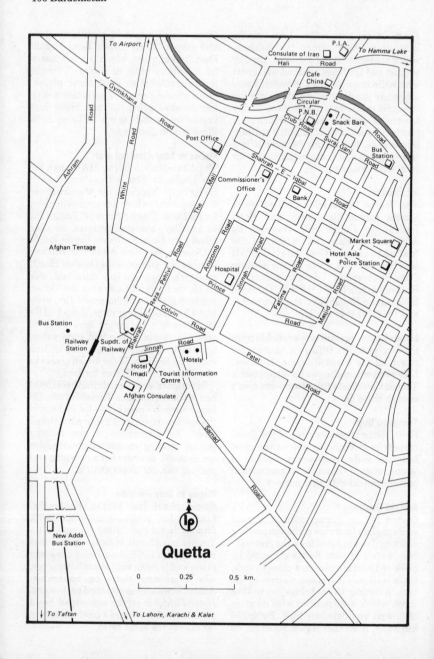

Places to Stay - top end
The *Lourdes Hotel* (tel 70168-9) on Staff College Rd is the best in town and the oldest established. Rates are from Rs 125 to Rs 250. It will soon be replaced as the flashiest by *Pearl Continental* which is currently under construction. The *Bloom Star Hotel* (tel 75178), Stewart Rd, has rates from Rs 90 to Rs 230. *Hotel Nile* on Jinnah Rd (tel 70736) is of the same standard and rates.

Places to Eat
All the cheap restaurants are along Jinnah Rd between the railway station and the city centre. A meal costs about Rs 8 to Rs 12, there is a cinema which also has cheap food, kebab and nan for Rs 8. Good, cheap local food can also be found in the bazaar area. In the city centre on Jinnah Rd there is an alley for *sajji*, lamb leg roasted from early morning till evening, for Rs 30 and up for a leg, price depends on size and weight.

The middle level hotels usually have restaurants which serve good western-style breakfasts and meals. There are other restaurants including *China Cafe* near the PIA and the Pakistan National Bank, also along this route are snack places. If you wish to have a splurge *Lourdes* and *Bloom* are the places.

Getting Away
Air The PIA office is on Jinnah Rd. These are some of the flights available:

Quetta-Karachi	four flights weekly	Rs 595
Quetta-Lahore	four flights weekly	Rs 715
Quetta-Peshawar	check flights weekly	Rs 540
Quetta-Islamabad	three flights weekly	Rs 755

Rail As usual for concessions obtain a Tourist Certificate from the tourist officer. The railway superintendent's office (tel 7017), is just in front of the station. From Quetta to Karachi there are four trains and to Lahore two.

Khokhropar (974 km)	sleeper	seat
air-con	Rs 585	Rs 340
1st class	Rs 235	Rs 138
2nd class	Rs 71	Rs 56

Lahore (1124 km)		
air-con	Rs 725	Rs 420
1st class	Rs 295	Rs 176
2nd class	Rs 91	Rs 69

For Karachi see section on Karachi.

Bus Taftan buses are on Shariab Rd, fare Rs 86, depart every couple of hours. For Chaman and Ziarat buses depart almost every hour from the General Bus Station on Circular Rd. Fare to Chaman Rs 10, Rs 18 to Ziarat.

Road Almost all the highways here, particularly the main one, the Karachi-Khuzdar-Quetta highway, Quetta-Chaman, the Quetta-Dera Ismail Khan highways, have been turned into federally controlled roadways. Almost all of them run through restricted tribal zones but it is now possible for foreigners to travel on public transport through these areas. For security reasons, if you have your own transport, it is advisable to follow public transport all the way.

Getting Around
Local There are a few taxis here, but the most common method within the city limits is by auto-rickshaw for Rs 5 or rickshaws Rs 3 and tongas are Rs 5 anywhere in the city. Generally there are no hassles about fare payments here, but it is still advisable to negotiate payment before getting on.

QUETTA TO IRAN
A train departs for Taftan every Saturday, fare Rs 48, and takes 36 hours, it stops about four to six km before the border town. It used to leave twice weekly for

Zahedan but since the Iranian Revolution entry into Iran has been stopped. It is a boring and uncomfortable journey with the added hassle of walking down to Taftan.

Buses, though cramped, are preferable to covering the 720 km from Quetta to Taftan. They depart from Quetta almost every two hours and the trip usually takes 24 hours, if you're lucky you may get fewer customs stops and do it in a few hours less, if you're unlucky, you may get more. It stops overnight in Nukundi for snacks and a rest. They have a shed here which provides blankets in winter.

The road is sealed as far as Yarmach and a little way on to Nukundi and cuts across a vast expanse of wasteland. In the opposite direction – from Taftan to Quetta – buses usually depart early in the morning, but if there are not enough passengers then later at 10 am or after lunch at 2 pm. It's quite a spectacular trip. The desert is flat and vast with undulating sand dunes looking like rolling waves, and the mountains, sky-blue in colour, seem very distant. You reach Nukundi around midnight and stop for a rest and something to eat. The following morning the bus leaves early and arrives in Yarmach before noon for lunch. From here the road is sealed and flat until just before Quetta. The bus is always stopped and searched for smuggled goods on the mountain road, and if it's a perfunctory inspection, you should arrive between 4 and 6 pm. A longer search may delay you until 8 to 10 pm.

Visas & Exchange Rates The Iranian Consulate in Quetta ordinarily does not issue visas, but it is still good for info on current events in Iran. Apply for your visa in Karachi if in the south; in Islamabad if in the north. Not so long ago the Iranian customs officers required foreigners to change US$150, even if they were just in transit for a couple of days, but this appears to be waived nowadays.

The Pakistan immigration and customs posts are at Taftan and those of the Iranians are in Mirjaweh, a checkpost scarcely a hundred metres away. Taftan used to be a *caravanserai* (camel caravan stopping place), but there are no more camel caravans on this route. There is a bank here which is closed on Fridays, but don't worry as there are money changers, unofficial of course, in teashops and hotels around here. You get good rates for your extra Pakistani currency, but much more if you have US dollars, sterling pounds or German marks. Current black market rate is 700 to 900 rials to the dollar, particularly with oil prices hitting rock bottom.

QUETTA TO AFGHANISTAN

There is one train daily to Chaman but buses depart almost hourly from the General Bus Terminus on Circular Rd and Suraj Rd. It's nearly 130 km from Quetta to Chaman. The road runs across flat, dry plains, then descends a few km before climbing to the mountains. Although the road is surfaced it is in bad condition in certain sections. It twists and turns through the Khozak Pass over dry, dusty country, and although it is less than 80 km from here to Chaman, it takes three hours to cross the pass, stopping frequently to pick up passengers and cargo. In the opposite direction the bus is stopped and checked thoroughly for smuggled goods.

Eventually you descend into flat desert and reach the small town of Chaman, which used to be just a little border village 20 years ago and although it is larger and more developed now, there is still no hotel, only muzzaffar khanas where you can spend the night if you arrive late.

It's walking distance from Chaman to the Afghan checkpost, but this is sealed up now, due mainly to the Afghan mujahadeen *jihad* against the Russian occupation troops in Spinboldak, 10 km away, and Kandahar about 24 km further away.

QUETTA TO PESHAWAR

Although there are trains and buses north to Fort Sandeman, the route to Peshawar via Bannu is a restricted tribal area. If you want to go into this region you need a travel permit from the Ministry of Home Affairs in Islamabad, but the chances of getting one are slim. Foreigners are not allowed to go past Ziarat either, although some travellers, 'unaware' of the restrictions, have made it.

Warning Note that in restricted areas there are no hotels, but you can stay at police outposts in the more civilised areas. It is extremely dangerous to travel around the wilder areas as witnessed by the circulars and photo displays of missing travellers, not only in Baluchistan but also the North West Frontier Province.

DERA GHAZI KHAN TO LORALAI

If en route to Peshawar via Dera Ghazi Khan and Dera Ismail Khan, get a Tourist Certificate to obtain a travel permit from the police station only for this section. The permit is often also issued by the Tourism Officer. The terminal for buses departing for Dera Ghazi Khan is on Cinema Street.

From Multan in the Punjab you can travel south-west to Jacobabad, then north-west to Quetta. If you have a travel permit you can go directly west through Dera Ghazi Khan. From this quite large town in the Punjab it is 270 km to Loralai. The bus leaves at 2 am and the fare is Rs 40.

The road is sealed but sections of it are in bad shape due to flash-floods during the monsoon. From flat semi-wasteland the route climbs up a mountain in a series of zig-zags. This mountain is quite unlike any to the north or west in composition or structure, appearing to have pushed straight out of the ground without tilting to one side with its strata horizontal. It is a continuation of the Sulaiman Ranges which make up the provincial border

between the Punjab and Baluchistan.

At the top you pass through Fort Munro beyond which the land flattens and then gradually slopes down into Baluchistan. Apart from a few patches of green it is generally arid with tiny villages tucked behind ridges that are almost invisible from the road. As you descend you can see the thin black ribbon of the tarred road stretching straight towards another mountain range to the left, where it turns south-west.

As you approach the mountain range the land becomes alien and mysterious, with a gusty wind that only stops for a short period during winter. Buses are often stopped by the powdery dust that cuts visibility to zero. Beyond this the landscape is less hostile and much greener. You can now see the nomads' tents, which look like huge beetles. Further down the track the tents are replaced by huts made of woven dry, yellow reeds. Two or three pieces of this make a hut, which can be rolled up in a trice and transported by camel.

After this, once again the landscape becomes barren and desolate until out of the sea of sand Loralai emerges. Although it is a major town in Baluchistan, Loralai is no bigger than Dera Ismail Khan, having only one bazaar, a few eating places and some muzzaffar khanas with rope-beds, most of them without toilets. It is not geared to tourists at all, but it's a fascinating journey getting there. You can wash the dust off yourself at *hammans* (barbershops) for a small fee.

LORALAI TO QUETTA VIA ZIARAT

Buses take nine hours to cover the 190 km to Quetta. Minibuses cost a little more but are about two hours faster. While the road is not bitumen, it is not bumpy. This is not a particularly exciting stretch of territory, but it is pleasant enough, crossing gently rolling land which is almost flat until the Chutair Valley. From there it begins to climb gradually up to Ziarat. Although the valleys are wider and the country greener, the area appears to be deserted. But once you start climbing up into the mountains you begin to see signs of settlement. The mountains are covered with junipers that are stunted, gnarled and twisted like desert trees.

The Chutair Valley is very picturesque with huts made out of big stones piled up from the base to form a low wall and branches of trees making the frame for the upper walls and roof. Juniper bark or long grass cover the frame. These huts have no windows and their primitive but attractive design is strikingly like the ancient Viking dwellings in Scandinavia.

Continuing on you reach the surfaced road, then suddenly come across the modern buildings of Ziarat. At 2500 metres, Ziarat is a popular hot season retreat with many expensive hotels which are heavily booked during the summer. There is no Youth Hostel either, so, unless you can afford the expensive *PTDC* complex, your best bets are the *Ziarat Hotel* or the *Grand Hotel* at Rs 20 per person. The former has a slight edge over the latter as it's quieter. Ziarat also has good treks including short hikes to Prospect Point about 5½ km away, and Fern Gorge which is 10 km.

From here the surfaced road meanders down through a narrow, barren valley to Kach. The rock formation here is rather fascinating with the barren, sandy countryside appearing more like a rock garden. In Kach, buses stop for passengers to get some refreshments and to do their *namast* (prayers) while the minibuses simply zip through. The valleys once again open up as you approach Quetta.

Warning Dacoitry (banditry) is rife along the Quetta-Loralai route, particularly near Loralai. Be careful.

QUETTA TO MAKRAN
The coastal region of Makran in the south of Pakistan is in the process of being developed with US assistance, and is

likely to be opened up to tourism in the near future. The land rimmed by the sea is barren and sandy with low, dry, hilly outcrops. Further inland the country rises from 600 metres to around 3000 metres in the north. It is a sparsely populated region, very hot in summer and freezing in winter. It's famous for its fine dates.

Since the ports on the Arabian Gulf became duty-free the desert region has become a smuggling area. During the British era only guns and ammunition were smuggled into the warring tribal areas, but today watches, television sets, radios, tape recorders, Japanese motorcycles, pens, refrigerators and innumerable other items are brought through this area into Quetta and all the way up to the North West Frontier Province. Due to the political turbulence in the region the western area of Makran is off-limits to foreigners and is likely to remain so for some time.

South of Quetta is Kalat, 122 km away. The paved road goes through the Lok Pass and continues on to Khuzdar, 144 km further on. From Khuzdar it is 220 km to Bela in the region of Las Bela. The road is paved all the way to Karachi via Sonmiani and is open to general traffic. However, if you have your own transport it is advisable not to go this way unless you are travelling in convoy, as it's too dangerous. It's safe enough to take the bus, but there are no tourist hotels yet, only muzzaffar khanas.

From Surab, a tiny village on the Kalat-Khuzdar Rd, a dirt track splits off towards Panjgur which is linked to Taftan by a camel caravan route. Khuzdar and Turbat are connected, and there are rough roads from Bela to Panjgur and the fishing villages. There is a jeep road from Pasni or Jiwani to Karachi, but it is closed to general traffic.

QUETTA TO LAHORE OR KARACHI
The trains for Lahore or Karachi start out along the same route as far as Sibi and the

Jacobabad Junction. You have to book air-con 1st class or 1st class sleepers two weeks in advance though, so you need time. If you haven't got the time, you'll have to use some ingenuity to make sure you get a seat. Get a concession ticket for the ordinary 1st class (unreserved coach) and arrive at the station early. Find a porter – they're obvious because they wear red shirts and an oval copper badge – and ask him to get you a seat. Make sure you show him your ticket so he knows what coach to get you on – and stick to him like glue. He will do all the hard work, struggling and jostling through the crowds and for just Rs 10 you'll get a seat. Make a note of his number to prevent later arrivals from claiming they have paid someone else for the seat.

At Jacobabad the trains turn north for Lahore via Multan or south to Karachi via Sukkur. From Quetta the train descends down to Sibi – about half-way to Jacobabad – passing a number of minor stations before reaching the Indus Plains. The mountains are forbidding, barren and desolate, almost primaeval in aspects. Except for tiny villages, mostly oases, everything is totally dry. The mountains close in around the rail tracks which slither through to the other side.

Fortresses top the low mountain crests manned by police forces led by the regional tribal leader. They generally wear grey quamis, shalwar and chappals, topped by an Australian-looking slouch hat with one side of the brim pinned up. As they are native to the region they are a far more effective police force than most others.

After what seems an interminable stretch of barren land, the train finally reaches the green plain, but in summer this is still uncomfortably hot. The train stops for about an hour here – the hottest region on the subcontinent – before going on to Jacobabad.

Archaeology

On the road to Quetta just before Bolan Pass is **Mehr Ghar**, another pre-Indus Valley Civilisation settlement. The neolithic tribes (6000 to 3000 BC) who settled here are considered to be the earliest known in the subcontinent. They apparently had trade links with the Indo-Gangetic people and the Iranian Asiatic civilisation, which indicates that they were a highly evolved and advanced people. They also are believed to have been the first to domesticate the buffalo.

The site was settled by Hindus later and then by Buddhists. The ruins of a stupa remain but the Hindu temple has now been converted into a mosque.

It was called by the ancient Chinese Buddhist pilgrims, *Polo-Leh* – Land of Mountains – but today is known as the Trans-Himalayas. This is the extreme western segment of the Himalayas, which spans the Indus and the Brahmaputra – a distance of 2400 km. It is about 500 by 800 km and makes up the immense corrugated region of the northern frontierland of Pakistan.

The Northern Territory is topped by the hump of the Pamirs on the side of the border of China, and right below it is the junction of the Hindu Kush and the Karakorams. The Hindu Kush splay out south and south-west straddling Afghanistan and Chitral in Pakistan, and while the Karakorams arch south-east right down to the valley of Ladakh where they are surrounded by the Ladakh, Deosai and Haramosh Ranges and the Indus River.

The Northern Territory covers an area that extends from Baltistan up to Darkot Pass and the fringes of Mastuj and Laspur in Chitral. In the region of Gilgit it is blocked by the Great Himalayan Range which slips in from the valley of Kashmir and spreads over the Diamar region, extending a little way beyond the Indus River to terminate just above the valley of Kohistan.

This is the upper northern highland, a craggy, arid, bleak area, where some of the highest peaks in the world are found, including K2, second only to Mt Everest. It is also one of the most glaciated regions in the world outside the Arctic and Antarctic.

The Hindu Kush cover the region of Dir, Bajaur and the eastern half of the Swat Valley and are bounded by the Altai Range and offshoots of the Himalayas to the south. Immediately south of the Great Himalayan Range are the Lesser Himalayas or Pir Panjal Range with an average elevation of 4500 metres where the peaks are always capped with snow. This range spreads from the valley of Kashmir right across Azad Kashmir, the Kaghan Valley, the Hazara and the western half of the Swat Valley. Right below the Pir Panjal are the Outer Himalayas which are contained by the foothills of the Hindu Kush to the west.

This is the sub-northern highland, lush green, a timber belt where some of the most beautiful valleys in the world are to be found. It is also where neolithic tribes settled in the foothills, a place where empires sprang up only to be wiped out and others to emerge.

In the incredibly inhospitable craggy region of the upper highland, neolithic tribes left vestiges of their Megalithic Culture. Down in the gentler sub-highland there is a concentration of archaeological sites from primitive rock shelters to great capital cities of empires.

The whole area was a crucible of different cultures, religions, art forms and racial stocks derived from the waves of successive invaders. It became the centre of Buddhism which influenced the religions of surrounding empires to a great extent, as well as their culture and art style, particularly those of Chinese Turkestan and Tibet.

The archaeological ruins, rock carvings and inscriptions, as explained by Dr Karl Jettmar of Heidelberg University, provide visitors with some perspective on the role played by the glacial Northern Territory of Pakistan in the development of world history.

THE SILK TRADE ROUTE

Neolithic trade routes linked this area with Persia, Central Asia and the Gangetic Plains and eventually became part of the Silk Trade Route between Rome, China and the Gandhara. Its main arteries ran east-west from the Gangetic Plains to Persia and south-north from Gandhara across the 'Suspended Crossing', which was how the ancient Chinese described the upper highland to Kashgar in Chinese Turkestan. The Silk Trade Route was named after the precious merchandise which was traded here – silk made from the threads of the mulberry worm, the weaving technique of which was a well-guarded secret of Imperial China for many centuries.

Before it became part of the Silk Trade Route, migratory neolithic tribes had already passed this way on their trading business and carved their impressions of animals on the rocks here. They were followed by other prehistoric, protohistoric and historic people: people from the Indus Valley Civilisation; Aryans; Achaemenians; Bactrian-Greeks; Scythians; Parthians; Sassanians; Hephthalites; Chinese and Tibetans – all of whom left their mark on this craggy gallery. Apart from scenes engraved into the rocks, there are numerous scripts including Pakrthi, Brahmi, Sogdian, Hanza-Haldeikish, proto-Sarada, Old Chinese and Tibetan.

THE KARAKORAM HIGHWAY

Distances

	km	hours
Rawalpindi-Abbottabad	117	2½
Abbottabad-Batagram	103	2½
Batagram-Thakot	28	½
Thakot-Beshum	28	½
Beshum-Pattan	44	1
Pattan-Camila	36	1½
Camila-Sazin	73	2
Sazin-Chilas	68	1½
Chilas-Jaglot	87	2
Jaglot-Gilgit	50	1½
Gilgit-Karimabad	112	3
Karimabad-Khunjerab Pass	209	3½
Total: Rawalpindi-Khunjerab Pass	955 km	22 to 26

The Karakoram Highway is almost a thousand km from the Hazara District of the Grand Trunk Rd up to Khunjerab Pass on the Sino-Pak border. It is linked by 24 major bridges and about 70 smaller ones.

The main route to the northern territory begins in Rawalpindi, at an elevation of 514 metres on the Grand Trunk Rd to the west. Here along the Sagjani, though the landscape is rapidly changing, are the remains of caravanserais of a bygone era. It continues through the Marghalla Pass where a memorial to Nicholson, a British officer, has been erected, on through Taxila to Wah, 43 km from Rawalpindi, where there is a Moghul garden with plane and cypress trees lining canals. It still has water basins and pavilions, but they are now in ruins.

On it goes to Hasanabdal, a busy crossroads, crowded with bazaars, hotels and restaurants. Here a Muslim shrine to Baba Wali Kandahari crowns a hilltop, at the foot of which is the Sikh shrine of Panj Sahib, which houses the hand impressions of Guru Nanak, founder of Sikhism. During the month of March thousands of Sikhs come to celebrate *Baisakhi*, a religious festival.

Along the way there are fields of yellow flowers, mostly mustard, sesame and rape plants. Just a little bit further on a road to the north heads off from the Grand Trunk Rd towards the Hazara District. On to Haripur, 35 km from Hasanabdal, and 22 km later is Havelian, a rail terminal noted for an impressive bridge which spans the Dar River, where the Karakoram Highway really begins its journey northward. From an elevation of 766 metres the road climbs for 15 km up to about 1200 metres into Abbottabad, then slithers down and on to Manshera, 26 km away.

On the northern slope of Manshera, at a road junction, are the moral edicts of Ashoka, inscribed on three large boulders. The edicts refer to avoiding wars and senseless killing, and stress compassion,

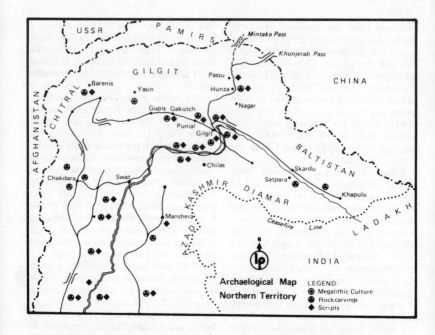

good deeds and self control. The highway meanders down to Batagram and then crawls in tortuous fashion along wooded ridges and spurs down into Thakot. From there it crosses the Indus and heads on to Beshum, a junction 28 km away in the Kohistan Valley, and continues on to Gilgit ending at Khunjerab Pass.

There is a police check point just before Chilas, and another just before Gilgit. The immigration and customs outposts are in Sust.

LOWER NORTHERN TERRITORY

The foothills of the Hindu Kush and the Outer Himalayas rear up from 1000 to 5000 metres above the valley of Peshawar and the Potwar Plateau in the Punjab. The valleys in Malakhand, Swat, Hazara and Azad Kashmir & Jammu are generally broad with undulating landscape, thickly wooded mountain slopes and ridges terraced for farming.

This luxuriant, heavily forested belt is where the monsoon dumps most of its rain in Pakistan. The climate is alpine, mild and pleasant – neither too hot in summer, nor too cold in winter, except in the higher reaches. Wheat, sugar, tobacco, fruits – apples, pears, peaches, plums and grapes – all grow in abundance. There are numerous wild animals in this region: leopards, black and brown bears, goral or wild mountain goats and markhors. Once there were also rhinos which the Moghuls used to hunt. But it seems they may have been rather too trigger happy as there are none around here now. However, there is a great variety of birdlife, which includes the *chikor* and black and grey partridges.

The valleys begin to narrow further up where the mountains crowd in on the rivers. The land becomes steeper and the skyline is serrated with peaks covered with snow, and the mountain sides are split with glaciers. Continuing north the forest belt terminates and the land loses its gentler aspects.

Historically this region is extremely significant, for it is where most of the neolithic tribes settled and evolved their cultures, an area conquered by Alexander the Great, where the Mauryan Empire had its beginnings, the great Gandhara Buddhist Culture emerged, where Akbar lost 8000 of his troops and where Winston Churchill failed to shoot a rebel only 20 metres away and had to beat a hasty retreat.

It's a land shared by the Pathans, the Kohistanis and other tribes: the cultural watershed between the south and the north.

AZAD KASHMIR & JAMMU

Azad (meaning free) Kashmir & Jammu is a long, thin slice of the state of Kashmir and Jammu. The border here is defined by a sensitive ceasefire line which has been the flash-point of India-Pakistan relations ever since Partition.

Three rivers converge here: the Kunhar, Neelum and Jhelum. The scenery is like any part of the Kashmir Valley, mountainous, luxuriant and beautiful. During the monsoon the landscape takes on a rainwashed appearance, with rivers rushing over rocky beds under clear, blue skies.

Azad Kashmir & Jammu is open to tourism from Pirpur and Kotli up to Muzzaffarabad and Khel in the north, but foreigners are not allowed within 16 km of the ceasefire line. They can only go as far as Noseri Bridge on the west banks of the Jhelum, and not beyond to Srinagar. The valleys of Neelum and Leepa, 55 km away, are superb, and are noted – among other things – for their unusual wooden houses, often three-storeys high and gabled like Alpine lodges. Unfortunately, only a small section of these valleys can be explored as they lie within the restricted zone.

MUZZAFFARABAD

This is the principal town in Azad Kashmir & Jammu and was once the administrative centre of the northern area. It is situated on the steep side of a mountain and spreads up the slopes on several levels, even the bazaar straddles three levels. There is one paved street but the town is scattered over the whole valley.

In Muzzaffarabad the Jhelum and Neelum rivers meet, and on the banks of the Neelum is a red fort, with another not far away on the top of a hill. Six km from here is the picturesque Banjora, near the tourist centre of Dhirkot. From Muzzaffarabad the road to Srinagar follows the Jhelum down under the Domel bridge. Just before you reach the Noseri bridge, if you wish, you can continue travelling north by bus via the west bank of the Jhelum River to Keran, Shardi and Khel.

Information

The Tourist Information Centre is in Dhirkot six km from the town centre of Muzzaffarabad.

Places to Stay & Eat

Middle level hotels are just around the bus station and the main bazaar. *Rainbow Hotel & Restaurant*, *National Hotel* and *Gilani Hotel*, Bank Rd, all have almost the same standard and rates, singles Rs 15 to Rs 20, doubles Rs 20 to Rs 25. *Farooq Hotel* on Secretariat Rd, not far away from here is of a similar standard and price.

More expensive hotels are *Al-Abaz Hotel* at the junction of the Neelum and Jhelum, singles Rs 75, doubles Rs 150. The *PTDC Motel* has the same rates and is near the old Fort.

AROUND AZAD KASHMIR & JAMMU

South of Muzzaffarabad is the Punch district where Kotli and Mirpur are situated. At Jangwan, 15 km west of Mirpur, to the south is the confluence of the Jhelum and the Punch rivers which are apparently good for trout fishing. In Mirpur places to stay are the *Alzaman Hotel* and the *Beyal Hotel* with rates from Rs 12 to Rs 30. Rawalkot in the centre of the Khunja Valley is at an elevation of a little over 2000 metres, in a valley shaped like an amphitheatre. It is linked with Rawalpindi via Kohala and Azad Pattan. In the valley of Samhani is *Baghzar Lake*, about 6 km long, and there is a Moghul Garden. On a hill is *Rohtas Fort* and not too far away is the *Mangla Dam*. In Rawalkot the place to stay is the *New Jenaid Hotel* (tel 626), Bus Station Rd, singles/doubles Rs 15/25. At Mangla Dam stay at the *Kashmir Point Hotel* (tel 37), Dino Rd, only doubles for Rs 20.

En route up north is **Chikor**, another hill staion, 40 km away from Muzzaffarabad, and about 5 km away is another forested hill resort, lovely and scenic, linked by road with Muzzaffarabad to the north and with Bagh in the Punch district via Sudham Gali to the south. Bus service continues up north.

Directly south of Muzzaffarabad is Bhatika, the gateway into the valley, a town with waterfalls, streams and irrigation channels, fragrant with sweet menthol in spring. It is linked with Balakot via Gari Habibullah and Athmugram, a town with a rest house on a hill. From here to the north in the Neelum Valley, 86 km away, the architecture and construction of the houses, which are made of wooden logs, begin to look distinctly Kashmiri. The staple food here is rice. Further up are the little towns of Salkhela, Barian, Qazi Nas, followed by Chaliana, which has an elevation of a little over 100 metres. Nosari is about 40 km away in the Neelum Valley.

The Neelum and the Leepa Valleys are very lovely, rich in fauna and flora, wooded with pine, deodar, and fir trees, and run for about 240 km in length with an elevation from 750 to 2500 metres, hemmed in by snow-clad mountains of the Great Himalayan Range.

Khel, located at the head of the Neelum Valley, is another hill resort with a rest house and a mosque, also a small bazaar. From here a trail leads to Shuntar

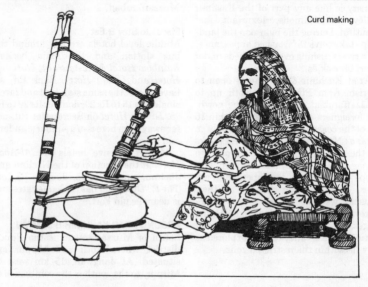

Curd making

Pass which continues on to Astore and Gilgit to the west. There is a jeep track to Tao Butt and further up are Janawai, Phullawai and Ahmad. It is accessible via the Kaghan Valley at two points; the Nuri Nari Hali Pass and the Ratti Gali. There are other minor passes which require the use of maps, mainly by trekkers. Another point is from Damurian which takes two days of hiking. Place to encamp on this trail is Dharian at 3000 metres elevation.

Getting There & Away

From Rawalpindi the 145-km trip by bus takes five to six hours and the fare is Rs 18. The bus passes through Murree to Bhatika, Dhirkot. From Jhelum there are also buses to Muzzaffarabad, 200 km to the north, via Kotli and Mirpur, the bus trip takes almost 10 hours. From Muzzaffarabad there are regular bus services to Neelum Valley to the north and to Gari Habibullah to the west towards Balakot, the 45 minute trip fare is Rs 3 to Rs 5. There are connecting miniwagons from here to Balakot. The bus station is just behind the bazaar and buses depart every hour for Rawalpindi, Kotli-Mirpur, Jhelum, Khel and Gari Habibullah.

HAZARA & THE KAGHAN VALLEY

Hazara is part of the North West Frontier Province, Pathan country, although geographically it forms part of the sub-northern region of the Malakhand, Swat and Azad Kashmir & Jammu. From the Indus Plains the land rises steeply to this area, then climbs less precipitously up north.

The way into Hazara from Rawalpindi is either via Haripur or Murree, the latter being the more popular with travellers. Although it is in the Punjab, Murree is really part of the sub-northern region. Burbhan, 10 km from Murree, is slightly lower at 1800 metres and has a Youth Hostel, but the bus service from here is irregular. This is a popular hiking place, though accommodation can be a draw-back in summer unless you have camping equipment and provisions.

Twenty-nine km away is Ayubia at 2600 metres above sea level. A tiny, summer hill resort in the Hazara region, it has a chairlift up to a mountain peak. Nathiagali, only eight km from here, is another scenic village worth visiting. All these hill resorts have moderately-priced hotels but tend to get packed out in summer.

From here you can continue north-east to Muzzaffarabad or north-west to Abbottabad, the principal town of the Hazara, 38 km away. Here the land dips down to 1200 metres, then flattens out before sloping gently downward to the north. The mountains recede along this pleasant route, whether you're heading towards Thakot and Baghram in the west or Gari Habibullah in the north-east.

If you decide to go north-east you come to Manshera, a city smaller than Abbottabad, but more beautiful in the traditional way. This is the site of Ashoka's rock inscriptions which are just by the roadside at a junction. In Manshera the places to stay are the *Nain Sukh Hotel*, singles/doubles for Rs 50/70, and the *Taj Mahal Hotel* which has a restaurant and charges Rs 15/25.

Approaching Gari Habibullah, 13 km further east, the mountains start to converge onto the road and the river, which squeezes through Balakot, 14 km away. This is the gateway to the Kaghan Valley and from here on, the valleys widen and narrow alternately.

Getting There

Buses for Abbottabad or Manshera are stationed at Pir Wadhai, Rawalpindi. It's a 3½-hour trip to Manshera from Pir Wadhai costing Rs 18. If you're heading for Balakot catch a bus from Manshera; it only takes an hour and the fare is Rs 10. From Balakot you can go to Naran by bus for Rs 22 to Rs 25. It takes about five hours. There is also a minibus service from Balakot to Kaghan, which takes 3½ hours and costs Rs 18. Kaghan is a rather nondescript town and it's better to take the direct bus to Naran.

BALAKOT

Though only a transit point situated at around 900 metres, Balakot is very beautiful. The surfaced road slithers out of the village following the Kunhar River through a valley with wide, terraced grain fields.

Information

The Tourist Information Centre is in the Tourist Lodge. The Tourism Officer here can arrange a jeep, particularly for a trip to Shogran.

Places to Stay & Eat

The *Youth Hostel* is on the right-hand side before you reach the Tourist Lodge and costs Rs 10 per bed. *Lalazar Hotel* is the next cheapest, only doubles for Rs 20. *Park Hotel* (tel 23), Kaghan Rd, has singles/doubles for Rs 70/105. The *PTDC Tourist Lodge* (tel 8), has rates from Rs 115 to Rs 175. *Seerab Hotel*, a newcomer, has competitive rates from Rs 15 up.

Getting Away

There are two buses daily to Naran at 6 am and 2 pm, there are also minibuses departing at almost the same time. It's five to six hours and costs Rs 16 to Rs 18. There is a bus service to Manshera for Rs 10, buses leave every hour but minibuses leave almost every ½ hour depending on the number of passengers, Rs 12. From Manshera buses to Rawalpindi are available, also to Beshum.

ROUTE TO NARAN

The bus speeds along the flat road for a while, before crawling up the steep mountain slopes. Squat mud and stone huts with flat roofs supported by heavy beams perch on narrow ledges with footpaths zig-zagging up the slopes.

In Kawai, 24 km away, a track turns left through a dense pine forest known as

Shogran – heavenly forest – up to a plateau 2400 metres high. At the edge of the meadow here are two rest houses which have a commanding view of the **Mussa-ka-Mussallah** – Praying mat of Moses – and **Malika Parbat**, which at 5290 metres is the highest peak in the Kaghan Valley.

Near Mahandri, 46 km away, the metal road peters out and becomes a dirt track, gravelly and rough in places, and basically just a jeep road used by trucks and buses to go to Naran. Approaching Kaghan, 14 km away, the valley gets very narrow. Kaghan, after which the whole region is named, is very small with a tiny bazaar lining one side of the main road. Snow begins to appear on the crests of mountains from now on and in several places there are greyish-black glaciers, virtually indistinguishable from the earth, which thaw in the summer heat and rain. They melt from below first, forming caves which eventually collapse. From Naran, where the sides of the mountains crowd in on the river, the road is jeepable only.

NARAN

The Naran Valley is 2400 metres above sea level, less than a km wide and only about five km long. Snow-crested mountains with slopes streaked with white glaciers border the valley. On both sides of the road and the Kunhar, the land is gently terraced and rises to wooded slopes. It is divided into two areas: the lower region where all the government administrative offices are located; while the bazaars, local hotels, restaurants, shops and the bus and cargo-jeep stations are on the elevated section. Clear blue streams cascade down the mountainside to join the Kunhar River. The valley is quiet, relaxed and has some of the loveliest scenery in Pakistan, but it is also very expensive. Primarily a trekking region, it is comparable with Nepal.

Information

The Tourist Information Centre is at the Tourist Camp site. If you want to hire a jeep for Saiful Muluk Lake this is the place to make enquiries. If you're trekking, bring camping gear and provisions. If you would like to try your hand at trout fishing in the Kunhar River, gear is available in the bazaar.

Places to Stay & Eat

The *Youth Hostel* is on the right side, three km before the village and costs Rs 15 per bed. The *rest house* has rooms for Rs 40 and local hotels have rooms for Rs 15 to Rs 25. There are also *muzzaffar khanas* which have charpois in the open for Rs 5.

The *PTDC Tourist Inn* has tents and huts or cabins with rates from Rs 120 to Rs 200 plus 15% surtax. The *Cottage Motel* is the most expensive and has rates from Rs 200 to Rs 1200.

The rest house has a kitchen available for cooking, but there are a few restaurants here with reasonable food for Rs 10 and up. The muzzaffar khanas are good value. Bring provisions and camping gear if you're going trekking.

Around Naran

Eight km to the east is **Lake Saiful Muluk**, which is about a km long and has midnight blue water afloat with ice during the winter. The lake is said to be inhabited by fairies and legend has it that Prince Saiful Muluk, a poet and philosopher, fell in love with one. It's a scenic spot surrounded by a carpet of flowers in spring and summer. The *rest house* here is very basic and it's preferable to camp if you have the equipment.

The village of Lalazar, 11 km north of the lake and at a slightly higher altitude, offers a magnificent view of Nanga Parbat. The area is covered with pines, hemlocks and spruce trees, and lots of flowers in spring and summer. There's a *rest house* here, and the village is also accessible via Batakundi.

Getting Away

There are two buses daily to Balakot. Departures are at 6 am and 2 pm, the fare is Rs 16 to Rs 18 and the trip takes six hours. You can hire jeeps from the PTDC Tourist Information Centre for around Rs 10 per mile plus Rs 200 per day, and Rs 5 per mile if empty on the return trip.

Cargo jeeps go over the Babusar Pass, but these are infrequent and irregular.

You can hire jeeps to Lake Saiful Muluk or horses are available for Rs 120 per day.

BEYOND NARAN

The Kaghan Valley, though less developed, is similar in topography to the Swat Valley. Both are terminated by the great mountains that form their border with the upper highland. In the Swat Valley there are trails that go over passes either into Dir, Chitral or Gilgit, while in the Kaghan Valley the trail has been turned into a jeepable track over the Babusar Pass into Chilas. On the road to Baghram, 65 km away from Manshera to the west and from Thakot to Beshum in the Swat Valley, the land becomes hilly and is girdled with low, green hills. In the monsoon it is remarkably like some places in East Africa.

BABUSAR PASS

This pass is 4067-metres high and closed for nearly nine months of the year. Officially it's open only from mid-July until the end of August, but it's already trekkable by late June. Late in July a few cargo jeeps, usually government supply vehicles, and some tourist Land Rovers cross over the pass into Chilas. Cargo jeeps are costly – even for a group of four – but the distance is trekkable. The route is gentle and easy going, but if you're tackling this trek in autumn, you will find that after you pass through Batakundi, most of the hamlets and villages are deserted as the majority of inhabitants have moved down to the plains. You may come across some Gujars in the process of moving their livestock down, but even the Afghan Kirghiz refugees who camp along the trail in summer have left by this time.

From the top of the pass it's a three-hour walk to the village of Babusar, which is also semi-deserted in autumn, but there are always a few people who remain. In the village there is a NAWO (Northern Area Works Organisation) *rest house* which has double rooms for Rs 60 or Rs 30 per person, and two more comfortable double rooms for Rs 90. There is also a *teashop*, which not only sells food but also has charpois for rent at Rs 5 a night. The latter is shut in autumn, and although the *rest house* is also closed then, the *chowkidar* will open it up for travellers. From Babusar you have a choice of walking to Chilas 18 km away or hiring a donkey for Rs 40 to get you there. You may catch a lift along the way on a tractor loaded with timber. It's a rough ride, but a lot quicker than walking. When you get to Chilas there are three *hotels* in the bazaar area, which have singles for Rs 10 and doubles for Rs 20. In summer you can get rooftop beds for Rs 5. There's also a *NAWO rest house* here with singles for Rs 30.

If you intend driving you'll have to make the trip in the six weeks or so from mid-July until the end of August. In autumn, when it's extremely beautiful, you can drive up to the top, but the pass itself is closed. However, the *only* vehicle able to negotiate the journey up and over the pass is a medium-sized Land Rover; it's not wide enough for a larger vehicle and only a four-wheel drive will make it. The way up is narrow with lots of hairpin bends. In places it is so narrow and so steep that jeeps have to back up three or four times to get around. There are two very difficult passages over glaciers where a winch is essential if you get into trouble, so make sure you bring one with you. It is advisable not to attempt this drive on a rainy day, or after it has been raining for a few days, as it gets very slippery and the

road slopes down the cliffside due to uncleared, minor landslides.

The alternative to either trekking or driving is to catch a PIA flight to Chilas, which has an airport, and take a bus from there to Gilgit. The not-so-pleasant alternative to trekking or flying can mean waiting for days – even up to a week – for cargo jeeps, tourist vans or Land Rovers. If you are not able to fly, trek or wait your only option is to retrace your steps to Manshera where you can pick up a bus for Beshum if you wish to travel up to the upper highland.

BESHUM

You can get to Beshum by bus or minibus in three to four hours from Manshera or Abbottabad. The route is scenic all the way up to the bridge where Aornos, believed to be the mountain where Alexander the Great relentlessly pursued native warriors, rises up above the Indus. Around here it is lush and green, but not much further on it becomes arid, rocky and almost barren.

Beshum is a little transit village now beginning to assume the features of a modern town and has the trappings of modern civilisation – petrol stations, cafes, restaurants, hotels, barbershops and bazaars. It is the junction for Swat Valley via the scenic Shangla Pass into Khwazakhela; Kaghan Valley via Manshera and Gilgit.

Places to Stay & Eat

There are still muzzaffar khanas here, but the cheap hotels are the *Azam Hotel* and the *Hazara Hotel* which have doubles only for Rs 20. The *International Hotel* has singles/doubles for Rs 40/60 as does the *Prince Hotel*, but the latter has better rooms, a pleasant atmosphere and a better restaurant. The *Government rest house* is a little out of town and has rooms for Rs 15.

Getting Away
There are buses and minibuses to Swat, Gilgit or Manshera.

They depart almost every hour. To Mingora is Rs 15 by minibus, to Gilgit Rs 60 and to Manshera Rs 15 by bus.

ROUTE TO GILGIT
Out of Beshum the Karakoram Highway stays on the western banks of the Indus, curling and meandering along, then slithering straight up, twisting again then sliding high above Pattan. It continues to corkscrew through rocky, narrow junctions of valleys until the sky opens out again. Across a bridge is **Camilla**, a tiny village worth a stopover for lunch or tea. Here the Karakoram Highway follows the eastern banks of the Indus, heads straight up, then twists through a rather barren valley.

Near where the Indus turns eastward is the village of Siazin, not visible from the highway. On both sides of the Indus from here are some extremely important archaeological sites. On the northern banks of the Indus are sites known as **Chilas I**, **Chilas II** and **Shatial Bridge**, which consist of rock carvings of animals and Buddhist stupas, engraved with ancient scripts, beginning with the primitive neolithic art style and the Bronze Age and progressing to the Gandhara period.

Sixteen km east and 10 km below Chilas, is **Huddar-gah**, another site. Numerous petroglyphs cover the cliffs from here up to Jaglot and down to the Alam bridge to the east, and the Kaghan Valley in Gilgit to the north. After crossing the bridge in Chilas the Karakoram Highway shifts back to the west banks of the Indus, leaving it near Alam bridge and continuing north to Hunza.

ROUTE TO SWAT VALLEY
It takes five to six hours by bus over the scenic, 2100-metre-high Shangla Pass from Beshum to Khwazakhela. The road is surfaced and starts climbing gradually before coming to a steep section and then again levels out and zig-zags gently upwards. The landscape here is brick-red, patched with green and the mountain slopes are generally terraced.

On the way down the scenery is the same until you reach the bottom of the valley where it starts to get dry, becoming green again near Khwazakhela, a busy intersection where the road splits north to Kalam and south towards Mingora.

SWAT VALLEY

Surrounded by towering hills it is a small state of large rocky tracts with only a little level ground here and there. Nature in all her bounty has blessed the Valley of Swat with a charm and verdure that rightly makes it a masterpiece of natural landscape ... (but) undisciplined and wilful life sinks man's morals to such a low depth that many a time his degeneration mars the natural beauty of his homeland as well.

Miangul Wadud Badshah Sahib, former ruler of Swat

Swat Valley, renowned for its scenic beauty, is also rich in archaeological relics. This was the apex of the triangular Gandhara region with its base running from the Peshawar Valley across the Indus to Taxila in the Punjab. Pottery, figurines and other artefacts which predate the Gandhara period have been discovered here and resemble Iranian finds from as far back as the 12th century BC.

In 327 BC Alexander of Macedon invaded this region, defeated the Hindu king, then continued on destroying guerrilla resistance by attacking the supposedly impregnable fortress at Ora or Aornos, now known as Udegram. Apparently, this was to teach them a lesson and convince other kingdoms along the way that capitulation was the best policy, a hint which Chandragupta of Taxila heeded.

Between 324 and 185 BC Buddhism spread widely throughout Swat and reached its peak during the Kushan era in the 2nd century AD. A great number of colleges and monasteries with innumerable stupas were built in the valley and a great quantity of Gandhara sculptural work was produced. It became – like Taxila – a sacred place for pilgrims from China and Tibet, the most famous being Xuan Zhang who, in the 7th century AD, recorded 1400 monasteries, with Ming Chili or Mingora having the largest. By this time the area was already in decline and much of it in ruins.

Following the successive invasions by barbarian hordes from the 5th century AD onward it fell into a 'dark age' from which it was never to emerge. Buddhism gave way to Hinduism which in turn fell to the onslaught of Islam in the 10th century and the whole region lapsed into barbarism. Babar unsuccessfully attempted to subjugate it, and the Sikhs who succeeded Babar, only managed to exert a tenuous hold on the land. It was with the British that peace was finally restored. As a reward for his co-operation the Akhund of Swat was given the upper half of the valley, Kohistan, for his administration. It remained an autonomous political agency right through until 28 July 1969.

Lower Swat begins from the district of Buner on the border of Mardan to the south and spreads north to Bahrain. Kohistan starts from the outskirts of Bahrain and continues up and beyond Kalam. The valley has an elevation from 1000 to 5000 metres and is generally scenic, green and fertile, stepped with terraces, rivers and snow-clad mountains. The climate here is pleasant, neither too hot in summer, nor too cold in winter.

Archaeological Route

South of Mingora the Karakar Pass, 1400 metres high, has a panoramic view of the Buner Valley where Emperor Akbar lost most of his 8000 troops. He had his revenge when he lured the Swatis down into the plains and routed them, but he didn't follow up his ambition to conquer the Swat region.

Mt Ilam, one of the highest mountains in Swat, was considered to be the seat of tribal deities in prehistoric times. The huge block-shaped rocks are believed to be tribal altars. South of Mt Ilam is Gumbat which has a Buddhist shrine and to the north in Shingardar is a Buddhist stupa. Two km further along is a rock carving of the Buddha.

Another archaeological site is the Gogdara area. There is a cave in this region which has rock carvings – most likely Aryan in origin – of two-wheeled chariots, dogs, horses, ibex, leopards, oxen and other animals. Higher up are some Buddhist carvings.

Along the Chakdara-Swat Rd are archaeological sites of the Gandhara period. At Haibatgram, eight km from Chakdara, are the ruins of a Buddhist monastery and a stupa. Seven km past Landaki in Nimogran is another Buddhist site and to the north of Birkhot Hill is Bazira, which in ancient times was sacked by Alexander the Great. The fortress at Bazira encloses a large, flat area and locals sell coins, arrowheads and statues to anyone who'll buy them.

Between Mingora and Saidu Sharif is Butkhara, an archaeological site with Buddhist ruins, considered in ancient times to be a shrine. From Mingora there is a side road which follows the Jambil River to the east. This valley is also dotted with Buddhist ruins and rock carvings. Panir is another Buddhist site, but at Butkhara II, Loeban and Matelai, 475 Aryan graves have been discovered. Towards the airport, the town of Aligrama is believed to have been an Aryan settlement around 1000 BC.

Bahrain is the furthest Buddhism penetrated in Swat, but there are very few relics left now. If you feel like a strenuous climb from Jahanabad Village up to Manglaur you will find a rock carving of a seated Buddha there.

MINGORA & SAIDU SHARIF

Like Islamabad and Rawalpindi, these are twin towns, but on a mini-scale. The more modern, Mingora is 1030 metres above sea level, and is a largish town with paved streets, rows of bazaars and shops and facilities such as banks, hotels, restaurants and an airport. Like Quetta it doesn't have any beautiful Moghul architecture, nor any imposing British structures. It is the commercial and business centre which extends to Saidu Sharif, the more traditional of the two, which is the administrative and educational centre of Swat. In Saidu Sharif is the palace of the former ruler. Between Mingora and Saidu Sharif is a museum, which has displays of the Gandhara culture. Just before the museum on the left is the road to Butkhara, which was once the site of several prehistoric, protohistoric and historic cultures. It's a quiet town which is slowly but surely developing.

Information

The Tourist Information Centre is in the Serena Lodge on Saidu Sharif Rd. The post office is on – surprise, surprise – Post Office Rd and the Pakistan National Bank is on the Main Bazaar Rd. The Gemstone Corporation of Pakistan, which deals in emeralds, is three km out of town on the way to Khwazakhela. There is a hunting season in this region which extends from mid-October to mid-March.

Things to Buy

The Swat Valley is a great place to buy handicrafts. It is famous for very fine and excellently designed embroidery work, for cut and uncut semi-precious and precious stones – particularly for emeralds – and mediaeval or village folk art, usually carved wooden furniture. It is also noted for old weapons – swords, shields and bows and arrows – heavy metal jewellery and replicas of archaeological artefacts.

Places to Stay & Eat

Cheapies and muzzaffar khanas do not accept foreigners. Medium class hotels are primarily on New Rd and Saidu Sharif Rd.

On Saidu Sharif Rd the *Park Hotel & Restaurant* is fairly clean and has rooms with fans and attached bathrooms for Rs 40 a single and up. The *Holiday Hotel* has the same rates and is recommended for its quiet atmosphere and friendly manager.

On New Rd the *Prince Hotel*, *Mehran Hotel* and *Rainbow Hotel* are all of a similar standard and price range.

The *Abasin Hotel* on Madian Rd and the *Meezan Hotel* on GT Rd are cheaper with rates from Rs 25 single, Rs 35 double.

The *Pamir Hotel* is a three-star hotel and has rooms for Rs 140 up to Rs 350. The *Serena Lodge* is a relic from the British era and has comfortable old-style rooms for Rs 180 to Rs 450.

About 16 km from Saidu Sharif is the *Marghazar Palace Hotel*. This white marble palace was once the residence of the former ruler of Swat and is now a four-star hotel with rates from Rs 140 to Rs 260. Even if you don't stay there it is worth a visit.

There aren't many eating places in Mingora except around the bus stations, where they serve mainly snacks. However, most of the hotels have restaurants with western-style breakfasts and mostly local meals except for the Serena Lodge and the Pamir and Maghazar hotels, where they serve Chinese and western food as well as local dishes.

Getting Around

With the arrival of Suzuki miniwagons, the tongas and auto-rickshaws have all but disappeared. Miniwagons ply between Mingora and Saidu Sharif, but in any case the town is small enough to reach most points of interest on foot.

Getting Away

Mingora has two bus stations: the General Bus Station on Grand Trunk Rd for points south like Mardan, Peshawar

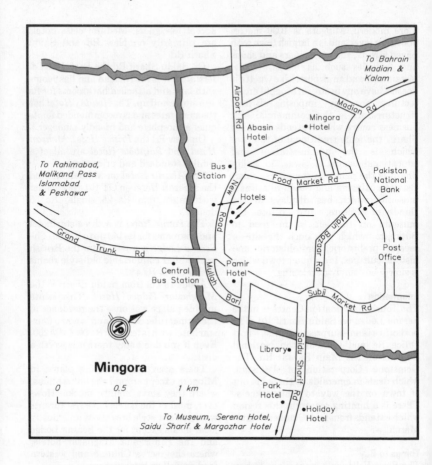

Mingora

To Bahrain
Madian &
Kalam

Airport Rd

Madian Rd

Mingora
Hotel

Abasin
Hotel

To Rahimabad,
Malikand Pass
Islamabad
& Peshawar

Bus
Station

New Road

Food Market Rd

Pakistan
National
Bank

Hotels

Grand Trunk Rd

Central
Bus Station

Mullah Bari

Pamir
Hotel

Main Bazar Rd

Post
Office

Subji Market Rd

Saidu Sharif Rd

Library

Park
Hotel

Holiday
Hotel

0   0.5   1 km

To Museum, Serena Hotel,
Saidu Sharif & Margozhar Hotel

and Rawalpindi as well as minibuses for Upper Swat; and another on New Rd, which is also primarily for transport to Upper Swat. The minibuses are more expensive but faster and cleaner than the buses from New Rd, which are filthy and take ages to get going. They also have long stops at villages en route. Mingora-Madian-Bahrain-Kalam costs Rs 8 by bus, and Rs 10 by minibus.

To Peshawar is Rs 15 by bus, Rs 25 by minibus. To Rawalpindi is Rs 25 by bus and Rs 40 by minibus.

UPPER SWAT

As you continue along the Swat River the valley narrows and the terraced grain-fields disappear and there's nothing to see but the granite walls of mountains and thickly wooded stands of large trees. The road is not particularly rough and you can still see traces of former attempts to seal it. The women in this area are generally not in purdah, but in buses they prefer to travel at the rear while the men go up front.

Upper Swat was previously known as

Kohistan. There are numerous different tribes in this region including the peoples of Utrot, Ushu and Kalam who are Bushkaris, and the Torwalis who live further south. The latter are adept in the use of slings.

The Bushkaris had no forts, but their villages were made in a peculiar fashion for security and defence. Usually built on steep hillsides in succession, one above the other, the buildings had flat rooftops built on the same level as the floor of the one above it, and the whole being interconnected by an outer wall. Inside the villages are a maze of passages, through which runs a stream. All the early houses were made of wood and any built outside the enclosed village were built without parapets – probably for protection.

The Bushkaris and Torwalis hold a similar belief to the ancient Persians and the Minoans of Crete – that the world rests on the horns of a cow, which causes earthquakes when it shakes its head from time to time at the sins of the inhabitants. They still believe in fairies who supposedly confer the power of prophecy on certain mortals, a theory which is also held in the upper northern highland.

In mediaeval times this region was known as the Land of Fugitives. In spring and early summer, Gujar nomads trudge north, loaded with pots and pans, herds of cattle, sheep, goats, chickens, dogs and horses. Children share the horses with the chickens, while the women tote large baskets on their heads and carry their babies in their arms. They dress in flamboyant printed fabrics; wear heavy, metal jewellery and are of sturdy build and ample proportions.

Along the way, a road forks off west to Kabal, where there is an 18-hole golf course at 870 metres which is open all year round. Further on another road cuts east to Malam Jaba, 2600 metres above sea level. The Austrian government had agreed to assist in setting up a ski resort here, but the rather grandiose scheme was abandoned recently, and Malam Jaba is now being turned into a hill station for tourists, diplomats and vacationing government officials. Experts considered that it was not only too small for a ski resort, but that the mountain was not high enough, nor was there enough snow to make it really viable.

The first town of importance is Khwazakhela, 26 km away, a busy, smallish intersection. If you want to stop off at Khwazakhela for a night, go and see Siraj Ahmad at Ajar Tajor & Co about his guest room. Check out the rural folk art of Swat Valley in the shop while you're there. From Khwazakhela there is a road to Beshum, a small village to the east. The main road continues to Madian 26 km away, but before reaching the latter there is another road branching east to Miandam, 10 km off the main road. At 1800 metres, Miandam is another scenic, little village. The *PTDC Motel* here costs Rs 100 a single and Rs 160 a double. Other hotels like the *Miandam Hotel* are more expensive with rates from Rs 120 to Rs 200. If you have the gear you can camp here. This is considered the most beautiful valley in Swat. There are some superb hikes up the mountains and along the stream here.

MADIAN

The valley becomes slightly claustrophobic at Madian, but it's very picturesque. At an elevation of 1320 metres, Madian is a popular town, both because of its beauty and the variety of accommodation available in the valley, along the streams, on slopes and ridges and high up into the mountains. Be careful to boil or purify drinking water from here to Bahrain and Kalam, or you could find yourself in trouble.

Places to Stay & Eat

Summer Hill Hotel is rather rundown, but still reasonably clean and has singles/doubles for Rs 15/20 with share bathrooms. *Hunza Inn*, on the banks of Swat

River, and *Hotel Insof* are similarly priced. *Muambakhan Food Shop & House Rentals* has rooms and huts for Rs 15 per person and is on the left-hand side going north on the main bazaar street.

The *Parkway Hotel* has singles/doubles for Rs 25/40 (Rs 15/30 in the off season). The *Shalimar Hotel* charges Rs 40/60 (off season Rs 20/40).

The *Mountain View Hotel* (tel 7) and The *Madian Hotel* (tel 34) are the places for a splurge and cost Rs 120 to Rs 270.

BAHRAIN

Only 10 km away at 1400 metres Bahrain is more developed, but not as attractive. From here the road is rougher and starts to climb steeply. The bare mountains close in on the road, which drops away precipitously to the river. This is still an interesting area for explorers, who could stumble on important archaeological finds. Thirteen km out of Bahrain and about three km before Madian, there's a trail that cuts off to the left then loops north to Jahanabad. High up on a cliff here, is a rock carving of the Buddha. It will take you about half an hour to climb up to see it.

Beyond Bahrain is Kohistan where the Pushto tribe gives way to the Torwalis and Bushkaris.

Places to Stay & Eat

Medium-class *hotels* here are more expensive than in Madian. The *Paris Hotel* on the banks of the Swat River is probably the best cheapie with dorm beds for Rs 15 and singles/doubles for Rs 20/25 with share bathrooms. It's pleasantly quiet with the sound of the river cascading below. The *Darol Hotel* is similarly priced.

The *Bahrain Hotel* (tel 33) and the *Five Star Hotel* have rates from Rs 60 to Rs 100 (off season Rs 30 to Rs 60). The *Abzhar Hotel* (tel 22) has rates from Rs 100 (half price in the off season). The *Deluxe Hotel* in the centre of town has much higher rates.

KALAM

The road levels off as the valley widens close to Kalam, 26 km from Bahrain. Kalam is at 2100 metres and is designed in two sections. The higher one consists of administrative offices and the police station and has more expensive accommodation. It slopes down gradually, terminating in a sharp drop to the main roadway and river.

Upper Swat or Kohistan belongs culturally to the northern region as the architecture of the old mosque and the carvings of wooden pillars, window frames and door jambs indicate. Although there is no road from here to Chitral or Gilgit, the upper northern cultural influence must have filtered in along the foot trails. This region is the boundary marking cultural changes from south to north.

Kalam has a tranquil air and a pleasant climate during the day, though nights tend to be cold. On a clear day you can see the 5918-metre-high Mt Falaksher from the upper section of the town. In the north-east of the valley its snow-clad upper slopes and peak rise above dense, lush forests. The river rushes through the town, right across from the old mosque.

Information

The Tourist Information Centre is in the Tourist Lodge.

Places to Stay

The *Khaled Hotel & Restaurant*, on the main road in front of the bus stop is the cheapest place in town with singles/doubles for Rs 25/40. Further up is the *Heaven Breeze Hotel* which has rooms with attached bathrooms for Rs 75/150. It's clean, quiet and has good food. The PTDC has a *Tourist Lodge* and several cabins for Rs 100 to Rs 140 plus tax. It has a mega-modern dining hall on the upper slope and a large lawn where camping is free. *Falaksher Hotel* and others up here are fairly expensive. Across the river are some nondescript hotels which are pricier than the Khaled.

BEYOND UPPER SWAT

Beyond Kalam where the Swat River splits, the road also forks, west to Utrot at 2225 metres and east to Ushu. To the north-west in the valley of Utrot is Gabral Valley which is excellent for fishing, while to the north-east is the valley of Ushu, which at 2286 metres also has great fishing streams. On the way up to Ushu there is a magnificent view of Mt Falaksher.

Trekking trails start from here to Dir, Chitral and Gilgit, but they're not recommended by the police and other authorities unless you're accompanied by a guide. See section on Trekking. There are regular bus services to these villages, which depart at 8 am and 2 pm. There are hotels here, but many still lack facilities. However, it's quite safe to rough it out here. Unless you're on a guided trek this is a dead end and you have no alternative except to retrace your steps, either to Khwazakhela or Mingora.

Getting Away

From Khwazakhela you can continue on to Gilgit or to the Kaghan Valley via Beshum. The way to Beshum goes over Shangla Pass, where there is a government rest house. At Alpurai there are a few local hotels.

To Kaghan Valley Buses leave Beshum almost every hour. There are minibuses and miniwagons plying between Beshum and Thakot, Batagram and Manshera. From the Kaghan Valley you can retrace your steps back to Balakot where buses and minibuses are available for Muzzaffarabad.

To Gilgit Buses depart Beshum every four hours. NATCO, the Northern Area Transport Company, have buses to Gilgit for Rs 60. There is a 50% discount for students on normal bus fares.

To Chitral & Peshawar From the General Bus Station, buses and minibuses depart almost every hour for Rawalpindi and Peshawar. If en route to Chitral, catch the bus to Chakdara where buses for Dir await the arrival of the Peshawar bus.

ROUTE TO DIR

Bajaur is still tribal and requires a permit to visit the area. It is still traditional and thus extremely interesting. One of the main towns here is Dir, a transit place, which used to be a stopover on the ancient Silk Trade Route that went through Bajaur over Nama Pass into Afghanistan and from there down to Central Asia and China.

In Chakdara, on the way to Dir, there is a fort known as **Churchill's Pique**, just after the bridge. The British dragged their heavy weaponry from here and marched into Chitral to quell the rebellion in 1885. Scattered in the surrounding area are archaeological sites of Aryan settlements along with their graveyards and Buddhist monasteries, stupas and rock carvings. One km after the bridge on the road to Dir is a footpath which runs west for about 1½ km to **Chat Pat**, another Buddhist site. Almost nothing is left here now.

On the north side of Damkat Hill are the ruins of a Buddhist monastery, and at the foot of it are rock carvings of the Gandhara period. Nine km further on there is a track that leads west to Talash Valley, which has the ruins of yet another Buddhist monastery and what's left of a stupa. At the extreme end is **Kat Kala Pass** which was used by Alexander the Great to enter the region. There's an old Hindu fort here.

Forty km further on is **Timargarha**, the site of more Aryan graves, made from elaborate stone slabs. **Ralambat** is another interesting place, once the site of Aryan settlements and later of the Achaemenians, Buddhists and Hindus. Houses excavated here have fire altars.

The paved road – segments of it have been washed away by flash floods – moves up gradually into rolling landscape with camps of Afghan refugees close to the foothills. It is only as you approach Dir that the mountains begin to tower over the road.

Dir

As a transit point, Dir is the administrative centre of the whole valley. It has a number of government buildings, schools and shops. Though still evolving, it has an atmosphere of never having quite made it into a major town. In this region the harvest and fruit season arrives earlier than it does in the upper north. This is timber country and as the road makes its way up to the 3075-metre-high Lowari Pass, the edges of the road are stacked high with wood.

Places to Stay & Eat

Dir is a pleasant, scenic spot for an overnight stay. It is also reasonably inexpensive with medium-class hotels near and around the bus station. Rooms are usually Rs 15 to Rs 25.

The *Al Hayat Hotel*, at the extreme end of the town near the bridge, is a nice place to rest and relax, but rather far away from transport if you're leaving for Swat, Peshawar or Chitral early in the morning. Local food here is similar to Afghan food with *nan* and the usual stewed mutton or beef in a tomato sauce.

Meals are always served with tea. You can also buy fresh fruit in the bazaar.

Getting Away

There are GTS buses, private buses and minibuses departing almost every hour to Swat, Chakdara and direct to Peshawar. The route to Chitral is plied mainly by cargo jeeps though some miniwagons do the trip. Bus fares are:

	Buses	Minibuses
Peshawar	Rs 22	Rs 25
Chakdara	Rs 12	Rs 15
Chitral	Rs 75 for cargo jeeps	

In early June, they cut glaciers in two or three places to open the Lowari Pass. The road is paved now but landslides can still block the road on occasions. The ascent is steep and twisting and affords fine views of the woods, streams and snowcapped mountains. Once over the pass, the descent is very steep down into the Valley of Chitral. In summer it can look like the freeways of Paris or London with waiting trucks, jeeps and cars jammed to a standstill, particularly if the pass is blocked by a landslide or a truck gets bogged.

Top: Lake Saiful Muluk, Kaghan Valley (PTDC)
Left: Chitrali man (PTDC)
Right: Chitrali woman (PTDC)

Top: K2, Pakistan's highest mountain and the second highest in the world (PTDC)
Left: Swat valley (PE)
Right: Buddha rock engraving, Kargah Valley, Gilgit (PTDC)

Gilgit –   Sust – china   200 rupees
9.00 am depart.

Upper Northern Territory

50 rps /day.

Where the forest belt ends the topography is radically transformed into granite mountains – bare of any vegetation – and jagged spurs that rise above fine dust and sand.

The landscape appears to be interminably crumpled, pockmarked with vast expanses of rocky deserts at 5500 to 6000 metres in the north, and desert steppes with scrub and tussocks of coarse grass in the middle regions which lie between 4500 and 6000 metres. It is characterised by escarpments, gorges, ravines, moraines and lakes, and crisscrossed by innumerable streams and rivers.

Up here the climate undergoes extremes in temperature, being dry-hot in summer and dry-cold in winter. The heat in the lower, arid regions becomes as intensely hot as quickly as it can become cold when clouds or the mountains shade the sun. In summer the temperature can vary from 35°C at 1500 metres to freezing at higher altitudes. It can also drop sharply with the slightest rainfall.

Up in the highest reaches of the mountains some of the rarest wildlife in the world exists: the markhor, urial, Marco Polo sheep and snow leopard. In the lower regions at around 2500 to 3000 metres there are prairie-like steppes where yaks are common and the abundant birdlife includes the crested hoopoe, hawks, falcons and eagles. The ground is covered with desert-like plants and there are forests of pines, firs, spruce, Himalayan cedars, willows and poplars.

The whole region is surrounded by great mountain ranges and is right in the vortex of the Hindu Kush in the west and north-west, the Karakorams to the north and north-east which cover 75% of the entire region, and the Great Himalayan Range to the south-east. These mountain ranges form a natural barrier to the summer monsoon causing rains to fall on the plains and the sub-northern area. They also protect the plains from icy, winter winds from Central Asia and Siberia. This is where some of the highest peaks in the world exist along with a few of the largest glaciers outside the polar regions. And running right across the territory, from Tibet through Ladakh, the mighty Indus flows westward, before veering sharply to the southern lowland, down and then out into the Arabian Sea.

The rugged gorges, often bare and narrow, sometimes give way to valleys or settlements of mud-stone huts that somehow exist in regions that seem too barren, bleak and desolate or too isolated and remote for human habitation. With its savage climate and primaeval quality, it must have been too desolate for human habitation for many centuries. But there is evidence of settlements of neolithic tribes that studied the stars and their movement.

Snowbound and sealed for nine months of the year, it was really only accessible in high summer. Astounding though it is, through this extremely inhospitable region routes were cut right down into the gentler lowland of the Indus Plains. These routes were not mere trails for migratory tribes but trade ways, predating the ancient Silk Trade Routes by at least a couple of millennia. It was from them that the Silk Trade Route finally evolved.

The major arterial road began at the foothills of the sub-northern region through Taxila and the Swat Valley, and continued up along the Indus through Gilgit and the valley of Hunza to the 5000-metre-high Mintaka Pass into Kashgar and Turkestan. Minor veins branched out in nearly all directions. This important section of the ancient Silk

Trade Route, along with the trails from Chilas to Passu and the Mintaka Pass, and those east to Satpara Valley and the Valley of Khapulu, and west through the valley of Punial and Gakutch and Yasin into Chitral, are all archaeological routes.

Rock carvings, calligraphy and engraved scripts – in historical sequence – and done in various art forms and styles, complement the written history of the different people and their cultures over a span of five millennia or more.

In the upper northern highland the important archaeological sites begin in the region of Chilas, which has numerous rock carvings and inscriptions dating back to the Achaemenian period (6th century BC), the Parthian (2nd century BC) and the Gandhara (2nd century AD). There are also some rock carvings dating to the Bronze Age. Here the art styles range from the ithyphallic, bi-triangular animal art form to the sophisticated style of the Gandhara culture. There are also Buddhist stupas and inscriptions from the first half of the 1st millennium AD.

It is a unique, natural art gallery which serves to throw light on the lifestyles of many different peoples – prehistoric, protohistoric and historic people. The only other places in any way similar, are the hills of the Bushmen in the Kalahari Desert or the cave-dwelling artists of Altamira in Spain.

There are some traces of pastoral, migratory Aryans passing this way; and the engraved Old Chinese script in western Turkestan records the passage of the Sakas who, it seems, could have settled in the Trans-Himalayas. It is possible that they became Hindus since Hinduism was replaced by Zoroastrianism, which in turn was replaced by Greek paganism. This is likely to have been spread by the settled communities in the sub-northern region who sought refuge up here. Later still, Buddhism held sway in this region, dominating the culture for a little under two millennia before being supplanted by Islam.

This upper highland emerges in history along with the Patola dynasty (4th to 8th century AD), but it is more than likely that the Patola dynasty was propped up by the Persian Sassanians in order not only to rule Bolor, but also to guard the Tarim Basin, an important crossroads of the ancient Silk Trade Route, through which Buddhism and the Gandhara culture were diffused to influence the religion, art and culture of Turkestan and Tibet.

The population was mostly Caucasian until the Chinese arrived in the middle of the 8th century AD after being booted out by the Tibetans in the 9th century AD, when racial stocks became mixed. When the Patola dynasty of Bolor disappeared it was replaced by the Empire of Dardistan, which also eventually fragmented.

By the 10th century Islam was already established in Chitral and was gradually spreading eastward. In the 16th century it spread from Kashmir and moved westward, and at about the same time, it moved in from Moghulistan in the north. The entire region became Islamic, but it comprised three different Muslim religious sects: the Shi'ites, Maulais or Ismailis, and the Sunnis. With the arrival of Islam, mirdoms evolved, and the kingdoms which emerged – largely because of religious differences – were always at war with one another until the arrival of the British.

Pax Britannica was established mainly because of Russia's expansion eastward, as it was considered likely that the Russian would carve out a share of the Indian subcontinent. The British consolidated the region, turning the more important mirdoms into political agencies, and establishing administrative centres and military cantonments in the area. They improved the trails and bridged rivers and gorges previously spanned by single-rope bridges. For the first time this region was explored, surveyed and methodically mapped.

It came under the direct administration of Kashmir, with the exception of Chitral which became part of the North West Frontier Province. In 1948 Gilgit and Baltistan booted out the Kashmiris and joined Pakistan. Geopolitics here have changed, but geographically it is still a strategic and sensitive area as the hump of the Pamirs is also the junction of Russia, China, Afghanistan and Pakistan.

Today this upper highland is developing at a fairly fast pace. The administrative centres of Chitral, Gilgit and Skardu have power supplied by numerous hydroelectric schemes, an improved road network and an air link with the south – most of the infrastructure of modern cities. The Karakoram Highway took nearly two decades to build with the assistance of the People's Republic of China. It roughly follows the old Silk Trade arterial route through this region. It is the lifeline to the south. But despite all these modern trappings, it is a wild, primitive land, still subject to the whims and vagaries of nature.

Cultural Orientation
You enter an entirely different world here. The population is generally a mixture of Caucasian and Mongoloid racial stocks, similar to those in Tajikistan, Xinjiang and central Asia. They are heterogeneous in culture, speech and religion, but superficially homogeneous in economic and social matters – this includes a universal belief in fairies and a liking for salted tea.

Traditionally they are endogamous – that is they forbid marriage outside their own group – and as a consequence they are inbred.

However, life is not harmonious. Conflict is no longer just religious, but is now beginning to manifest itself in political and cultural rivalry, which flares up occasionally in shooting and rock-throwing incidents.

Generally, life in this region is rough and basic, demanding not merely physical fitness, but a 'personal quality' from travellers to enable them to face difficult situations and circumstances.

It is a conservative, tradition-bound society, so the rule 'when in Rome' applies very strictly here.

Economy
The economy is mainly agrarian and 75% of food requirements are produced locally. The main exports are fruit and herbal plants to the south in the Indus plains and to the north in Xinjiang in China, where barter trade is conducted through the Khunjerab Pass. However, the main source of income is tourism.

Tourist Season
This extends from spring through summer, that is mid-February to mid-October, particularly for mountaineering, trekking and rafting expeditions. The best time is between August and October. Summer and autumn are the fruit and fishing seasons, but swimming in the rivers is forbidden – it's very dangerous as the water is running high and fast then. Summer fruits include apples, apricots, mulberries, walnuts, peaches and grapes, while in early autumn pears are abundant.

Restrictions & Permits There are restricted areas where permits are required from the Ministry of Home Affairs in Islamabad. These are mostly required for mountaineering, trekking and rafting groups, and also for anglers.

Expired visas cannot be extended up here. The commissioner and the police superintendent can only give permits to stay in the area for a period of seven days.

Information
There are Tourist Information Centres in every major town, along with hospitals, libraries, fisheries offices, polo grounds, tourist curio shops and bazaars.

Banks The Pakistan National Bank in Skardu and Gilgit deals exclusively with foreign currency and travellers' cheques, but only in pounds sterling or US dollars. Rates offered are usually less than bank rates in the lowland. With the possible exception of banks in Chitral, you would probably lose about 10% in exchange. So be sure to take enough rupees with you to last your visit.

Mail Postal services are still not reliable, particularly for parcel post. To put it bluntly they're erratic.

Telephone & Telegrams Domestic and international calls are okay, except that you are likely to end up shouting to be heard. Telegrams arrive, but they're often mislaid or not handed over.

Things to Do
Mountain Climbing/Trekking/Rafting This is no mere back-to-nature area, but a back-to-the-wilderness region. It's an explorer's, trekker's and rafting enthusiast's playground. See the Trekking chapter for details.

Northern Territory Jeep Tour Jeep tours of the Northern Mountain Zone are arranged by tour and travel agencies in Islamabad, particularly by *Karakoram Tours*.

These jeep tours cover the sub-northern area of Kaghan, Azad Kashmir & Jammu and the Swat Valley; or the upper northern region of Hunza, Gilgit, Gojal, Nagar, Naltar, Yasin, Ishkoman, Ghizer and the valley of Chitral. They usually last for two to three weeks or more.

Fishing The streams and rivers of the Northern Territory are well known for trout fishing. Trout – the best sport fish – was introduced at the turn of the century and snow, brown and rainbow trout are all found here.

Fishing licences must be obtained from the Bureau of Fisheries in Gilgit, Gupis, Astore, Skardu, Khapulu or Chitral. For foreigners it is US$2 or Rs 32 per day, US$12 per week, US$40 per month. Rules and regulations are printed in the licence. Fish less than 22 cm in length must be put back in the water. Check if you can fish on Fridays in any area. Apparently there are fishing wardens who are very particular about observing Friday as a day of rest.

Rods, tackles, flies, etc are all obtainable from fisheries offices as is information on good fishing spots. Equipment is also available for hire or purchase in the bazaars and is often of better quality.

Entertainment There are cinemas in Gilgit, Skardu and Chitral which mostly screen local and Indian films, and the occasional western movie. There are polo tournaments in the month of June, August and November, and in Chitral and Gilgit they put on *buzhkasi* tournaments, a game that involves top-speed riding carrying the headless body of a goat from one end of a large playing ground to the other and back again without losing it to opponents or dropping it. This rather gory game was re-introduced by the Kirghiz Afghan refugees.

Things to Buy
The local handicraft industry isn't as developed as it is in lowland Pakistan, and consists largely of woollen rugs called *namda*, long stockings with geometrical designs and woollen Chitrali, Gilgiti or Balti caps. You can also buy various antiques – mostly weapons – including Mongol bows, Russian matchlocks and slim curving swords dating back to Ivan the Terrible. Also available is an assortment of folk jewellery, but they no longer manufacture musical instruments.

Places to Stay & Eat
There are 1st class, middle level and bottom range hotels and restaurants, as well as travellers' inns. But if you've got camping gear, bring it with you. It's also advisable to bring some supplementary food.

Getting There

Air PIA has two to three flights daily to all major centres in the Upper Northern Territory.

Flights are dependent on weather conditions: the most certain and regular times being from September into October.

There are no concessions on flights here: fares are already subsidised by the government.

Road NATCO and other bus lines offers four bus services daily between Islamabad and Gilgit. There are also buses and minibuses from Peshawar to Dir and cargo jeeps from Dir to Chitral.

The Karakoram Highway which links Islamabad with Gilgit is open all year round. However, the Chitral route over the Lowari Pass is only open from early June till mid-October. After this the only way to get to Chitral is by air and flights are often fully booked for two weeks ahead.

The Karakoram Highway, built with the assistance of the Chinese, is surfaced from Islamabad up to the Khunjerab Pass. The Gilgit-Skardu road is now surfaced as is the Dir-Chitral route. However, the Gilgit-Chitral road is not sealed and after Teru there are only tracks to Chitral, through some of the most hair-raising mountain roadways in the world. The rest of the roads are bumpy, potholed and 'hairy' in places zig-zagging steeply up the sides of sheer granite walls, across swaying suspension bridges, and suddenly disappearing around acute, narrow corners. Often in spring roads are blocked by landslides which can take a couple of days to clear away.

Getting Around

NATCO has buses linking Gilgit, Skardu and Hunza. There are other buses and minibuses, and occasionally, cargo-jeeps to Chitral and other minor towns and villages. There are also ponies and donkeys for hire, along with their owners who act as guides.

Getting Away

To Afghanistan The borders with Afghanistan are closed and there are police check points along them.

To India There is still no trekking access through the ceasefire line, which is guarded by volunteer UNO observers.

To China The border through the Khunjerab Pass, over 5000 metres high, opened on 1 May 1986. NATCO and PTDC buses and land cruisers ply between Sust and Pirali in Xinjiang, just across the Khunjerab Pass. One way fare is Rs 160 by minibus, more by PTDC land cruisers.

BALTISTAN

Baltistan, 26,000 square km in area, is right below the serrated, jagged and glaciated ramparts of the Karakorams. Once part of Ladakh, it was known as Tibet-i-Khurd – Little Tibet.

Archaeological exploration has proven that it was encompassed by the Silk Trade Route. Rock carvings have been discovered along the road between Gol and Khapulu, and Skardu and Satpara Lake. The trade routes here split in Skardu with one leading to Satpara over the Deosai and Burzil Pass (5000 metres high) into Kashmir and another leading to Gol. At Gol it forks again with one trail leading to Khapulu, the other to Kharmang into Leh.

Between the 9th and 16th centuries it belonged to Tibet, being part of Ladakh until conquered by Muslim Shi'ites from Kashmir, who introduced Islam here. The story goes that one of the more daring rulers pillaged the fringes of Kashmir and married a Moghul princess called Gul Bibi. While her husband was away conquering the northern area, Gul Bibi built a superb garden with an aqueduct. So jealous was her husband of her achievement and so warped his mind that he condemned her to death. But the story does have a happy ending, for ultimately she was reprieved and her engineering skills were eventually acclaimed.

Baltistan consists of five valleys: Shigar, Skardu, Rondu, Khapulu and Kharmang. The most interesting are the valleys of Shigar and Khapulu with Rondu and Kharmang being the most isolated. The whole region is the most important mountaineering and trekking area in the Upper Northern Territory. It is here where K2, the second highest in the world, and Siachen, the largest glacier in this part of the globe, are to be found. It is also the gateway of the mighty Indus River.

Until recently with the exception of Hunza, Baltistan was the most isolated region of the upper highland. There used to be three overland routes into the region. The first via Muzzaffarabad through Smaro, Khel, the Shuntar Pass (4200 metres), over the Deosai Plateau into Satpara. This route is closed to foreigners. The second route is through the Kaghan Valley over the Babusar Pass (4067 metres) through Astore, the Deosai Plateau and past Katchura Lake. The third route via the Karakoram Highway through Beshum into Skardu is longer. This route is now traversable by truck.

This region would still be cut off were it not for its air link with Rawalpindi. Weather permitting, PIA has two, occasionally three, flights daily to Skardu with Fokker-27s. Although flights are uncertain and liable to be cancelled even as they approach Skardu, they still remain the best way of getting into Baltistan.

It's a spectacular flight, turning eastward towards Islamabad from Rawalpindi, skirting the Marghalla Hills, then climbing north-east. The little plane gets close to the immense mass of Nanga Parbat (8125 metres) which broods over the surrounding mountains, many of them rising higher than the F-27's flight altitude. Finally in a canyon

where the Indus flows westward, it descends into a rather arid, sandy area.

SKARDU

Skardu is the principal town of Baltistan. It is a dry, dusty little place on the banks of the Indus with the **Rock of Skardu**, on which is perched the fort, **Karpochu**, towering above the main street. This is lined with low-roofed structures and wooden box stalls which make up the bazaar area. Princess Gul Bibi's aqueduct is long gone, replaced by a drab-looking concrete structure.

Beyond it, the main road continues. On the left side is the polo ground and right at the foot of the Rock of Skardu, by the banks of the Indus, is a little village. Nearby it is possible to camp. Further down on the the left are the PTDC K2 Motel and a government rest house. Where the road to Satpara veers away to the right are government offices including the Pakistan National Bank, another rest house and the police station. The road continues on to Khapulu and Shigar.

Skardu is 2300 metres above sea level and has a pleasant climate. However, a blustery wind can rise up in spring and summer, stirring up the dust and blowing until evening. Of the three administrative centres in the Upper Northern Territory it is the least developed, but it is now changing at a faster rate than either of the others.

There is a continuous flow of mountaineering and trekking expeditions here from spring through summer until early autumn, but mountaineers and trekkers do not seem to hang around long. Most rush through to the mountains and on return get away quickly.

Information

The Tourist Information Centre is at the K2 Motel (tel 104). The PIA office is on New Bazaar St, as are the banks, post office and telegraph & telephone office.

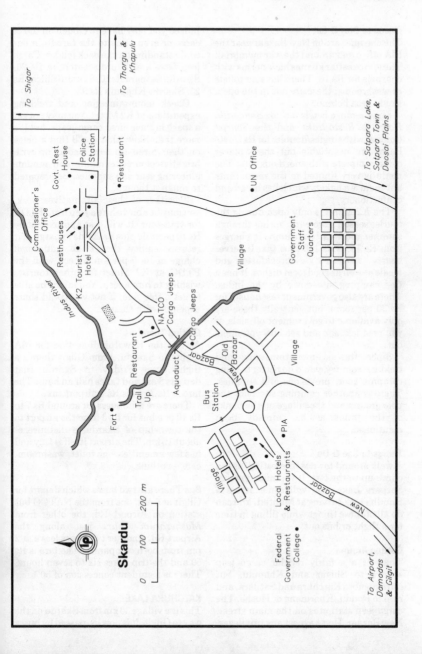

Places to Stay & Eat

The cheapies are on New Bazaar near the PIA office and around the war memorial. These muzzaffar khanas have dorms with charpois for Rs 10. There have no toilets or washrooms; these are out in the open, sandy area behind.

Middle-range hotels include *Shangrilla Hotel & Restaurant* and the *Tourist Cottage* with singles/doubles for Rs 25/40. Rates are negotiable but these places come complete with enormous rats. The menu is very limited in the restaurants but there is a bakery which has bread and confectionery.

The *K2 Motel* is only open during the tourist season from early spring through summer until early autumn. It charges from Rs 75 to Rs 150 plus tax. It serves hearty western-style breakfasts and meals as well as good local dishes. It has a free camping site down by the Indus. There are also government *rest houses* for Rs 30 per room, but generally these are only available to government officials. If you're stuck, ask and see how you make out.

Since this is mountaineering and trekking country, you'd do better to bring camping gear, provisions and supplies. There is another camping site near the polo ground and the village on the banks of the Indus as has already been mentioned.

Things to See & Do

A walk around town is interesting, as is a climb up to the fort. If you hike down to Satpara Lake, you will come across a Buddha rock carving at Mantlal. You can do all of these things while filling in time for a flight or bus out.

Getting Around

There is a a fairly regular cargo jeep service to Shigar and Khapulu, but infrequent to Katchura and Satpara, and rare to Rondu, Kharmang or Hushe. The cargo jeep station is on the main street, New Bazaar. Don't expect any privileges.

Indeed you may have to crouch on top of cargo or even cling to the tarpaulin bar while standing on the back fender. Cargo jeep fares are: Skardu-Katchura Rs 20, Skardu-Satpara Rs 10, Skardu-Shigar Rs 25, Skardu-Khapulu Rs 35.

Check mountaineering and trekking expeditions at K2 Motel. You may not get a space in their hired cargo-jeeps, but it's more than likely that you'll find a place on their hired tractors loaded up with brightly-coloured camping and mountaineering gear and supplies. Be prepared to rough it though.

If neither of these alternatives work, you may be able to hire a jeep from PTDC for your tour. It will cost approximately Rs 10 per mile plus Rs 200 day charge. If it returns empty there's an additional charge of Rs 5 per km. Check with the PTDC at K2 Motel for other tourists wishing to hire a jeep. You might be able to get a free ride, if not you could share expenses with them.

Getting There

Air See the Rawalpindi section for PIA flights to Skardu. From Gilgit there's a flight every Friday to Skardu that departs 8 am and takes half an hour. The fare is Rs 75 plus Rs 5 airport tax.

There are minibuses for around Rs 7 to Rs 10 or a bus for Rs 3 from the airport to the township of Skardu, a distance of about 16 km. The airport itself is tiny and has few amenities – no toilet, washroom, cafe – nothing.

Bus There are two buses which depart for Gilgit at 6 am, one from the NATCO bus station on Airport Rd, the other from *Masherbrum Tours* just along the Airport Rd. Another two buses leave at 2 pm from both companies. The fare is Rs 50 and the trip takes six to seven hours. There is a student concession of 50%.

KATCHURA LAKE

This is a village 30 km from Skardu on the way to Gilgit. It is now by-passed by buses heading for Gilgit as the road has been moved to the right bank of the Indus following the construction of the new bridge three km from the village.

There is a luxurious five-star hotel here called the *Shangrilla Tourist Resort*, considered by the proprietor, a retired brigadier, to be heaven on earth. That aside, it's worth a visit just to see the set-up. It consists of a complex of cottages, four-room lodges, camping ground, shops and a restaurant with local and western cuisine. It also has a library, fish hatchery and a mini-zoo. If you like aircraft, you can stay in the old Dakota which crash landed at Kachura Lake decades ago, and is now converted into a tourist cottage.

Resort rates are from Rs 200 to Rs 1000. There are half rates for children and free transport from the Skardu airport and back. If you're interested check for an advance booking at Shangrila Reception Centre, (tel 6 6936), 14/N Murree Rd, Rawalpindi.

It's an ideal place for relaxing, particularly if you're keen on fishing. You can also go swimming, take a short trek or walkabout or a tour by jeep of some of the valleys in Baltistan.

SHIGAR

Shigar is 32 km north of Skardu at an elevation of 2316 metres. Five km out of town on the road to Khapulu there is a turn-off to a sandy wasteland, which leads down to a bridge and up into Shigartang – the desert plain of Shigar. The road is dusty, desolate and rough, and jeep passengers hanging from the rear often have to jump off to lighten the load for the steep climb up.

Shigar is a pleasant little village with a nice climate. Set in a lush, green valley 2300 metres above sea level, the atmosphere of cascading rivers dominates the atmosphere. One of my strongest images of this place is students sitting in the grounds of the modern school, singing sad songs about faraway places and inspiring mountains. On the left-hand side of the

road is a traditional **Tibetan mosque**, topped with a star-shaped tower. Near here are two or three wooden box stalls which comprise the bazaar, and right beside the Shigar Nallah (stream) is the *Karakoram Hotel & Restaurant*, which is really only a muzzaffar khana.

Up a rocky plateau are the ruins of a castle, now a crumbled pile of rocks, and across a little wooden bridge is the *teshildah* or administrative heart of the valley. The old part of the city consists of houses of quaint Ladhaki design. The architecture in old Shigar is distinctly Tibetan in style. Around the fringes are modern buildings like the rest house, the hospital, government staff quarters and a hydro-electric plant.

Dr Karl Jettner of Heidelberg University discovered a Buddhist settlement here two years back, which dates from the 5th to 6th century AD. It has monastic complexes, 20,000 rock carvings and 2000 inscriptions along with a representation of a Chinese pagoda and Chinese inscriptions indicating friendly relations with China. Inscriptions found here include Brahmi and Tibetan dating from the 8th to 10th century. Work in still in progress and the good professor turns up every August to work at the site.

It's pleasant and relaxing here with only the sound of the cascading stream and singing birds, like the mynahs and the *hazardastan*, a lovely yellow bird streaked with brown, usually called *mayon* in Chitral. The rest house is clean and furnished but has limited food – bring some with you if possible. There is also a lawn here where camping is possible. A nice way to spend some time is to walk around the environs, but there's nothing much to do here.

This is the gateway to Dassu 80 km away and to the trekking route to Concordia via the Baltoro Glacier. Out of Shigar a trail forks off the route to Dassu down to a bridge where it continues to the other side of the valley. There are a few interesting villages on this side of the valley. Many children from around here – particularly infants – are dressed in traditional attire and headwear. It is also the setting off point for Khapulu.

KHAPULU

Situated 103 km to the east and at 2560 metres, this valley is considered to be the most stunning in Baltistan, and is regarded by the natives as the Garden of Eden. The desert plains along the River Shyok are reddish in colour. In 1892 the Earl of Dunmore, a British explorer who spent a year crossing the Karakorams, wrote that the Shyok Valley 'was more beautiful than anything I have ever seen in my life ... magnificent and on an enormous scale, larger than anything even in the Rocky Mountains of America.'

Cargo jeep transport is frequent, twice daily at 7 am and 2 pm, but quite often loaded to capacity. The route to Khapulu is similar to the journey to Shigar, and while rough and bumpy, the discomfort is offset by stunning scenery. It can be roughly divided into three sections. The first wanders through archaeological petroglyphs, then through a narrow valley which broadens further up the Shyok Valley and on past the Humayun Bridge. This section is crossed by numerous irrigation canals.

Khapulu is the principal town of the Shyok Valley with villages built along gentle slopes shaped like an amphitheatre. It has a small bazaar, and perched on elevated land overlooking the valley near the polo ground is the palace of the former ruler. Villages near Khapulu are **Shaling** and **Chakchang**. The people here belong to the Nurbuksh Sufi faith and their mosque is of a particularly interesting design and well worth a look.

The people, language, culture and architecture in this fascinating valley are distinctly Tibetan. Part of its fascination lies in its summer festivals when the tradition of presenting offerings to the fairies is made. They also perform two special dances at these festivals: one a flower dance called *mindak*; the other a sword dance known as *stamno*. Another magical element of Khapulu and its people is their use of the serpentine stone as an antidote to snake bites. They crush it into powder, apply it to the wound and it works.

There is a furnished *rest house* here which has tolerable food, but *Shyok Inn*, once an alternative accommodation spot, has been turned into a clinic by an elderly Austrian couple. Accommodation is sometimes possible when they are not there. Camping is possible near the rest house, or if you don't have camping gear and are finding accommodation a problem see Alam Dar, nephew of the former rajah. He might be able to arrange something for you.

Khapulu is a starting point for treks to the north and east, particularly to: Hushe and the valley of Masherbrum, the river valley of Dansam to the east, and the Kondus Valley which also leads up to the Baltoro. The sights on the plateau here are simply stupendous.

There are also a number of walks around Khapulu: along the Shyok, the village, and in the surrounding plateaux above the village where there are stunning views of the snowcapped peaks of the Karakorams.

SATPARA LAKE

Eight km south from Skardu and 2400 metres above sea level, this lake is halfway to the town of Satpara. It is quite possible to trek there and back in a day. The only building apart from a watchman's hut is a forlorn-looking *PTDC Tourist Motel*. There is a small island in the middle of the lake, which is topped by a low, mud-stone hut. Trout fishing is possible.

From the lake the road continues to the town of Satpara and beyond to the south is the Deosai Plateau. This is a beautiful plateau but a special permit is required to visit there. However, the PTDC will organise day excursions by jeep for those interested.

GILGIT-HUNZA

Like Baltistan, the entire Gilgit-Hunza area is in the shadow of the ramparts of the Karakorams. Sandwiched between Chitral and Baltistan, it is 26,500 square km and spreads up to the Hindu Raj Range and the Khunjerab Pass in the north, to the fringes of Mastuj and Laspur in the west, down to Darel and Tanger in the south and the Nagar Valley and the Rakaposhi and Bagroth Range in the east.

It has a number of high mountain peaks which include Mt Distaghilsar (7895 metres), the Momhilsar (7342 metres), Rakaposhi (7788 metres) and the Haramosh (7479 metres). It also has huge glaciers, such as the Hispar and Batura. Both the mountain peaks and the glaciers are in the western region of the Karakorams in the valleys of Shimshal, Hunza and Nagar.

Further west, below the Hindu Raj Range, is the Ishkoman Valley, and beyond is the Yasin Valley. All these valleys in the north, from Shimshal to the Khunjerab and Mizghar, and from the valley of Nagar across Passu, down to Chalt, and right up to Ishkoman and Yasin, comprise what is known as the Hunza region. It is divided into three linguistic areas: the southern or lower Hunza from Shishkhat up to Chalt speak Shina or the Gilgiti language; the Hunza proper from Chalt up to Karimabad and west to Yasin is the area of the Burushuki-speaking people; and in Upper Hunza from Gulmit to Khunjerab the language is Wakhi.

South of Chalt from Bagroth Valley, right through the Punial-Gakutch river valleys to Darel and Tanger in the south, and beyond Shandur Pass is the Gilgit region. The people in these valleys speak Shina and are generally Shi'ites.

This entire area used to be known as

Bolor during the Patola dynasty which collapsed when the Chinese arrived in the 8th century AD. With the arrival of the Tibetans in the 9th century AD, it was referred to as Dardistan which declined and fragmented into several mini-republics, which in turned evolved into mini-kingdoms. With the arrival of Islam in the 10th century they developed into mirdoms, which appear to have been constantly at war with one another. At this time it became customary for women to work the fields while the men stood guard or fought battles. Despite being devout Muslims, they were fairy-worshippers until two decades ago.

The opening of the Karakoram Highway – which roughly follows the old Silk Trade Route through this region, branching east towards Leh and west through Punial and Yasin into the Oxus to Samarkhand – wiped out traditional customs, the social caste system and ways of celebrating festivals and beliefs. As a result it is now a society caught between two worlds – the conflict of traditional Islamic culture and progressive revolutionary trends.

GILGIT

The 240-km road between Skardu and Gilgit is now sealed and follows the Indus River down featureless and often bleak valleys. It is fairly narrow and can be exciting depending on your driver, though it's not dangerous, but flash floods or avalanche can make the road impassable for days. At the Alam Bridge, the road joins the sealed Karakoram Highway.

From Jaglot the road meanders through rolling green landscape into Gilgit, in the centre of the upper highland. Gilgit is larger and more developed than Skardu, and has all the usual trappings of an administrative town: government offices, rest houses, banks, hotels, a polo ground, bazaars, tourist shops, teashops and a couple of cinemas.

Originally the capital of Bolor and the centre of the Patola dynasty (4th to 8th

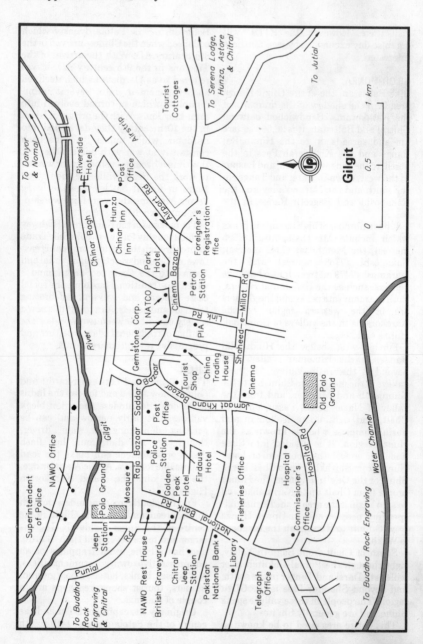

century AD) and of Dardistan (9th to 10th century AD), it was a transit trading centre of the ancient Silk Trade Route. It was still a slave-trading area until the arrival of the Sikhs and the British in the middle of the 19th century, and was Buddhist until around the 17th century when it was invaded by the Shi'ite Muslims from Baltistan.

Historically it is an important archae-ological site and part of its history is recorded in the Gilgit Manuscript discovered in the area above Nowpur near the Kargah Valley. This was written during the Patola period in Sanskrit-Persian script and inscribed on birch bark. On a rocky cliff in the Kargah Valley is a carving of the Buddha executed during the Tibetan period, and further up the valley is a cave inscribed with rock carvings. In the village of Danyor is a house which contains a boulder covered in inscriptions that record the lineage of the Buddhist rulers of Bolor, dating back to the 7th century.

Gilgit is a reasonably quiet, pleasant town through which the river of the same name flows. Spanned by one of the longest suspension bridges in Asia, the Gilgit River heads south, joining the Hunza River and finally the mighty Indus. The people living here now are predominantly Ismailis from Hunza and a large group of Sunnis, a situation which makes for social conflict at times.

Of all the administrative centres in the Northern Mountain Zone of Pakistan today, this town is the most important geographically, being right in the centre of the highland. It is a major junction for the Gilgit-Sinkiang barter trade. As a gateway to China through the Khunjerab Pass, Gilgit has prospered and developed rapidly over the last few years.

Information
The Tourist Information Centre is at the PTDC-run Chinar Inn, within walking distance of the airport. Check with them for cultural programmes, and transport to Pirali in Xianjiang, China. The PIA office is on Cinema Bazaar.

You can cash travellers' cheques at the Pakistan National Bank, and for books on the northern area and handicrafts, check Gulam Mohammed Beg's shop on Jamaat Khana Bazaar and Dad Ali Shah in front of the Park Hotel.

The China Trading House, Jamaat Khana Bazaar, is good for Chinese silk and porcelain. The Gemstone Corporation has a display room on Cinema Bazaar, opposite the PIA office.

Things to See & Do
Walking around the town is fascinating. For a start there's the bazaar area to explore, or the handicraft shops and the China Trading House. Then there's the Gilgit River banks and Chinar Bagh, an interesting but not very well-kept garden, which has a patch of sandy beach and a pavilion. There's also an old British cemetery or you can wander up to the Serena Lodge in Jutial, which has a balcony with splendid, panoramic views over Mt Rakaposhi, Diran and Deobani – particularly interesting late in the afternoon.

You can also go on a tour of the old town centre, site of the old fort, though nothing much is left except a lone tower in a military cantonment. Kargah Valley has a rock carving of the Buddha, and in the vicinity of Nowpur is Giri Yashani, the site of a Buddhist settlement where the *Gilgit Manuscript* was discovered in 1931. It is on the Punial road via the Rajah Bazaar. On the way there's a trail off to the left just before the suspension bridge, turn down it and you will see the rock carving of the Buddha, over nine metres up on the cliff face. The figure itself is about three metres tall and is framed in a pentacle.

Near the hydro-electric plants is a cave which has numerous rock carvings. On the way back follow the water channel along the mountainside. The trail from Gilgit to the water channel begins just opposite the airstrip. If you take this route, don't follow the water channels up the valleys to the left, just continue straight in a northerly direction or you could get lost.

Another pleasant walk is to the village of Danyor, a few km beyond the Gilgit River over a suspension bridge and through a tunnel. Ask around for the house where the boulder with historic inscriptions is – if you can't find it this is still a pleasant, relaxing walk.

There is a waterfall, two to three hours walk from town. Go south of the water channel in the opposite direction of the route to the Kargah Valley. Keep following the water channel as it ascends and goes through a gorge. There are three or four water channels at different levels here, take the top one and follow it to the end where you will find the waterfall.

In the first two weeks of June there are polo tournaments, both in the mornings and the afternoons; and in the first week of August there is a polo match in Shadnur Pass between Gilgit and Chitral. At this time there are cargo jeeps going to Shadnur Pass from both Chitral and Gilgit. At other times the cargo jeep service is rare. In the first week of November is another polo tournament. Included in the programmes are games like *buzhkazi* that were re-introduced by the Kirghiz Afghan refugees. These games are usually enlivened by a small band of musicians playing pipes, trumpets and drums.

In the old days there used to be a specific polo day, a day when women took their revenge on those who had wronged the community. Sitting on low-roofed, stone huts all along the way to the polo ground, the women would wield long sticks and flay their enemies with great accuracy and vigour. Most often the latter included the village ruler, traders and merchants, who tended to pay ransoms to get off lightly.

Fishing

The Bureau of Fisheries is just over the road from the Pakistan National Bank. If you want to fish you must get a licence from this office. See Samiullah Khan and check with him about restrictions, etc, for over-zealous fishing officials could ruin the day for you even before it's begun if your papers are not in order. Make sure they are. The usual rates for fishing gear is Rs 10 per day with a Rs 500 deposit. You can also hire gear, apparently of better quality, along Saddar and Rajah Bazaars. Try the place just opposite the Post Office and the Police Station where rates are Rs 10 per day with a Rs 250 deposit.

Good fishing grounds close to the town are **Kargah Nallah** and **Gilgit River**. Further away **Bashiret Nallah** is also popular with anglers. Twenty-two km from Gupis and 44 km south of Darel and Tanger, **Batesh Nallah** is renowned for golden trout, while to the west, **Phander Lake** is also a popular trout fishing area.

Places to Stay – bottom end

Accommodation can be a problem during summer, though new hotels have eased this. The *Jubilee Hotel* on Airport Rd, has double rooms only for Rs 40. Western-style breakfasts and local meals are available.

Down an alley off Jamaat Khana Bazaar, the *Firdous Hotel* has doubles for Rs 20 and charpois in the garden for Rs 8. Only local food here. The *Tourist Cottage* in Jutial (tel 376), has singles/doubles for Rs 20/35, and dorm accommodation with share bathrooms for Rs 15. You get western-style breakfasts and the best dinners in town here. It is very popular and is generally packed with local people and tourists in summer. You can also camp on the lawn and there is parking space. The *Lalazar Hotel* is right in town and has similar rates.

Places to Stay – middle

The *Vershingoom Hotel* on Airport Rd (tel 2991) has a restaurant with Punjabi specialities and occasionally shows videos in the courtyard. Singles/doubles are Rs 40/60, an extra bed Rs 20 and verandah beds Rs 15.

Sargin Inn near the airport is new with carpeted rooms, a dining hall, and a large lawn and parking space. Rates are from Rs 45/90 for singles/doubles, Rs 165 for 4-bed rooms.

Masherbrum Inn on Airport Rd has double rooms only for Rs 50 to Rs 80. The *Golden Peak Hotel* Bank Rd (tel 876), has dorms for Rs 40 and double rooms for Rs 70. This used to be the palace of the Mir of Nagar. It has a pleasant atmosphere, serves meals and has a parking lawn.

Places to Stay - top end

The *Serena Lodge* Jutial (tel 331), 2½ km away from the town centre, is the poshest hotel in town. The architecture is central Asian and it has rooms from Rs 360 and up.

The *Chinar Inn* Chinar Bagh (tel 562) is run by the PTDC and has rates from Rs 150 to Rs 225. It has a relaxing atmosphere and there is a restaurant with excellent cuisine.

The *Hunza Inn* Chinar Bagh (tel 814) has a restaurant and camping ground, double rooms only from Rs 150 to Rs 250. The *Riverside Tourist Lodge* also on Chinar Bagh, is a new building with a campsite and dining hall. Singles/doubles are Rs 80/110, a two-bed tent is Rs 30, single Rs 15. The *Park Hotel* on Airport Rd (tel 679) has a restaurant and doubles only for Rs 105 and up.

Places to Eat

The food tends to be more central Asian here and noodles predominate in the local diet. However, traditional food is harder to find these days with the incursion of lowland food, but you can still have it specially prepared for you in some restaurants and villages.

There are a number of local restaurants along Cinema Bazaar which serve good cheap food, mostly of the Afghan variety – stewed meat in tomatoes with nan or chappatis and washed down with tea. There's also an excellent bakery in the same street.

The *Kasghar Restaurant* on Saddar Bazaar in an alley opposite the new mosque offers Chinese or Kasghari meals at very reasonable prices, as well as Pakistani and western dishes.

But as already mentioned the *Tourist Cottage* is *the* place for dinner. The menu is a mixture of Chinese, Pakistani and western food, which includes *daudo* – the Gilgiti version of noodle soup – rice, chappatis, salad, french fries, sliced roast mutton and beef, chicken or mutton curry and dahl. Desert is usually custard pudding with apricots and nuts, or sometimes apples, and all this is washed down with jasmine tea or coffee. The menu may vary from time to time, but it's always good value.

Breakfast is served any time, but dinner is put out on a long table between 7.30 and 8.30 pm. In summer the tables are out on the lawn and you may be lucky enough to see an aurora in the sky to the north. Manifested by a white light rising over the mountains and eclipsing the stars, it is considered to be electrified gaseous matter in space, and looks rather like a fluorescent light. The Tourist Cottage has a relaxed, social atmosphere and should not be missed.

If you somehow tire of the Tourist Cottage tucker and want to do an expensive gourmet tour, then there is the *Serena Lodge* or the *Chinar Inn*.

Liquor Alcohol is not available here. If you have your own supply, drink it in your hotel room. The thing to drink here is *Hunza Water*, and it comes in two varieties – grape and mulberry. The former is a cloudy-green colour and sweet, the latter reddish in colour and tasting rather like dry wine. Make discreet enquiries if you want to try some, there are places beyond the reach of the police and the fundamentalists.

Getting Around

There are miniwagons plying between Jutial – the Tourist Cottage – and the centre of town for Rs 1. If they have to diverge from the usual route – to go to the airport or the commissioner's office for instance – the fare varies between Rs 5 and Rs 10.

Gilgit is a starting point for mountaineering expeditions, trekking parties and tourism. It has miniwagons, vans, buses and cargo jeeps going in all directions.

NATCO has buses and cargo jeeps for most places in the area. It also has jeeps for hire at Rs 10 per mile, Rs 200 day charge and Rs 5 per mile if returning empty.

The PTDC Tourist Information Centre at Chinar Inn also has jeeps for hire at the same rates. They are new and comfortable, but only have space for six passengers. Rates are not negotiable, but you can be assured of excellent service and assistance.

There are other private jeeps for hire, but they are not as reliable as NATCO or the PTDC. Suzuki wagons are also for hire. They are good on paved roads but not really suitable for rough roads up to the remote villages.

Getting Away

Air Gilgit is linked by air with Rawalpindi. Try and get a seat on the right-hand side up the front of the plane or down the back, as the flight path is quite spectacular, following the Indus River up the Kaghan Valley and over Babusar Pass.

The *PIA* office, on Cinema Bazaar, schedules two F-27 flights daily between Gilgit and Rawalpindi depending on weather conditions. Departure times are usually around 10.30 am, 1 pm and occasionally, 3 pm. The fare is Rs 160 plus an airport tax of Rs 5.

PIA also has one flight a week to Skardu every Friday at 8 am. The fare is Rs 75 plus Rs 5 airport tax.

Bus The NATCO office is on Cinema Bazaar and has four buses daily to Rawalpindi, departing at 6 am, 11 am, 5 pm and 10.30 pm. The fare is Rs 86 and the trip takes 18 to 21 hours. There is a 50% concession available to students.

There are other buses that depart daily for Rawalpindi from Cinema Bazaar, Jamaat Khana Bazaar, Saddar Bazaar and Rajah Bazaar. There are air-con coaches (Rs 110) and minibuses, but they are not regular and departure often depends on availability of passengers.

North

To Sust NATCO has a bus daily to Sust (Rs 22, six hours), departing at 6 am and 12 noon. There are minibuses for Rs 40, and the PTDC coach for Rs 160. The route is via Ganesh, Gulmit and Passu.

To Karimabad Direct buses no longer do this route. Take the bus to Ganesh and continue from there. Besides the NATCO bus, there are many minibuses and miniwagons leaving Gilgit for Ganesh almost every hour from 6 am to 3 pm. The trip takes 2½ hours and costs Rs 16 by bus, Rs 20 by minibus or miniwagon.

Nagar Cargo jeep service to Nagar is fairly regular and costs Rs 25. If you are trekking it is advisable to take the bus to Ganesh and start the trek from there.

To Chalt The cargo jeep service is infrequent. The fare is Rs 16. It is advisable to take the bus or wagon for Ganesh and get off at the bridge for Chalt.

To Naltar Cargo jeep service here is irregular and costs Rs16. As an alternative you can take the bus to Ganesh and get off at Nomal and trek from there.

East

To Skardu There are four buses a day to Skardu for Rs 60. Student concessions are available. Both NATCO and Masherbrum run services.

To Bagroth The cargo jeep service here is irregular and costs Rs25. Check the bazaar or NATCO for transport.

To Astore Frequent cargo jeep service for

Rs 50 and an additional Rs 25 for the return trip. The trip is dusty and bumpy and takes four to five hours. If there are no jeeps to Astore take one to Jaglot where there are many jeeps to Astore and Rama.

South

To Jaglot There is regular transport here for Rs 10, two hours.

To Chilas Regular bus service for Rs 22, three hours.

To Darel & Tanger Cargo jeep service only from Chilas.

To Rawalpindi Regular bus service via Beshum for Rs 86, 18 to 21 hours. To Beshum costs Rs 70.

North-West

To Imit Irregular cargo jeep service to this town for Rs 30, via Chatorkhand in the Ishkoman Valley.

West

To Punial, Gakutch, Gupis, Phander and Yasin Regular cargo-jeep service to all these places. Fares in same order are Rs 15, Rs 20, Rs 30, Rs 55 and Rs 45.

To Teru Very irregular cargo jeep service here for Rs 60.

To Chitral The cargo jeep service along this route is very rare. On the Teru-Chitral route cargo jeeps are also rare. The Shandur Pass on the Chitral road is only open from early May until mid-November.

At the time of the polo match between Gilgit and Chitral during the first week of August, cargo jeeps are regular, but once that is over, it is difficult to get there again. In early autumn you may be able to get a ride on the cargo jeeps that take Chinese goods to Chitral from Gilgit.

Valleys Around Gilgit

On a tour of this region if you don't have an itinerary organised, it is difficult to know where to begin. There are so many beautiful and interesting places. They are all scenic but some have their own particular attraction which may be anthropological, archaeological or historical.

BAGROTH VALLEY

There are no regular cargo jeeps to this valley, 40 km east of Gilgit. The road is partly sealed and runs along a picturesque, narrow valley, terminating before the Bagroth Range.

Get off the jeep at a foot-bridge and climb up a steep path to the first village, about three km off the road.

In this valley and the adjoining one, Haramosh, there are numerous ruins of altars comprising stone pillars set up like *menhirs*, which were supposed to house the protecting spirit of the village, usually an ancestor of one of the local people. This is an indication that the people from these valleys practised a mixture of fairy and ancestor worship.

The latter was probably introduced by the Chinese in the 8th century AD. Despite the fact that Islam is acknowledged as the religion of Pakistan, until two decades ago various forms of syncretic faiths were practised openly. Today, you would be lucky to find any villagers

willing to admit to such forms of worship or even to talk about them, but if you're interested in religions, you can take a look at some of these stone altars on a ridge near the village of Datuche in Bagroth Valley.

The traditional houses here have no windows – not even for ventilation – and use round poles with steps cut in them for ladders. The huge box on top of these strange houses is used to store meat after cattle have been slaughtered during their winter festivals.

A jeepable road leads from this village to the government rest house about two km from the glacier. **Deobani** is visible from here but the **Chogolungma Glacier** is a disappointment, being dark grey, almost black in colour, and thawing in summer. Although it is 2500 metres high, it does not get much snow in winter.

ROUTES SOUTH

The Karakoram Highway follows the Gilgit River south, then the Indus, to Jaglot, the transit village to Bunji, Astore and Skardu. From Jaglot a trail leads down to a bridge and on to Bunji and Astore. The road to Skardu is four km north of Jaglot at the Alam Bridge. A few km south on the Karakoram Highway is the Rakhiot Bridge, which is the setting off point for **Fairytale Meadow** or the base camp of **Nanga Parbat**.

Just before Chilas is another starting point to the base camp of Nanga Parbat on the Diamar side. The highway passes Chilas, which is off the road and a transit point for Darel and Tanger, then goes through a route covered with petroglyphs, past Siazin, a police check-post, and another before Camilla. It continues to Patan and finally reaches Beshum.

DIAMAR

This is the last region in the Northern Territory to be defined by the ancient name of Dardistan, an empire which emerged on the disappearance of Bolor. Historically Dardistan covered the whole of Gilgit as far as Chitral to the west, with the exception of Baltistan which was then under the Tibetans, east to the edge of Kashmir, and south as far as Chilas.

Situated immediately south of Baltistan and south-east of Gilgit, this is where the western bastion of the Great Himalayan Range slips in from the valley of Kashmir, extending some way beyond the Indus to Darel and Tanger and finishing just in front of the ramparts of the Hindu Kush. The area is dominated by Nanga Parbat, known locally as *Diamar* – Naked Mountain – which is now the accepted name for Dardistan.

Nanga Parbat soars to 8125 metres and is the eighth highest mountain in the world. The only peak within a hundred km radius, it stands out like 'some huge marble cathedral ... above all meaner buildings – a sight never to be forgotten. It is the culminating point of the Kashmir Ranges, linked with the central chain of the Himalayas as it turns southward running parallel with the Indus,' wrote Arthur Neve, an English explorer and travel guide writer.

It has been dubbed a killer mountain by climbers and has taken a toll of more than 50 of those attempting to conquer it, beginning with A F Mummery, who led the first British expedition here in 1897. After this disastrous attempt, Norman Collie, his companion, was to write:

The sunshine and beauty were gone; savage, cruel and inhospitable ...The dominant sensation in this strange land is that of fear and abhorrence; and what make it all the more appalling is that this thing before one is there in all nakedness; it has no reserve. There is nothing hidden. Its rugged insolence, its brutal savagery, and utter disregard of all the puny effort of man, crushes out of the mind any idea that this spot belongs to an ordinary world.

Dardistan or Diamar is also known as the Land of Fairies and Nanga Parbat is believed to be the home of the Queen of Fairies. According to legend, she lives in a castle made of solid, crystal-clear ice, and is guarded by gigantic frogs and snow snakes over 100 km long. Women from the surrounding valleys were so frightened of attracting the envy and jealousy of the fairies, they refused to wear brightly-coloured clothes. Today, like the women in Hunza and Laspur, they wear black or white headgear to indicate marital status – black means they are married, white means unmarried.

Summer nights are clear and starry up here. But in mid-July the monsoon affects the area causing occasional snow-falls. During winter the temperature can plummet to –40° or –50°C.

CHILAS

Chilas is the administrative centre of Diamar, 122 km south of Gilgit where the Indus veers westward, before it turns sharply south to the lowland of the Punjab just beyond Siazin.

Chilas is a large, sprawling town where the momentum of development seems to have slowed. There is no real town centre, the rest house, police station and commissioner's office are spread around the town. In the old days the Sunnis used to murder Shi'ites travelling south. Today, conflict has diminished, but has never disappeared.

The Indus, which runs east to west, delineates the border between the sub-northern and upper northern region. Petroglyphs along this route appear far more numerous than any other archaeological site in the area. You will come across them just below Chilas at the confluence of the Butogah and Thakgah rivers, on the south bank of the river, between Chilas, Shatial and Thor on the north bank, and at Soniwal, Huddur and the village of Thalpan.

Chilas is a transit point for trekkers going over the Babusar Pass into Kaghan, to the base camp of Nanga Parbat on the Diamar side, to the archaeological sites, and to the valleys of Darel and Tanger.

DAREL & TANGER

Near Shatial, a trail leads down to the banks of the Indus. It crosses over a bridge and continues to the valleys of Darel and Tanger, which are immediately north of Chilas.

The inhabitants speak Shina and have much in common with the Kohistanis, and like the Pathans, they are armed to the teeth. In summer they have a peculiar custom of segregating men and women, probably a method of birth control. Most marriages tend to occur in winter. They live in houses fortified with tall towers like those in Waziristan.

Both valleys are fertile and relatively rich, but a lot of their wealth is wasted on litigation due to continual feuding. In the past, like Kohistan, this was rebel territory where strangers would not dare to venture without being accompanied by a powerful police contingent.

Spring is brief, and by the middle of June the harvest is over. The main crops are wheat, barley and millet and there are also abundant fruit orchards.

Archaeology

Fogit-i-Run is the site of an early Buddhist settlement and further on at Ghor, there is a sculpture of the horse-god Talban that is worth looking out for. From Ghor to Seo along the banks of the Indus are numerous ancient rock carvings and scripts.

The trails in Darel and Tanger, which once went right up to Gupis, Ghize and north Badakshan, are dotted with archaeological sites.

The Departments of Agriculture and Forestry have government offices here, and there is a rest house. This is also a trekking region so make sure you have camping gear and provisions.

ASTORE

Astore is 115 km south-east of Gilgit, perched on a green, wooded ridge at about 2800 metres. It has precipitous cliffs which drop straight down into the Astore

Nallah. It's a small place with the usual government offices, banks, schools and basic local travellers' inns

There are no tourist facilities here so far, although it is a transit point for trekkers to Rama, Rumpur, Muzzaffarabad, the Deosai Plateau, Chilas and Gilgit.

Trekking permits are not required for Rama or Rumpur, but they are for Muzzaffarabad and the Deosai Plateau. See the Trekking section.

Note that travellers have to register at the police checkpoint here.

There are lots of different kinds of fresh fruit available including a local taste treat called *chilgoza*, strawberries and raspberries. There is also a wide variety of wildlife and birdlife around. Among them are ibex, musk deer, snow leopards and peacocks.

Getting There

Of the four districts of the upper northern highland, the area of Diamar is the least developed. Its administrative centre, Chilas, is a long way west of Astore, another main centre, also at the foot of the north-eastern flanks of Nanga Parbat. Eight km from here is Rama, a small scenic village.

There is no direct transport from Chilas to Astore, but there is a direct cargo jeep service from Gilgit and Jaglot. About four km before you get to Jaglot heading from Gilgit is the Alam Bridge where there is a road to Skardu. About two km further on a trail leads to a bridge over the Gilgit River and continues on through Bunji for Astore.

Having passed the bridge, the trail climbs up to a flat, desolate sandy plain, strewn with detritus, beyond which is Bunji. After Bunji it crosses Saitan Nallah and continues into the mountains along the Haramosh and Deosai Ranges, following the Astore Nallah upstream. This flows south-west to join the Indus. The valley is long, narrow, arid and featureless in sections, broken occasionally

by patches of green where villages and human settlements have cropped up.

There are several small villages with hotel signboards and rest houses along the way. From here on you will come across postmen called 'runners'. Their job is to carry the mail five km on foot – although often they hitch rides on jeeps – then pass it on to a colleague in a kind of postal relay system, introduced by the British. This idiosyncratic system continues despite the introduction of a modern postal system throughout the rest of the region.

Approaching Astore the bare granite walls become sparsely wooded with junipers and alpine scrub and the sky begins to open up. The junipers eventually give way to pine trees.

RAMA

To get to Rama from Astore you go via a road by the school building and then through a scenic valley eight km on. It zig-zags up steeply taking a jeep 35 minutes to cover the distance, and hikers almost two hours. To hire a jeep from Astore costs around Rs 200.

The country, at 3200 metres, is lush green and wooded with many fine grazing meadows. The rest house is three km from the village and is basically used by government officers only. It is also the only building in the area.

You will come across numerous shepherds with flocks of sheep and occasionally cattle, but at this height you will not be able to see Nanga Parbat, unless you climb another 200 metres up to the lake. From here you can catch a glimpse of Chongra Peak. There are two lakes close to the glaciers and beyond it another, larger one.

After crossing a bridge, you will find a shepherds' village on the right side, and Sango Sar Lake, which is fed by the glaciers and has good trout fishing.

The area is dotted with snow-covered glaciers, and sections of it are filled with moraines and scarred with ravines. In summer it is still cold and often drizzling with fine rain. In winter the shepherds leave their villages and move further down, as the land becomes blanketed in metres of snow.

ROUTES NORTH

From Gilgit the old route starts across the suspension bridge, follows the right bank of the river to the village of Danyor, and from there heads into Nomal, a transit village to the Naltar Valley 27 km away. It continues to Chalt, 51 km from Gilgit, following the left bank of the Hunza River upstream. The Karakoram Highway runs parallel to it on the other side of the Hunza River, but at the junction of Chalt it veers north through granite walls blasted from the mountainside.

east

NOMAL

Nomal is 27 km away from Gilgit on the west bank of the Hunza. It is on the old route, used before completion of the Karakoram Highway. It is possible to trek to Nomal along this route. If not trekking, to get there take a bus to Ganesh and get off at Rahimabad which has a muzzaffar khana for overnighting. The river has to be crossed by raft for Rs 1.50.

NALTAR

This is an alpine valley, 14 km from Nomal. It's set in a forest, has crystal-clear lakes, and is encircled by snowcapped peaks. Naltar also has a ski resort, a rest house and a few shops, but they're often closed. To stay at the rest house, prior arrangement must be made in Gilgit at the NAWO or Forestry Dept office. There's also a local hotel with a few beds and tolerable food. However, it is closed from late autumn until mid-February.

This is the starting point for treks up the Diantar Pass into Chalt or to Ishkoman via Naltar Pass and Pakhora.

CHALT

Chalt is roughly 50 km from Gilgit, 24 km from Nomal and about 62 km from Karimabad. Another starting point for trekkers, there are trails to Baltar Glacier, Diantar Pass via Bar and Naltar via the Chaprot River Valley. It has an old rest house with a guest book which dates back to the 1930s – well worth reading.

HUNZA VALLEY

Seven km east of Chalt, the Karakoram Highway veers north and climbs gently up the Rakaposhi Range.

The Chinese influence is obvious along this stretch of road, and is particularly noticeable in the bridges which are made with railings and posts, and decorated with stone lions' heads. About 500 members of the Sino-Pakistan labour force are believed to have lost their lives in the construction of this road and there are numerous memorials – distinctly Chinese in character – commemorating the deaths.

You are now going through a section of the old Silk Road described by the Chinese as the 'Suspended Crossing'. At the village of Jeethal, 16 km from Gilgit, you will come across cliff faces that are decorated with carvings of animals. Along a tributary of the Hunza River, some way up, are large flat rocks which depict ibexes, markhors, horsemen and other hunting scenes. Forty-eight km further on at Sonikot, there is a boulder with two stupas carved on it. *Ganesh*

Two km out of Hunza is what is called the **Sacred Rock of Hunza**, a rocky ridge of barren mountain between the Hunza and Hispar rivers, which, according to Dr Karl Jettmar, appears to have been a frontier post. Basically a rocky gallery divided into four sections, it contains a multitude of engraved scripts – mostly in Kharosthi and Brahmi – and carvings of animals, warriors and men on horseback. There are more petroglyphs all the way to Gulmit, Passu, through the Kilik and Mintaka passes and into western Turkestan.

Here, despite its name, the all-weather highway and its 70 bridges are subject to landslides, avalanches and blockages from shifting glaciers, which can take days – sometimes weeks – to clear or cut detours around. It may even be necessary to blast the glacier off the road. However, the road is not particularly steep and it is scenic all the way, passing through tiny hamlets and offering glimpses of the majestic Mt Rakaposhi from half-way up.

The Valley of Hunza is divided linguistically – the Lower Hunza which starts from Shishkhat up to Karimabad, and Upper Hunza, known as Gojal, which begins from Gulmit and goes up to the Khunjerab Pass. In Lower Hunza Burushuski is spoken, whilst Wakhi is spoken in Gojal. They are all Ismailies with the exception of the inhabitants of Ganesh and the Nagar Valley who are Shi'ites. This is due mainly to the continuing influence of the Balti in this area of the Hunza.

Hunza was one of the most isolated regions in this part of the world. It was cut off from the south by a deep gorge in the area of Nilt where the passage was actually hanging or 'suspended', now gone of course with the construction of the Karakoram Highway. Its traditional links were with central Asia via the Wakhan and Badakshan valleys and with Chinese Turkestan via the Kilik and Mintaka passes. This was where the *Thum* or Mir of Hunza fled when the British invaded.

Hunza was a tributary of Imperial China and the Mir had favoured the traditional ties with the governor of Xinjiang. In 1887, Sir Francis Younghusband became the first European to set foot in the region. He came to negotiate with the Mir for an end to the brigandage in Baltistan, but also to determine the extent of Russian influence and of course to extend British influence.

Due to the harsh environment and the severity of their lifestyle, people here practised a form of natural birth control,

which involved the women leaving the husband's bed and no intercourse until each baby was completely weaned. The groom's mother would accompany the newlyweds on their honeymoon as guide and teacher, for they considered marriage too important to be left to chance. The women here wear round caps, seven to 10 cm high, embroidered with bright floral or geometrical designs, usually with bright red or maroon as the predominant colour, and similar to those worn by the women in Phander and Laspur in Chitral. Like the Chinese they beat drums during a lunar eclipse to drive away the dragon, which they believe is devouring the moon.

Rubies and garnets are found in this region. Early in December of 1891, following the successful assault on the fort at Nilt, Colonel Algernon Durand, the commanding officer, was wounded. When the bullet was finally extracted, it turned out be a garnet enclosed in lead. 'There were sacks full of similar bullets within the fort,' wrote an Englishman in the expedition.

Most of the people from this region are Ismailis and until the 1950s, continued to practise their own culture and hold their own traditional festivals. These festivals were similar to those of the Kalash Kafirs, consisting of a kind of *mardi gras*, involving much feasting, drinking and dancing, dressed in very brightly coloured clothes. In spring they would hold a festival known as *Thomothaleno*, a night procession, lit by flaming torches and celebrating the death of an evil-doer.

Once again the completion and opening of the Karakoram Highway marked the end of these customs, and eventually brought about the complete merging of the valley with the rest of Pakistan. The death of the last mir shortly after the opening of the highway also signified the end of mirdom.

(looking s-w
Baltit to Rakaposhi)

Old Fort Tower, Hunza

The Ismailis

On his last visit to Kadir Qum, Mohammed the Prophet announced to the faithful that Ali, his son-in-law, was his chosen successor. This was known as *Id Agadir*. Conflict arose soon after the death of Mohammed which brought about the murder of Imam Ali and the defeat in the Karbala when Imam Hussein was also murdered.

The Shi'ites, belonging to the Shia sect of Islam, hid themselves from the Caliph and moved towards Persia. They remained united until the sixth Imam, Jaffri Saddique, who had two sons: Mora Kazim, the elder and Ismail, the younger. Here the split began. The followers of Mora Kazim and those of Ismail Ashraf split irreconcilably, mainly on the belief that the Mahadi, the 12th Imam, who disappeared mysteriously, will return on the day of judgement and rule with justice and love.

The Maulais or Ismailis refused to follow this. They believe that their Imam should be here for the spiritual and earthly guidance of the faithful. They believe that the prophethood of Mohammed, *Nebereth*, was the last and that the Imamat mission was to interpret the teachings of the prophet according to the changing times and conditions.

Their creed appears to be based upon the *Kelam-i-pir* which compares with the *Mithaq*, or Covenant of the Initiated among the Druse of Lebanon, according to Dr G W Leitner. They believe in the undivided chain of life in the elements, plants and animals. They have blind obedience to their spiritual leader who is their link with Allah. Like the Hindus they believe in transmigration of the soul. Upon death a good man proceeds to a higher form of life and an evil man risks becoming an ass, ox, plant or even a stone.

During the Crusades (9th to 15th centuries) the Ismailis became notorious as the *Hashishsims* of the Old Man of the Mountain. They drugged their victims and sent them to murder Ismaili enemies. This is the origin of the word assassin.

Nazir Khozrum from Balkh, an Ismaili preacher in the 10th century, began spreading the tenets of the Ismailis in Iran, Afghanistan, Xinjiang and Russian central Asia.

The original Ismaili tribe appears to have come from Persia and were identified with the early white Huns. The Ismaili tribes in the same century began their migration across Afghanistan along the Oxus in the Badakshan and Wakhan Valleys, over the Hindu Kush, the Pamirs and the Karakorams into Chinese Turkestan and into the Valley of Hunza where they settled.

There are no more than a million Ismailis in Pakistan, yet many of the richest families in Pakistan are Ismailis, most of them being industrialists, bankers and businessmen. Amongst the three major Muslim sects they appear to be the best organised with federal councils on regional, national and international levels.

Fairy Worship

Long before the Ismailis came to Hunza, fairy worshipping was practised. The origins of fairy worship are uncertain though the best theory is that it came with the Aryans who settled in the valleys of the Trans-Himalayas. Another theory is that it was brought by the Greeks, but this is less tenuous as they did not settle in the upper highlands for long, as did the Aryan Sakas.

Past Aliabad on the way to Ganesh, there is a trail off to the left leading up to Haiderabad, a small village perched high on a ledge. This region of the Ultar Range was once a ruby-mining area, and like almost every hamlet and village in the Hunza Valley, a centre for fairy worship. Haiderabad has a sacrificial altar known locally as a *haligan* where ibexes were offered to the fairy goddess or godmother in ritual ceremonies. The people from these parts believed that fairies were a ghoulish lot who thrived on viscera and warm blood.

There are a number of other villages around here that have similar altars including Nominabad just up from Ganesh, Ganesh itself and Altit. By the glacier in Passu, right at the entrance of an amphitheatre-like valley there is another *haligan*, and on the trail to Shimshal Valley, half-way to the village, yet another. Many have specific names which may possibly refer to their own particular fairy goddess. For example the altar in Altit is known as *Ahaz Ziarat*; the one in Ganesh as *Bulchi Toko*.

Although traditional fairy worship is slowly disappearing, there are still festivals throughout the year where the walls, posts and pillars of houses and huts are painted with ibexes, markhors and Marco Polo sheep, and the altars bedecked with pennants and flags, as a kind of appeasement to the fairies.

NAGAR VALLEY   Shiia Muslims

Nagar is 19 km east of Ganesh, and about 26 km from Aliabad across the Hunza River. The valley covers the area to the west in the Diantar Valley, to the south as far as Chalt and to the east beyond Hopar extending up to the village of Hispar.

The former rulers of Nagar were scions of the royal families of Baltit. The original rulers were two exiled brothers from Persia, whose rivalry began a tradition of bloody conflicts. Thus many aspects of traditional life continue to this day, such as the womenfolk tilling the soil while the men stand guard and prepare to do battle. The former ruler still lives in his palace here, though no longer as a ruler.

Nagar Valley is one of the more popular areas for walking, but it is mainly a starting point to other trekking regions like Hopar and Hispar to the east, to Shayyar in the south and to the base camps of Distaghilsar and Momhilsar to the north.

There are two routes into the valley: one via Pisan and Minapin villages and the other is via the Hunza Sacred Rock beyond Ganesh. The Minapin route is used by cargo jeeps coming from Gilgit, and the Hunza Sacred Rock route is mainly used by trekkers or tourists on hired jeeps from Karimabad.

As you enter the valley it is deep and narrow with steep, rocky walls and therefore there is no vegetation at lower levels. The valley lies in the shadows of the great mountains, mainly made up of gorges, ravines and moraines. On the banks of the Nagar River are tents of nomads panning for gold. The trial ascends and crosses a bridge. From the bridge the trail climbs steeply and vegetation becomes more prominent. Up ahead are villages and farms with the Golden Peak towering above them.

Nagar village is a cluster of mud-stone huts with a few modern buildings on the edges. There is a government rest house here but if you wish you can continue on for another 7 km towards Hopar for a sight of Bualdar Glacier, which is now melting and cracking in the process. There is another rest house in Hopar. Prior arrangement should be made in Gilgit but it depends on the discretion of the kindly chowkidar.

There are very few cargo jeeps to Hopar. You have to trek in to Hopar and out again to the village of Nagar where cargo jeeps are available, though infrequent. However, from Nagar it is an easy walk down to Ganesh. If you don't wish to backtrack, a trail goes off towards Shayyar, Pisan and Minapin. This is a jeep track but there are other trails off the main track to Shayyar which taper off into narrow valleys. There are rest houses in Pisan and Minapin, and across the bridge the trail continues up to the Karakoram Highway where you can catch jeeps, buses or wagons to Gilgit or Ganesh.

GANESH

Whether coming from Sust in the north or from Gilgit en route to Karimabad, you arrive in Ganesh. It is a tiny Shia village with a general store, hotel, teashops and a tourist camp. Most of the buildings are of mud-stone and there are some underground dwellings that can be identified by the ventilators sticking out of the ground. They are used mainly as shelters for domestic animals during particularly harsh winters.

Buses, jeeps and wagons stop here, but when the link road connecting Aliabad with Karimabad via Haiderabad is completed, there will be direct transport to Karimabad.

It is a transit stop to the north and south and the trekking areas in the entire Hunza Valley. After 2 pm there is no more transport out, only incoming transport in the evening.

Places to Stay & Eat

Yadgar Hotel is fairly clean and pleasant. It serves meals in the teashop and has singles/doubles for Rs 15/25. The Tourist Camp has tent beds for Rs 10. It also has a teashop.

Since this is a Shia village, the stores sell cigarettes. Buy your supply of cigarettes or tobacco here before going to Karimabad, Gulmit, Passu or Sust. Ismailis have recently been prohibited from smoking or dealing in tobacco.

by Aga Khan ??

KARIMABAD

The town nestles on a corner of the Ultar Massif overlooking the Karakoram Highway and Ganesh. From the highway it is almost straight up, with tiers of flat narrow ledges where villages are stacked one above the other, their mud-stone huts packed tightly together against the granite flanks of the Ultar.

Over the last six years Karimabad has been gradually transformed into a touristed village with growing bazaars, cafes, restaurants, modern hotels and banks, as well as more schools and training colleges. It now has electricity and paved streets, and is expanding horizontally and vertically along the narrow winding streets.

However, despite the progress and modernisation, it has also become more fundamentalist and the women wear chaddor and the men are banned from smoking.

Karimabad has a commanding view of the entire Hunza Valley. The panorama includes the towering Rakaposhi along with Diran and Golden Peak to the left, the Shayyar Peak, Deobani and Hacinder Peak to the right, and above all this are the Ultar Peaks and glaciers. It is the loveliest area in the valley.

A trail leads up to another village called Baltit where the 8th-century Baltit Fort is perched on an upper ledge and looms like a sentinel over the whole valley.

The fort, designed along Tibetan lines, was remodelled in the middle of the 19th century and looks more like a castle than a fort. Originally the 1st floor was used as a storage room and grain depot, with a jail and kitchen above it, and the upper floor was the mir's official room. From here the balcony offers a commanding view of the whole picturesque valley, which is dominated by Rakaposhi. The smoke-darkened interior is lit by only a few small windows and to get there you must climb equally smoke-blackened ladders. The wooden window frames, doors and posts are ornately carved.

It is built of heavy wooden beams, covered with twigs and branches and a mixture of sand and mud. A Tibetan-style star-shaped tower surmounts the building. Only a few decades ago Huk Gukkur, a *bitan* or local seer, was jeered at for predicting that the castle would be empty one day. Today, it is just that, an ill-kept and poorly managed museum with a collection of old swords and scimitars, old Chinese porcelain, photos of the mir and of some English noblemen. It exudes a feeling of mediaeval gloom.

+ graffiti all over

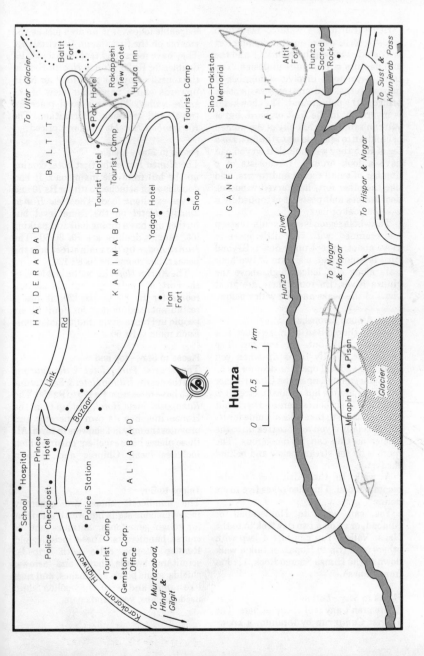

Hunza

To Ultar Glacier

Baltit Fort

BALTIT

HAIDERABAD

Link Rd

Bazaar

ALIABAD

School • • Hospital

Prince Hotel

Police Checkpost

• Police Station

Tourist Camp

Gemstone Corp. Office

Karakoram Highway

To Murtazaabad, Hindi & Gilgit

Park Hotel

Rakaposhi View Hotel

Hunza Inn

Tourist Hotel

KARIMABAD

Tourist Camp

Yadgar Hotel

• Shop

Iron Fort

Tourist Camp •

Sino-Pakistan Memorial

GANESH

Altit Fort

Hunza Sacred Rock

ALTIT

To Sust & Khunjerab Pass

To Hispar & Nagar

Hunza River

To Nagar & Hopar

Glacier

Minapin • • Pisan

0   0.5   1 km

Below Baltit is a watercourse which leads to Altit, where another smaller fort is located. This was built in 1503 and the architecture is Kashmiri in design. The track down to it involves a number of hairpin turns, and crosses a suspension bridge to the polo ground. The chowkidar is invariably in the fruit orchard, but if you can't find him, ask any of the women or children to take you up to the fort. For a fee of Rs 5 they will unlock it so you can have a look around. It consists of a number of small rooms and towers, and like the other fort, has carved windows, door frames and posts. It is topped by a wooden goat or ibex.

The whole region is spectacularly steep and cramped, with very little space to move about, except up or down. Beyond Altit is Amotabad, a six-km or two-hour walk along cliff ledges high above the Hunza River. En route there are great views of the peaks and the valley below.

Walks Around Karimabad

A walk to the old Baltit fort is a must. It is a steep climb but not too far. The chowkidar usually turns up when you need him and will open the door for Rs 5.

Or you can trek up to the Ultar Glacier to the shepherd's hut at 3000 metres. It is about five to six hours there and back, but it is advisable to take a local guide for Rs 40, especially if you want to trek up to the glacier as this can be dangerous. The route is by the stream below and behind the fort.

A walk to the Altit fort is also recommended. This also takes five to six hours.

You can walk to Haiderabad or Aliabad, or go on a two day trek to to the Nagar Valley. You can hire a jeep with others for a trip to Hopar, or talk a walk down to the Hunza Sacred Rock, 1½ km from Ganesh.

Places to Stay - bottom

There aren't any real cheapies here. The *Tourist Camp* run by Ibrahim, a know-

Mountain Lodge (?)

ledgeable fellow, is in an area just as you emerge on the first tier on the climb up. They have rooms and tent beds for Rs 10, doubles for Rs 30. *Hunza Health Food* in the tourist camp has good food for Rs 15 upwards and a panoramic view of the entire valley. This is a good place for travel and trekking information. The *Karimabad Hotel* is similarly priced.

Places to Stay - middle

opp. Tourist camp

The *Hunza Inn* is the first hotel coming up the hill from the main road. It had doubles with attached bath for Rs 70 and serves excellent food. The *New Hunza Tourist Hotel* on the same level but further up, has a dining hall and parking lot. Singles/doubles are Rs 30/50. The *Hunza Lodge* up the main street near the bazaar, has rooms for Rs 80/120.

The *Karim Hotel* up on the last level to the Fort, is nondescript but has modern rooms for Rs 80 to Rs 120. It has a restaurant and dorms for four to six people in Hunza-style traditional rooms. Each room is Rs 50.

Places to Stay - top end

The *Tourist Park Hotel & Restaurant* and the nearby *Hilltop Hotel & Restaurant* both have rates from Rs 125 to Rs 150. The *Rakaposhi View Hotel*, just up from the Hunza Inn, has its own generator and provides the only hot showers in town. All these places have excellent cuisine which includes local, Chinese and western dishes.

Things to Buy

The handicraft shops are generally inconspicuous stalls but worth a look at for rough gemstones, antiques and of course handicrafts. These include: old Russian steppe rifles with tripods, scimitars, swords, bows and arrows, shields, stone bowls and dishes, and rugs like *namda* and pattu, the woollen fabric used for caps, vests and coats.

GOJAL - UPPER HUNZA
History

Long before the Ismaili influence, one of the nomad rulers, Quli Kutor, in the Wakhan Valley was exiled into Ishkoman where he settled with his followers. They lived a pastoral existence, tending their animals and crops. Though they remained beyond the Pamirs on this side of the Karakorams, they maintained social, cultural and economic ties with Tajikistan and the Wakhan Valley. With the tribal movement of the Ismailis across the Oxus, like the Uigurs, Tajiks and the Wakhis, they fell under the influence of the Agha Khan in the 9th to 10th centuries AD.

The Gojal became tributary to the Mir of Hunza in a very simple fashion. The Mir visited them often, received gifts and in return he became the leader whom they looked upon for justice and succour in times of crisis. The court language used was Burushuski, which evolved out of a mixture of the Kurutz tribe's language from Persia, the Bartaling from Russia, the Browng from Kashmir and the Dramatin tribe from Tartary.

The linguistic and cultural affinity remains unchanged between the Gojal people and the Wakhis, the Uigurs and the Tajiks in Xinjiang in Chinese Turkestan. They speak the same language and have almost the same attire, particularly the women who still wear caps similar to those found in Taskurgan in Tajikistan, where the people have remained nomads, tending their herds and living in *yurts*, round tents made of woollen fabric.

Like the Wakhi-speaking people and the Tajiks, the Gojal womenfolk embrace and kiss each other by way of greeting, like the French. When meeting an elder, the children curtsy, kiss the elder's hand and then press it to their forehead.

Unlike the Karimabad womenfolk, the Gojal women do not wear chaddor or purdah. Unlike some regions where women are never seen outside the home and are strictly forbidden to talk to men or strangers, the Gojal women enjoy a relative freedom unheard of in much of Pakistan.

Population

The Gojal population is less than 18,000. Because of limited land resources, they have adopted a very effective system of birth control. Unlike the valleys of Nagar, Hunza and Baltistan they do not appear to have suffered from continuous inter-breeding. Until the revolution in China, there were intermarriages between the Gojals and the Wakhans, Tajiks and even the Uigurs. With the opening of the Khunjerab Pass, social and trade relations have been resumed.

Geography

The Gojal area stretches from Hussaini up to Mizghar and the Khunjerab Pass, and from the Shimshal Valley it spreads across Gulmit towards the valley of Ishkoman beyond the Chapursan River, and to the Boroghil Pass in Chitral. This is an area, like Baltistan, with some of the largest and longest glaciers in the region, such as the Batura Glacier and the Passu Glacier, which is considered the most beautiful. The Batura peaks are the most impressive and beautiful in the valley. Wildlife and birdlife are abundant.

It is linked with the Wakhan Valley and Xinjiang by high mountain passes with an average height of 5000 metres. To the north-west are the Kilik and Mintaka passes, and to the north-east are the Khunjerab and Shimshal passes.

Economy

Economic life is based mainly on agriculture - wheat, barley and black peas; animal husbandry - goats, sheep, yak and cattle; and the handicraft industry - *namda*, a rug of pressed, not woven, wool with some painted designs or embroidered patterns, and *pattu*, a woven woollen fabric. Tourism is increasingly becoming a major source of income.

Fauna & Flora

The wildlife includes ibex, markhors and the ural, which resembles a woolly sheep and is now becoming extinct, though there are numbers of them in Gilgit and Baltistan.

Birdlife includes the *ram chakkhor* known as the mountain snowcock. It is as large as a chicken and has dazzling, bright plumage. The *Chikkhor* is smaller, about the size of a pigeon, and is a game bird. Other birds include falcons and eagles.

Gojal Food

The staple food is wheat, barley and the many fruits that are grown in the region.

The food is similar to that found in central Asia and Xinjiang, mainly noodles , with dried yoghurt known as *kurut* and taken with *patti*, a bread similar in texture, and even taste, to German brown bread. *Nighan* is another type of bread, thin and round in shape.

The main meal is known as *ghazikh*, made of potato, cabbage, turnip and pumpkin with beef or mutton. It may be followed by *chamosh*, a cold Wakhi drink made from ground apricots.

Pest is another local drink made from dried apples that are crushed then fried with barley, mixed with flour and milk, and then turned into a powder. Four teaspoons of this mixed with water, makes a tasty, nourishing drink. They also drink yak milk in this region.

Gojal Festivals

Before sowing time *(bofani)* the Gojal gather at the mosque to pray and prepare *helma*, a paste of wheat, which is painted on the pillars of the mud-stone houses. There is also a harvest festival – *ginani*.

A Gojal Fairytale

A hunter and a fairy fell in love with each other. But, such is the ephemeral nature of fairies, she had to leave. She told him to be patient and wait for her, and on no account should he search for her. Days, weeks and months passed until the forlorn lover could wait no longer. He went to look for her in the *nari-ghaz* – garden of the fairies. When he found her, she told him that because he had not taken her advice he would soon die. Within four days he had lost not only his love, but his life. The moral? Have patience and don't fall in love with fairies.

GULMIT

Gulmit is 32 km north of Karimabad. On the way up, the Karakoram Highway becomes more rugged as it passes through narrow gorges, but suddenly it opens up into a broad valley.

At Gulmit the land is terraced and slopes gently up to the foothills. From the highway a jeep track meanders up through grainfields to the village. The top level is fairly broad and contains the old part of the village – the palace of the Mir, the mosque, bazaar, hotels and the local museum.

It used to be the second capital of the valley of Hunza, where the Mir held court in winter, considering local problems and arranging the hunting for the season. Now it is the main centre of the Gojal Valley.

The Mir's palace is well maintained and may well become a hotel one day and join the new hotels that have cropped up amidst the grainfields. There is a growing air of prosperity about the village and a new school, hospital, college and even a library have been built.

There is nothing spectacular here but it is a pleasant village with excellent hotels and food. It is becoming more popular with local tourists than Karimabad.

Gojal has fine weather from March to October, but it gets very cold from November to February due to the northern wind called the *duma*.

Places to Stay & Eat

The *Tourist Cottage*, just off the highway

to the left, is the best for budget travellers. It is comfortable, has good food and information. A tent bed is Rs 15, singles/doubles are Rs 40/60, and a four-bed room is Rs 100.

The *Village Hotel*, a little way up a trail behind the Tourist Cottage, is the next best. It serves excellent meals for Rs 40, and is in a building that belonged to the brother of the Mir of Hunza. The rates are Rs 75 to Rs 150, slightly higher in the new building.

The *Marco Polo Inn* is the most expensive in town and is usually booked out with local tourists.

Walks Around Gulmit

The village is quite interesting with old mud-stone and wood mosques, the Mir's palace, the library, museum, the old village and the ruins of the Andhra Fort. The latter is on top of the hill just behind the palace; a trail leads up to it from the old part of the village.

Or take a walk across the suspension bridge. The left trail leads to Ghuliarabad, though this is a risky trail as there always seems to be a cascade of rocks; the trail on the right leads to Mazimbad village, two hours walk away.

If you're interested in archaeology, there are engraved rocks up the side of Chamangul Nallah. This is a hard day's walk there and back.

Or walk to Kamaris near Gulmit Glacier, then on to Gulkin village, up and across Gulkin Glacier near Hussaini, then up to Burit Lake and back to Gulmit. This is a full day's walk.

Getting There

Gulmit is a ½-hour bus trip from Karimabad, Rs 5. Buses leave Gulmit from early morning until 2 pm only.

PASSU

Passu is on the right side of the highway and slopes down to the banks of the Passu River. It appears like an oasis, luxuriant with fertile fields. It is 125 km from Gilgit,

and a further 35 km from Hunza.

At 2900 metres it is slightly higher than Gulmit. It is mainly a setting off point to the trekking areas in the valley. There are also short walks around the village.

Passu will soon be supplied with electricity from the hydro-electric plant under construction at Khaibar. However, there is a plan underfoot to shift the entire population to another area further up, with the village being turned into agricultural land and fruit orchards.

A little way beyond Passu is the confluence of the Shimshal, Chapursan and Batura rivers. At this confluence the trail to the valley of Shimshal begins.

Places to Stay & Eat

The *Shishpar Hotel* is at the start of the village and is fairly isolated. Just behind it is the snout of the Passu Glacier. It is new and clean and has singles/doubles for Rs 35/60. The owner cooks a good breakfast and is good for trekking information. The *Passu Inn* just opposite the village has the same rates as Shishpar. Gulam Mohd also prepares good food here.

The *Batura Inn*, about a ½ km up the road on the right hand side, used to be the base for the Chinese who built this section of the highway. This is the most isolated and the cheapest. It has four doubles with two attached bathrooms, serves good food and is pleasantly situated on the river with lots of space for camping and parking.

At twilight in spring, there are singing frogs across the Passu River. They sound more like hornbills than frogs – they don't croak, they sing, and they seem orchestrated. Their plaintive frog songs ring out in chorus, then stop and only one sings – a solo from the tenor frog – and then they all start up again.

Walks Around Passu

There are walks to Abdeghar and on to Shikhargha; or to the Shimshal gorge; or down and around the village. There is also a walk to the pond. The route starts on the right just before the bridge, if going south; if coming from the Shishpar Hotel it is on your left. The trail follows a stream towards the snout of the glacier. It is dry, dusty and rough and takes an hour to walk to the pond. At Yunz, along the trail, are shepherd's huts.

The Burit Lake walk takes nearly a whole day. Before commencing see Azimshah at the Shishpar Hotel. He can give you good information and you may wish to have one of his hearty breakfasts before setting out. The trail is behind the hotel. On reaching Burit Lake the trail leads up to a rest house which is usually closed. Nearby is Burit village. From here the trail zig-zags down to the Karakoram Highway and the village of Hussaini, where there is a hot spring and a shrine to Pir Shah Talib. If you don't want to backtrack, you can follow the highway back to Passu.

The Passu Glacier walk takes about one hour to reach the glacier. Then it's 1½ hours to climb over the moraine and across the Batura Glacier. Approximately a three-hour walk. There are two trails – the high and low trails – the low trail is simply across the moraines. Continuing to the meadows of the upper reaches takes another two days. This is a trek which requires food and camping gear.

However, if you are on your way to Gulmit there is a trail from Burit Lake which continues up the ridge and then down and over Gulkin Glacier , then up and over Gulmit Glacier to Gulmit. (See the Trekking section).

Getting Away

Transport out here is between 8 and 10 am. If you intend reaching Pirali or Taskurgan on the same day, be sure to depart early for Sust as the immigration office for outgoing travellers is open only till 11.30 am. It is only 1½ hours by bus to Sust, and costs Rs 5. Moreover you still have to book a seat in either NATCO or PTDC buses which depart at 12 noon.

SUST

The Karakoram Highway continues to be in excellent condition on the way to Sust, though the vagaries of nature could wash away sections of the highway. It remains scenic and for the most part is flat all the way to Sust, where the valley suddenly opens up.

Sust, at an elevation of 2975 metres, is higher than Passu and the valley is broader, though there is less arable land as the Khunjerab River flows out here in several streams.

It has the air of a frontier village, like Taftan on the Iranian border. However, Sust is not really a border village, it is just a customs/immigration checkpost. The border is still some 50 km further north.

To the right is the Shaheen Hotel with tents out the front, the mosque and school (madrazhi) are on a slope, and at the level of the highway are the customs buildings and post office. To the left are long, low structures where the immigration office, teashop and stores are located. The PTDC tents and tourist office are also on the same side of the river.

The set up is improvised and still very disorganised with a minimum of facilities and amenities, but in case of delay the tourist officer, Nasrullah Khan, can give you a tent, arrange food and water and even transport. The village has been hurriedly set up for international business with the opening of the Khunjerab Pass, without adequate or essential facilities being provided.

Places to Stay & Eat

The *Shaheen Hotel* has tents with beds for Rs 15. *PTDC tents* are free at the moment, but they will eventually have a motel and office here. The place for eats is at the teashop near the immigration office. Fried eggs, paratha and tea is all you'll get. Expect hotel and food rates to spiral. The alternative is to zip through non-stop to or from Passu.

IMMIGRATION & CUSTOMS

Open every day from 8 am to 11.30 am for outgoing travellers. It takes 2½ hours by bus to reach the Khunjerab Pass and another hour from there to Pirali. The Chinese authorities want you to arrive before evening to enable them to make the necessary arrangements, such as hotel accommodation, food and transport to take you to Taskurgan. A visa for China is essential. Get it in Islamabad, they will not issue visas at the border. The Khunjerab Pass is open for international tourism from 1 May to 30 October every year.

Note that bicycles are allowed into China, as are motorbikes and tourist vans if properly documented and you have an approved Chinese international driving licence. The usual international driving licence is not sufficient, for motorists have to be able to read Chinese traffic signs when driving in China. All the paperwork should be done when you apply for your visa.

For incoming travellers the immigration and customs offices are open until 5 pm. The bank is closed on Fridays but if you have a few FEC (Chinese Foreign Exchange Currency), you can change them with outgoing travellers.

At present customs officers are not particularly strict on liquor brought in from China, nonetheless there are those that also like a drink and your bottles might just get confiscated. Like the Pakistanis, have your fill in Xinjiang before departing from Kashgar or Taskurgan.

ROUTE TO KHUNJERAB PASS

NATCO and PTDC buses depart at 12 noon for Pirali, 86 km away to the north in Xinjiang, Chinese Turkestan. The trip takes 3½ hours and costs Rs 160. It is advisable to take food and water with you as it is not available on the way.

The Karakoram Highway continues to be well paved and passes Khudabad, just a km from Sust, then Khaibar, Murkhun and Abghat in a craggy narrow valley. At Bely a trail splits off the highway north-west to Peshit and Irshad Unwin Pass. From the same trail another forks away to the village of Mizghar, Kalamdarchi Post and Murkushi, and the 4700-metre-high Mintaka Pass. This is the ancient Silk Trade Route up here.

There is a dramatic change on the route up – the valley gets very narrow and dark as the sun is blocked by the high granite walls of the highway. Five km away is a petrol station where the highway narrows even more and the air becomes dank and cold. Another 5 km away is the Wildlife Checkpost for the Khunjerab National Park and a hundred metres away at Dhee, is the military checkpost where passports are checked for exit stamps.

A little way beyond Dhee the route starts zig-zagging upwards, climbing more than 2500 metres up to the Khunjerab Valley which is perennially covered with snow.

Khunjerab Valley translates from the Khirghiz as Valley of Blood, for this was the area where the Kanjuts of Hunza plundered the camel caravans. They were supposed to guard the valley and make it safe for the trade caravans that made their way through here en route to Kashgar or Leh. They were to collect taxes for their trouble but it appears that this was not enough and they degenerated into plundering the passing caravans.

At the border, two police guard the frontier from their lonely outpost. From here the Sino-Pakistan Friendship Highway continues across snowfields for 10 km to a military checkpost. From here it is just over 30 km to Pirali.

Going just to the Khunjerab Pass, at 5275 metres, is allowed, but unless you have your own transport it is not possible to make it up and back in the same day. Even if you did make it up in a hired jeep, you would probably wish that you had your Chinese visa and could follow the route beyond the border on to Pirali, then Taskurgan, then Kashgar, and then ...

GILGIT TO CHITRAL

The road from Gilgit to Chitral was once a vital section of the Silk Trade Route, with minor trails branching off to the north for the Darkot and Boroghil passes. It then continued towards Bukhara and Samarkhand. Today, just a few km from the Kargah Valley in the Punial River Valley is **Buber**, site of a number of rock carvings and engraved scripts. At Gakutch there is a trail which forks off towards Imit in the Ishkoman Valley. Along this route is **Hatun**, another archaeological, petroglyph site.

Between the valleys of Vershinghoom and Yasin is **Gupis** where there are stone formations of the megalithic culture, which have continued to baffle archaeologists over the years. You can't miss them as they are about 10 metres in diameter and about 1¼ metres high.

The 400-km road to Chitral is only just jeepable. It goes north-west then dips down slightly to Teru, 190 km away, the last fair-sized village before the border of Chitral. On this route from Gilgit you pass Punial, 34 km away; Singal, 54 km; Gakutch, 72 km; Gupis, 109 km; Phander, 168 km; all of which have rest houses and are good trout-fishing spots. At Gupis a road branches off to Yasin across the Punial River, proceeds to a tiny village called **Takht-i-Taus** and beyond is **Dasht-i-Taus** – the Desert of Peacocks. From here the route splits into several tracks, one continues to Ishkoman, Naltar and Hunza, while another leads to the 4500-metre Thui Pass, 19 km away, another to the Darkot Pass, 22 km away and 4690 metres above sea level.

Unless you take it easy, stopping at villages and doing some fishing, this is a long trip. Getting a ride is tricky as cargo jeeps using the route usually start full and do not have room for more passengers at intermediate villages. If you do fluke it, an additional Rs 10 will get you a front seat and cover luggage charges. Most travellers try to make it to Yasin, then cross the passes into Chitral.

From Rajah Bazaar in Gilgit the road is unsurfaced and the country is lined with stone walls and large fruit trees. Only eight km further on is a shaky suspension bridge where you have to get off the cargo jeep and walk across. The country road continues beyond Buber to Punial where a policeman will enter your name and passport details in a register. At Singal you make a tea stop and again register with the police.

Beyond this village the road becomes more dramatic, climbing up steep mountainsides and running parallel to the river far below. Here you will see several hanging bridges – usually made of a single strand of wire-rope – which are used by locals to haul themselves across while seated on loops. You will pass a more modern bridge at Sher Quila and from here the road begins to climb in earnest.

Across the Punial River, a trail leads to the Valley of Ishkoman from Gakutch. In the village of **Rosan**, before Gupis, are the petrified remains of a pair of dragons on the upper strata of a cliff face. Legend has it that they so angered a saintly old man when they began devouring children that he put a curse on them and turned them into stone.

Just before Gupis and the confluence of the grey Punial River with the clear blue water of the Yasin River, is a bridge which leads to a track on the other side that goes through barren, rocky country into Yasin.

YASIN VALLEY

It is not more than 134 km away but it takes almost seven hours by cargo jeep. A tiny village 2500 metres above sea level, it has a few shops and a well-furnished rest house where you can get food. The fort-palace of the former ruler of the region is down on the banks of the Yasin River.

Takht-i-Taus, another tiny village further north, has a small bazaar and a post office. Past this village is Dasht-i-Taus, which is close to Darkot where the English explorer, Captain George

Hayward, his interpreter and five porters were all murdered on 17 July 1870. Years later Frederic Drew, author of *Jammu & Kashmir*, took his remains and buried him in the British cemetery in Gilgit.

Higher up the route splits into several tracks: one continues to Ishkoman, Naltar and Hunza; another leads to the 4500-metre-high Thui Ann Pass, 19 km away; and a third veers towards Darkot Pass, 4690 metres above sea level, and into the Chitral Valley. In late spring or early summer both Thui Ann and Darkot are still impassable and are often still slushy with melting snow in late summer. Only at the end of summer and early autumn do they become passable.

If you are unable to get through, your only alternative is to backtrack to Gupis, which has a rest house. But you may be able to get a jeep to Phander on the same day. Cargo jeeps leave Yasin at 7 am and arrive 45 minutes later in Gupis.

PHANDER

Phander is a pleasant little village known as Tiny Kashmir, and less than 40 km from Gupis. From Gupis – a long, spread out village – the road starts to get rough, but once you leave Shashi it gets very rugged, even for jeeps.

The rest house on the hill above the lake is reserved for officials, but more often than not it is closed altogether and rarely accepts foreigners. Get off the jeep about four km before the main village. There are some hotels with basic facilities where you can put up for the night or for a few days. The cargo jeep service usually finishes at this point, but occasionally continues to Teru.

Across the bridge a trail leads to a broad opening to the north, which eventually turns westward towards the 5009-metre-high Chumarkhan Pass and the Zagar Pass, just a little north of Shandur Pass, which is 3730 metres high. See the section on Trekking.

TERU

Teru is almost 32 km from Phander and it takes almost two hours by cargo jeep to get there. A little less than half-way is Ghizer, a tiny village where the trekking route to Kalam in the Swat Valley begins. See the section on Trekking.

Teru is 3100 metres above sea level and is bitterly cold at night. There are two small shops which are hardly ever open for business and a rest house, which also appears to be closed most of the time.

Perched on a slope north-west of the rest house is the Agha Khan Primary School. The school master here will give you a bed if you're having difficulty finding accommodation. If you're not organised for trekking, for a small fee or present, he can also arrange a horse and guide for you at less than the usual rate of Rs 100.

SHANDUR PASS

Shandur Pass is about 24 km from here, and it's another 16 km down to Laspur. One of the most scenic routes in the region, it dips gradually down to a small hamlet six km away. The latter is the last settlement before Laspur. It's a fairly broad valley, with flat meadows, hedged on both sides by brown and gun-metal blue, snow-flecked granite mountain slopes. There is no danger here from possible avalanches.

You will hardly see a soul along this road except, occasionally, a few men working on the jeep track or perhaps some nomads camped along the wayside. You may also come across a few local trekkers in woollen caps, urging their pack donkeys to go faster or occasionally men on foot or horseback coming from Laspur. Other than that, no one.

The mountain streams are clear, cool and safe for drinking. There are horses grazing along the river banks and higher up you will see herds of black, woolly yaks. The route swerves away from the valley and follows another river upstream to the pass. The pass is very narrow and has sheer granite walls that are usually topped by clouds.

The pass opens up as you turn into a broad valley. Soon you will reach a small lake, which is riddled with mosquitoes – not a good spot to camp. Here, too, the weather is changeable, often drizzly, but beyond this point the sky is blue and often there's a pale, watery sun. Not much further on you will come across another, bigger lake, and in the distance you can see a silvery-grey mountain. About here the land begins to open up and is either rich red or chocolate brown in colour, but barren. The route meanders around the lake to the great rocky flanks of mountains where the road is surfaced. It leads straight on to Chitral.

On the way down to Laspur the trail drops abruptly into an arid, dusty, gravelly region, slopes steeply for about five km, then levels off. In the distance on the rim of a ridge is a patch of green, surrounded by huge bare mountains. This is Laspur. The trail continues to be rough, rocky and precipitously steep as it zig-zags down.

CHITRAL VALLEY

Chitral, about 11,500 square km in area, is 80 km at its widest, 50 km at its narrowest and 400 km long from south-west to north-east. It's shaped rather like a crooked little finger and has an altitude ranging from 1000 to 4000 metres. Right in the Hindu Kush, it borders Nuristan to the west and Badakshan to the north in Afghanistan.

The extreme south is lush green with gently rounded slopes, is cloaked in pines and firs, has fertile terraced valleys, and a climate similar to Kashmir. Heading north the landscape gradually changes, becoming more arid. Higher up it is barren, craggy, desolate and inhospitable, and the temperature never gets hot but can dip precipitously to below freezing in winter.

Here the Panjkur Plateau joins the Kasghar Valley in Mastuj and beyond

Boroghil Pass is the Yarkhund Valley where the Yarkhund River flows south to join the Mastuj. Below Mastuj Valley is the Kho Valley and further west is the Tirich Mir Valley which runs northward for about 96 km, gradually looping north-eastward to join the Turikho Valley, then flows south to meet the Kasghar Bala. The Turikho Valley, which runs from the south-west to the north-east and parallel to the Yarkhund River, is a fertile area covered with cedar trees.

It is here that the sheer cliff faces of the valleys meet and you will see foot bridges made of plaited osier. The Kasghar River which rises to seven metres in summer is the natural borderline between the Valley of Chitral and Yasin. Seven km below this junction are the valleys of Chi Trai and the Ludkho Valley. The Kasghar Valley is interesting but it is a restricted area. There are forts here with ramparts over nine metres above ground level and towers that rise 4½ metres above the parapets.

The region is dominated by the majestic Tirich Mir, which at 7750 metres is the highest mountain in the Hindu Kush. Like Nanga Parbat it has several peaks. It is also believed by the local inhabitants to be the home of the fairies. The guards of this fairy palace are visualised as giant frogs known as *bugzai* rather than snow snakes which are supposed to guard the fairy domain of Nanga Parbat. If you are not frightened by the giant frogs, then Tirich Mir apparently has other, more malicious and more whimsical guards. These are fairies who tempt any unfortunate and thirsty adventurers who do manage to get there with bowls of milk or blood. Legend has it that those who accept this hospitality never return home.

Like Baltistan, Gilgit and Hunza this was a region traversed by the ancient Silk Trade Route from Dir and Gilgit in the east to Ferghana and Bukhara. The village of Barenis has rock carvings, engraved proto-Sanskrit script and evidence of primitive settlements, probably Aryan, dating back to the 4th century AD. There are also Buddhist settlements and rock carvings here.

Buddhism existed in Chitral until the 9th century AD during the time of Jaipal, King of Kabul and Chitral. Afghanistan – in the Hindu Kush – was part of the Moghul Empire until it lost power in the latter part of the 18th century. The British tried to annex it, unsuccessfully, and subsequently the Durand Line was cut across the Hindu Kush to separate Afghanistan from Chitral, which eventually came under the administration of the North West Frontier Province.

Recorded history begins here with Yue-Chi tribes, who were Hephthalites or White Huns who invaded Kattor and Gebrek, now known as Kafiristan and Peshawar Valley. Having conquered these regions they established the Kingdom of Little Yue-Chi, and in the 5th century AD they conquered Balkh and Gandhara and occupied Chitral, which later fell to the Uzbekhs. In the middle of the 8th century AD the Chinese came, and in the same century it was invaded by the Muslims. But the southern areas of Lotkah, Chitral and Drosh did not adopt Islam until about two centuries later, with Kafiristan – Land of Non-believers – remaining outside its fold to this day. Islam wiped out all the colourful traditional customs and festivals of the Chitralis.

In the 1880s this region came under the suzerainty of the Maharaja of Kashmir, and fell into British hands, becoming an autonomous political agency of the North West Frontier Province. In 1885, stirred up by the Pathans in the south, the Chitralis rebelled and besieged the British forts, but were reconquered by Sir George Robertson.

It retained its autonomous political agency status until 1966 and eventually in 1970 became a district of the Malakhand Division of the North West Frontier Province. In April 1972 the mirdom of Chitral was completely abolished.

LASPUR

From Shandur Pass the first town in Chitral is Laspur. As you enter the village the trail appears to turn away, but then crosses a dry riverbed and makes a U-turn back into it. The streets here are narrow and gravelly, and the village is hardly visible for trees.

Laspur is situated at an altitude of 2600 metres and is so small it doesn't have a single shop – not even a teashop – or inn. The rest house is often closed, but camping on the lawn is possible. Villagers will offer their huts to travellers for nothing, but food is very limited.

This is the setting off point for trekking routes to Mastuj, Madaghlast, Kalam and Teru.

Early on the day after arriving hike up to Harchin, 11 km away. Cargo jeeps are rare along this route, particularly from spring to early summer, but the road is easy going and follows the Sorlaspur River upstream. Harchin is a fair-sized village, with a few government buildings, local inns and teashops. From here there is a regular cargo jeep service to Mastuj.

MASTUJ

Sixteen km away, Mastuj is a hikeable distance through a remarkably narrow, arid, barren valley. This is where the Mastuj and Yarkhund rivers meet. Approaching the village the trail crosses numerous irrigation channels. At 2400 metres, Mastuj has a small bazaar and a teashop which also serves as a travellers' inn. There is a *Tourist Cottage* here, but it's expensive and it's preferable to camp if you are equipped.

At the foot of a mountain not far from the village, is the fort-palace where the retired ruler of the region still lives. On the side that opens out onto a lawn is a guest room, in disrepair, but still furnished. There is a guest book at this place, which dates back to the 1930s with comments like: 'Had a super-duper time', from an Australian geological party in 1951, or more recently, 'This place seems to be the end of the world – traversed frightening road to come to a warm reception'.

In the spring of 1895 this fort was one of those defended by two British officers, Lieutenant Moberly and Captain Bretherton, until relieved by the force of Colonel Kelly who came all the way from Gilgit.

Mastuj is also a setting off point for trekking routes up to Darkot, Thui Ann and Chumarkhan passes into Yasin, Laspur and Chitral. There is more variety in food here, but it is advisable to bring camping gear and supplementary provisions all the same.

CHITRAL

This is a mini-version of Gilgit with the same physical surroundings, bazaars, polo ground, government offices, banks, hotels and restaurants along a single main street, Shahi Bazaar.

It used to be an important stopping point on the ancient Silk Trade Route, and like Gilgit was a slave-trading centre. One of the local legends reveals that a female slave owned by a Chinese was raped by a Chitrali, bringing about the destruction and depopulation of the valley and consequently turning it into a tributary of China.

The mosque on the banks of the Mastuj River has been recently constructed in a Moghul style, but the adjacent Chitral fort which is Central Asian in design, is literally falling apart with age. It's been converted to a police station but looks more like a museum with the muzzles of 1860s cannons jutting out from the corner of an outer hall.

Like Gilgit, the town bustles through spring, summer and early autumn, but by mid-October, when the Lowari Pass gets snowbound, it's completely cut off from the rest of the world; even though it is connected by air link to Peshawar, 200 km away, this service is severely affected by weather. A long tunnel has been designed to pass through the mountains, but it appears that construction work is being held up due to financial difficulty.

Information

The Tourist Information Centre is at the PTDC Tourist Lodge. Foreigners have to register with the police superintendent immediately on arrival.

You also need a travel permit for the places you wish to visit, which you can get from the deputy commissioner's office. It's supposed to be free but they usually charge Rs 25 which you can bring down to Rs 10. If you want to do any fishing, you must get yourself a licence which will cost Rs 16.

The post office, banks and police station are all along an alley leading to the river. The PIA office is in the next alley.

Things to See & Do

Walk along the river bank to the old fort and the mosques and continue on to the polo ground. Also check out the bazaar while you're here, it's colourful and fun.

The summer palace of the ex-mir which sits atop a 2700-metre plateau is well worth a visit, but the climb is tough going. It has been turned into a hunting lodge, and you can get a magnificent view of the Tirich Mir and Raja Kush from here.

Also worth going to are the polo matches which are put on each weekend at 4 pm and 5 pm.

You can buy semi-precious gemstones from a number of shops along Shahi Bazaar.

If you're in the area between April and September, Ludkho River in Garam Chasma is great for trout fishing.

Places to Stay & Eat

Government rest houses here are mainly for officials only. If you want to treat yourself try the *Mountain Inn*, the most expensive in town. There's a PTDC

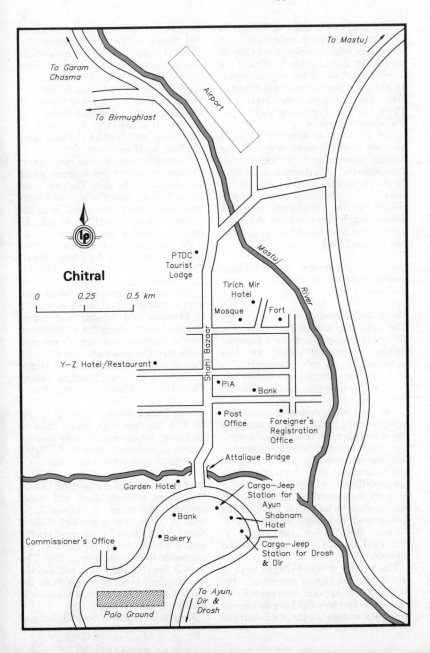

To Mastuj

Airport

To Garam Chasma

To Birmughlast

PTDC Tourist Lodge

Chitral

0   0.25   0.5 km

Tirich Mir Hotel

Mosque

Fort

Mastuj River

Y-Z Hotel/Restaurant

PIA

Bank

Post Office

Foreigner's Registration Office

Shahi Bazaar

Attalique Bridge

Garden Hotel

Cargo-Jeep Station for Ayun

Bank

Shabnam Hotel

Bakery

Cargo-Jeep Station for Drosh & Dir

Commissioner's Office

To Ayun, Dir & Drosh

Polo Ground

Tourist Lodge with rooms for Rs 75 to Rs 150 and a very good restaurant. Just beyond the Attalique Bridge, en route to the District Commissioner's office, is the *Garden Hotel*, which has singles/doubles for Rs 15/25, share bathrooms and reasonably good western-style breakfasts. *Tirich Mir View Hotel*, near the mosque, is also worth checking out.

The *YZ Hotel & Restaurant*, on an alley off Shahi Bazaar, is now under Afghan management. It has singles/doubles for Rs 15/25, charpois on the lawn for Rs 10, and meals are Rs 10. On the right-hand side, heading towards the polo ground is the *Shabnam Hotel & Restaurant*. It provides basic, double or dorm accommodation for Rs 10 per bed, and has good food.

Liquor This is a dry area, except for local brews produced in the Shugur and Kafiristan valleys.

Mastuj-Chitral Road
The cargo jeep service from Mastuj to Chitral is frequent and it's a fantastic journey, incredible even by this mountainous region's standards. It's more perilous than the Gilgit-Astore jeep track but comparable to the Shandur Pass-Laspur trail.

The jeep track crosses a suspension bridge over the Yarkhund River and takes the mountain road, then fords a shallow but swift stream, where passengers hanging from the rear have to jump off and wade across. After this it climbs up a craggy defile where in 1895 a small British military contingent was trapped by the rebels, while on its way to reinforce the beleaguered defenders of the fort in Chitral. Just before the village of Shanewal the road gets even steeper and zig-zags up.

The perfect pyramid-shaped peak of Tirich Mir, the highest mountain in the Hindu Kush, appears unexpectedly at this stage. But you will have no time to enjoy the scenery as the road starts to drop crazily down the outer wall of a sheer cliff, similar to the road to Laspur after Shandur Pass. The hairpin turns are tight even for jeeps. They have to stop and back up at each turn on this frightening descent. There's just time to get your breath back at the village of Shanewal, when, once again, the road drops away steeply. It's like the blue train in Darjeeling (India), which also has to stop and back up at each turn.

Eventually you get to the valley where it meanders past a few bazaars, which have very little for sale. The next main village is Buni, which is built in a fairly wide, long, green valley and is in the process of being turned into an administrative centre for upper Chitral.

Further along are Reshun and Maroi where the jeeps stop for a lunch break. The rest of the way down to Chitral is fairly unexciting.

Alternatively there is a paved road from Laspur to Chitral, which runs south of Harchin and Mastuj and passes through Ustur, joining the main Chitral road at Koghozi. However, it's not used much except by motorists since it is quite a distance to Ustur. It forks near Ustur to Madaghlast, Kalas and Drosh, by-passing Chitral and continuing to Lowari Pass.

Getting There & Away
Air PIA has two F-27 flights daily to Peshawar, which cost Rs 150 plus an airport embarkation fee of Rs 5. Flights are subject to weather conditions.

Road Cargo jeeps to Dir cost Rs 65. Lowari Pass opens in early June and closes around mid-October. It is possible to walk in if the pass is blocked. Take a Suzuki wagon from Dir up to where the road is closed. From this point a trail follows the river up and over the pass. The snow is deep but the trail is well defined and the climb is not too steep. From the top the descent is steep and the snow is slushy but not too deep.

Fares to other places from Chitral are:

Ayun, Rs 10; Birer, Rs 15; Bumburet, Rs 15; Garam Chasma, Rs 15; Mastuj, Rs 35.

The Shandur Pass is open from early May until mid-November. Cargo jeep pick up stations are at Shah Bazaar for Garam Chasma, Mastuj and other northern villages, or just past the Attalique Bridge on the left for Ayun, Birer, Bumburet, Drosh, Ashret and Dir. Mastuj to Chitral is Rs 75 for front seats.

The PTDC has jeeps for hire at the usual government rates. They also arrange and organise treks. Private agencies are a little cheaper but not as reliable or responsible.

BIRMUGHLAST

Fourteen km west of Chitral at an elevation of 2700 metres is Birmughlast. It's a steep four-hour climb up to the little old fort, which is looked after by an old man and his grand-daughter, who live in a mud-stone hut nearby. They will offer visitors tea, and sometimes curd and bread.

Most people leave the trek up until late in the afternoon when it's cooler and then camp overnight. The view is magnificent, particularly on a bright, moonlit night. It's cold here though, so you need a good sleeping bag and some extra food. Trek back early next morning.

GARAM CHASMA

North-west of Chitral, 45 km and 1½ hours by jeep, is the natural hot spring resort of Garam Chasma. It's a delightful, restful little village at an elevation of 1900 metres. Until half-way up, the road is surfaced, but from then on it's narrow and dusty though very scenic.

It passes Shugur where *Shogur Water* is still distilled, then crosses a suspension bridge. On the right as you approach the village, almost hidden by trees, is an old fort, which once used to guard the route into Afghanistan.

The village itself has a tiny bazaar, local hotels, restaurants and teashops. It is a hilly region with a number of mud-stone bathing huts through which the spring water courses. The low-roofed mud huts line the river and it will cost you Rs 5 to bathe. There are pleasant teashops here with tables and benches overlooking the river.

The way to the Afghan border goes through a lush, open field, which is a good site for camping. The rest house is often closed, but there are cheapies like the *Mohat Hotel* which has dorm beds for Rs 10. There's very little choice in food.

Note that there are police check-points along the border here. You may meet some Afghan mujahadeen.

KALASH VALLEYS

South-west of Chitral, 35 km away, are the deep, mysterious valleys of the Kalash people, where the Kafirs, or 'unbelievers' have carried on their traditional culture, religion and way of life for 2000 years without change.

Particularly striking are the Kalash women in their coarse, black cotton, ankle-length clothes and headwear decorated with cowrie shells, beads and buttons or tiny bells hanging from the end of a tail piece. The headwear and dress are strikingly similar to those worn by a tribe in Ladakh, except in Ladakh they adorn them with turquoise. This is not surprising for in the Times of Trouble in the 4th century AD, Dardic tribes migrated towards Leh via Baltistan.

The people in these valleys are often called the Children of Nature. They lead simple lives, surviving on subsistence farming, small flocks of sheep, and a few goats and cattle. They also have fruit orchards. They live in windowless, mud-stone huts and only just participate in the cash economy.

They celebrate their religious festivals in January and May with group dancing, feasting and drinking, and are regarded by many as pagans. Some of their gods are similar to those of the Romans and

Greeks, though they strongly believe in ancestor worship and use wooden effigies for this purpose. Their rectangular coffins are made of thick hard wood, the lids seldom being nailed down, but more often held down by large rocks. The coffins are generally laid out in the open at the foot of nearby mountains.

One theory of their origin is that they are descendants of the Greek troops of Alexander the Great, who settled in these valleys with their Persian wives, after wearying of the long military campaign which began in Egypt and continued all the way across Persia to the Indus. This is highly controversial however, and there is no *bona fide* proof of it. What is likely, is that they were settled in the lowlands for a long time and, following the death of Ashoka, were driven further and further up with successive waves of invasions.

The whole style and dress of the women is similar to the Gandhara bas reliefs you can see in the Museum of Peshawar and this would seem to indicate that is where their origins lie.

Kafiristan consists of three isolated villages within a radius of 18 km. **Bumburet**, the largest is about five km long and about half a km at its widest. It is approximately 35 km from Chitral and accessible by jeep. Bumburet is sandwiched between **Rumbur**, 11 km away and the second largest village , and **Birer** the smallest, which is five km to the southeast behind a massif. Birer is also accessible by jeep from Chitral via Bishala.

The village of Bumburet has quaint water-run mills, a trout hatchery, and is more developed than the other two. It also has several cheapies like the *Peace (Pax) Hotel* which offers free rope beds and charges only for food, meals are Rs 15 to Rs 20. *Kalash Water* may also be available, but be discreet. There are also many middle level hotels with restaurants with rates from Rs 15 up.

The valleys of Birer and Rumbur are very narrow with villages built on steep ledges with mud-stone huts in tight clusters, or perched on hilltops and narrow ridges with sheer cliffs. All these valleys have a mysterious and timeless aura about them.

Getting Around

From Bumburet there is an occasional cargo jeep that goes to Rumbur. But if you don't want to hang around waiting for public transport, it's within walking distance. At Rumbur there is a two-room hotel with six beds for Rs 10 per per person. The food is limited, but it is an interesting valley to explore. You can walk from Bumburet to Birer via the massif, but it's a steep climb, followed by a precipitous path down. There's a small *hotel* here with just three rope-beds for Rs 5 per person. Once again, food is very limited, so bring your own.

Trekking

Introduction

The Northern Territory of Pakistan is cragsman's country with many opportunities for mountaineering and trekking. Since it's covered with fast-flowing, turbulent rivers, including the Indus, it also offers numerous different kinds of rafting and white watering. Skiing is another outdoor activity which can be pursued here. What is more, it's an anthropologist's and archaeologist's paradise.

Recently, the western extremity of the Himalayas has become a playground for mountaineers, trekkers, rafting and skiing enthusiasts. It's larger, craggier, more barren and more glaciated than the eastern Himalayas. Neither the terrain, nor the culture of this region are easy to grapple with. Trekking routes often seem much more straightforward than they are, their dangers underestimated, and the culture, in the process of being transformed, can too easily be taken for granted.

It is a land of uncertainties, where schedules cannot be strictly adhered to, and where women turn their backs and refuse to talk to male strangers for fear of being killed by their own kin. It presents enormously varied experiences, some anticipated, others surprising. But any undertaking needs forethought and organisation, and physical fitness and mental toughness, if you are to conquer the challenges of this rough region.

The Mountains

The Upper Northern Highland with the great mountain ranges of the Hindu Kush, the Karakorams, the Great Himalayan Range, and further south the Lesser and Outer Ranges, contains more than 120 peaks with an average height of 6550 metres. Some of these are still unclimbed and unnamed.

Many of the highest peaks – among them, some of the highest in the world like K2, Nanga Parbat and Hidden Peak – are barely visible. Even when you're right underneath them, the view from the deep valleys is obstructed by the high foothills, whereas the magnificent Annapurna Range in Nepal is wholly visible in all its grandeur from Pokhara. Rakaposhi and neighbouring Diran Deobani are occasionally visible from the Karakoram Highway, as is Nanga Parbat which can also be seen from the air, from Fairytale Meadow and from the Rupal Valley on the Diamar side; and Tirich Mir, which is visible from Chitral. But by and large, most are remote and hidden by surrounding mountains. For example, it is a two-week trek to Concordia, the inner sanctum of the Himalayas, to see K2.

K2 or *Chogori*, as it is known locally, is hemmed in by the Gasherbrum, Masherbrum and Kangri Peaks, which have an average height of almost 8000 metres. Hidden Peak was only discovered in 1934, which is how it got its name. These mountains are more difficult to scale technically and more dangerous than any other mountains in the world, not only because of their physical structure, but also because of the unpredictability of the weather.

Before being conquered, they invariably took their toll in human lives. At the end of the 19th century, Italian and American mountaineering expeditions attempting to scale K2 and Broad Peak were both defeated by weather conditions, which confined assault parties to their tents, causing illness. One person in each party died as a result. Even experienced mountaineers such as Eric Shipton, one of the great mountaineers, and Hermann Buhl, Austrian conqueror of Nanga Parbat in 1954, were killed in this glacial region.

Masherbrum, immediately to the south, is called 'Doomsday' or 'Judgement Peak', because it is a killer mountain. This description was also coined for Nanga Parbat originally, when A F Mummery and two Sherpas perished on the first British mountaineering expedition there in 1897.

More recently, in the summer of 1982, a Swiss mountaineering party failed to scale Kangri Peak because they found the peak had iced over and it was technically impossible. They hammered away at the ice covering for two hundred metres, only to give up when they discovered they could not break the solid ice which capped the summit.

Most of the great peaks are in the Karakorams in the Aghil Range east of the Muztagh in Baltistan. K2, Gasherbrum, Masherbrum and the Kangri Group are all concentrated within an area of 24 square km. To the west, in the valleys of Hunza, Nagar and Gilgit are Distaghilsar, Malangute and the Batura Peaks, which are regarded as being among the most beautiful mountains in the world. To the south are the Rakaposhi, Diran and Haramosh, and in Diamar, south-east of Gilgit, is the last western segment of the Great Himalayan Range where Nanga Parbat, majestic in its solitude, reigns over minor peaks. In Chitral, the Tirich Mir is the highest mountain in the Hindu Kush.

The Valleys

The valleys at the feet of these great mountains are deep and narrow, and do not seem to run in any specific direction, but all over the place. Often their junctions are not only forbidding but confusing. They are anywhere between 16 km and 48 km long, covered in rocks and cascading rivers, and occasionally scarred with ravines, gorges, moraines and glaciers. They usually open out into a sandy wasteland with long, craggy, arid escarpments, or flat plains strewn with detritus; or sometimes into fan-shaped

meadows with ridges that are lushly cultivated. Finding the way into some of these valleys is not only circuitous and tortuous, but also involves climbing high passes.

Only a few valleys, like Chitral and Gilgit, are below the usual 2500-metre elevation. Most are between 2500 and 3500 metres, which means attaining extraordinary heights quickly, and tends to make climbers and trekkers forget the necessary acclimatisation period before moving on to higher altitudes. Changes in the ecological level are significant up here, particularly over passes.

The craggy, barren and arid nature of the valleys seems interminable at times. Sir Francis Younghusband, who explored this region extensively in the latter part of the 19th century, used to run uphill to see the snow-covered ranges to refresh himself after the desolate march through these featureless valleys.

The western segment of the Himalayas is corrugated not in a spectacular manner like Nepal, but in a regular fashion where the great peaks tower above surroundings at an average height of 6500 metres.

The Rivers

Eric Shipton wrote, that to describe this region was to indulge in superlatives, for everywhere you look are the highest, longest and largest mountains, glaciers and rivers in the world.

The Indus, known as the 'Father of Rivers' or the 'Lion River', has its source in Lake Manasarowar at the foot of Mt Kailash in Tibet. It begins its 3300-km odyssey roaring out of Tibet, crossing Kashmir and Ladakh in a north-west direction, and closely skirting the border of China. Looping west, the Indus forces its way through constricting granite walls, and rushes onwards. By the time it enters Baltistan it has already gone 800 km, descended around 3500 metres and still has a 1500-km journey ahead, through deep gorges and some of the bleakest, most barren and most scenic areas in the world. When it gets to the Upper Highland of Pakistan it veers off at a sharp 90° angle and then plunges 1500 metres into the lowland of the Punjab, crossing through Sind and finally sweeping into the Arabian Sea.

On the way through Baltistan it is joined by the Shyok River, and further west by the Hunza, Gilgit and Astore rivers. Turning to the south, it is joined by other tributaries like the Swat and Kabul rivers.

There are other rivers in the region: the Ishkoman and the Harambul in the Valley of Hunza; the Yarkhund, Sorlaspur and Mastuj rivers in Chitral; and the Punial, Hunza and Gilgit rivers in the Valley of Gilgit. Because they are mountain rivers they are all turbulent and fast flowing, particularly in summer. But for sheer adventure, none beats the Father of Rivers.

The Glaciers

Of the entire Himalayas, the Trans-Himalayas of the Northern Mountain region of Pakistan has the most glaciers. The Karakorams consist of 25% glaciers, while in Baltistan there are some of the largest and longest glaciers outside the Arctic and Antarctica.

The Siachen, near the border of Ladakh, is about 74 km long and the largest glacier in this part of the world. Others include the Baltoro, Biafo, Hispar and the Batura, all roughly 58 km in length. They run parallel to the Karakorams and arch up from the Valley of Ladakh, north-westward over Baltistan to the Hunza Valley.

Many of the glaciers are thawing slowly and, as a result, are shifting and sliding into the valleys. Some are inert masses of ice and rocks sculpted by wind, sun and rain into weird, often beautiful shapes, which vanish suddenly leaving only moraines in their wake. In this region it is possible to travel over 100 km without ever setting foot on earth, particularly along the Biafo-Hispar segment, which

runs from Ashkole to the Valley of Nagar, a distance of 240 km. It takes approximately 10 days to a fortnight to do this trek.

Apart from the Batura, which is just off the Karakoram Highway, the rest of the gigantic glaciers are remote and difficult to reach.

Warning

Note that unless you're oriented to travelling on glaciers, it can be extremely dangerous, particularly in summer when they are liable to develop fissures and collapse into yawning crevasses. When they do collapse, the explosion reverberates around the valleys. Unless you know what you're doing, this region can not only be daunting, but terrifying.

The Seasons

Spring arrives in mid-February, and the weather begins to get warmer. By March it is pleasant, the valleys are turning green and it's the time for festivals. The April downpours are renowned, and often whole mountainsides are dumped down on the road, blocking them for days. In May, snow and glaciers begin to thaw, and streams and rivers start to swell, the villages and towns stir into life, and mountaineers, trekkers and tourists trickle in.

June marks the beginning of summer and temperatures soar to over 38°C in the lower valleys, but it is still pleasant in the higher reaches. This is the season for polo and tourism. The rivers become fast-flowing torrents and the shepherds move upland with their stock. By mid-July the monsoons are inundating the plains, though they don't have any effect on the high country. The temperature starts to drop by mid-August, and the high mountain passes are clear of ice and snow.

In September, autumn moves in and tourists start to move out, just when the climate is becoming pleasant and the valleys beautiful. The rivers and sky clear and the stars are sharp, dense and dazzling. There's a crispness in the air by October, and the trees turn amber, through russet to brown. By November the valleys are cold and stark and the tourists have disappeared.

In December it starts snowing and winter sets in. It's quiet and cold and the temperature sinks to as low as -20°C. Daylight only lasts for between four and six hours and the valleys are dark and desolate.

Maps
Good trekking maps are difficult to obtain in Pakistan. However, the Pakistan Survey Maps, available near the post office in Murree, are better than none at all. In Gilgit, there are shops and even hotels that have photo-copies of trekker's maps of this region. You can also try *Feroze & Sons* in Rawalpindi, or the *American Bookshop* in Peshawar. However, your best bet is to try specialist mountaineering and trekking bookshops at home before you leave.

Books
Apart from *Pakistan – a travel survival kit*, there are several guidebooks on Pakistan, but most of the books on the Northern Territory are written by British explorers and are 'historical', covering the geology, anthropology and archaeology of the area. However, there are two excellent guidebooks that are highly recommended. They are *The Trekker's Guide to the Himalaya & Karakoram* by Hugh Swift (Hodder & Stoughton, London, 1982), and *Himalayan Odyssey* by Trevor Braham (George Allen & Unwin, London, 1974).

Travel guidebooks are available at *London Books,Feroze & Sons*, Saddar Bazaar, Rawalpindi; and the *American Bookshop* in Peshawar. Apart from travel guidebooks, rare or specialised books are available in Gilgit at Ghulam Mohammed Beg's bookstall, Jamaat Khana Bazaar, and Dad Ali Shah's *Hunza Handicraft Shop*, Airport Rd, in front of the Park Hotel.

Trekking Agencies
There are a few trekking and mountaineering agencies in Rawalpindi, and a few local operators in the Northern Territory. The *Pakistan Tourism Development Corporation* (PTDC), *Karakoram Tours* and *Mrs Waljis Tour-Trek Agency*, all have offices in Islamabad and Rawalpindi. The former is a quasi-government corporation; the latter two are operated by private companies.

They all assist in clearing trekking parties through immigration and customs, preparing advance hotel bookings, fixing formalities with the Ministry of Tourism, booking flights to central points, arranging alternative transport and providing camping gear if required. They also arrange for the storage of equipment, for supplies to be sent on ahead of the party, work out an approximate cost of the tour or trek on enquiry, and even provide medical kits and trekking equipment if necessary. They handle large parties of up to 50 and over, and treks that last a month or more.

Enquiries on trekking or mountaineering can be made from any travel agency, but the PTDC has offices in some overseas countries, and failing that, the Pakistan embassies and consulates provide literature which sets out the terms and conditions for obtaining permission to trek or climb a mountain in Pakistan. Also included is detailed information on fees, insurance, cancellation charges, porterage, equipment, clothing, supplies and foreign exchange.

Useful Addresses
Islamabad & Rawalpindi
Pakistan Tours Ltd, Flashman's Hotel, The Mall,Rawalpindi.
Travel Waljis Ltd, Box 1088 Waljis Building, 10 Khayaban Suharwardy, Islamabad.

Karakoram Tours, F-7/2, Street 19, 1-Baltoro House, Islamabad.

Sitara Travel Consultants, Box 63, 25-26 Shalimar Plaza, Rawalpindi.

Gilgit
Ghulam Mohammed Baig, Box 516, Jamaat Khana Bazaar.

Ibrahim Baig, Tourist Camp, Karimabad.

Nasir Sabir, World Mountain Adventure, Tourist Cottage, Jutial.

Abdul Karim, Tourist Cottage, Jutial.

Other
If you want to trek in both open and regulated zones, and intend applying for a permit before you head off to Pakistan, don't forget that it takes three months minimum for it to be processed. However, if you are in Pakistan already, you will have to wait at least a month for your permit to come through, unless you are a member of a small group, in which case it may only take four or five days. For detailed information on terms and conditions of trekking, get hold of the brochure published by the Ministry of Culture & Tourism, Islamabad, Pakistan.

Mountaineering
Mountaineering clubs wishing to scale any of the peaks in the Northern Territory have to meet special requirements and conditions. Applications must be made at least a year in advance between 1 January and 31 October, and it's done on a 'first come, first served' basis. All applications to climb K2 must be made two years in advance of the intended date of the expedition through any Pakistan Embassy or Consul's Office.

Equipment & Supplies
Non-consumables can be imported free of duty on condition they are taken out of the country when you leave. Consumables – including liquor – are allowed in free of duty as long as they are to be consumed. Anything left has to be taken out with you or burned. You are not allowed to sell non-consumables or give them away, except to institutions with government approval.

Remember, walkie-talkies and radio-transmitter sets for communication between party and district headquarters are indispensable for large parties attempting to scale major peaks.

Royalties
These vary according to the heights of the peaks.

For a mountain of 6000 to 7000 metres costs Rs 15,000; 7000 to 7500 metres costs Rs 20,000; 7500 to 8000 metres is Rs 25,000; 8000 metres and above, except K2, is Rs 35,000 and K2 costs Rs 45,000 or approximately US$3000.

Should a foreign mountaineering club join up with a Pakistani one, the royalties are halved. Concessions are made to small parties attempting the smaller peaks.

Foreign mountaineering expeditions must be accompanied by at least one English-speaking member to obviate communication difficulties. There must also be at least one doctor in a large expedition, or a medical assistant if it's a small party.

Liaison Officer
A liaison officer is usually detailed with large trekking or mountaineering, rafting, skiing, or even filming expeditions over hazardous or strenuous and restricted regions. Like high-altitude mountain guides and high-altitude porters, they have to be provided with insurance, equipment and supplies.

Rafting & Skiing
The same restrictions and permit requirements apply to rafting and skiing expeditions. There are no agencies in Pakistan that handle rafting or skiing parties. You should either join an agency overseas – there are a number in the USA, particularly in California, and in the UK – or, if you're in Pakistan, approach the PTDC for assistance.

Rafting or skiing equipment is not locally available here and has to be imported. Once again the same customs rules and regulations apply to rafting and skiing expeditions.

A liaison officer is also detailed by the Ministry of Tourism to rafting and skiing parties, but it's highly unlikely that the liaison officer will make it through the whole trip, particularly skiing parties.

Rivers Open for White-watering

The Indus from Jaglot to Thakot
Kunhar River from Naran to Kaghan
Swat River from Bahrain to Saidu Sharif
Chitral River from Butkhaila to Dir
Hunza River from Aliabad to Gilgit

Filming & Photographic Expeditions

Aerial photography is allowed only if the pilot or liaison officer is informed beforehand. Photography and filming of military sites and local women is strictly prohibited.

In the Northern Territory the customs rules and regulations also apply to photographic or filming expeditions. But there is no restriction or permit requirement in the rest of Pakistan.

A liaison officer is usually assigned to filming parties, but seldom to photographic expeditions except in restricted regions.

Mountain Guides

The Northern Territory has some of the finest high-altitude mountain guides in the world. Considered the equal of the Sherpas of Nepal are the Balti mountain guides, and more particularly, those from Hunza. A particularly skilled guide is Nasir Sabir, who accompanied the successful Waseda Mountain Expedition to K2 in the summer of 1980, and in the summer of 1982 topped both Broad Peak and Gasherbrum with Reinhold Messner.

Porters

At low altitudes the porters' maximum load is 25 kg over a distance of either 10 km or a day, which must include rests of about five to 10 minutes' duration. If a night camp is struck before the traditional 10 km to 13 km has been covered, the shortfall has to be made up the next day.

High-altitude porters must be provided with insurance against accidents, camping gear – tents, sleeping bags, boots, food – and medicine.

Maximum Load

5000-6000 metres altitude	25 kg
6000-7000 metres altitude	17 kg
7000-8000 metres altitude	14 kg
Above 8000 metres	12 kg

This load has to be carried up at each level (advance base camp) and back to base camp or lower level base camp on each trip. Porters have to sign an undertaking of good behaviour, particularly for mountaineering expeditions as they can ruin an expedition by refusing to move on unless paid more, and negotiation could go on *ad infinitum*.

For your own benefit check the references of any prospective porter/guide. It is advisable to choose one who comes with good credentials and recommendations. It is often better to hire porters for short distances only – i.e. to the next village only – as there will be local porters waiting there who know the area well. Of course, this is only possible if you are trekking by stages over a long route from valley to valley.

If a porter has served you well, be sure to recommend him in the notebook he keeps for such commendations.

Porter Registration Generally for locally hired porters, registration with the police is not necessary, but there are areas where this is vital, particularly areas north of Kalam in the Swat Valley, Darel and Tanger in the sub-northern region of the Northern Territory.

Porter Rates through Agencies
US$25 for guides per day plus food
US$20 for porters at high altitudes per day plus food
US$15 for low-altitude porters per day plus food
US$20 for cooks per day plus food

Official Government Rates
Porters at low altitude	Rs 75 per day plus ration or Rs 25 in lieu of ration
Porters at high altitude	Rs 100 per day plus ration or Rs 30 in lieu of ration

There are also applicable rates for rest days, sickness or injury and return journey rates. The rates can vary between regions, eg the rates in Chitral are slightly lower than those shown, in Gilgit they are slightly higher.

Tour & Trekking Agencies Service Fees
US$300 for two to four people
US$400 for five to 10 people
US$500 for 11 to 15 people
US$600 for more than 15 people

Vehicle Hire
Jeeps	Rs 10 per mile
Tractors	Rs 15 per mile
Toyota Jeeps	Rs 12 per mile

These rates are for Baltistan; Gilgit and Chitral are slightly lower.

Trekker's Requirements
Personal Quality Up in the Himalayas, which begin where the Alps end, physical fitness is not enough. Stan Armington notes in *Exploring Nepal*, a more or less hassle-free country for tourists, that both trekkers and travellers 'must have the ability to adapt to unusual situations, to accept confusion and lack of certainty'. This advice is applicable to the whole of Pakistan, but particularly to the Northern

Territory, where in addition a trekker must have almost infinite understanding and be able to stay cool and positive.

Insurance Trekking and mountaineering insurance is obtainable in Pakistan, but it is preferable to get it in your own country from your trekking or mountaineering agent. The policy for illness, accidents and luggage, must cover trekking and mountaineering emergency services such as helicopter evacuation and hospitalisation. If there is an accident up here, a helicopter rescue is more-or-less inevitable, particularly in remote areas. This is a clause which is indispensable in the insurance policies of individuals, group trekkers and mountaineers, and rafting and skiing enthusiasts.

Insurance for the liaison officer, mountain guides and porters is obtainable from local insurance companies in Islamabad.

Visa Usually a one-month visa is enough, but if you're likely to go trekking for over a month, it is advisable to get a three-month visa.

Also it's a good idea to take into account possible delays of up to two weeks because of unpredictable weather conditions. Flights could be cancelled or the Karakoram Highway blocked.

Ways of Trekking In contrast to Nepal, Kashmir and Ladakh, the craggy, barren, glacial trekking region of the Northern Territory is sparsely populated.

Villages, hamlets and shepherds huts are few and far between. Moreover, they are not tourist-oriented. With the exception of a handful of local people who would offer overnight accommodation and food to trekkers, the Muslim society is closed to outsiders.

What Stan Armington describes as the 'living-off-the-land' approach to trekking in the Eastern Himalayas is simply not possible here. The one exception is if you're trekking along the main jeep tracks which have local travellers' inns or government rest houses. Out in the true trekking regions, you are virtually walking on untrodden ground along tracks which have only been used by villagers themselves. Trekkers must bring food supplies with them, which means careful forward planning is vital. You must take into consideration the availability of food, distances from village to village and trekking time.

What to Take

Camping Gear Thorough preparation in organising a trip and knowing what to bring can mean the difference between an enjoyable and a miserable trek.

Comfortable boots and thick woollen socks plus cotton inner socks are essential. Trekking trousers must be made of strong material and not too tight. Longjohns, preferably woollen, a crew-neck or polo-neck woollen pullover (sweater), light woollen jumper and windbreaker, and woollen shirts and cotton underwear are musts. Warm gloves and a raincoat make the difference between relative comfort and sheer misery.

Your tent must be light, have a flysheet, and preferably be waterproof. A waterproof, down sleeping bag with an inner cotton sheet and ground pad with waterproof groundsheet are also essential.

Mountaineering food is recommended: dehydrated, sealed and packed food and the usual essentials. In summer fruit is available and you can also get milk, curd, cheese and, occasionally, eggs from shepherds. Bring some fishing rods and obtain a fishing licence as the rivers are full of trout.

The kind of rucksack you take depends on what is most comfortable for you. Generally packs with frames are too large and cumbersome, but some individuals prefer them. Whatever you choose, make sure it's big enough to contain all the essentials. You should also make sure that everything is tightly packed, so that you don't have clothes, food and equipment moving around. Rucksacks must be made of strong material for rough travelling.

Odds & Sods Useful items include a torch, candles, matches or lighters, spoon and fork, Swiss Army knife, needle and thread, leather sewing awl with extra strong thread for running repairs on packs and boots, a tube of glue or adhesive tape for other repair work and a nylon cord for laundry and other uses.

Health

Staying in good physical shape is of primary importance to any traveller, particularly when roughing it, trekking, mountaineering, rafting, skiing, fishing or filming in this rugged terrain.

One simple way of maintaining your health is to be very careful about the water you drink. Well-known Netherlands mountaineer and trekker, Egbert Bardoel, suggests the following precautions in order of preference: boiling water for 20 minutes; filtering which involves taking a mini-filter with you; or purifying with tablets – there are a number of brands you can choose from, most of which taste terrible and only last six hours, but do not have any negative side effects. It is also advisable to add lemon juice if you have any available. Iodising is also a practical, efficient way of purifying water. It kills amoeba, giardia and bacteria. Iodine for this purpose comes in tablets or solution and produces safe drinking water in 15 to 20 minutes.

Bardoel believes garlic is the best natural antibiotic for all-round good health measures. It fortifies the digestive system, increases resistance to diseases – especially stomach problems, dysentery, etc – cleanses the blood, protects the liver, wards off colds and has no negative side effects. He recommends a minimum of three cloves or pills a day and double that if you are having trouble. The cloves have to be cut in tiny pieces or chewed, and if you're concerned about being given a wide berth by the rest of the party, keep your breath fresh with celery.

An excellent book that covers all aspects of health whilst mountaineering is *Medicine for Mountaineering* edited by James A Wilkerson (The Mountaineers, Seattle, 1975).

Common Diseases Apart from travel fatigue and sore feet, influenza and intestinal infections (particularly giardia) are the most common afflictions for trekkers and mountaineers.

Be sure you have the following in your medical kit: iodine for cuts and bruises or contusions; Tetracycline Hydrochloride, 250 mg capsules are excellent antibiotics for influenza, bronchial or respiratory infections and abdominal ailments; Fasigyn for gut problems or giardia; Flagyl for amoebic dysentery; Lomotil for diarrhoea; Strepto-magma and dehydration salt for diarrhoea and other gut problems; antihistamines for high-altitude respiratory congestion and APC tablets for headaches, muscle pains and fever. Terramycin is a good cream for skin infections and wounds; Multifungin footpowder; Moleskin or Telpa Pads for blisters and Dextrose tablets for exhaustion or travel fatigue.

To counteract scabies Benzyl Benzoate is good; and take some insect repellent for bedbugs, mosquitoes, sandflies and fleas. Ophthalmic ointment for sore eyes; skin cream to prevent lips and skin from cracking or flaking; gauze, cotton, bandaids and some rolls of adhesive and elastic bandages for sprains.

Physical Aids A good pair of sunglasses to protect your eyes from the glare of sandy wasteland or snow; a hat, preferably made of cloth, scarves which are large enough to cover your head and nose against dust storms or cold winds, are all essentials.

Vitamins B and C are also indispensable. If possible, carry your special medicines in your pocket or keep them in a handy side-pocket of your rucksack, so that you can get at them quickly if necessary.

Checkups Be sure to have a medical checkup before heading off into the mountainous wilderness of Pakistan. As a special precaution it may be a good idea to have an injection of Gamma 16 (immune serum globulin 16.5%), a prophylactic against diseases and infections for a period of 20 days.

For the inexperienced, getting fit is also necessary. Choose a rugged place and go for regular five-km hikes several weeks before you go. Make sure this includes rock climbing.

Altitude Sickness

Dr Karl M Herrligkoffer, successful expedition leader to Nanga Parbat and Broad Peak in 1953-54, and again to Nanga Parbat from the Rupal side in 1982, believes the same advice applies to mountaineers, trekkers and skiers in high altitudes.

Atitude sickness begins at the level of 3300 metres and is caused by lack of oxygen, and thus of pressure, at higher levels. The body has certain faculties that adapt to any changed environmental conditions. Dr Herrligkoffer writes that the body 'reacts as it would to any physical exertion: the heart beats faster and the blood circulates more quickly. Lack of oxygen makes the body lethargic and the climber's will-power and orientation decreases. The comparatively small physical exertion involved in pitching a tent or preparing food loom large and call for a tremendous effort.

The degree of acclimatisation varies widely with the constitution of the individual. It may also be affected by the enormous fluctuation in the outside temperatures and the damaging influences of the sun radiation.

At higher altitudes there is a loss in carbon dioxide. The carbon dioxide acts as the normal regulator of the breathing function by stimulating a rhythmical activation of the breathing muscles without the conscious intervention of the brain. A diminished carbon dioxide content of the body may cause a disturbance in the breathing function in the following manner: after a long pause respiration starts with very shallow breaths, which gradually increase into a very deep and panting breathing movement known as *Cheyne-Stokes* breathing.

On the physical side, the disturbance of proper brain-functioning may cause severe headaches, vertigo, sickness and vomiting. The subjective mental phenomena may be equally marked: the climber suffers from feelings of great lassitude and general lack of will-power. Lapses of consciousness may occur, and the faculty of reasoning is affected . . . The normal activities of consciousness are considerably restricted and a diminution of the rational critical powers may lead to a serious underestimation of objective dangers . . . '

At 7000 metres acclimatisation becomes impossible and at 7600 metres you reach what is known as the 'death zone' and, 'a climber may have a race with death to conquer the peak'.

Trekkers must not on any occasion try to climb over 3000 metres in one day. If you ignore this advice, you risk having altitude sickness compounded with pneumonia. Note that treks in this area start at an elevation of around 2300 metres to 2600 metres and can easily ascend 750 metres or more in a few hours. So watch your breathing and mental condition. Slow down when you start getting a tight chest or a headache.

Too much alcohol before climbing is verboten. This is a region which teaches you to accept your limitations and not to over-extend yourself. Moreover, this mountain wilderness cannot be hurried through, or out of, or up. Above 3650 metres you need two days of acclimatisation before going any further. If you

haven't spent enough time in acclimatising yourself, you will soon begin to feel the symptoms of altitude sickness.

The safest method of approach is to climb an average of 300 to 400 metres only each day.

The first symptoms of altitude sickness are persistent headache, nausea, loss of appetite, sleeplessness, shortness of breath, fatigue and increased output of urine. As soon as you become aware of these symptoms, descend at once to rest before ascending again at a slower pace.

Headache and breathlessness are early symptoms and should not be ignored. If you develop a headache, assume that this is altitude sickness and do not ascend further until the symptoms have cleared, usually in one or two days. Headache is often dismissed or blamed on some other condition, and if ignored can lead to serious results. If the symptoms persist or worsen, descend at least to the level at which you felt well. If severe symptoms have developed, that particular trek should be abandoned.

More severe symptoms include an abrupt decrease in urinary output, gross fatigue, severe headaches, breathlessness, coughing blood or foaming saliva. This indicates pulmonary oedema or water-logged lungs.

Other possible symptoms are extreme weariness, vomiting, staggering walk, irrational behaviour, drowsiness or unconsciousness. This indicates cerebral oedema or water-logged brain.

In either of these cases, *you must descend at once*. With the former you might recover and be able to continue the trek, but with the latter the trek must be abandoned altogether.

This warning cannot be stressed often enough or strongly enough: 'Don't go too fast, too high'.

In the summer of 1982 a Japanese doctor died on Ultar Peak of altitude sickness compounded by pneumonia. A Swiss doctor who fell to his death from Nanga Parbat was suffering altitude sickness, but insisted on following the rest of the team up. Many accidents that occur are due to negligence in getting acclimatised.

The effects of altitude sickness are often subtle and can worsen dramatically if ignored. Do not ascend if they develop, no matter how minor. However, altitude sickness rarely strikes suddenly and the progress of symptoms is steady. Relax and enjoy your trek if you're feeling well and be prepared to rest for a day or two if you're not.

Trekking Zones

The Northern Territory has always been a sensitive region because of its geopolitical importance. By and large, trekking and mountaineering expeditions, and this includes rafting and skiing parties as well, are not allowed outside the boundaries of the 15-km ceasefire line in Azad Kashmir & Jammu, and are restricted to staying within about 30 km of the Chinese and Afghanistan borders.

Circumstances and conditions along borders are subject to change, so suss out the latest information before you set out. At present trekking regions are divided into three zones – free, open and restricted. The free zone covers unrestricted areas with general elevation, not exceeding 6000 metres and permits and guides are not necessary. The treks are generally easy ones of two days and up to a week, and are considered simply as walkabouts. The open zone covers unrestricted areas but the altitude is higher than 6000 metres, and treks go over a period of two weeks to more than a month. They rate from moderate to strenuous, a high-altitude guide is necessary, and often a permit is also required. The restricted zone covers areas prohibited to foreigners in border regions above 6000 metres, where trekking is very strenuous and covers a period of over a month. Usual

prerequisites are a permit, porters and high-mountain guides. Often a liaison officer is detailed to the expedition or party by the Ministry of Culture & Tourism.

This region has become increasingly sensitive since the Russian invasion of Afghanistan. Some trekking areas have been deleted from the official list approved by the Ministry of Culture & Tourism. These are strictly off-limits to foreigners – indefinitely, probably until the situation is resolved.

Heading Off

Before setting off into the unknown of open or regulated zones, trekking or mountaineering expeditions have to register with the Foreigner's Registration Office at Rawalpindi or Islamabad and at the Police Station in the administrative town of the region where they are going to trek. They must also notify the same offices when they are intending to depart.

The Northern Territory is a particularly special trekking area, not merely because of its vastness, ruggedness and weather conditions, but also because of the special cultural, social and geopolitical conditions. Attention is drawn to these facts, not only for reasons of safety, but also for increasing the pleasure of trekking up here.

Essentially this is a peaceful place, but it is in the process of undergoing enormous changes – always unsettling – initiated partly through the influx of tourists in recent years. This has been further complicated by the situation in Afghanistan, which has led to many refugees from the Wakhan region entering Pakistan, and is made all the more complex by international pressure on Russia to get out of Afghanistan. Added to all this is the pressure being put on Pakistan by the US to eradicate the cultivation of poppies and plug one of the main narcotics sources.

Like most mountainous trekking regions in the world – Latin America, Africa, Nepal, Ladakh and Kashmir – a few

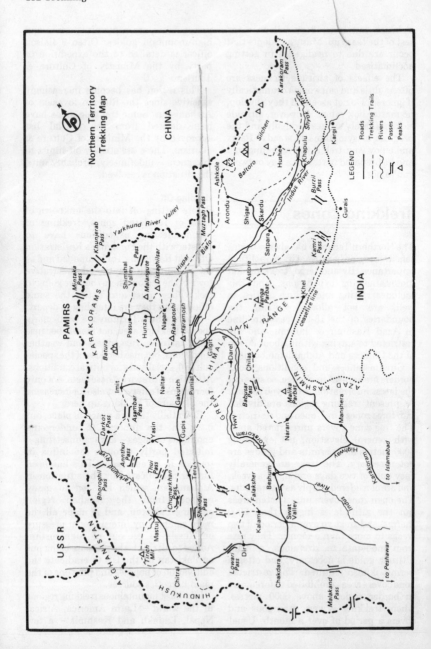

Northern Territory
Trekking Map

CHINA

Karakoram
Pass

Silchen

Hushe

Shyok

Baltoro

K2

Ashkole

Indus River

Kargil

Arondu

Shigar

Skardu

Khapulu

Burzil
Pass

Yarkhund River Valley

Muztagh Pass

Satpara

Kamri
Pass

Khunjerab
Pass

Pass

Hispar

Biafo

Astore

Gurais

Mintaka
Pass

Shimshal
Valley

Malangute

Distaghisar

PAMIRS

KARAKORAMS

Passu

Nagar

Hunza

Rakaposhi

Haramosh

Nanga
Parbat

RANGE

INDIA

ceasefire line

Khel

Batura

Imit

Naltar

Gakutch

Gilgit

H I M A L A Y A N

AZAD KASHMIR

Darel

Bhoroghil
Pass

Darkot
Pass

Asambar
Pass

Yasin

Gupis

Punial

Teru

GREAT

Babusar
Pass

Chilas

Malika
Parbat

Mansehra

Annthui
Pass

Thui
Pass

Chunarkhan
Pass

Shandur
Pass

Naran

Karakoram

HWY

Yarkhund River

Mastuj

Falaksher

Beshum

Karakoram Highway

Indus River

to Islamabad

Tirich Mir

Chitral

Lowari
Pass

Dir

Kalamm

Swat
Valley

AFGHANISTAN

HINDUKUSH

Chakdara

Malakand
Pass

to Peshawar

USSR

LEGEND

Roads

Trekking Trails

Rivers

Passes

Peaks

trekkers have disappeared mysteriously up in this region. People trekking on their own or in small parties should be particularly aware of this danger. Always double check with the police, tourist officers or mountain people themselves about which areas are risky and whether or not you need a guide.

Try to see the headman or the teacher in villages along the way to let them know you are in the area and ask permission before camping. Once permission has been granted you are automatically under the protection of the whole village. They will also be able to give you some good tips on dangers, weather, food, etc. If you take some small gifts with you and hand them out as you go, it always makes for better relationships. If you're not camping near a hamlet or village make sure you choose a site that is not in danger from landslides or flash floods.

Up here the Islamic culture takes on a special character. Local women should never be photographed or even approached, and if they turn away do not try to follow them. Apart from being frightened of foreigners, they also dread being caught talking with strangers by male members of their family or clan. This is not true of the Kalash Valleys of Birer, Bumburet or Rumber in Chitral.

Try to avoid any discussion on sensitive political matters, or religious tenets. Communal clashes occur here from time to time. The mountain people are friendly, hospitable and trustworthy, but there are rules to be observed on a trekking trail. Always greet them first and take time to shake hands with everyone in their party. Never approach them with suspicion, be friendly and smile. While this approach may not work all the time, it generally does.

Most successful mountaineering or trekking expeditions get on well with their mountain guides and liaison officers, so energy should be put into establishing a rapport and mutual trust and confidence from the outset.

If possible bring a gas stove and some portable gas with you. As the country up in this region is arid, rocky and barren, plants and trees are precious and wood is in short supply. Also make sure you leave your camp sites clean when you leave.

If you are trekking independently it is important to bring some food. In the more populated areas food should be readily available in local tea shops, but the variety is very limited. Even rice can be a rare commodity up here. The mountain people are naturally hospitable, but it is important not to abuse this hospitality.

Both the inexperienced and the uninitiated in trekking and rock climbing would be wise to start with easier routes. It's quite possible for middle-aged, and fit elderly people, to go on trekking expeditions in this region, but take it slowly at first. Do not cover any more than 10 km a day, rest often and increase the distance covered gradually day by day.

People trekking should walk together, keeping each other in view. Do not allow anyone to lag behind, and if you're with a guide, never get ahead of him. Those left behind can become confused, lose their way or, at the very least, are quite likely to injure themselves in their hurry to catch up.

In a glaciated region guides are indispensable because it is so dangerous, particularly if you're unfamiliar with such phenomena as fissures, cracks and crevasses. Never disobey the guide in glacial, mountain regions. Most of the porters are veterans of trekking expeditions, and know exactly what to do. What's more, they will do almost everything but trek for you – from choosing the best and safest camping sites, finding water and obtaining food, to carrying the equipment. The majority are frightened of receiving poor references, so they work very hard. Do not abuse them because of this.

Good preparation and good luck!

Lower Northern Treks

AZAD KASHMIR & JAMMU

The distance between Muzzaffarabad and Khel is accessible by road, but beyond Khel it is a restricted area.

Khel-Naran Trek

This is a two-day trek in a free zone. It is an easy to moderate trek at 3000 metres and a porter or guide is not necessary. It can be undertaken all year round except during the monsoon.

The route from Khel is either via Ratti Gali, Nuri Nali Hali Pass, or Damurian. Camp at Dharian, 3000 metres in elevation.

Khel-Chilas Trek

This takes six to 10 days and you need a permit, guide and porters. Setting off point: Muzzaffarabad. It is a restricted zone; strenuous trek at an elevation of 6000 metres. Best time to do it is from July until September.

From Khel to Moti it's 24 km; turn north-west to Domel; 2½ hours easy travelling with huts along the way. The trail forks at a stream, one path leading to Astore, the other to Chilas.

It is 16 km from Moti to Kalan ascending gradually to a pass, 4000 metres high.

Between Kalan and Paloi there is a steep climb of 32 km. The route goes north then west; then north again for 1½ hours, ascends a pass at 4900 metres; then turns west into a valley, descending to 3300 metres. After walking another four hours you will reach a lake. Once you've passed the lake there is a 2½-hour descent through cultivated land, then through pine forests. Paloi is situated at an elevation of 3150 metres.

It is 16 km between Paloi and Bunar which takes about 4½ hours to cover. After 2½ hours you will reach the village of Kilbai, which is surrounded by walnut trees. The trail splits at Kilbai with one path leading to Bunar and the other over Mazeno Pass to Tarshing.

The trail to Bunar follows the right bank of the river and leads into the village at 1850 metres above sea level after a two-hour trek. There's a good view of Nanga Parbat from here.

From Bunar Village to Bunar Tarao it is 19 km or five hours; gradual descent to a plateau, then down and across the river. Follow the trail along the Indus to Chilas, elevation is 1650 metres. The left bank of the Indus is sandy and stony.

From Bunar Parao to Chilas it's 27 km or 5½ hours.

(From Major Arthur Neve, *A Tourist Guide to Kashmir & Skardo Etc*)

SWAT VALLEY

Ushu-Paloga Pass Trek

This is a five-day trek and a porter/guide is necessary. Setting off point: Kalam. Free zone. Moderate to strenuous. Elevation 5000 metres. Time from June to September.

Trek to Ushu at 3250 metres, a valley with beautiful meadows and cedar forests. Ten km further to the north is Matiltan. From Ushu the twin Batin Peaks, 6000 and 6250 metres respectively, are visible on a clear day. There is an old fort here.

Six km further up is the village of Paloga at the junction of the Ushu and Paloga Rivers. The trail goes through pine forest and about eight km on you come to Falaksher Nallah, where up ahead Falaksher, 5918 metres, is framed between steep walls of the valley forested with birch.

At about 4000 metres there is a shepherd's hut and from here the trail is over moraines. Falaksher Glacier is visible from here. The trail leads up to the Paloga Pass at an altitude of 5000 metres.

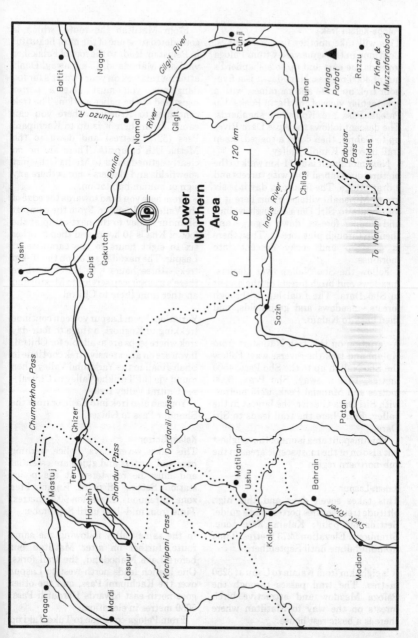

Paloga-Kalam Trek

This will take another five or six days. Continue in the same valley from Paloga towards the east and up to a shepherd's hut at 4000 metres. Next day it is a five-hour trek up scree and moraines, with a spectacular view of the Batin Peaks. Up Paloga Pass are Kohistani shepherds. The descent follows the Apse Dara River up to Gabral, then down a rugged, steep trail into the Kandia Valley.

Next morning it is an 11-km walk to the picturesque Gabral Fort with turrets and a drawbridge. The following day it is six km to Mirishahi village. From here it is four hours to Siri Dara through walnut and juniper forests, down a gorge and then up through pine forests. Then there is a steep and rocky descent into moraines.

Follow the Sho Nallah over glaciers, meadows and birch forests on the ascent to Sho Dara. The final lap is through forests, meadows and grainfields, and then back to Kalam.

A variation on this trek is to start from Kalam and trek the reverse way. Follow the Sho Nallah up to the Sho Pass, 4500 metres, 14 km away. Sho Peak, 6000 metres and Mankial Peak, 6275 metres, with Siri Dara Glacier, the largest in the valley. From here the trail leads to Siri Dara.

This unspoilt area is one of the roughest but also on of the most scenic areas in the sub-northern region.

Kalam-Laspur

This takes seven days and this high altitude trek requires porters and a guide. Setting off point: Kalam. Free zone. Strenuous. Elevation 5273 metres. Time from mid-June until September.

It is eight km from Kalam to Ushu at 3250 metres. The trail passes through the Paloga Meadow and attractive birch forests on the way to Matiltan where there is a basic rest house.

From Matiltan the route, which is considered to be one of the most beautiful in Pakistan, leads to the foot of Falaksher via Lake Mahodand, 15 km away. Don't attempt this trek on your own; it's far too dangerous, you must take a porter registered at the police station. The trek continues to Kruederi where you can camp. From there it is up to Kachipani Pass (5273 metres) and down to the Metha Uth campsite. There are no no clearly defined paths to Metha Uth – just snowfields and glaciers – nor is there any sign of human habitation.

From here you head towards the edge of the Valley of Shandur. From the camp at Shandur Valley to the next camp at the foot of Kha is 10 hours and then another six to eight hours to the campsite at Laspur. The next day set off on the 10-km trek – three hours – to Harchin where there's a cargo jeep service to Mastuj and another from there to Chitral.

Variation: From Laspur you can continue trekking to Koghozi, a three to four-day trek where jeeps are available for Chitral. If you are on an extensive trek continue to Shah Jinali in the Yarkhund Valley, then round via the Turikho Valley to Chitral – see Chitral Valley trek.

You can also trek into Yasin or from the Shandur Pass to Ghizer.

Kalam-Ghizer

This takes seven days, police warning here and porters and guide are essential and must be registered at the police station. Setting off point: Kalam. Free zone. Strenuous. Elevation 5030 metres. Time from mid-July until September.

In the same valley following the same route, further on after Matiltan but before Lake Mahodand, the trail forks. One branch leads north-west to Laspur over the Kachipani Pass, and the other goes north-east towards Dardarili Pass, 5030 metres in elevation.

From Paloga continue to Tuka Taki up

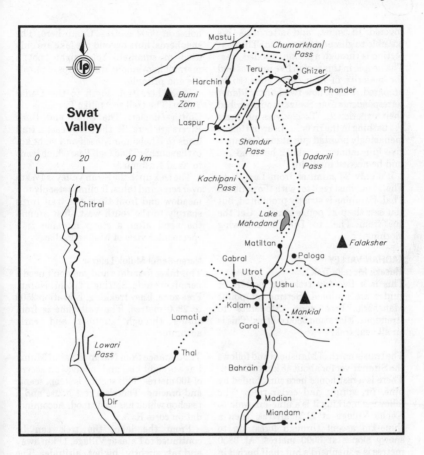

Swat Valley

0   20   40 km

Mastuj
Chumarkhan/
Pass
Teru
Ghizer
Harchin
Phander
Bumi Zom
Laspur
Shandur
Pass
Dadarili
Pass
Kachipani
Pass
Chitral
Lake
Mahodand
Matiltan
Falaksher
Gabral
Paloga
Utrot
Ushu
Kalam
Mankial
Lamoti
Garai
Lowari
Pass
Thal
Bahrain
Dir
Madian
Miandam

to Birchwood Meadow. Beyond, the trail starts to get rough and it is hard going over snow fields and glaciers. The trail continues on to Bashgor Gol, Gor Laspur, Langar, then down into Teru and Ghizer.

From here you can either continue to Laspur over the Shandur Pass or down to Phander in the opposite direction. From Phander you can do an extended trek to Gilgit via Pingal, Jubal and Gupis.

Kalam-Utrot-Dir
This takes three days and no permit is necessary, but police warning here.

Porters and guide are essential. Setting off point: Kalam. Free zone. Fairly strenuous. Elevation 2225 to 4500 metres. Time from June until September.

It's five km by bus from Kalam to Utrot, which is situated 2225 metres above sea level north-west of Kalam. There is a rest house in Utrot. Further west is the valley of Gabral where the trout fishing is excellent.

From Utrot it's a one-day trek to Lamoti, but there is no defined trail. The first phase is up a steep pass, sometimes covered in snow, and after this it's possible to glissade for one km. The next section is through a scenic, wooded area. The people in this region live in caves and the majority of men carry guns, so be prepared. This is how two Lonely Planet correspondents from Switzerland described their experience: 'Troglodytes up there . . . bathing in the river . . . bearded fellow menacingly pointed gun at me. Got up to give him money . . . shook his head . . . said he needed medicine!'

It's only 20 minutes from Lamoti to Thal. You must register with the police in Thal. Camping is strictly prohibited, but you can sleep at police station. Get the bus from Thal to Dir the following morning.

KAGHAN VALLEY
Musaka Musalla Trek

This is a five-day trek and porters or guides are optional. Setting off point: Manshera. Free zone. Moderate to strenuous. Elevation 3850 metres. This is an all year trek.

The trail is north of Manshera and follows the Siran River for about 45 km to Domel. There is a rest house here surrounded by pine, fir, spruce and cedar trees. The following morning it is a nine-km walk to Kacha Village at 2125 metres, then a three-km ascent through forest up to snowy slopes at 3000 metres. At 3850 metres is a shepherd's hut, half buried in snow in winter. Next day ascend a ridge, taking 2½ hours, to the white dome. Backtrack to Manshera.

Naran-Siran Valley Trek

This is a five-day trek and a guide is necessary. Setting off point: Naran. Free zone. Easy to strenuous. Elevation 4500 metres. Time from June to September.

The trail is along the valley above Naran through a forest three km long. Malika Parbat can be seen from here. Then go over a snow bank where there is a rest house at 3500 metres. Camp here. The shepherds' huts beyond the lake are only used in summer. You might spot a marmot here among the clumps of purple iris and primula.

From here trek south to the Dadar Valley. The trail to Malika Parbat is via Chitta Glacier. The Siran and Burji Rivers are here. To the south-east a trail leads to Khobamar Massif and eight km to the south is Thad Gali Pass which leads to Azad Kashmir.

The trek up to the Siran Valley is 1½ km over scree and talus. It climbs steeply to a meadow and from there the trail turns sharply to the south-west. Just around the bend after a steep moraine is a spectacular view of Malika Parbat.

Naran-Saiful Muluk-Lalazar

This takes four days and you don't need a permit or guide. Setting off point: Naran. Free zone. Easy trekking. Elevation 2500 to 2800 metres. The best time is from spring through summer and early autumn.

The distance from Naran to Saiful Muluk Lake is eight km, and involves an ascent of 400 metres. This section is steep, scenic and bracing. There's a rest house and a teashop which has basic food. Accommodation costs Rs 5.

From the lake, the trek can be continued to Lalazar Village, 11 km away and at slightly higher altitude. The country along this part of the trek is shaded by trees and forests and carpeted with flowers in spring and summer. If you have time spend a couple of days in the village; it's a beautiful spot and there's a rest house there.

From Lalazar trek to Battakundi where the jeep track continues north to Babusar Pass into Chilas. Sixteen km to the south is Naran.

DIAMAR
Chilas-Babusar-Naran

This takes five to six days and you don't

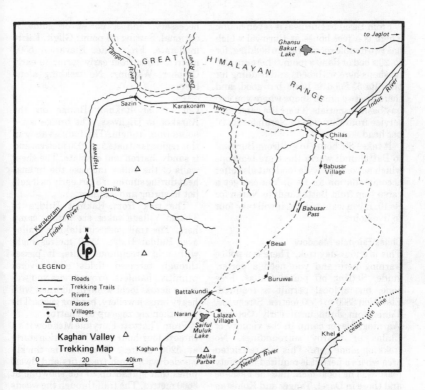

Kaghan Valley Trekking Map

LEGEND
- Roads
- Trekking Trails
- Rivers
- Passes
- Villages
- Peaks

0   20   40km

need a permit or a porter or guide. Setting off point: Chilas. Free zone. Moderate. Elevation 2900 to 4067 metres. Time from mid-June to early October.

From Chilas to the village of Babusar it's 18 km or from six to eight hours of steep climbing. There is a cargo jeep service between Chilas and Babusar for Rs 20. It's four hours of steep climbing from the village to the top of Babusar Pass, 4067 metres, and another three to four hours to Gittidas. The huts in this region have their walls and floors thickly padded with dried grass, which make them very cosy. Food is limited to corn or barley chappatis, lassi or curd and tea. The people in this village are friendly and hospitable. They will not accept money, but appreciate small presents of sugar, knives, needles and thread, medicine, etc.

From here you can do a short side trip to Luluzar Lake, a 2½-hour walk. There are no villages along the way, but there are camping spots and occasionally you will come across Gujar nomads with their herds of livestock.

From Luluzar Lake it takes half an hour to get to Besal which has a teashop that supplies basic food. You can sleep on their padded floor for Rs 5 a night. Cargo jeeps occasionally go as far as Besal nowadays to bring supplies from Naran. A jeep to Naran costs around Rs 30.

Note that the trek from Babusar Village through Gittidas to Besal is pretty steep and rough for 12 hours, but the scenery en route is magnificent.

From Besal to Buruwai is seven hours. There is a rest house at Buruwai which has two double rooms, but no bedding, for Rs 20 a bed or Rs 40 a room. There are also teashops here with beds and bedding for only Rs 5. Food is basic but good, and there are two small shops where you can buy basic essentials. There is a cargo jeep service from Buruwai to Naran for Rs 20 per head.

It takes 3½ hours to get from Buruwai to Battakundi where there are teashops which not only provide food but also offer accommodation for Rs 5. You can get a cargo jeep from Battakundi to Naran for Rs 10. If you want to trek, it will take four to five hours.

Chilas-Fairytale Meadow

This is a four-day trek. There is a police warning here and you need a porter/ guide. Setting off point: Chilas. Free zone, but a local permit is required. Elevation 3800 to 5500 metres. Strenuous. Time from June until early October. Warning: Never camp in the vicinity of Chilas or nearby surroundings. No trekking alone here. This is a restricted area where a permit is required for safety reasons. The local men, like the Pathans and those in Darel, Tanger and Kohistan are always armed.

From Chilas trek to Bunar along the Indus River, then on to Jungal and Khusto, and finally Fairytale Meadow. The trail is rough, arid and dusty.

From Fairytale Meadow you can proceed to Behal Camp, then up to the Nanga Parbat base camp. You could easily spend a couple of days here, or even more if you decide to climb higher to the Buldar Peak camp and summit.

It is another four days trekking down to Rakhiot village on the Karakoram Highway from the Fairytale Meadow via Thatto village.

Rakhiot Bridge-Fairytale Meadow

This takes four to five days, no permit is

necessary, and a porter or guide is optional. Setting off point: Gilgit. Fairly moderate. Free zone. Elevation 5500 metres. Time from early spring to early October. Warning: No trekking alone here.

Get off at Rakhiot Bridge on the Karakoram Highway. The bridge is 2½ hours from Talichi. The Indus Valley in this region is situated at 1000 metres, and is sandy, barren and desolate. The sheer walls of the valley increase the intense heat during summer. Start early as it gets hot in spring and summer.

The trek from Rakhiot Bridge to Thatto Village takes six hours; camp here. The trail goes via Rakhiot Valley over Buldar Ridge, 2950 metres high, with arid precipitous cliffs. It passes through terraced fields and several primitive hamlets. Around here you will come across local women, adorned with heavy brass jewellery, herding goats. The path then zig-zags up to Thatto.

From Thatto to Fairytale Meadow it's a three to four-hour walk. Vegetation starts at 3200 metres. The area is thickly wooded with birch trees, firs and dwarf pines that spread up to the snowline at 3600 metres. The trail through the woods spirals steeply up to Fairytale Meadow. There's a good view of the north-west section of Nanga Parbat from here. Two days backtracking.

Further up at 4500 metres is the interim base camp. It takes another day to get up here and back to Fairytale Meadow, but the view of Silver Pinnacle to the right of Diamar Gap and the 5900-metre high Ganalo Peak is spell-binding.

Harchu-Rama-Astore

This takes three days. You do not need a permit and a porter is optional. Setting off point: Gilgit. Free zone. Fairly moderate. Elevation 2800 to 3800 metres. Time from June until September.

Harchu, 16 km before Astore, is on the

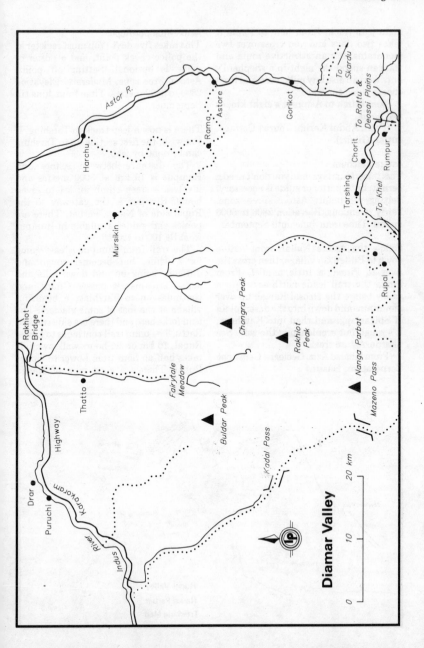

Diamar Valley

main jeep track. From here to Rama it takes two days and you cross over two mountains. It's an attractive route and you can spend the night in a shepherd's hut. You can also buy milk, curd and local cheese along the way.

From Rama to Astore it's eight km, or two hours.

(From Abdul Karim, Tourist Cottage, Jutial, Gilgit.)

Astore-Katchura

This takes four days, and you don't need a permit, but a porter or guide is necessary. Setting off point: Astore. Free zone. Fairly strenuous. Elevation 2800 to 5000 metres. Time from June until September.

Follow the Astore Nallah from Astore down to Bullen Ga village, then cross the river to Finna, a little hamlet. From Finna the trail leads north-east into a valley before the Deosai Range, up over mountains and down into the desert plain of Shigartang, and then into Katchura. It's rough but scenic along the way. See Skardu-Astore trek.

(From Khaled Aziz, Geologist Gemstone Corporation, Dassu.)

Astore-Rumpur-Rupal

This takes five days. You must register at the police check point, and a porter or guide is optional. Setting off point: Astore. Free zone. Moderate. Elevation 2800 to 3800 metres. Time from June till September.

There is now a jeep track to Tarshing. If you wish, the first section up to Tarshing can be done by jeep.

The distance between Astore and Rumpur is 19 km at 3000 metres and involves a steep climb for six to seven hours. Rumpur is the gateway to the Rupal side of Nanga Parbat. There are ponies and guides available in Rumpur from Rs 100 to Rs 150.

The trail from Rumpur is easy-going for a while, but becomes rough and difficult, going up and down hills and across streams. It passes Churit and continues on to Tarshing, a beautiful village at the foot of some glaciers. The trail forks here and there is a side track to Rattu. The main trail continues to Lower Rupal, 10 km or 2½-hours walk away. It takes half an hour from Lower to Upper Rupal. There's a good view of Nanga

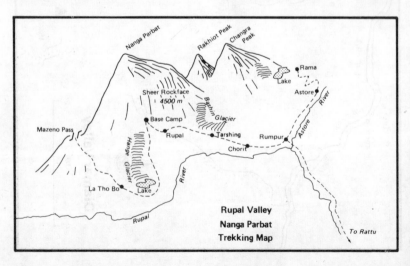

**Rupal Valley
Nanga Parbat
Trekking Map**

Parbat's Rakhiot Peak from Upper Rupal. The trek from here to the base camp at the foot of Nanga Parbat takes four hours. There's fresh spring water nearby.

Rupal is on the south side of Nanga Parbat, and there are numerous wolves preying on the sheep and goats in the vicinity, which contribute to its eerie 'other-world' atmosphere. From the base camp you get a spectacular view of the Nanga Parbat's sheer rockface, which rises 5000 metres straight upwards.

Around Base Camp

Base Camp to La Tho Bho (A Place to Live)

To get to this shepherds' hamlet, it takes 1½ hours to cross Bashing Glacier. On the right is a lake, and one km further up is a larger lake, which has clearer water, but it's full of frogs. At the end of another glacier are some beautiful stones – probably semi-precious. Ponies are available in Rupal for this trip.

From La Tho Bho a trail leads to Shakeri Pass, at 5000 metres.

Around Nanga Parbat

Dr Herrligkoffer says it is possible to walk around the great mountain in two weeks via Shakeri Pass, but extremely difficult via Mazeno Pass, at 6000 metres, Diamar Glacier, Patro Glacier, Rakhiot Glacier and Buldar Valley.

If you wish to cut the trek down, walk down into the Indus Valley to Rakhiot Bridge from Rakhiot Glacier, and catch a bus back to Gilgit. From Buldar Valley continue trekking around Nanga Parbat to Tarshing, then back to Rupal Valley.

Dr Herrligkoffer saw the Swiss doctor fall to his death while filming his own team's progress up ... found the scattered pieces of the body, buried them.

Good food at the base camp: cheese and beer. We had a ride around to La Tho Bho and back. When we left we were stacked up with German tinned foodstuff.

Rein Hilhorst, Mountaineer, Amsterdam.

Other Treks

The following treks are from Major Arthur Neve's *Tourist Guide to Kashmir-Skardo, Etc* published in the early 1900s, and updated with material collated from travelling officials and scientists, particularly on the Astore-Deosai route.

Tarshing-Chilas

This takes seven days and you need a permit, porter and a guide. Setting off point: Astore. Free zone. Strenuous. Elevation 6000 metres. Time from mid-June until September.

It's 22 km from Tarshing to Kaonagod along the Rupal Nallah; and 15 km from Kaonagod to Zambazi; over Mazeno Pass at 6000 metres; then 16 km to the Bunar Valley before descending to the Indus Valley. The trail up and down is rugged and tough, but the scenery is spectacular.

The route from this part of the Indus Valley to Chilas is easy.

Astore-Rattu

This is a four-day trek – two days up and two days down – and you need a permit and a guide, a porter is optional. Setting off point: Astore. Restricted zone. Moderate. Elevation 2800 to 3200 metres. Time from June until September.

From Astore to Rattu it's 34 km. There is a fine view of Nanga Parbat past Mons and Chagam, after crossing Rupal Nallah, which has huge granite boulders and moraines. The latter indicate that glaciers once filled the ravine, which turns right towards Nanga Parbat. The chocolate-coloured river is spanned by a wooden bridge. Not much further on the trail splits, with one branch leading to Astore, the other to Churit and Tarshing.

The tiny hamlet of Fopun, and its entire population of a hundred, was completely wiped out by an avalanche in the spring of 1983.

Astore-Arondu

This takes six days and you don't need a permit, but a porter and guide are essential. Setting off point: Astore. Open zone. Strenuous. Elevation 5600 metres. Time from June until September.

It's 23 km from Astore to Thingeh; and another 15 km from Thingeh to the campsite. Leave the main *nallah* (river) after 12 km, and go north. The campsite is situated at 4000 metres and the ascent is steep. It's 18 km from one camp to the next. There's a steep climb to 5600 metres. Traverse the glacier, then descend to some stone shelters along a rough route through snow and rocks. Then there's a long trek of 29 km through several villages to the camp at Mendi, followed by a steep descent to the Indus River. From here it is two km into Arondu.

Reverse Trail via alternative Route Mendi to Balamik, 19 km; a fairly easy trek or six to eight hours by pony. From Balamik to Baltal is a 10-hour trek which passes through a village about two hours below the camp. Between Baltal and Thingeh it's an easy eight-hour ascent to the pass, apart from the last stretch into Thingeh, which is hard-going. From Thingeh to Astore it's 23 km.

Astore-Deosai

This takes seven to 10 days and you need a permit, porter and a guide. Setting off point: Astore. Restricted zone. Strenuous. Elevation approximately 5000 metres. Time from June until September.

From Astore to Gorikot it's 10 km heading south-east; steep trail up to 2000 metres. At Gorikot, there's a steel-cable suspension bridge about 65 metres long. The trail goes up to a 4456-metre-high pass, descends to villages along a stream; and cuts through a luxuriant valley speckled with goats and cattle before arriving in Gudhai, 26 km away. From Gudhai the route goes through hamlets so tiny they mostly comprise wooden huts. There are numerous scenic spots along the way. From here to Bubin it takes nine hours along grassy, wooded country and across streams. Then it's another 10 hours to the campsite by the side of a ravine.

Bubin-Skardu At Bubin the trail splits up: the lower trail goes to Chilim over Deosai into Skardu, 50 km away. The rest house in Chilim is occupied by UNO observers. The wooden bridge at this spot used to be dismantled every year for firewood in winter and rebuilt in spring. From Chilim you go up to Chachok Pass, 4595 metres, then to Deosai Plateau, at 4800 metres and about eight square km in area, and from there to Satpara, a distance of 20 km. The distance between Satpara and Skardu is 16 km.

The Deosai Plateau is open from mid-July until mid-September and offers spectacular scenery of the surrounding snow-capped peaks. Keep your eyes open for marmots, and for black and brown Himalayan bears. You may be lucky enough to see some bears fishing in the streams here.

Bubin-Katchura The upper trail from Bubin winds gradually up Alampir-La, 5500 metres high; campsite is at 4300 metres. From here to Thlashing Span Hut it's 12 hours through steep, snowy terrain; then a long descent over snowfields for 2½ hours to Barapani, a rocky valley dotted with huts. Just before you reach Satpara, the trail splits, one path going to Katchura.

Note that this is a restricted area, and the majority of people who supplied this information were government officials or scientists on location, who travelled by jeep – none had done this trek on foot. The information concerning distances, names of villages, and time needed to cover the territory – either to Skardu or Katchura – is therefore incomplete.

Astore-Srinagar

There used to be a trail linking Astore to Srinagar via Burzil Pass at 4500 metres, through Gurais on the other side of the ceasefire line, across Kashmir & Jammu.

Baltistan Treks

Satpara Lake-Deosai Plateau

This takes two days, a permit is required, but porters or guide are optional. Setting off point: Skardu. Restricted zone. Fairly moderate. Elevation 4600 metres. Time from mid-June until September.

In 1963 Skardu was linked with Diamar via Deosai Plateau by a rough, narrow jeep track, which is open only in summer. The trek up to Deosai Plateau from Skardu usually takes two days, and while this side of Skardu is not a restricted zone, the Deosai-Diamar side requires a special permit from the Ministry of Culture & Tourism.

The route from Skardu to Satpara Lake has been surfaced, but it's just a dirt track up to Satpara Village, 16 km away. The trail continues to Deosai, 20 km further on and 4800 above sea level. You can hire a jeep from the PTDC to take you up to the Deosai Plateau and back, or backtrack by foot, if you don't have the special permit to cross over into the Diamar region via the Deosai Plateau.

If you wish to go to Deosai Plateau, to be on the safe side, check with the Tourist Officer at the K2 Motel in Skardu. Note that there is also an officer here from the Ministry of Tourism, who might be of some assistance.

Skardu-Astore via Alampir La

This takes six days, and a permit, porter and guide are necessary. Setting off point: Skardu. Open zone. Fairly strenuous. Elevation 5500 metres approximately. Time from mid-June until September.

Get to Kachura from Skardu by jeep – 32 km – then it's a two-hour easy walk to Chakke Village. From the village follow Chakke River which is renowned for trout. A number of villages are scattered along the trail and as you start climbing through summer pastures you will see many yak. On the third day out of Chakke you arrive at Alampir La at 5000 metres. The ascent is tough and rough, but the view of Nanga Parbat to the south and the Deosai Plateau to the east is magnificent.

From here you descend to the village of Khane at the foot of the pass, then it's another six to eight-hours walk to Gudhai in the Astore Valley. From Gudhai it takes a few hours to walk to Astore, where there are jeeps available for Gilgit.

Alternative Route

This was recommended by Major Arthur Neve decades ago.

From Skardu to Shigartang is a two-day walk; Shigartang-Ordukas, 18 km; an easy trail initially, then a steep ascent to a rocky path at 4350 metres; Ordukas to Chumik, 15 km; seven km up a snowy trail, then over Bank Pass, 5350 metres. Be careful – in summer there are crevasses in the glaciers here; steep ascent for eight km up 1500 metres to Chumik. From Chumik to Thingeh it's 17 km; a gradual descent of nine km along the right bank of Herpo Nallah, another two km across a wooded plain, easy going for three km, then a difficult trek to Gutumsar Village. From here it's another three km to Thingeh at 2850 metres. There's 23 km between Thingeh and Astore; 12 km easy going, through hamlets, hard-going for 1½ km, reasonable for three km, then a steep ascent. The trail crosses Astore Nallah, ascends and then traverses a ravine into Astore.

Alternative Route

See route via Mendi, Balamik, Baltal above, also recommended by Major Arthur Neve.

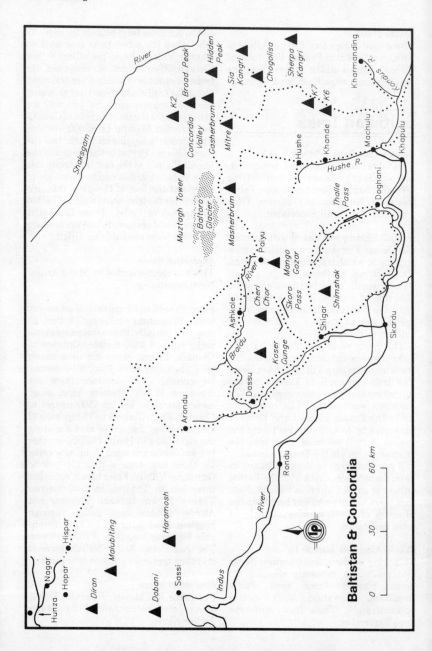

Baltistan & Concordia

Skardu-Shigar

This takes one day and you don't need a permit, but a porter is necessary. It is also possible to take a jeep if you prefer.

Skardu-Thalle Pass

This takes five days, you don't need a permit, and a porter and guide are optional. Setting off point: Skardu. Free zone. Fairly strenuous. Elevation 5335 metres. Time from June until August.

From Skardu to Balaghar the route is reasonably easy. Ascending to Upper Thalle it becomes more difficult but there are spectacular views of the Karakorams. From there it goes to Brooq and finally on to Thalle La Pass at 5335 metres.

This is as far as this trek goes, but actually you can continue trekking on to Khapulu in the east or Shigar to the north-west. Either route is another five to six days trek.

Skardu-Skoro Pass

This takes seven days, a permit is not necessary, but a porter and guide are essential. Setting off point: Skardu. Free zone. Strenuous. Elevation 5500 metres. Time from July to September.

From Skardu you go to Dongla, then on to Dassu. From the latter you reach Chakpo along the Braldu River and then trek to Chango and camp or continue to Ashkole. The next section – from Ashkole to Skoro Pass at 5072 metres – goes through villages along the way. Then the trail loops down through Shigar Meadow and continues to Shigar, where you can catch a jeep back to Skardu.

Alternative Route

Set off from Skardu to Baha; on to Dassu and Chakpo. From Chakpo the route is via Chago and Ashkole to the base of Skoro Pass. It then goes up to Skoro Pass and finally loops down into Shigar.

Skardu-Masherbrum Base Camp

This takes two weeks. You don't need a permit, but a porter and guide are indispensable. Setting off point: Skardu. Open zone. Strenuous. Elevation approximately 4500 metres. Time from July until September.

Head off to Doghani from Skardu; then on to Thalis. From here you trek to Khande, Hushe, Wachack and Frozen Lake. Then go straight to the Masherbrum base camp.

Returning, backtrack to Khande and from there to Khapulu where jeeps are available for Skardu.

Skardu-Sherpigang Glacier

This takes two weeks. You need a permit, a porter and a guide. Setting off point: Skardu. Free zone. Strenuous. Elevation 5500 metres. Time from July to August.

This is in the same valley and along the same route as the preceding trek. But from Doghani take the trail to Shaling; then on to Thalis; to Khande; Halde; Thagas; Brooq; Latchit; Kharmading; Khor Kondus; and to the snout of Sherpigang glacier. It's an awesome trail.

Return by backtracking to Khande, and from there to Khapulu where you can catch a jeep back to Skardu.

Skardu-Khapulu

This takes five days. No permit, porter or guide necessary. Setting off point: Skardu. Free zone. Fairly easy. Elevation approximately 3000 metres. Time from early spring to early autumn.

This route is along the main jeep track. From Skardu to Khapulu it's 102 km. The ascent is gradual and gentle along the Indus River from Skardu to Gol, which is situated at the confluence of the Indus and Shyok rivers. There's a bridge over the Shyok River at Gol and you pass through several hamlets along the way.

From Gol to Quresh and on to Karpakhs takes four hours. During June and July you get a good view of the Masherbrum from Quresh. After Quresh, the first village en route to Khapulu is Barra, which has numerous springs and streams and is a great place for trout fishing. Then on to Khapulu and beyond is Sarmo, 18 km to the east.

SHIGAR VALLEY
Shigar-Dassu

This takes four days and you don't need a permit, porter or guide. Setting off point: Shigar. Free zone. Fairly moderate, even easy. Elevation approximately 3000 metres. Time from early spring to early autumn.

Shigar is the gateway to Concordia via Dassu, 80 km away. From Shigar the trail goes through a fertile area of grainfields, poplar trees and hamlets, then down an escarpment by the Shigar River. The valley is broad and sandy, and the river is broken into little streams.

The most direct route to Dassu is along the right bank, heading upstream, but there is an alternative approach from the other side of the valley. Just out of Shigar is a track that leads straight down to a bridge, which spans the broad, sandy valley streaked with streams. There are numerous lush areas and quiet little villages with huts of wattle and mud over this side. You will also see a number of women and children, dressed in traditional costume. Even the babies wear the traditional headgear, richly embroidered and embellished with metal buttons and other metal objects.

If you go south the jeep track leads to Katchura, while if you head to the north it finishes at the end of the valley. Near where the jeep track ends is a trail which goes for some distance before branching off in two directions, one track going to Arondu, the other leading to Dassu. At the end of the jeep track across the sandy, river valley are four little bridges, which link it with the main jeep track to Dassu.

On the main track direct from Shigar are some orchards. It begins to get arid and barren again along the escarpment, before ascending to a rather claustrophobic, but lush green valley. From here it descends into a boulder-strewn stream. Jeeps and tractors dive into it, and have to lumber up a steep bank. You can cross the river by foot, jumping from boulder to boulder. There are also two long poles here, which you can use to cross to the other side.

The country around here has abundant fruit trees and terraced grain fields. The rest house is clean, modern but basic, with several beds and one western toilet plus local loos. The food is limited to eggs, chappatis and tea.

Close by is the camp of the Gemstone Corporation geologists, who are hospitable and friendly. If you let them know in advance, they will make food available. Don't leap to the assumption that war has broken out if you hear an explosion – they're just blasting for gems. Take a look at the Corporation's collection of unpolished stones – quartz, tourmaline, aquamarine and others.

Crowds of porters are camped, more-or-less permanently, on wooded hillsides, near the road and rest house, as there is a continuous shuttle of mountaineering expeditions and trekking parties going in and out. You'll see tractors, crammed with bright red and orange packs, equipment and supplies, plying back and forth; and loads of liaison officers either paying off or recruiting porters.

The jeep track continues for about eight km past this spot, but treks to Concordia start here. The area has recently been surveyed to see whether it's possible to make it up to Ashkole, which would cut the trekking time to Concordia by three to four days.

Note It's advisable for individual travellers who wish to join trekking or mountaineering parties to check with the PTDC at K2 Motel, Skardu, before going to Dassu – or at Hushe in the Khapulu Valley. There are chances of getting accepted, but it's essential to have your own camping gear and provisions, and it's necessary to hire a porter for this trek.

Dassu-Ashkole-Concordia

This takes 26 days, and you need a permit, a guide and porters. Setting off point: Dassu. Restricted zone. Strenuous. elevation 2590 to 4267 metres. Time from June until the end of August.

This is a 26-day trek through a restricted zone – 13 up and 13 down – and it's strenuous. The most popular trek in the entire Northern Territory, it could be done in 16 days, but you would need the other 10 days to recover.

From spring through to early autumn the shuttle of trekking parties and mountaineering expeditions is continuous. There are tough-looking guys trudging up with pick-axes, armed to do battle with the mountains, and followed by a retinue of porters, guides and liaison officers. However, most trekking parties comprise elderly or middle-aged westerners, accompanied by a few younger people, generally their sons and daughters.

Usual setting off time is 4 am – occasionally earlier – going through until 6 pm or 7 pm.

It's approximately 57 km from Dassu to Ashkole. On the first day you cover the 15 km between Dassu and Chakpo, which takes about six to eight hours. It's fairly strenuous in sections. The trail goes through barren country across streams and glaciers, but the terrain along the banks of Braldu River is quite gentle with only occasional steep sections over moraines, through gorges and narrow passes. There is a danger of falling rocks or avalanches on this stretch. It's very hot near the Braldu Gorge.

Between Chakpo and Chango is the toughest segment of the entire trek,

ascending about 665 metres through desolate, barren country, before descending to a village. It's a six to eight-hour walk.

From Chango to Ashkole it's an easy three-hour ascent through grassland, farms, mulberry and apricot orchards and irrigation canals, then up glaciers, along sheer precipices and ravines, and past a hot spring. Ashkole is the last village on this trek.

The section from Ashkole to Korofan is where you begin to enter the wilderness of glaciers, deserts and lofty peaks. It's easy crossing the glaciers to the campsite at Korofan, which is on the far side of Biafo Glacier. The site is surrounded by trees and has a fresh water spring.

Between Korofan and Bardomal there are numerous small streams to ford and then you will come to a rope bridge in bad repair. This is operated by a *haji* – a Muslim, who has been to Mecca – who charges Rs 10 per person plus Rs 5 a pack. While this is considered to be excessive by the local government, there is no way they can persuade the haji to bring his rates down as the only alternative to crossing at this spot involves another two to three days detour via the Dormundu Glacier. Immediately after the bridge the going is difficult for eight to 10 hours.

From Bardomal to Paiyu the elevation is around 3500 metres. There are a few streams to cross and a rocky area to cover down to Paiyu, which is on the south side of Baltoro Glacier. The camping area here was once a green, wooded area, but is gradually being denuded of trees, and beginning to be littered with campers' rubbish – mostly lavatory paper.

The trek continues from Paiyu to Liligo, taking about six hours, before crossing Baltoro Glacier. The camp at Liligo is just off the glacier and offers a view of Paiyu Peak and Trango Towers.

The next campsite along is Urdokush at 4350 metres. The going is rough and steep, with many ups and downs. There is also a difficult stream to cross. The camp is not far from the glacier on the south side and is rather like an oasis. The view of Paiyu Peak, Trango Towers to the north, and Baltoro Cathedral is stunning.

Between Urdokush and Goro there is another tough stretch over stony ground. The camp here is at the junction of Muztagh and Baltoro Glaciers. There are spectacular views of Muztagh Tower to the north, Masherbrum Peak to the south, and Gasherbrum IV to the east.

The elevation between Goro and Concordia is 4665 metres, but the trek to Concordia Valley is fairly easy. The valley itself is hemmed in by K2, Broad Peak, the Gasherbrum Group, the Golden Throne and Chogolisa. This is where all the glaciers meet. The camp is on a ridge of a glacier and has a view of Masherbrum to the south and Muztagh Tower to the north.

From here you can go on to the base camp of Chogolisa – an eight-hour trek – or take a side trip to the base camp of K2 or Broad Peak.

To return, backtrack over the same route or, for those of tougher stuff, when you reach Chogolisa continue to trek south into the Khapulu Valley.

Concordia-Khapulu

This is an extra two to three weeks with the same requirements as the preceding trek. This trek requires more supplies, stamina and courage.

From Concordia continue trekking south to Chogolisa, then a side trip to the Gasherbrum Glacier and back to Concordia. Backtrack to Goro where a trail veers south towards Yarmanondu Glacier and continue up Masherbrum La. This is a very dangerous region here, with avalanches and crevasses in summer.

Continue onto Ghondogoro, Dalzan Camp, then Rose Meadow and finally down to Hushe. From here it is another two days trek via Khande and Shaling to Khapulu.

Other

The weather in this area is unpredictable; even in summer there's intermittent snowfall, hail and rain.

Keep your eyes open for rubies, garnets and other semi-precious stones, along the way.

Concordia was so-named because it is the junction of Siachen, Baltoro and other minor glaciers like the Godwin Austin, the Gasherbrum and the Masherbrum. The valley itself is broad and surrounded by the white, snowy walls of slopes and peaks. This is the inner sanctum of the Himalayas; the approach to the mighty peaks of K2, the Gasherbrum and the Kangri. Most trekkers are tempted to climb up to the base camps of K2 or Broad Peak. Left of the valley is a grand view of Marble Peak. Once you get to Concordia, it takes another three hours to trek to the Minor Peak base camp.

Alternative Routes

Major Arthur Neve gives the following seldom trodden trails, previously used only by the British military explorers and other early 'sportsmen' in the region. These trekking routes are in both open and restricted zones where permits, porters and guides are needed. As well, there's usually a liaison officer detailed to trekking parties. If you intend undertaking a climbing, trekking, rafting or skiing expedition it is best to check with the PTDC for detailed information on formalities before you go.

Shigar-Ashkole

This takes 17 days and you need both permit, porter and guide. Setting off point: Shigar. Restricted zone. Strenuous. Elevation approximately 5000 metres and over. Time from June until August.

From Shigar to Yuno is 32 km, along an easy trail shaded by willow trees; over a sandy, stony plain with streams to be forded. From Yuno to Koshuma – opposite

Dassu – it's 19 km along a similar stretch of sandy, stony country; near Wungo, the trail ascends, then follows a canal and crosses the Shigar River to Dassu; between Koshuma and Chukpa there's 16 km of difficult trekking to the rope bridge below Biano. There's a better trail on the right via Dassu; Chapku to Ashkole, 25 km of rough, stony trekking. Crossing the stream here takes 1½ hours; another two streams further on take another 1½ hours, four hours from Chukpa altogether. At Pakore use the rope bridge to cross from the left bank of the Braldu River to the right bank.

Alternative Route This was used by British explorers and was completed in three easy stages from the second camp at Thal Brock via the lower route to Ashkole, returning via Skoro La.

When Domordo Nallah can be forded it takes nine hours from Ashkole to Bardomal. If Domordo Nallah can't be crossed on foot, there is a long detour to a bridge. Camp at Korofan. The second day out, there's a six-hour march between Biafo Glacier and Domordo Nallah; from Bardomal to Urdokush it's 15 km, up over Baltoro Glacier; and from here it takes six hours to get to Liliwa following the bank of the river over boulders, past a small lake; then to Chober Zechen it's three hours over glaciers, before crossing to the other side of the moraine to Urdokush, which is another three hours. There's a good campsite here.

Crossing the glacier from Urdokush takes four hours; then you'll get to Muztagh Lunka at Conway's Piale Glacier. Ascending Muztagh over the glacier and getting to Muztagh Spang-La takes 11 hours. On the left banks of Lobsang Blangra is a grassy slope. Follow the glacier at the foot of the pass for four hours. There is a difficult three-hour ascent to the summit at 6335 metres, and particularly difficult descent north of Chang Tong.

Return to Shigar by backtracking over the same route.

Alternative Return Route From Ashkole to Pakore is 3½ hours; Pakore to Hu five hours; Hu to Dassu six hours; Dassu to Simu six hours. In the old days you had to cross the river by raft to get to Shigar, but today there is a trail straight down to Shigar from Dassu. Moreover the river is now shallow and has two bridges spanning it.

Shigar-Baltoro-Muztagh Pass

This is an exploration route undertaken by Sir Francis Younghusband, which takes 16 days. A permit is necessary and a liaison officer is detailed. Porters and guide are essential. Setting off point: Shigar. Restricted zone. Strenuous. Elevation over 6000 metres. Time from June until August.

It's 1½ hours from Shigar to Hashu; head upstream to cross the nallah, from here it takes approximately nine hours to get to the campsite, which is about 100 metres above a steep grassy slope, just below the snowline. From the camp to Ashkole is another long trek – 10½ hours – up a 1000-metre-high snowy and rocky region; then two hours to the summit of the 5078-metre Skoro La. On the north side of this is a glacier-filled valley; the trail leads through snowfields for three hours, then down to some hamlets and into Thal Brock, 6½ hours from the summit. From here there's a steep drop into scenic Braldu Valley and the rope bridge below Ashkole. This takes two hours.

Shigar-Mango Gussar

This takes 14 days. You need a permit, and a porter and guide are necessary. Setting point: Shigar. Open zone. Fairly strenuous. Elevation 5073 metres to 6288 metres. Time from June until August.

From Shigar go to Khutti Skoro, then on

to Dassu. From Dassu either head for Biano or go directly to Chakpo. On reaching Chakpo, you have a choice of going straight to Ashkole on the same day or going to Chango. The next stage is Mango Gussar Peak.

Return by backtracking to Dassu or the Skoro Pass (5078 metres).

Shigar-Choktai Glacier

This long trek takes a month. A permit is necessary and a porter and guide are essential. Setting off point: Dassu. Restricted zone. Strenuous. Elevation between 5407 metres and 5833 metres. Time from June until August.

Trek from Dassu to Chakpo; then to Chango or Ashkole; from here to Korofan, Panmah, Panmah Glacier, Chiring Glacier, Drinsang Glacier. From Drinsang Glacier trek to Nobande; then to Sobande Glacier; to Skam Pass (5407 metres); on to Singang Glacier and Singang Pass (5833 metres); and finally to Choktai Glacier.

Backtrack over the same route.

Shigar-Snow Lake

This takes 16 days. You need a permit, and a porter and guide are necessary. Setting off point: Dassu. Free zone. Strenuous. Elevation 5000 metres. Time from June until August.

Along the same valley and route, but when you reach Ashkole take the trail to Drinsang; then go on to Mongo; and from there to Biafo Glacier, Singang Glacier and finally Snow Lake.

Note that this trek is also the route of the Nagar Valley trek. Backtrack to Dassu over the same route.

Shigar-Shusbun Glacier

This is a 10-day trek through open zone. You need a permit, and a porter and guide are necessary. Setting off point: Dassu. Strenuous. Elevation 6462 metres. Time from June until August.

Once again this trek is in the same valley, but take the trail to Hohlungma Glacier to the base of Ganchen Peak (6462 metres); then to Tsilbu Glacier and on to Shusbun Glacier.

Backtrack to Dassu.

Shigar-Haramosh

This is a 10-day trek through open zone. A permit is not necessary, but you need a porter and guide. Setting off point: Shigar. Fairly strenuous. Elevation approximately 5500 metres. Time from June until September.

Go to Molto from Shigar; then to Chutran, Arondu, Chogolungma Glacier and to the base of Haramosh Peak 11 (6217 metres).

Backtrack over the same route to Shigar.

Dassu-Arondu

This takes one day and you don't need a permit; porter and guide are optional. Setting off point: Dassu. Free zone. Strenuous. Elevation 4500 metres and over. Time from June until September.

From Dassu to Mendi, the main village in Arondu, it takes five hours to trek along a difficult trail down through a riverbed, then a steep ascent up to a ridge at 3665 metres. Another alternative is from Damodas on the Indus to Arondu, which is apparently only two km.

This is a starting out point for the Nagar Valley over Hispar Glacier. Formerly used by British sportsmen, it's an alternative to the Ashkole-Nagar route, but the climb up the Biafo-Hispar Glaciers is extremely difficult.

Shigar-Nagar Valley

This takes two weeks through an open zone. You need a permit, and a liaison officer is assigned to each party. Often, in winter or early spring, they do not go the whole way. Porters are necessary, but high altitude guides generally refuse to do this trek in winter, sometimes even until early spring. Setting off point: Dassu. Strenuous. Elevation over 5600 metres. Time for trekking from early spring in late May until September, all year round for high altitude skiers.

In the winter of 1978 four Americans skied from Ashkole to the Nagar Valley over the Biafo and Hispar Glaciers, with the liaison officer assigned to the party unable to make the entire journey. An American couple also made it through on skis in the early spring of 1980. Less fortunate were the 50 brigands from the Nagar Valley who perished on this glacier in the mid-19th century.

If you are in Shigar take a jeep to Dassu. From Dassu you go to Chakpo along the same trail to Ashkole. At Ashkole take the trail to Drinsang; then on to Mongo; Biafo Glacier; Hispar Pass (5151 metres); Hispar Glacier; Nagar Valley and on to Ganesh where cargo jeeps and buses are available for Gilgit.

Alternative Treks

This is another of the old British 'marches' of Major Arthur Neve via Shigar's western branch, the Basha. There are trails on either bank, but Major Neve preferred the route along the left bank. It involves crossing the stream to Gulapore, and a three-day walk, climbing all the way. However, there is now a direct route to Dassu from Shigar, and from Dassu it is only two to three days walk to Ashkole.

At Ashkole the trail splits up with one route heading west to Biafo Glacier, the other branching eastward to Concordia or Muztagh Pass. The Biafo Glacier is north-west of Ashkole and linked to the Hispar Glacier by a snowfield. It is also traversable from the Nagar Valley, but the usual way to go is via the western route.

From Shigar to Koshuma is a six-hour trek along fairly flat, but stony ground; and from there it's 1½ hours to Hashu;

another 1½ hours to Alchori, and another 1½ hours to Tshildi, and an hour to Koshuma from the latter. There is a magnificent view of the peak of Koasar Gan from Koshuma.

The next stage is an eight-hour trek from Koshuma to Chutran through a wide valley, where there is a confluence of rivers, then it's 1½ hours to Yuno. When you reach the Braldu River cross the bridge and walk for 2½ hours across the flat, stony plain until you come to another bridge over the Basha River. From here it's 1½ hours to Tisser. High up on the left are some waterfalls, and opposite is the gorge of the Braldu River. There's a sharp ridge here, then trek up Braldu Valley for 1½ hours. The first stage is easy, scenic; the second is over sand and stones to Chutran. The word Chutran means 'hot water' and there are hot springs and baths here. You will also notice white marble in this region.

It takes three hours to get from Chutran to Doko Sibri, the first half through cultivated land, followed by an easy walk through walnut groves to Dogoro; then half an hour to Sibri and another half-hour to Doko, 2000 metres above the river. Just beyond the village is a camping site. From here it's an easy descent to Gulapore, but below Tisser, the trail is rough and dangerous. Cross a stream into Doko. From Doko to Arondu it's four hours along slopes, 2½ hours up and down, turning left when the valley widens. At first the valley is stony and barren, later it is cultivated. When you get out of the valley it's another two hours to Arondu across a stony, sandy plain and several streams.

Arondu is the last village in the Rondu Valley. About a km west of Arondu is the rather dirty-looking snout of the Chogolungma Glacier. To the south, overhanging the village, is Tipor Glacier. Over many years these glaciers have shifted quite a distance, and more recently they have started to recede. The village is at an altitude of 3265 metres.

This completes the first half of the trek to Nagar Valley via the Biafo and Hispar glaciers. Trekking above Arondu is difficult as it involves technical rock climbing. This is probably why today skiers generally start their trip at Ashkole, and go straight across the glaciers to the Nagar Valley.

Arondu-Nagar Valley

This route via Kiro Nallah goes north out of Arondu to Domak. Follow a narrow trail over the Chogolungma for two hours; and continue to Beg Bransa for another half an hour. There's a campsite at Harimach, which is a 2½-hour ascent over moraines and along a glacier, followed by an hour walk through a grassy forest of birch trees. Domak, at an altitude of 3835 metres, has some picturesque stone huts. From Domak to Katche Bransa takes four hours along grassy slopes, and another hour to a meadow and polo-ground known as Shagram. From here you go through the junction of Huches Alchori Glacier and Kiro Glacier, which takes 1½ hours. Beside the moraine is a grassy, hollow region, the campsite at Tasuwacha. Wood and water are available at this site. Not far from Tasuwacha is another grassy hollow. Cross the glacier to Katche Bransa at 4664 metres here.

From Katche Bransa trek to Strathu Bransa. It involves a walk of 4½ hours across the middle of the glacier, followed by an hour's ascent of a moraine, then another hour climbing and crossing to Ding Bransa at the foot of a spur to the north. Climb up this spur for 1½ hours, then head down the side of the glacier. From here you trek in a north-west direction – be very careful of crevasses in this area – on a rugged trail up to the next spur. Once you reach this spur it's another two hours to the campsite at Strathu. Strathu is perched high on a steep and tiny platform 5335 metres above sea level.

It takes 1½ hours to get from Strathu Bransa to Galefang Bransa. One hour's easy trekking up a snowy valley to Nushik Col where you get a good view of the mountains in Hunza. Backtrack about a hundred metres then turn east up a steep, snowy ridge to some large rocks – very good sheltering place at 5600 metres. Beyond the rocks is a steep, icy slope traversable in an hour, and another easy slope, 160 metres. There are often avalanches in this vicinity, so be careful and keep alert.

The best time to go is in mid-June as there are lots of snow bridges over Zur Briggan. By early July there's only one snow bridge left and by September, none at all. There are crevasses ranging from three metres to 14 metres wide in this region. If there are snow bridges descend to the side of the glacier, and cross over to Haigutum or Hai Kuru on the left of Hispar Glacier – 1½ hours. There's a snowy lake here. From the glacier to the Hispar Valley takes a day, then it's another day to Nagar about 20 km away. The total distance is about 240 km.

Shigar-Khapulu

This takes three weeks. You don't need a permit, but a porter and guide are necessary. Setting off point: Shigar. Restricted zone. Strenuous. Elevation over 5000 metres. Time from June to August.

From Shigar to Khapulu it's about a hundred km through hamlets. Take the Kaniskhar trail, onto Bransa to the Thalle Pass. The trekking is strenuous to Thalle Pass, at 5335 metres – hard-going all the way, but the scenery is spectacular.

Continue down to Thalle Goma, Balghar, on to Hushe; and from Hushe to Shiescho, on to Gondogoro, Dalzan, Manzila and up the Masherbrum La (pass). Backtrack down to Manzila, Gondogoro, Dalzan, Atosar, then Ghondonstan and back to Hushe. It takes another two days via Khande and Shaling to Khapulu.

Variation: This is via Thalle Pass but the route goes straight down to Khapulu. A porter and guide are optional. Free zone. Fairly strenuous.

Trek from Shigar to Ashir, then on to Brun Bhaim, Thalle La, Doghani, then on to Khapulu. This is on the south side.

Or take the north side. Ascend to Dassu via Skoro La or the usual Ashkole route to Concordia. Khapulu is the usual destination point, but treks here usually take over a month.

Khapulu-Hushe

This trek is only four days return. A porter or guide is optional. Open zone. Time from June to October.

Just before Humayun Bridge is a trail that veers to the north. It's actually a jeep track which goes all the way to Hushe, but there are very few cargo jeeps in this area. Mountaineering expeditions and large trekking parties on their way to Masherbrum generally go directly to Hushe. Others on foot usually rest up in Khapulu for a while.

From Khapulu head straight up north. This can be difficult as the Shyok River gets swollen in early spring. Getting over the Shyok by *zakht* – a raft floated on four or more goatskins filled with air – is an extremely dicey proposition. In May and June the river recedes and you can walk across the river, when the riverbed becomes an expanse of pebbles almost two km wide.

There is an alternative route via Humayun Bridge, but it's 40 km east from Khapulu. This is necessary when the river is swollen.

In summer you can cross the river at Yugu to Shaling just on the other side of the Shyok. Go through the Balti settlements which are often hidden by chestnut, mulberry and walnut trees. It is refreshingly luxuriant against the arid background. It is also possible to go direct to Machulu by crossing at Gol, thus avoiding the barren Indus-Shyok area. There is also a bridge at Talli on the way to Hushe, but it is often in disrepair.

From Shaling the next village on is Machulu, a distance of 18 km. There's a NAWO rest house here, built in an attractive spot, which has fairly good food. It's a little expensive but there are spectacular views of the valley and Masherbrum Peak.

From here it's half an hour to Asherpe, then on to Hushe across the river of the same name. This is a full day's walk along the jeep track.

At 3250 metres, Hushe has only three or four trees – almost nothing grows in this area – a few huts and very friendly inhabitants. You can hire low and high altitude porters and guides in Hushe, and the shops provide basic trekking needs as well as food and a few beds. This is an enchanting village with forests of juniper between glaciers, snowfields and snow-clad mountain massifs.

To return, backtrack to Machulu, or continue on to Masherbrum Valley.

Hushe-Masherbrum Base Camp

This takes one day each way. You don't need a permit and hiring a porter or guide is optional. Setting off point: Hushe. Strenuous. Open zone. Elevation between 3500 metres and 5600 metres. Time from early spring to early autumn.

Hushe is the setting off point to the Masherbrum base camp, and the trail to Concordia, which goes over the Masherbrum La to the Baltoro Glacier. The Masherbrum La region is covered in snow all year round, and because the marked trails are fading, they now use sticks as markers. This used to be a popular trail, but it has diminished in importance and is hardly used today. Even mountaineers and trekkers scaling the Kangri Group usually take the Dassu-Ashkole-Concordia route nowadays. It takes 11 hours from Hushe to the

Masherbrum base camp along this dangerous, difficult, rocky and glacial trail, overhung with ice-cliffs. In summer crevasses crack and cave in. It's a rather daunting trek but porters and guides know it well.

Other Treks
A short distance beyond Humayun Bridge on the Hushe jeep track, there's a branch going east to the Saltoro River, north of Shyok in the direction of the Siachen Glacier and the Kangri Group. Above the Hushe and Saltoro Rivers are some extraordinarily beautiful peaks. The trail along the Saltoro leads to the Muztagh Range at the end of the valley and offers spectacular views.

Around Khapulu
There are a number of short treks in the surrounding area and villages along the Shyok. On a nearby plateau above Khapulu you can get a magnificent view of snowcapped peaks.

Machulu-K6 Base Camp
This takes 18 days through an open zone. You need a permit, and porters and guide are also necessary. Setting off point: Machulu. Fairly strenuous. Elevation approximately 5500 metres. Time from June until August.

If you're in Skardu get a jeep straight to Machulu; jeeps are also available to Machulu from Khapulu. Alternatively it takes three or four days on foot to get from Khapulu to Machulu by Humayun Bridge and then three days across the Shyok River via Shaling. From Machulu cross the Hushe River to Halde; then go to Sinu; and from there to Thang. From Thang trek to Lachit in the Kondus Valley, then on to Lachit Meadow and finally to the K6 base camp.

Halde has a teashop with beds that you can rent for the night, and at Thagas, near the Kondus Valley, there are some very hospitable and friendly school teachers, who will almost certainly put you up.

To return, backtrack to Machulu.

Machulu-Ghandugurup Valley
This is an eight-day trek through open zone. You need a permit, and porters and a guide are a must. Setting off point: Machulu. Fairly strenuous. Elevation approximately 5600 metres. Time from June until August.

You go through the same valley, but from Machulu trek up to the village of Hushe. From here go to Ghandugurup Valley via Cholinga Glacier up the Baltoro side in the direction of Shigar from Masherbrum. On the same trail going north towards Trinity Peak is Gondoroko Valley. This is a longer route in the vicinity of the Biarechi or Biarchedi Glacier. A detailed map of this trek is indispensable.

Backtrack over the same route on your return.

Machulu-Gharkun Peak
This takes 16 days. You need a permit, and porters and guide are indispensable. Setting off point: Machulu. Open zone. Strenuous. Elevation approximately 5800 metres. Time from June to August.

Cross the Hushe River to Halde from Machulu; then trek to Paron; Dansam; Unak; Gyang Glacier, and finally to the base of Gharkun Peak (6620 metres).

To return, backtrack to Machulu.

Machulu-Chumick Peak
This is a 24-day trek through an open zone. You need a permit, and porters and a guide are indispensable. Setting off point: Machulu. Strenuous. Elevation approximately 6000 metres. Time from June until August.

Follow the same route through the valley until you reach Unak, where the trail forks. Take the branch leading to Goma; from Goma trek to the snout of Ghayari

Glacier; then to the snout of Bilafond Glacier; and on to the base of Chumick Peak (6754 metres).

Backtrack over the same route.

Machulu-K2 Base Camp-Dassu

This is a month trek and a permit, porter and guide are essential. Setting off point: Machulu. Restricted zone. Strenuous. Elevation 5800 metres. Time from June till August.

In the same valley and over the same route, but from Bilafond Glacier take the trail to Ali Brangsa and from there to Bilafond Pass.

Note It is now not possible to go as far as Siachen or Sia La as this area is under Indian control. Military skirmishes have stopped but the area is controlled by the Indian army. You have to proceed to Abruzzi Glacier, but the best thing is to check with the Ministry of Tourism before starting off on this trek.

Continue down to Concordia via Baltoro Glacier, then on to Paiyu, then Bardomal, Korofan, Ashkole, Gomboro and finally Dassu.

Variation: You need not continue down to Dassu, but can take the trail to Shigar by the Skoro Pass.

Machulu-K12 Peak

This takes 24 days through an open zone. You need a permit, porters and a guide. Setting off point: Machulu. Fairly strenuous. Elevation approximately 5600 metres. Time from June until August.

In the same valley and along the same route, but after you get to Bilafond Glacier take the trail to Garamcha Valley. From there trek to the base camp of K12 (7468 metres).

Backtrack over the same route.

Machulu-Dansam Peak

This is a 20-day trek through an open zone. A permit is required, and porters and a guide are necessary. Setting off point: Machulu. Strenuous. Elevation approximately 5800 metres. Time from June until August.

In the same region and along the same route, but when you reach Goma take the trail to the foot of K13; then go to Dansam Peak at 6660 metres.

To return, backtrack over the same route.

Machulu-Sherpi Kangri Peak

Another 20-day trek through an open zone. A permit, porters and guide are necessary. Setting off point: Machulu. Strenuous. Elevation 6000 metres. Time from June until August.

In the same valley and along the same route, but from Unak take the trail to Lachit; from there to Kharmading, Khor Kondus; Sherpigang Glacier; to the base of Saltoro Kangri Peaks 1 and 11 (7706 and 7742 metres respectively); and on to the foot of Scarpi Kangri and Sherpi Kangri Peak at 7380 metres.

Backtrack over the same route to return.

Machulu-K7 Base Camp

A 16-day trek through an open zone. You need a permit, and a porter and guide are indispensable. Setting off point: Machulu. Fairly strenuous. Elevation around 5600 metres. Time from June until August.

Take the trail to Khane from Halde; then go to Hushe; Charaksa Glacier; and the base of K7 at 6935 metres. If you're in Khapulu, cross the Shyok River and walk along the banks of the Hushe River to Halde; then on to Hushe, etc.

Backtrack over the same route on return.

Machulu-Dassu

This is a one month trek through a restricted zone. A permit is necessary, and a liaison officer is detailed to each party. Porters are also a must. Setting off point: Machulu. Strenuous. Elevation approximately 6000 metres. Time from June until August.

In the same region and along the same route. At Kharmading take the trail along the Kondus-Kabiri river valley to the base of Chogolisa Peak; continue from there to Vigne Glacier in Concordia Valley, then trek towards Ashkole, and finally to Dassu.

Alternative Route

Once again on the same route, but branch along the trail to Trinity Glacier from Charaksa Glacier. From Trinity Glacier trek to the foot of Trinity Peak at 6800 metres; then on to Vigne Glacier; Vigne Pass; Baltoro Glacier in the Concordia Valley; Ashkole and then Dassu.

Machulu-Mitre Peak

This takes 20 days through an open zone. You need a permit, and porters and guide are necessary. Setting off point: Machulu. Fairly strenuous. Elevation 5500 metres and over. Time from June until August.

From Hushe take the trail to Aling Glacier; then trek to the foot of the 6553-metre Daube Peak; on to the base of Itwar Peak (6400 metres); then to the base of Hunch Peak at 6553 metres; and finally to the base of the 5944-metre Mitre Peak.

On your return, backtrack over the same route.

Khapulu-Sia La

An 18-day trek through a restricted zone. You need a permit and a liaison officer is detailed to each party. Porters and guide are also essential. Setting off point: Khapulu. Strenuous. Elevation is approximately 5400 metres. Time from June until August.

Take the Khapulu trail east towards a bridge across the Shyok. Then follow the trail along the Hushe River banks; cross the Saltoro River to Halde; from Halde to Tagas and then to Kharmading, the last village on the trail. There is a campsite in some fruit orchards in the Kondus Valley. This is a very remote and isolated area. The villagers cling to their traditional customs and culture, but are extremely hospitable and friendly.

It takes three days to trek to Kharmading. From there it is another three days to the base of the Kondus Glacier, where the campsite is surrounded by the stunningly beautiful peaks of Chogolisa and K12. Cross the Kondus Glacier from there. This is tough in sections and fairly strenuous. On the second day out from the Kondus Glacier you will reach the foot of Sia La (5665 metres).

The scenery here is out of this world, with superb views of Saltoro Range, Sia Kangri and the Siachen Glacier.

Backtrack over the same route on your return.

Warning Never attempt to cross the ceasefire line into Indian Kashmir by following the Indus River into Kargil or Leh. With the Siachen Glacier changing hands, it is at present a very sensitive region.

In the summer of 1983 an American, weary of hanging around in Skardu for his flight to Rawalpindi, was caught trying to cross the ceasefire line by UNO observers. He was returned and kept under escort until his plane arrived and departed. If you do make it across, you might end up being shot on the other side or – better, but nonetheless dangerous – having to do a lot of fast talking to explain yourself.

Upper Northern Treks

HUNZA VALLEY
Ganesh-Nagar

This is a one day trek through a free zone does not require a permit or a guide. Setting off point: Ganesh. Moderate.

Elevation 2400 metres. Time from early spring through early Autumn.

The route is via the Hunza Sacred Rock. A little way up the Karakoram Highway a trail veers to the left and crosses a bridge, then turns south before heading west. The trail follows the Nagar River through a very narrow valley past a bridge where gold panners are camped. The trail continues on to Hispar village for another 12 km. From the bridge up to Nagar Valley the trail is steep and passes through arid country, but higher up it becomes luxuriant and the trail levels off and opens into a broad valley.

To return, you can backtrack or proceed to Hopar for the Bualtar Glacier, then backtrack and take the Shayyar route towards Minapin and Pisan and then back to the Karakoram Highway.

Karimabad-Ultar Glacier

A four-day trek through an open zone. No permit is necessary, porters are optional but a guide is indispensable. Setting off point: Karimabad. Fairly strenuous. Elevation 5600 metres. Time from June to September.

Follow the trail that runs on the left of the stream behind the old fort in Baltit. It stops just beyond the bridge, then continues up a very rugged stretch over a gorge to the left. Depending on pace it should take from half a day to a day to climb up to the shepherds' hut at 3000 metres. The trail is steep, but very scenic.

If you start early in the morning, it's possible to return on the same day. But you can camp here and climb to the top of Ultar Glacier with a guide the following morning. The trail continues to ascend, then forks. Both branches lead to the glaciers, one being easier but taking longer than the other. The more difficult trail goes right to the top of the glaciers – there's a dark mica glacier and a snowclad ridge nearby.

After crossing two small glaciers, you have to scale a dangerous cliff. When you reach Ultar Glacier, you're 6000 metres above sea level and the world around you is pristine white. The view of the Hunza Valley from this glacier is magnificent. Guides usually cost Rs 40 a day, which you usually have to pay on the spot. Ultar Peak is a towering 7329 metres, but there are other peaks on the same massif that are even higher. The Ultar base camp is at 4500 metres above sea level, but Karimabad is situated at 2500 metres up, so it's only 2000 metres further on.

Make sure you get acclimatised before doing this trek. In 1982, a Japanese doctor on a mountaineering expedition died of altitude sickness compounded by pneumonia.

At the Ultar base camp there is a flat grassy patch with a view of some peaks to the north, probably part of the Batura group.

Be very careful going down. Take it slowly as the going is difficult.

Aliabad-Hacinder Glacier

This trek takes two days through an open zone. A permit's not necessary, and neither are porters or a guide. Setting off point: Aliabad. Easy. Elevation 2800 metres. Time from June until September.

The trail begins at Hasanabad River, 1½ km south of Aliabad on the Karakoram Highway. Follow the Hasanabad River westward, then turn south to Hacinder Valley, an extraordinary region consisting largely of pebbles and boulders, that must once have been a riverbed or the site of a gigantic glacier. There is a trail leading up a slope to Hacinder base camp. Other trails in the same region go to Thosdaro and Hacinder Glaciers. Campsites along this route are known as *harabasa*.

(From Khaled Aziz & Akram Huna Baig, Gilgit.)

Sultanabad (Hini)-Passu Peak

A 14-day trek through an open zone. Permits are not issued, but if you are allowed to do it, porters and guide are a must. Setting off point: Sultanabad. Strenuous. Elevation approximately 4800 metres. Time from June until August.

If starting from Ganesh jeep it to Sultanabad, south of Aliabad. The trekking route is via Muchichul Glacier; the base of Batura Peak at 7785 metres; Hasanabad Glacier; the base of Shishpar Peak (7619 metres); and then to the foot of Passu Peak at 7284 metres.

On return, backtrack over the same route to Sultanabad or continue along Passu Glacier to Passu village on the Karakoram Highway. There are wagons and buses going to Karimabad from here.

Karimabad-Shishpar Valley

This is a seven-day trek through an open zone. A permit is not required and a porter or guide is optional. Setting off point: Karimabad. Moderate to strenuous. Elevation 4600 metres. Time from June to August.

Trek to Khudabad Harai and on to Wazirkhan, then Khatar Harai, Punu Harai and finally ascend to the top of Punu. Camp here and backtrack over the same route on the return trip.

Aliabad-Mutsutshil

This is a ten-day trek through an open zone. A permit is not required but porters and a guide are essential. Setting off point: Aliabad. Strenuous. Elevation 4800 metres. Time from June to August.

From Aliabad trek to Mose near Tochi Glacier along the Hasanabad Nallah and on to Gaimaling, six hours over moraines and across glaciers. From Gaimaling it is six hours over the meadow to Bakur and then an easy seven-hour trek across

glaciers to Batakshi. The trek then takes you to a lake that is believed to be the home of fairies – humans drown here, so beware! The trail continues on to Shendar, seven hours away.

To return, backtrack over the same route.

GOJAL – UPPER HUNZA VALLEY

Gulmit-Bulkish Glacier

This is a six day trek through an open zone. A permit is not required and a porter or guide is optional. Setting off point: Gulmit. Fairly strenuous. Elevation 4500 metres. Time from June to August.

From Gulmit trek to Rajab Hill, on to Sirkhum-Vek, then Bulkish Glacier up to Ganz and Dashil. From Dashil continue over glaciers to the shepherds' hut. Then it's a rugged descent to Bubin, Surugingal and finally back to Gulmit.

Gulmit-Passu

From Gulmit it is possible to walk to Passu via Husseini on the Karakoram Highway. The trekking route, however, is via Kamaris where you start to cross the Gulmit Glacier, then down the valley and up again over the Gulkin Glacier to the village of Gulkin near Hussaini. From here continue up to Burit Lake. The trail along the lake is easy though narrow. It opens up to the snout of Passu Glacier. From here a trail leads down to the Karakoram Highway into the village of Passu.

This trek takes more than a day. It's not particularly scenic but nonetheless it is a pleasant walk.

Passu-Shimshal

This takes five days through an open zone. No permit is necessary, and porter and guide are optional. Setting off point: Passu. Fairly strenuous. Elevation 2800 metres to 3200 metres. Time from June until September.

You set off in a north-easterly direction

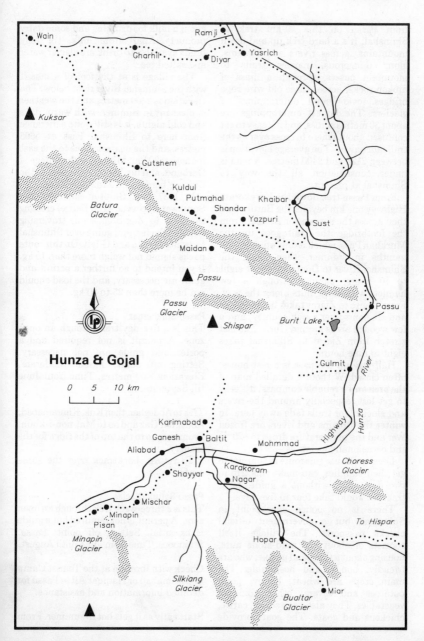

Wain
Ramji
Gharhil
Diyar
Yasrich
▲ *Kuksar*
Gutshem
Kuldul
Putmahal
Shandar
Khaibar
Yazpuri
Sust
Batura Glacier
Maidan
▲ *Passu*
Passu Glacier
▲ *Shispar*
Passu
Burit Lake
Gulmit

Hunza & Gojal

0   5   10 km

Hunza River
Karakoram Highway

Karimabad
Ganesh
Baltit
Aliabad
Mohmmad
Shayyar
Nagar
Karakoram
Choress Glacier
Mischar
Minapin
Pisan
To Hispar
Minapin Glacier
Hopar
Silkiang Glacier
Miar
Bualtar Glacier
▲

from Passu on this 80-km trek to Shimshal. It's a hard trek up and down mountains, across rivers and streams, along dangerous, narrow trails to mountain passes, through a mass of broken rocks, across three old wire-rope bridges, over small outcroppings of glaciers. The largest outcroppings are about 30 metres across, and it's easy to get confused about where to cross over as the trail fades away. The average elevation is between 2125 and 2400 metres. A road is under construction all the way to Shimshal at present.

From Passu trek down the Karakoram Highway one km beyond the Batura Inn, then across the suspension bridge. From the footbridge the trail goes up the Murkhan Pass, which is only open for two months in summer, then along the Shimshal River to Donte for about eight to 10 hours, passing through a few hamlets with stone huts along the way. From Donte to Ziarat takes between five and six hours over rough country, and a few wooded areas around Gurn. The last stretch from Ziarat to Shimshal takes eight to nine hours.

Half-way up the pass is a rest house, often closed. Without a detailed map of the area and a reliable compass, it's easy to get lost, especially around the rivers and glaciers for trails fade away here. In winter the streams and rivers are frozen over and the temperature drops to -20°C and occasionally as low as -35°C.

Locals, who use this route in summer to get their supplies, can make this trip in two days, but, without a guide, most trekkers would take four to five days.

There is no police checkpoint in Shimshal, but a government official checks passports. The village itself consists of about 100 mud-stone huts, housing about a thousand people, who are friendly, honest and hospitable. The main crops are wheat, barley, peas, potatoes and several other kinds of vegetables. They also keep sheep, cattle, chickens and goats. The goats provide enough milk for drinking and some dairy products. Apart from milk, the only fluids available to drink are glacier water and salted tea.

The village is at the foot of a massif with the Shimshal River right below. The elevation is 2400 metres and the weather is pleasant in summer, with warm days and cold nights. It is still quite a distance from here to Shimshal Pass at 5665 metres, and the nearest place to the east is another 80 km. Midway is the village of Darband, and further on is the pass to the Chinese border and Muztagh Range.

In 1937 Eric Shipton surveyed the Surukwat Basin via Aghil Range, crossing the pass to Zug-Shaksgam, traversing Braldu Glacier, and going over Shimshal Pass into Hunza and Gilgit. On this route packs should not weigh more than 15 kg. If you intend to go further a permit and guide are necessary, and the load should not be more than 25 to 30 kg.

Passu-Shikhargaz

This is a five-day trek through an open zone. A permit is not required and a porter and guide are not necessary. Setting off point: Passu. Moderate. Elevation 5000 metres. Time from June till September.

Trek to Abdeghar, then Kuk, Khuramabad, Abdeghar Gaz and on to Maj-non-i-khun. From here go to the top of the ridge for the scenery.

To return, backtrack over the same route.

Passu-Batura Glacier

This is a three-week trek through an open zone. A permit is not required but a guide is essential. Setting off point: Passu. Strenuous. Time from June until August.

Check with Ibrahim at the Tourist Camp in Karimabad or Haqiqat Ali in Passu for detailed information and assistance.

Start early as it gets hot in summer. From

Passu it's six hours to Zertbin then an eight-hour walk across moraines and meadow to Yazakpert. There is a settlement here with views of Batura Glacier and peaks. Continue on to Kuldul shepherds' hut and then on to Shelmin at the junction of the Pupshikarga and Shirin-maidan valleys. You can take a side trip to Morthorn then back to Shirin-maidan.

The trek continues to Gutshem camp where snowclad peaks are visible and then to Yuksgaz over moraines. Camp at 4000 metres. Up on the highest ridge are views of the Batura glaciers and peaks and you may see yaks and ibexes.

Retrace the route back to Ludpur and Pupshikarga through narrow valleys and over moraines. At 4500 metres there are magnificent views of the glaciers and peaks.

Continue to Yudshgaz and camp here. Backtrack to Pupshikarga at the extreme end of the Batura Valley.

The trail continues over moraine and talus back to Gutshem, then Kuldul and down to Patmahal where there are shepherds' huts and a fine view of the Batura Peaks. Continue on to Nangarchi over glacier and back to Shirin-maidan. Then it's on to Khirghiz-Washk, Molunghil and finally back to Passu.

This is a very rough trek and it is advisable to take it slowly.

Passu-Kalamdarchi

This is a ten-day trek through a restricted zone. A permit is required and porters and guide are indispensable. Setting off point: Passu. Strenuous. Elevation 5250 metres. Time from June till August.

From Passu trek to Kallapani. From here it's nine km to Khaibar and another five km to Gircha. The trek continues on to Sust where the valley opens up suddenly.

You can bus or jeep it to Sust now, from where it is 60 km to Mizghar and beyond is Kalamdarchi, once the fort/customs post for the Khunjerab Pass.

Khunjerab Valley

This is a restricted area and a special permit is required.

From Shimshal Valley a trail leads to Kulamudi in the Yarkhund Valley heading north-east towards China. Another trail branches off towards the Pamirs. There are numerous wild yaks and ibexes to be seen. To the north-east are tribes of Pakposhes and Shakshahs, who live at an altitude ranging from 3000 to 3250 metres. Very little is known about these peoples, though it appears likely they are of Aryan descent. They are fair-complexioned and speak the language of the Chagatai Turks.

North of Hunza Valley is Sirikol Pass. Kilik Pass, at 5000 metres, is wide enough for horse and camel caravans, and is now used by Afghan Kirghiz refugees. Much further up is Mizghar Pass, which now has bridges spanning the rivers.

In 1878 Chinese rule was re-established in Kasghar and brigandage on trading caravans to Leh ceased. But towards the end of the century Chinese power declined and brigandage on this route and in Baltistan was resumed, until the British arrived.

To the north-west is the Karumbar River Valley, which is 40 km across. The river joins up with the Ishkoman Valley at Darkot Pass. On the other side of Ishkoman Pass at 4350 metres, is the Oxus River, situated in the Badakshan region or what is now known as the Wakhan, a narrow strip of land which separates Russia from Pakistan by just 16 km. This area is mainly inhabited by the Kirghiz tribes, who sought refuge in Pakistan when the Russians invaded Afghanistan.

Right above the Batura Valley is the Lupghar River Valley and further north is the Chapursan River Valley. The setting off point is Sust, however these areas remain restricted and require a special permit, mainly due to their proximity to the borders of Afghanistan and China.

CHALT VALLEY
Chalt-Baltar

This is a seven-day trek through a free zone. A permit is not required, and porters and guide are optional. Setting off point: Chalt. Fairly moderate. Elevation from 2800 to 3200 metres. Time from June to September.

Chalt is 48 km from Hunza and 54 km from Gilgit, where the Hunza River veers southward at a 90° angle to the Karakoram Highway. The bridge here spans two gorges. To the south are the villages of Chaprot and Nilt. The latter, conquered by the British in 1891, was the last fortified village guarding the route to Baltit.

A jeep track from the bridge leads to Chalt. Turn right at the blue signboard – written in Urdu – just before you come to another bridge crossing a tributary. Go past the forest ranger's office, which appears to be perpetually closed, and through some apricot orchards. Climb a trail above the stream, then cross the bridge.

From Chalt to Budalas – a long, sprawling village – takes two hours. Near Budalas is a sulphur spring. Continue along the jeep track, and as you approach Das, you'll get a view of Rakaposhi. The section between Budalas and Das takes three hours. Stay on the jeep track after crossing to the left bank of the Bolas Das River; the tributary splits up here, and the stream to the left leads to the Diantar Valley. About a third of the way along is another bridge. Keep to the jeep track. Getting to Bar from Das takes 1½ hours. Bar can also be reached by another route, which branches off about a hundred metres past the bridge. The jeep track ends at Bar, which is a very picturesque village. There's a campsite here.

About an hour out of Bar on the way to Shunghe, the trail becomes difficult to follow – it seems to fade away. Press on and you'll come to a bridge, and cross over to get to the right bank of the river. It's

another hour from here to Shunghe, a shepherd's hamlet consisting of a few mud-stone huts. Getting to Baltar Glacier from Shunghe takes another five to six hours.

The next part of the trek is tough going. As Ronald Mis of California puts it, be prepared to 'tighten boot laces and prepare for a really rough trail. Without a guide, good luck!'

Trek right up to where a stream flows out from beneath a glacier, that is covered with scree. Above is a beautiful meadow. There are shepherds' huts here. The view is superb and there are plenty of places to camp. There is another trail via the left bank of the Baltar Nallah, but it's said to be even rougher. What's more there are no villages along this trail.

It's almost 50 km from Chalt to Baltar Meadow through deep, narrow valleys and across streams. Baltar Glacier is steppe-like, about four km long and three km wide. As you climb the snowclad slopes to the snowline at 4000 metres, the birch forests of the meadow give way to junipers. Above and all around, snow capped peaks rise up to 6775 metres. The meadow is 2500 metres above sea level, carpeted with flowers and there are numerous vividly-coloured small birds darting about. There are also ibexes and bears up here. To the west is Kukay Glacier.

On the return trek, start early in the morning from Baltar Meadow and follow the shepherds. They are so fit they seem to skip, hop and jump over rocks all the way down to Das – for 12 hours! Camp overnight in Das.

Das-Diantar Pass-Naltar

This is a five-day trek through a free zone. A permit is not necessary, but you do need a porter and guide. Setting off point: Das. Fairly strenuous. Elevation 4800 metres. Time from August until September.

The trail drops down to a little bridge between Das and the Diantar Valley;

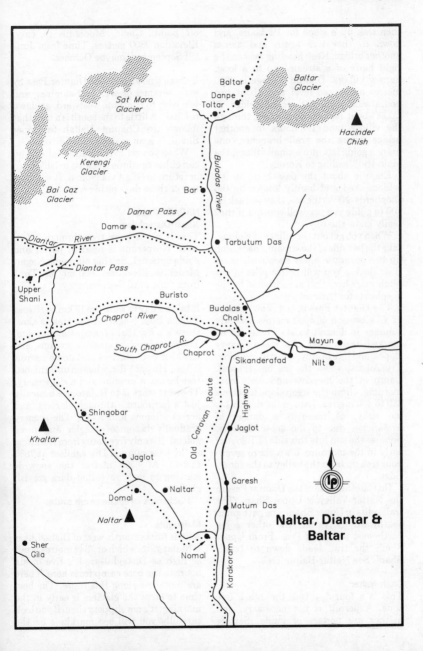

Naltar, Diantar & Baltar

then trek up a slope for 1½ hours, and down to the river again and across another bridge. Keep heading west on the right bank of a stream, up to a long, narrow village. Diantar Village is 3350 metres above sea level and about two hours walk from the second bridge. It takes about half an hour to get through the village, and 1½ hours to another bridge where the trail branches, one branch going left into a small village, the main trail leading to Korong.

Enquire about the pass here, as it's seldom used and hardly known by the shepherds. Nevertheless, they will ask Rs 100 to guide you up, well worth it if they really know the way.

When you get out the village of Korong, take the left side of the stream, then climb up to a meadow where shepherds graze their flocks. You will notice piles of dry birch twigs here that are gathered by the shepherds for their own use.

The Diantar Pass is in a snowy massif at an elevation of 4800 metres. In early summer it doesn't exist. There are no marked trails over the steep, snowy slopes, and late in July, it is still iced over. Try August when the ice has thawed. Camp in the meadow and early next morning, climb the steep slope for about 350 to 400 metres. Late in the day this is too risky, as there is a danger of avalanches due to the snow thawing, because the sun hits this side of Toloybar early in the morning. It's a six to seven-hour trek up from the valley to the snowy ridge.

On the other side of the Diantar Pass in the Naltar Valley is Upper Shani. The trail splits in Upper Shani, one path going southward to Naltar, the other going north-west to Naltar Pass. From Upper Shani the trail leads down to Lower Shani. See Naltar-Baltar Trek.

Chalt-Naltar

This is a four-day trek through a free zone. A permit is not necessary, and neither are porters or guide. Setting off point: Chalt. Moderate to easy. Elevation 2800 metres. Time from June till September, maybe October.

If there's no sign of the Diantar Pass by early summer or even mid-summer, and you wish to continue westward, go down to Chalt. A little to the south is a trail that follows the Chaprot Nallah to Upper Shani. It is an easier and safer route.

When you get to the Naltar Valley, you can either continue trekking to Ishkoman or return to Gilgit via Nomal. It will take two or three days either way.

NAGAR VALLEY
Nagar-Distaghilsar

This is a one-week trek through a free zone. No permit is needed; porter and guide optional. Setting off point: Nagar. Moderate. Elevation 3800 metres. Time from June until September.

It takes a day to walk the 18 km to Hispar Village from Nagar. If the trek is slow, there is a *harabasa* (campsite) en route. The route involves crossing streams, and trekking over glaciers and down narrow ledges. Hispar Village has an unfurnished rest house, a mosque and a dispensary. The next stage is to Bularong - basically just a *harabasa* - through glaciers, and across streams and rocks. The scenery gradually becomes craggier and more glacial. It's only five hours from Bularong to the base camp of Distaghilsar at 7885 metres. At 6500 metres the snow is starting to melt revealing dark-greyish glaciers.

Backtrack over the same route.

Malangute

A little further north-west of Distaghilsar is Malangute, which at 7342 metres is not as high as Distaghilsar. It's five or six hours to the base camp from here. There are moraines along this route. The best time to cross the glaciers is early in the morning; it's not slippery then. If you look carefully you will see markhors on the high, sharp ridges. There is vegetation from 3000 to 5000 metres, and there are quite a few of these impressive-looking animals in this area. Some of them are as tall as 1½ metres and have huge horns.

Nagar-Rondu-Ashkole

A two-week trek through open zone. A permit is necessary as are porters and guides. Setting off point: Nagar. Fairly strenuous. Elevation 5600 metres. Time early spring for skiers; mid-June until September for trekkers.

In the village of Hispar the trail splits up: one branch leads north to the base camps of Distaghilsar and Malangute; the other towards the east over Hispar and Biafo Glaciers, which cover 112 km together. About midway along it forks again, and one trail leads down to Rondu, the other continues to Ashkole. It goes through the 5830-metre Hispar Pass, passes a snow lake, and covers a distance of 240 km altogether. The beauty of this region has been described by Martin Conway as one of the 'wonders of the earth'. See Shigar-Nagar trek.

Nagar-Barpu Glacier

This is a 10-day trek through a free zone. No permit is required, and porter and guide are optional. Setting off point: Nagar. Moderate to difficult. Elevation approximately 5800 metres. Time from June until September.

The first section between Nagar and Shishken is gentle trekking through apricot orchards and villages. Along the way you get a fine view of the Rakaposhi Range. Shishken is on the other side of Kapel Glacier – an easy four to five-hour walk.

From Shishken walk to Lake Rush, where you can camp above Barpu Glacier at 5000 metres. It's a picturesque area, the water is crystal clear and the green slopes are dotted with flowers. There are views of Malubiting Peak (7292 metres),

Golden Peak, Miar Peak at 6824 metres and Barpu Glacier, which slopes down towards Nagar Valley. From Lake Rush trek to Chokotans. It's too hot in summer to do this trek during the day; better to start off in the afternoon. Camp at Chokotans, a beautiful area with spring water, streams, flowers and juniper trees. Trek from here to Gridindil. Crossing the Barpu Glacier takes two to three hours. The campsite – at 5800 metres – is known for its wildlife. There are several peaks nearby that are easy to scale, should you wish to do so.

Backtrack over the same route.

Nagar-Malubiting

A 12-day trek through a free zone. No permit is necessary, and porters and guide are optional. Setting off point: Nagar. Moderate. Elevation 5600 metres. Time from June until September.

From Nagar trek to Buldar Glacier; and continue to the base of Diran (7279); Barpu Glacier; Miar Glacier; the base of Miar (6824 metres); and finally to the foot of Malubiting (7292 metres).

Backtrack over the same route.

Nagar-Khanibasar Glacier

This is a 14-day trek through a free zone. A permit is not required, but porters and guide are necessary. Moderate. Elevation 5200 metres. Time from June until September.

From Nagar trek to Hispar about 20 km to the east; then on to Hispar Glacier; Kunyang-Pak Glacier; Pumarikish Glacier; Jutmaru Glacier; and finally Khanibasar Glacier.

Backtrack over the same route.

Nagar-Bualtar Glacier

A one-day trek in a free zone. Permit not necessary; and porters and guide not required. Setting off point: Nagar. Elevation 3200 metres. Time from June until October.

From Nagar the trail leads south-eastward to Hopar, eight km away, in a broad, beautiful valley with mud-stone huts scattered on the slopes. CIDA (Canadian International Development Agency) is doing a lot of good work here. There's a rest house here with beds and even a kitchen. From Hopar, it's a steep uphill trek across streams. The trail continues beyond the rest house, uphill and then down steeply into the canyon and the Bualtar Glacier. The glacier is cracked and melting and will eventually leave only moraines. Golden Peak towers above it and there are good views of Barpu Glacier and Diran.

Backtrack for the return route. On approaching Nagar, on the left side of the road junction, is the palace of the former Mir of Nagar.

Nagar-Pisan

A two-day trek through a free zone. Permit not required, neither are porters or guide necessary. Setting off point: Nagar or Aliabad. Moderate almost easy. Elevation 2800 metres. Time from early spring until October.

On the Karakoram Highway in the Hunza Valley a road branches off to the right before Aliabad and leads to Nagar village via Pisan and Minapin. It's possible to to take a bus and get off at this road or trek it all the way from Aliabad. From Nagar there is a trail through Shayyar to Pisan and Minapin. It climbs steeply along narrow ledges before descending into Minapin. It's off the main jeep track which you can also take to Minapin.

The trail to Minapin is an alternative to backtracking over the same route to Ganesh. On approaching Minapin and Pisan from Shayyar, this trail runs along a narrow shelf above the Hunza River. From the Karakoram Highway it's about five km from the bridge.

There are rest houses in both villages, above which are the Minapin and Pisan Glaciers on the flank of the Rakaposhi Range.

Nine km to the south of the Karakoram Highway Bridge is the village of Dudimal. This is on the same shelf as Pisan, and is interesting because of its packed mud-stone huts which are huddled along narrow ledges.

Minapin Glacier Trek

This is a four-day trek through a free zone. No permit is necessary, nor is a guide, and a porter is optional. Setting off point: Minapin rest house. Moderate. Elevation 4600 metres. Time from early spring until September.

About a km up, turn right to Taghafari, a beautiful meadow just below Diran. The trail follows the glacier to Rakaposhi base camp. Better to do this in the late afternoon as it's too hot during the day in summer. There are settlements at Hapkhund and Tagaya, but from here to Taghafari the trail gets narrower and more difficult. Turn up to Kacheli, another wooded meadow. There are lots of flowers here and no snow until you reach the 4500-metre level. From the top of the moraine of Minapin Glacier you get a stunning view of the 5200 and 7700-metre icy walls of Rakaposhi and Diran that stretch to around 30 km in length.

The following day cross the glacier in the middle. Follow the glacier, which is flat, until you reach another green, wooded meadow, closely surrounded by mountain peaks. There seem to be continual avalanches on these mountains, so be very careful. You will also see Rakaposhi, seamed with glaciers, towering above the rest, its slopes covered in pines, fir trees, willows, alpine scrubs and flowers.

It's possible to climb further up to another meadow at 3554 metres, and be transported to a world of ice, snow, rocks and streams. There is a campsite just above Kacheli at 3600 metres. Backtrack over the same route to return.

Trekkers can continue on to Rakaposhi base camp from here, or the base camp of Minapin Peak (7279 metres). There are tremendous views of surrounding valleys from these camps.

Pisan Trek

This is basically just a gentle stroll. There is a trail leading out of the nearby village of Pisan, which goes up the glacier to a meadow. It's a gentle climb. The meadows on this side are lower than those on the Minapin side. There are lots of flowering plants, trees, medicinal herbs and butterflies here.

GILGIT
Gilgit-Bagroth

A five-day trek through a free zone. No permit, porters or guide are necessary. Setting off point: Gilgit. Easy. Elevation not over 3000 metres. Time from early spring until early October.

Bagroth is 46 km east of Gilgit, through deep, scenic valleys that are lushly green and have flat, terraced ridges and precipitous cliffs. The jeep track from Gilgit is paved in sections, generally easy going, and finishes at Bagroth.

The trail continues through meadows, ascending gently to grain fields. Cargo jeeps ply this route, but if you're trekking all the way, go from Gilgit through Danyor across the Chinese Bridge to Oshikhandas. From there it's eight km to Snakar, three km to Datuchi. Away to the right is Oshikhandas, and right of Datuchi is Farfu, 1½ km away. Nearby is a fresh water spring. Then it's 2½ km to Chirah, and on to the unfurnished NAWO rest house.

Cross the bridge then climb up to the edge of the valley. There's a grey-black glacier to the left, and right in front is Diran, capped with snow.

Note that off the main jeep track there are other trails across the grain fields to the rest house.

Follow a narrow trail up a steep slope,

then descend to Chirah; around the mountain is Gasunder. There are glaciers and pine forests around this region. To the left is the dark-grey Henerchi Glacier, and nearby is Bulchi. Left of Gasunder is Gutumi Glacier – also slate-grey – beyond is a bridge and just after the bridge is Buyofor Glacier. Continuing to the right is Chargo Glacier, to the left is a footpath to Burchi Glacier. At the foot of the glacier is the village of Burchi. Further on is Kardi Glacier. The trail takes you back to Gasunder, Farfu and the rest house from the latter.

It's possible to explore the valleys in more depth by following the trail from Henerchi Glacier. This leads to Nagar Valley and there are wooded areas along the way where you can camp. It's advisable to get hold of a detailed map of the area before you set out. There are lots of semi-precious gems around in this region – mostly aquamarines. Accommodation is possible with villagers, but don't count on it. Take camping gear and provisions with you.

If you decide to go to Bagroth, check at the Tourist Cottage in Jutial, Gilgit before you set off. You may be able to hitch a lift on a tractor – occasionally tractors go there for a day or two in spring, summer and early autumn. If you manage to hitch a ride, be prepared to rough it. Take a warm jacket and a scarf, especially during the cold season.

Gilgit-Haramosh Base Camp

This is a 10-day trek through a free zone. A permit is not necessary, and porters and guide are optional. Setting off point: Gilgit. Easy. Elevation 3200 metres. Time from June until September.

Take a jeep from Gilgit to Jaglot, or a bus up to Sassi. Trek to Shah from Sassi; then on to Bahut; Ishkapal Glacier; and to the base of Haramosh (7406 metres).

Backtrack over the same route on return.

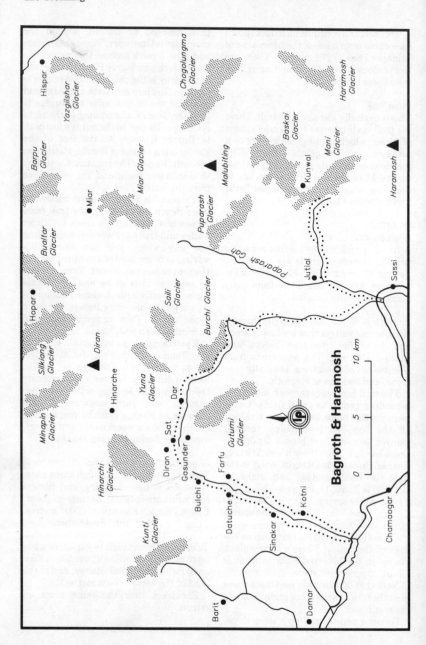

Gilgit-Phuparash Glacier
An 18-day trek through an open zone. A permit is not necessary, but porters and guide are essential. Setting off point: Gilgit. Moderate. Elevation 5600 metres. Time from June until September.

Get a jeep from Gilgit to Jaglot where the trek to Hanochol starts. From there you trek to Sassi; Dache; Ishkara; Mani Glacier; Baskai Glacier; the base of Laila Peak (6218 metres); the base of Malubiting Peak (7452 metres), and finally to Phuparash Glacier. Backtrack over the same route on return.

Variation: From Gilgit trek to Pharpui, up to Chargo Meadow; Darchan; Jutsar; Jutial village; Burchi village; on to Baskai Glacier and then to the base camp of Malubiting Peak. From here continue on to Kutwal Lake, a good place to stop over, then on to Ishkere village, Dasso and finally back to Sassi.

Gilgit-Chogolungma Glacier ✓
This is an 18-day trek through a free zone. A permit is not required but porters and guide are essential. Setting off point: Gilgit. Fairly strenuous. Elevation 5600 metres. Time from June till September.

Trekking route is provided by Qurban Ali, a mountain guide from Dasso, Karamosh Valley.

From Gilgit take a jeep to Sassi, two hours away. From Sassi to Dasso is a six to eight-hour trek. The next day trek to Ishkere, then Kutwal Lake, then on to the foot of the Haramosh Pass. From here it is an eight-hour trek to the top of the pass at 5600 metres. It is then four hours hard trekking across the Chogolungma Glacier. Camping places here are known as Laila Camps. Continue on to Arondu, then Doko and the following morning trek to Tisar. From Tisar cargo jeeps are available for Skardu.

Variation: From the Haramosh Pass take the trail to the base camp of Laila Peak, then down to the base of Bolocho Glacier, then on to Tisas and from here to Arondu, Sesko, Niaslo and finally Tisar.

This is a fascinating trekking region. The villages here are still very traditional and there is an abundance of wildlife in this hardly explored area. Beyond the village of Dassu it is particularly scenic with lakes and forests and there is trout fishing as well.

Gilgit-Rakaposhi Base Camp
This takes 10 days through an free zone. A permit is not necessary, and porters and guide are optional. Setting off point: Gilgit. Moderate. Elevation 6000 metres. Time from June until September.

Take a jeep to Danyor from Gilgit; then trek to Bilchan; the base of Dobani (6143 metres); the base of Diran (7279 metres); and finally to the base camp of Rakaposhi.

Backtrack over the same route on return.

Jaglot-Gazhu Bahut Lake
A two-day trek in an open zone. No permit, porter or guide necessary, but don't trek alone here. Setting off point: Gilgit. Moderate. Elevation 3200 metres. Time from early spring to autumn.

Take a jeep from Gilgit 43 km south along the Karakoram Highway to Jaglot. It's a little beyond the confluence of the Gilgit and Indus Rivers. The jeep track turns right and goes inland for about eight km where the trail continues to Gazhu Bahut Village. Higher up is the lake. It's 18 km of difficult trekking, up and down hills and across rocky riverbeds, or as John Knight of London describes it, 'Really not too rough a trail but still quite tough'.

This trek is particularly suitable for anglers as the lake is well-known for golden trout. Check with the fisheries bureau in Gilgit.

Chilas-Darel & Tanger

This is three days through an open zone. No permit, porter or guide necessary, but do not trek alone in this area, neither should you camp. Setting off point: Chilas. Easy. Elevation not above 2400 metres. Time from early spring until early autumn.

Jeep it out to Siazin or follow the trail beyond the bridge at Chilas. But check with the superintendent of police at Chilas before setting off as this area has a long-term reputation for being dangerous – the feuding among native tribes is continuous. At one time even archaeologists could not work here without being accompanied by a police contingent. The houses are all fortified with tall towers and, like the Pathans, the men are armed. The local inhabitants appear to actively spurn progress, though there are now government offices – mostly for the departments of forestry and agriculture – and rest houses. The villagers' attitude towards foreigners has apparently softened and they are reported to be quite friendly. However, check for the latest info before you go.

The country is lush, green and fertile, full of grain fields and fruit orchards. The narrow mouth of the valley opens out into conifer forests, and the trail along both valleys is dotted with innumerable archaeological ruins. There are apparently routes that lead to Gupis and Ghizer over Khanjer Pass. Nearby is Fogit Village, also known as Dar-I-Run, an archaeological site of Buddhist ruins.

NALTAR VALLEY
Naltar-Chalt

Seven days of strenuous trekking through an open zone. No permit necessary, porter optional but guide indispensable. Setting off point: Naltar. Elevation 4800 metres. Time from mid-July until September.

If you're in Gilgit and there is no cargo jeep service available to Nomal or Naltar, take the Hunza or Passu bus. Tell the driver to drop you off at Rahimabad, also known as Maltum Das, on the Karakoram Highway. There is a little *inn* here where you can get bed and breakfast for Rs 16. Early next morning cross the river by raft; the fare is Rs 1.50 per head to Nomal.

From Nomal it is 16 km to Naltar, up a gentle trail to an altitude of 3222 metres. Go to Domal on the south side of the river and Jaglot on the north; continue to Bichgari at 3400 metres; and Shingobar at 3745 metres. The bridge is a little difficult to find, but it's just behind a small wood. Naltar is a ski-training area with a tiny hotel and a rest house, which requires advance booking in Gilgit. There is also a small shop here.

From Naltar to Naltar Lakes along the the river of the same name is 12 km or four hours trekking through pine forests. You will see numerous species of birds along this trail including the snowcock, monal pheasant and Himalayan pika. There are also ibexes in this area. You will come across nomads who will sell you milk and butter.

The lakes are 4675 metres above sea level, and there are shepherds' huts nearby that are primitive but dry. The lakes are full of trout, so take some fishing gear with you. From the lakes the trail ascends gradually for six to eight hours up to Lower Shani, a scenic wooded area with a view of the peaks of the Hindu Raj to the north. There is an ideal camping spot in a wooded area in Shani. There are also hamlets here where porters and guides can be hired, and milk and eggs are available. The trail climbs gently from Lower Shani to Upper Shani. A small, dark glacier is on the left, and after about two km the trail forks, with one branch going north-east to Diantar Pass, the other east to Chaprot and Chalt.

There are two ways to get to Chalt. The first is via Chaprot from Upper Shani; the second via Diantar Pass. Set up camp at

Upper Shani, a beautiful spot which offers a good view of Khatta Peak. There are numerous ibexes around here.

The trail from Chaprot to Chalt is fairly easy from early spring till early autumn. But the route via Diantar Pass is tough-going and is usually used by trekkers continuing to Baltar Meadow. Trek up to Distar-Bar and camp overnight. From Distar-Bar go towards Diantar Pass (4800 metres), an extremely difficult section, which calls for stamina and a good guide.

Guides are available in Lower Shani or Diantar village on the other side for Rs 100 to Rs 150. Once you get over the pass, you descend to summer pasture land, 300 metres above the village of Diantar. From here you go down to Budalas River, then turn south towards Chalt; or north to Baltar Meadow and Glacier.

From Diantar village there is also a trail leading straight up to Baltar Meadow and you don't have to go all the way to Budalas. You can come back this way on your return via Bar and Das villages.

On the return trip if there are no cargo jeeps in Chalt you can cross the bridge to the Karakoram Highway and take a wagon or bus for Gilgit.

Naltar-Pakore

Seven days through an open zone. No permit is necessary, and porters and guide are optional. Setting off point: Naltar. Moderate. Elevation 4500 metres. Time from June until August.

In the same valley and along the same trail north, but out of Upper Shani on the third day of the trek, the trail splits, with one branch leading to Diantar Pass, the other to Naltar Pass at 5150 metres. Take the one to Naltar Pass. From here there is a gradual ascent over rather rocky and glaciated terrain to Khori Bort. There is a good camping spot here with commanding views of Rakaposhi, Dobani and some of the peaks of Nanga Parbat in the far

distance. From Khori Bort to Pakore the trail is easy-going for two days. From here the trek to Chatorkhand is only one hour via Hayul Gol (5250 metres).

There are jeeps going to Gilgit from Chatorkhand, but you can continue trekking to the Valley of Yasin via Asambar Pass if you wish.

YASIN VALLEY
Chatorkhand-Yasin

A five-day trek through an open zone. No permits are required, porters are optional but a guide is necessary. Setting off point: Chatorkhand. Moderate. Elevation 4500 metres. Time from June until September.

The cargo jeep service from Gilgit to Chatorkhand is irregular and infrequent, but a large group can hire a jeep. However, Chatorkhand is in trekking distance from Gilgit via Naltar and Pakore, or from Gilgit via Punial and Gakutch where a jeep track cuts through the valley, north to Chatorkhand. Chatorkhand has a teashop and a tiny bazaar.

From Chatorkhand the trail leads to Asambar Aghost (4432 metres), Muduri and then Sandhi. From the latter it is eight km or 2½ hours trek to Yasin.

There's a jeep service from Yasin to Gilgit or Gupis.

Yasin-Mastuj

Ten days of strenuous trekking through a free zone. No permit is necessary, and porters and guide are optional. Setting off point: Yasin. Elevation 5000 metres. Time from June until September.

From Yasin to Taus Nazbardeh; then on to Askarthan; Shikhan; Nazbar Pass (4977 metres); Ano Pass (3483 metres); Haringal Shal; Zagar Pass (5009 metres); Anoshal; Dakshal; Chapchirgah; Chapali; and Mastuj. This route is hardly ever used, and the area is uninhabited except for shepherds.

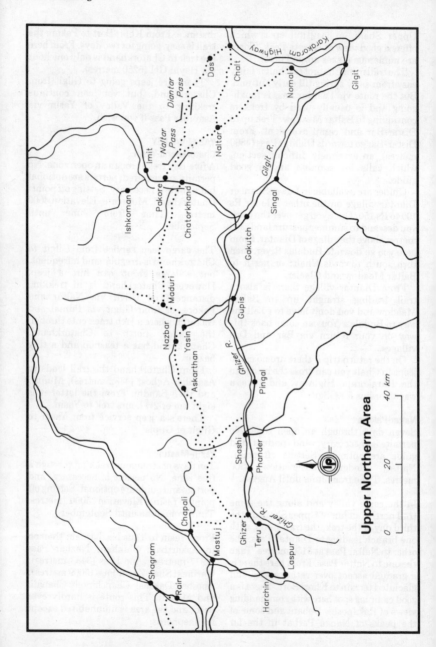

Upper Northern Area

0   20   40 km

Phander-Mastuj

A three-day trek through a free zone. No permit necessary, and porters and guide are optional. Setting off point: Phander. Moderate to difficult. Elevation 5000 metres. Time from June until September.

Take a jeep from Gilgit to Phander where the trek into the Ghizer Valley starts. The trail goes via the Chumarkhan Pass (5009 metres).

At Phander, 3030 metres, cross the bridge into a wide open valley. The trail turns west up to Chumarkhan Pass. You will arrive at a a shepherds' hamlet at the foot of the path and from there it's a one-day trek into Mastuj. The scenery to the north of the Hindu Raj Range is magnificent. See Chitral-Yasin Trek.

Ghizer-Darel & Tanger

A six-day trek through an open zone. Permit and porters not necessary, but a guide is essential. Setting off point: Ghizer. Strenuous. Time from early spring till early autumn.

From Phander trek to Ghizer, beyond Shiashi and 15 km before Teru. There is a trail from here that goes through narrow valleys into Siazin. Alternatively there is a route midway to the Darel-Tanger Valley. See the Chilas-Darel & Tanger Trek.

Teru-Laspur

A one-day trek through a free zone. No permit, porters or guide necessary. Setting off point: Teru. Easy. Elevation 3720 metres. Time from early spring until mid-November.

There are no cargo jeeps for Teru from Phander. You can hire one or trek via Ghizer. From Teru continue to Shandur Pass (3720 metres). It is a 30-km trek.

From Laspur the trek can be continued to Harchin 10 km further on, or 2½ hours along an easy route. You can get jeeps to

Mastuj from there. Alternatively you could head off in the direction of Ustur, Koghozi and Madaghlast. See Chitral Valley treks.

CHITRAL VALLEY

Chitral trekking regions are usually restricted zones, but generally all trekking permits are obtainable from the Deputy Commissioner's officer in Chitral.

Kalash Valleys

The traditional setting off point for any of these treks is always Chitral. But treks can start in any of the three valleys, or even Ayun.

From Ayun trek to Bhishala, 45 km away in the Birer Valley; and from there to Bumburet, then Rumbur. Backtrack to Bumburet where you can catch a cargo jeep to Chitral.

Alternatively you can start at any point along the jeep track to Bumburet. There is a trail along the northern tributary of the river – near where it forks – which leads to Rumbu; then up to Bumburet, Birer and back into Chitral.

Below are some of the more popular treks to do between early spring and early autumn around the Kafiristan Valley, where the elevation does not exceed 3500 metres. Many of them are fairly easy walks. 'Living-off-the-land' is almost possible, but it's best to bring along extra provisions.

Birer-Bumburet-Rumbur

Six days through a restricted zone. A permit is necessary, obtainable from the Deputy Commissioner's Office in Chitral. No porter or guide needed. Moderate.

Take a cargo jeep from Chitral to Birer, 45 km away. From Birer trek up the massif into Bumburet. It's only nine km up, but it takes four to six hours to get there because the trail is so steep. From Bumburet to Rumbur is 11 km, or three to four hours easy walking. You can either backtrack to Bumburet or take a jeep, then trek up to Birer, the third of the Kalash towns. See section on Kalash above.

On return, trek back to Ayun or catch a jeep to Chitral.

Garam Chasma-Birmughlast

A two-day trek through a restricted area. A permit is necessary, but no guide or porters are needed.

There is a regular bus from Chitral to Garam Chasma. Trek to Birmughlast and continue back to Chitral.

Birer-Birmughlast

A six-day trek through a restricted zone. Permit necessary, porters and guide optional. Setting off point: Chitral. Moderate. Elevation 2400 to 4500 metres. Time early spring until September.

Take a jeep from Chitral to Birer. Then from Birer the trail goes up to Chumbai Pass (1150 metres), before descending rather steeply to the Bumburet Valley. From here you walk through a long, narrow valley and across a footbridge, which consists of a single pole, into Brumbutu, where there is a rest house with a limited choice of food. There is more choice when you get to Bumburet. Continue northward; the trail south leads to a tiny village known as Krakal, and beyond Krakal is the Afghan border. Between Bishala and Bumburet there is a six to eight-hour trek.

You can continue to trek to Rumbur from Bumburet passing through hamlets along the way. It only takes about three hours. From Rumbur go down to Bashagan, over Utak Pass (4647 metres), and then to Birmughlast.

At Birmughlast the trail splits, one branch leading to Chitral, the other to Garam Chasma.

Bumburet-Garam Chasma

This is a one-week trek through a restricted zone. A permit is required, porters are optional but a guide is a must. Setting off point: Bumburet. Moderate to strenuous. Elevation 4647 metres.

Take a cargo jeep from Chitral to Bumburet.

At the south end of Bumburet is a small village called Brumgram or Burumgram, which has a teashop and a tiny general store. There's a trail leading north-west from here through uninhabited valleys along the banks of the Chumarsan River. It climbs up to the 4647-metre Utak Pass, which is open from mid-June until mid-September, then down into Putrik Village and into Garam Chasma.

After a day's trek, the trail forks, one branch leads to Garam Chasma, the other loops down into Rumbur. The Brumgram route is stunningly beautiful, but the area is not inhabited so it's easy to get lost or confused. If you haven't been able to get hold of a detailed map or compass, hire a local guide or porter. It's only a day's trek over two low passes from here to Rumbur. This is a variation on the route to Rumbur via the Burumgram trail. From there you can either go to Birmughlast, Garam Chasma or Chitral.

Be careful not to stray across the border into Afghanistan.

SHISHI VALLEY

This valley is at the southern end of the Hindu Raj range and has luxuriant forests of pine and juniper, but in the upper reaches it takes on the usual aridity and ruggedness of the Trans-Himalayas. The main town is Drosh which is linked by a jeepable road with Chitral. To the north are Madaghlast, Ustur and Koghozi.

Chitral-Phargam Pass-Laspur

Eight to ten days trek through a restricted zone. Permit necessary as is a porter or guide. Setting off point: Chitral.

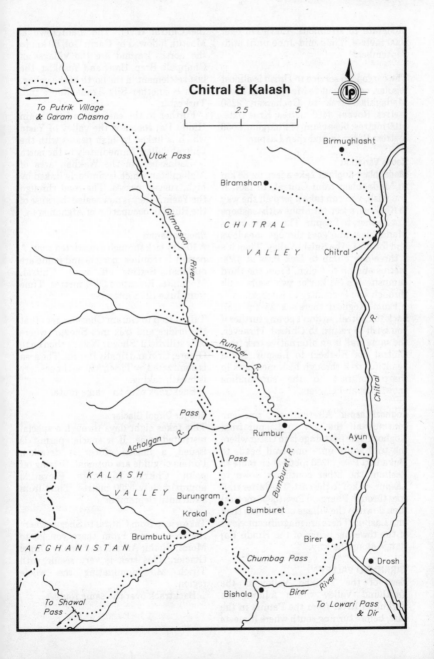

Chitral & Kalash

0   2.5   5

To Putrik Village
& Garam Chasma

Utok Pass

Gitmarson River

Birmughlasht

Biramshan

CHITRAL

VALLEY

Chitral

Chitral R.

Chitral

Rumber R.

Pass

Rumbur

Ayun

Acholgan R.

Pass

Bumburet R.

KALASH

VALLEY

Burungram

Bumburet

Krakal

Birer

Brumbutu

Chumbag Pass

Birer River

AFGHANISTAN

Bishala

Drosh

To Shawal
Pass

To Lowari Pass
& Dir

Moderate to strenuous. Elevation over 5000 metres. Time mid-June until mid-September.

The cargo jeep service to Drosh is almost regular, or jeep out to Madaghlast. From Madaghlast trek to Gocharsar, 3250 metres; Roygal, 3460 metres; Krue Uzte, 3100 metres; base camp of Phargam, 5056 metres; Rahman and then Laspur.

Route Variation

Madaghlast-Koghozi Take a jeep for 86 km to Madaghlast from Chitral. In fact, if you wish, you can take a jeep all the way to Koghozi, a jeep terminus with teashops – or further, to Laspur. The trek starts in Madaghlast and goes through meadows and forests in the Shishi Valley. Then it's a three-day climb to Dok Pass at 4500 metres and on to Golen. From the third campsite it's 5½ km or two hours walk through scenic country to Koghozi.

From Koghozi there's a 25-km trail back to Chitral, so don't go any further if you wish to return to Chitral. However, the same trail is an alternative trek from Chitral via Koghozi to Laspur. It's a beautiful trek through lush meadows in sharp contrast to the surrounding snowfields and glaciers.

Koghozi-Laspur Alternatively you can continue all the way to Laspur from Koghozi. The first stage is to Ustur where the trail splits up – one trail heads to Dukadaki Pass (3250 metres) en route to Reshun, the other continues down to Laspur, 48 km to the east. The latter trail goes through Phargam Pass (5056 metres) then down to the village of Rahman then into Laspur. There are magnificent views of the towering peaks of the Hindu Raj Range along the way.

YARKHUND VALLEY

East of the Turikho Valley is the Yarkhund Valley which follows the Yarkhund River from the Pamirs in the east, before turning south where it meets the Chitral River. The main town is Mastuj, followed by Gazin Gol, 60 km to the north. Beyond are the villages of Chappali, Brep, Bang and Yoshkist, the last settlement in the north of the valley. This is another Silk Trade Route into Turkestan.

Further to the east beyond the main Hindu Raj Range is the valley of Yasin which is linked by high passes with the Chitral Valley. Immediately to the north is Badakshan in the Wakhan area of Afghanistan which is similarly linked by high, rugged passes. The road through the Yasin Valley is now sealed, because of the Russian occupation of Afghanistan.

Shogur-Barum

A 10-day trek through a restricted zone. A permit is requires, porters and guide are optional. Setting off point: Chitral. Moderate. Elevation 3200 metres. Time from June till September.

Take a jeep to Garam Chasma, get off at the bridge and trek into Shogur, where they still distil 'Shogur Water'; then on to Ojhore; Orin and finally Barum. The area is dominated by Tirich Mir so the scenery is breath-taking.

Backtrack over the same route.

Shogur-Dirgol Glacier

This takes eight days through a special restricted zone. If a special permit is issued, a liaison officer is detailed. Porters or guide are optional. Setting off point: Chitral. Moderate. Elevation approximately 5200 metres. Time from June until September.

Take a jeep from Chitral to Shogur where the trek starts. From there you go to Momi; Shahi; Arkari; and finally Dirgol Glacier. This trek is very scenic with Tirich Mir dominating the whole region.

Backtrack over the same route.

Shogur-Suzum

Four days through a restricted zone. Permit necessary, porter and guide optional. Setting off point: Chitral. Easy to moderate. Elevation approximately 4800 metres. Time from June until September.

Take a jeep from Chitral to Shogur or further on to Suzum Valley. If you get off at Shogur the trek goes to Suzum via Ovir; then on to Kosht. It's a scenic trail with views of Tirich Mir along the way.

Backtrack to Shogur or catch a jeep back from Suzum to Chitral on return.

Shogur-Purisht

A relatively easy four-day trek through a restricted zone. Permit necessary, porters or guide optional. Elevation approximately 4800 metres. Time from June until September.

Through the same valley and along the same trail, but take a jeep to Garam Chasma from Chitral. The trek goes through attractive country to Purisht.

Backtrack to Garam Chasma on return.

MULIKHO-TURIKHO-TIRICH VALLEYS

The village of Shagram divides this region in two: the lower area is Mulikho and the northern area is Turikho. Shagram was the former royal village used mainly during the hunting season. The route up is via Warkup or Drasan, a fair-sized village with jeepable tracks going all the way to Rain, where there is a Buddhist stupa near the polo ground.

In spring the region is carpeted with flowers amongst clusters of poplar trees, but further up the landscape is barren except for the patches of greenery that stand out like oases.

Tirich Valley begins beyond Rain. Here the main villages are Melph, Tirich and Kot. The valleys of Zivar and Uzhnu lead to the glacial regions in the north-west and the village of Rua at 3125 metres.

Beyond Rua is Moghlang, the last settlement to the north.

To the north-west of Chitral are the main ramparts of the Hindu Kush which demarcate the border between Afghanistan and Pakistan. Tirich Mir (7750 metres) is the highest mountain in the region and further north are Noshaq and Saraghrar.

Tirich Mir Valley

This is a seven-day trek through a restricted zone. A permit is required and porters are necessary. Setting off point: Chitral. Elevation 4500 metres. Time from June till September.

From Chitral take a jeep to Drasan, then trek to Rain, 6 km to the north. Porters are available here. The route to the Tirich Valley is 3 km out of Rain in the direction of Zani Pass (3250 metres), up a flat-topped ridge with a spectacular view of the Hindu Raj massif. Continue on to Shagram (there is another village of the same name on the Turikho side) and beyond is the Tirich Glacier which is about a day's hard walk.

You can backtrack over the same route or continue down to Banduk and on towards Tirich Mir base camp. Return to Chitral via Barum.

Turikho Valley

A two-week trek through a restricted area. A permit is required, porters and guide are optional. Setting off point: Chitral. Moderate. Elevation 3500 metres. Time from June till August.

From Chitral catch a jeep to Warkup or Drasan and then 6 km on to Rain. En route are the villages of Melph, Tirich and Kot, then through the glacial regions of Zivar and Uzhnu and finally Rua (3250 metres). It is a three day trek to Rua. Continue to Moghlang and camp in the shepherds' huts there. Then it's on to Bala Bugdu via Rahazan Gol. There are more shepherds' huts at Bala Bugdu.

Continuing east you reach Shah Jinali; it is a day's walk up to the Shah Jinali Pass. To the south is Yoshkist in the Yarkhund Valley and further south are Brep and Mastuj.

Route Variation An alternative trek from Turikho Valley to Yarkhund Valley is over Kot Pass (5000 metres). The best route is via Lasht Kot (Cloud Plains). It is advisable to have a porter/guide if going over the pass, where the scenery is spellbinding. The last village here is Djzig, then across a river and a little way on is Brep. Or from Chitral trek to Maroi and Barenis to Drasan.

You can either backtrack or continue trekking to Shah Jinali and then down to Mastuj, where you jeep it back to Chitral.

Chitral-Turikho-Yasin

A long 26-day trek, ranging from moderate to strenuous, through restricted territory. Permit, porters and guide are essential. Setting off point: Chitral. Elevation 4400 metres. Time from June until September.

Take a jeep from Chitral to Drasan or Parpich. The latter is 57 km north of Chitral, Drasan is only 14 km from Kosht in the Mulikho Valley or Lower Kho. In the village of Rain you can hire porters and guides for expeditions to the peaks in the west of Turikho Valley. It's a two-day trek from Rain to Shagram.

Alternatively you can get a jeep from Chitral to Warkup Village, and then it's a two to three-day trek to Rua, at 3000 metres, on the west bank of the Turikho river valley. There are villages and streams along the trail, and the tributaries to the north-west lead to glaciers. Notice the ibexes in the upper reaches. At a village six km from Warkup there is a rock carving of a Buddhist stupa.

Up towards Turikho Valley via Zani Pass (3000 metres) there is a flat ridge, 24 km long, which offers a view of Tirich Mir and other mountain peaks. Camp here. Not much further on is Moghlang and a shepherds' hamlet. Beyond Khot Pass (4600 metres) is Khot Valley, which leads into Yarkhund Valley. The best route is to the north through Lasht Khot village. Once you get out of the valley the route becomes confusing as there are trails leading in all directions. You need a local guide to take you through this extremely scenic section.

From here you go down the valley through another village and across a stream into Brep, a village which has a teashop-inn. To the south is Mastuj, but at Gazin you can go to Yasin Valley via Thui Ann Pass (4499 metres), and into Shotaling, Mushk, Harph and then Yasin.

Another route is from Mastuj via the Chumarkhan Pass (5009 metres) or Zagar Gol, just off Chapali village, 12 km north of Mastuj, across a bridge, up a gradual ascent to the pass at 1150 metres. Once you reach the Yasin Valley go either to Shiashi or Phander in the Ghizer Valley.

Another variation of this trek is from Warkup to Mastuj in the Turikho-Yarkhund valleys which takes eight to 10 days.

Chitral-Shah Jinali-Yasin

A 24-day trek through a restricted zone. A permit and porters are necessary and a liaison officer or mountain guide is detailed. Setting off point: Chitral. Elevation 4400 metres. Time from June until August.

Take a jeep to Istaro from Chitral. It's possible to get a jeep all the way to Uzhnu via Shagram in the Mulikho Valley. Note that there is another *shagram* – polo ground – in the Turikho Valley.

From Uzhnu go to Phurgram; Shah Jinali; over Shah Jinali Pass (4300 metres); and then to Ispru; Shosht; Lesht; Dobargar; Gazin; and Brep in the

Yarkhund Valley. From Gazin there is a trail over the Thui Ann Pass into Shotaling, Mushk and Harph in the Yasin Valley.

This trek to Yasin is a variation of the preceding one. There are many different trails going from Chitral to Shah Jinali, but all of them end in Mastuj – see above. You can trek back to Chitral or catch a jeep from Brep or Mastuj all the way. Another variation is to go to Yoshkist Village, just north-east of Shah Jinali Pass. Here the trail forks off east to Darkot Pass, or alternatively, to Brep and Mastuj.

Warning Whether or not you hire a guide, before heading off on a trek check with the tourist officer in Skardu, Gilgit or Chitral for more information. The situation in these areas is constantly changing and this should be anticipated.

Always ask about the availability of supplies, distance between villages and towns, fares or rates and border situations.

Note The trekking region up here is vast and in preparing this section it has not been possible to personally cover all the trails which have been written up in this book. However, careful research has been undertaken both from books, brochures *et al* and from other trekkers. The former includes trekking brochures put out by the PTDC, literature on trekking and mountaineering published by the Ministry of Culture & Tourism in Pakistan, and books on anthropology, history, archaeology, geology and on general exploration of the region.

Index

Map references are in **bold** type

Temperature

To convert °C to °F multipy by 1.8 and add 32

To convert °F to °C subtract 32 and multipy by 5/9

Length, Distance & Area

	multipy by
inches to centimetres	2.54
centimetres to inches	0.39
feet to metres	0.30
metres to feet	3.28
yards to metres	0.91
metres to yards	1.09
miles to kilometres	1.61
kilometres to miles	0.62
acres to hectares	0.40
hectares to acres	2.47

Weight

	multipy by
ounces to grams	28.35
grams to ounces	0.035
pounds to kilograms	0.45
kilograms to pounds	2.21
British tons to kilograms	1016
US tons to kilograms	907

A British ton is 2240 lbs, a US ton is 2000 lbs

Volume

	multipy by
imperial gallons to litres	4.55
litres to imperial gallons	0.22
US gallons to litres	3.79
litres to US gallons	0.26

5 imperial gallons equals 6 US gallons
a litre is slightly more than a US quart, slightly less
than a British one

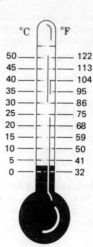

Lonely Planet Newsletter

We collect an enormous amount of information here at Lonely Planet. Apart from our research there's a steady stream of letters from people out on the road. To make the most of all this info we produce a quarterly Newsletter (approx Feb, May, Aug, and Nov).

The Newsletter is packed with down-to-earth information from the pens of hundreds of travellers who write from first-hand experience. Whether you want the latest facts, travel stories, or simply to reminisce, the Newsletter will keep you in touch with what is going on.

Where else could you find out:
- about boat trips on the Yalu River?
- where to stay if you want to live in a typical Thai village?
- how long it takes to get a Nepalese trekking permit?
- that Israeli youth hostel stamps will get you deported from Syria?

One year's subscription is $10.00 (that's US$ in the USA or A$ in Australia), payable by cheque, money order, Amex, Visa, Bankcard or MasterCard.

Order Form

Please send me four issues of the Lonely Planet Newsletter. (Subscription starts with next issue. 1987 price – subject to change.)

Name and address (print) . . . .

. . . .

. . . .

Tick one

☐ Cheque enclosed (payable to Lonely Planet Publications)
☐ Money Order enclosed (payable to Lonely Planet Publications)
Charge my ☐ Amex, ☐ Visa, ☐ Bankcard, ☐ MasterCard for the amount of $. . . . .

Card No . . . .   Expiry Date . . . .

Cardholder's Name (print) . . . .

Signature . . . .   Date . . . .

Return this form to:
Lonely Planet Publications   *or* Lonely Planet Publications
PO Box 2001A   PO Box 88
Berkeley   South Yarra
CA 94702   Victoria 3141
USA   Australia